DEVELOPMENT AID CONFRONTS POLITICS

THE ALMOST REVOLUTION

THOMAS CAROTHERS | DIANE DE GRAMONT

DEVELOPMENT AID CONFRONTS POLITICS

THE ALMOST REVOLUTION

CARNEGIE ENDOWMENT

FOR INTERNATIONAL PEACE

WASHINGTON DC ▪ MOSCOW ▪ BEIJING ▪ BEIRUT ▪ BRUSSELS

Carnegie Endowment for International Peace
1779 Massachusetts Avenue, N.W.
Washington, D.C. 20036
202-483-7600, Fax 202-483-1840
www.ceip.org

To order, contact:
Hopkins Fulfillment Service
P.O. Box 50370, Baltimore, MD 21211-4370
1-800-537-5487 or 1-410-516-6956
Fax 1-410-516-6998

Cover design by Jocelyn Soly
Composition by Cutting Edge Design
Printed by United Book Press

Library of Congress Cataloging-in-Publication Data

Carothers, Thomas, 1956-
   Development aid confronts politics: the almost revolution / Thomas Carothers and Diane de Gramont.
      pages cm
   Includes bibliographical references and index.
   ISBN 978-0-87003-400-8 (pbk.) -- ISBN 978-0-87003-401-5 (cloth) -- ISBN 978-0-87003-402-2 (elect)
   1. Economic assistance--Political aspects. 2. Economic assistance--Government policy. 3. Economic development--Political aspects. 4. International economic relations--Political aspects. I. Title.

   HC60.C2953 2013
   338.91--dc23

                                    2013003672

CONTENTS

THE WAY FORWARD

CONCLUSION

FOREWORD

When we think about the noble aim of development assistance—reducing the devastating poverty that cripples the lives of so many people around the world—the idea of a potentially constructive role for politics in this endeavor may at first seem an oxymoron. We are all too familiar with the United States and other aid providers playing politics with aid—channeling large quantities of it to some governments that are unwilling or unable to make good use of it, for domestic reasons or to shore up strategically useful partnerships. And we know how development dollars can fall prey to corruption or the narrow political designs of unhelpful leaders in developing countries, undermining their governments' ability to help the poor.

Yet as Thomas Carothers and Diane de Gramont show in this magisterial, sharply perceptive book, a transformative movement is under way in development aid, one that is all about integrating politics both into what aid tries to do and how it tries to do it. The movement is an attempt to get beyond the technocratic, apolitical ways of thinking about developmental change that have dominated foreign assistance for decades and so often produced disappointment or outright failure. It is an effort both to carry out politically smart development programs that take local realities into account and to infuse positive political values into our basic conceptions of what aid can and should achieve. As the authors chronicle in their examination of the evolution of aid from the 1960s to the present, the new politics agenda got its start in the 1990s as the Cold War straitjacket that had long constrained aid dropped away. It has made significant though inconsistent progress in the ensuing twenty years. Yet despite the power of these new ideas, deeply entrenched obstacles in the aid business raise serious doubts about whether the attempted transformation will succeed.

Here, the authors offer both a fresh perspective on the history of development assistance and an insightful account of the cutting edge of efforts to renovate aid. Readers familiar with Thomas Carothers' writings will not be surprised either by the breadth of this ambition or the success of the book in fulfilling it. Over the past twenty years he has produced one field-defining book after another on core components of democracy support, including rule of law assistance, civil society aid, and political party support. His decision to take on the broader domain of development aid, in particular the changing role of politics within it, is a natural extension of his earlier work. He has been joined in this undertaking by Diane de Gramont, a gifted young researcher who joined Carnegie's Democracy and Rule of Law Program in 2010 and quickly demonstrated a level of analytic acuity and intellectual maturity far beyond her years.

In an age of ever-increasing pressure on think tanks to chase after headlines and reduce findings to quick digital bits, Carnegie is proud to balance its embrace of the opportunities new communications technologies provide with an enduring commitment to producing research that reaches deeply and stands for years. In the best of cases this is work that helps change the dominant paradigms that guide entire policy domains. This book is a shining example. I am proud Carnegie is offering it to the international policy community and of the role that I am confident it will play in shaping basic policy choices and outcomes.

–Jessica T. Mathews
President
Carnegie Endowment for International Peace

ACKNOWLEDGMENTS

We are grateful to the Norwegian Agency for Development Cooperation and the John D. and Catherine T. MacArthur Foundation for their generous financial support that made the writing of this book possible. We also thank the UK Department for International Development for early research support that helped introduce us to the topic. At the Carnegie Endowment, Saskia Brechenmacher made substantial contributions to the underlying research, Zoe Benezet-Parsons, Amina Edwards, and Tiffany Joslin provided helpful support in many areas, the Carnegie publications team, including Ilonka Oszvald and Jocelyn Soly, ably saw the manuscript through production, and Carnegie president Jessica Mathews provided the institutional leadership that made Carnegie the ideal environment for this project.

Special thanks to Larry Garber, Adrian Leftwich, Mark Robinson, Petter Skjaeveland, and Graham Teskey for their tremendously useful comments on an earlier draft. We are also grateful for the valuable assistance we received along the way in many forms from Kaya Adams, Per Øyvind Bastøe, Helena Bjuremalm, Bella Bird, Derick Brinkerhoff, Robyn Chomyshyn, Noha El-Mikawy, Poul Engberg-Pedersen, Nancy Estes, Verena Fritz, Francis Fukuyama, Annabel Gerry, Claudia Hernandez, Ann Hudock, Stefan Kossoff, Benjamin Latto, Brian Levy, Sarah Lister, Susan Loughhead, Barry Lowenkron, Sarah Mendelson, Mary Page, Laure-Hélène Piron, Chris Pycroft, Keith Schulz, and David Yang. We are indebted to the numerous practitioners, scholars, and activists in many parts of the development community who shared their insights with us in interviews or informal conversations.

Diane thanks her parents for their unwavering love and encouragement and her great-aunt, Carnzu Clark, for her strong support for this book. Tom thanks Andrea for completeness, and believing.

INTRODUCTION

CHAPTER 1

THE NEW POLITICS AGENDA

INTRODUCTION

Ever since its early years, international development assistance has had an uncertain and uncomfortable relationship with politics. The emergent community of organizations that Western governments set up in the 1950s and 1960s to carry out aid programs in what was then called the Third World embraced a conception of development centered on economic well-being and defined their central mission as fostering economic growth. They initially hoped that economic growth in poor countries would produce political development, which they defined primarily as liberal democracy. That political ambition receded quickly, however, when authoritarianism spread widely in the developing world during the 1960s. To fulfill their central economic mission, aid organizations held fast to what can be called "the temptation of the technical," the belief that they could help economically transform poor countries by providing timely doses of capital and technical knowledge while maintaining a comfortably clinical distance from these countries' internal political life. These views took hold strongly in those early years, exerted a powerful influence throughout the intervening decades, and are still prevalent in the development aid community today.

This preference for an economic-centric, technocratic approach to development is understandable. While economics appears as a rational, scientific domain, politics seems to imply inevitable entanglement with the irrational side of human affairs—with ideological fervor, nationalistic impulses, and other volatile passions. Economics emphasizes consensual ideas, like the universal appeal of prosperity and the tragedy of poverty. In contrast, politics is all about conflicting visions and objectives. Economics deals in definite goals, with easily measurable signs of improvement. Politics is about subjective values, with signs of progress hard to agree on, let alone measure. Many development aid practitioners fear that the more political assistance appears to be, the harder the time they will have building or maintaining productive relationships with governments throughout the developing world. They hope that emphasizing economic goals and technical methods will help them avoid controversy and overcome local suspicions within developing countries about what these putatively well-intentioned outsiders are really up to.

Yet the effort to keep development aid away from politics has weakened the endeavor. Aid agencies have too often failed to grapple with the political complexities of the countries where they work and of the inherently political nature of processes of developmental change. This has led to numerous problems, including:

- *Misunderstanding the causes of developmental problems*, for example, assuming that a developing country government's failure to distribute needed medical supplies to a particular region in its territory is due to a lack of transportation capacity rather than some underlying sociopolitical factor, such as animus on the part of the ruling party toward the local elites of the region in question or a desire to distribute medical benefits disproportionately to political supporters.

- *Failing to pay attention to or strengthen domestic institutional capacity to carry out development programs*, for example, implementing food projects over decades that deliver nutrition to poor people but do not address the persistent inability of the state to prevent or cope with famines.

- *Trying to insert solutions conceived from the outside that lack domestic buy-in while failing to identify and thus help facilitate local impetus for change*, for instance, setting up formal consultative mechanisms for selected government actors to discuss policy with citizens but then limiting the citizen side to elite nongovernmental organizations

(NGOs) while neglecting other forms of representation in the society and other actors—like trade unions, religious groups, or traditional leaders—who have the political strength and legitimacy to represent collective social interests.

- *Overlooking how technocratically rational institutional reforms may threaten powerful domestic political interests and thus go nowhere*, like how a plan to rationalize the personnel structures in a ministry and increase meritocratic appointments may not move forward despite the cost savings and other benefits it would bring because it would reduce the patronage opportunities for the minister in charge.

- *Not anticipating unintended harmful political consequences of socio-economic reform efforts*, such as how a hurried, large-scale privatization program in a resource-rich country with weak legal institutions may create a new class of oligopolistic, predatory elites who end up capturing the political process and blocking further reforms.

- *Ignoring the broader aspirations of citizens beyond economic success, such as popular desires for political dignity and empowerment*, leading to an aid effort that helps a country achieve certain economic changes but neglects profound underlying tensions on other, more political, matters. These tensions can keep mounting and eventually blow up and derail the economic reform process while also undermining the local reputation of the development actors that were behind it.

Warnings about these dangers of excluding politics from development aid did surface during the initial decades of the aid enterprise. Articulate early dissenters highlighted shortcomings arising from narrow technocratic approaches and called on aid providers to think and act more politically. But these voices failed to gain much traction. They ran up against a strong head of apolitical steam behind the still-expanding world of development aid as well as a frozen Cold War context that encouraged many developmentalists to try to isolate what they viewed as an idealistic endeavor from the contamination of politics of all types.

It was only in the 1990s that the door to politics significantly opened in the development aid world. In those years some assistance practitioners long frustrated with the persistent developmental failures of many poor countries managed to push onto the aid agenda the simple but powerful idea that failures of governance—a term adopted as a relatively nonthreatening, apolitical way to talk about such clearly political issues as governmental incentives, structures, and actions—are the underlying cause of chronic underdevelopment and must be addressed by aid providers. Without minimally effective government institutions to support sustainable development, progress is likely to remain out of reach for many countries. This insight flourished in a new international context that was suddenly much more favorable to a political lens on development work. Thanks to the end of the Cold War, Western donors were no longer inhibited from politically criticizing many aid-receiving governments out of fear of losing their support in the anti-Soviet cause. They also no longer faced the automatic assumption that any effort to talk about politics in developing countries was just a cover for geopolitical machinations. In addition, the rapid, heartening spread of democracy in the developing world in those years undercut the old idea that authoritarian politics were normal for poor countries and revived in Western policy circles the appealing idea that liberal democracy and economic development naturally go hand in hand.

Many changes followed in the aid world. Throughout the 1990s and the first decade of the new century, most major aid organizations adopted political goals alongside their socioeconomic ones. Sometimes they formulated their goals in terms of improving governance, but often they went further and came out openly in support of democratic governance or democracy itself. They established a whole new arena of openly political aid programs aimed at reforming political institutions and processes, from parliaments and judiciaries to elections and political party development. In their socioeconomic work, they began exploring and adopting more politically informed methods. These included developing new analytic tools for understanding the political contexts where they worked as well as efforts to facilitate locally rooted processes of developmental change, such as fostering citizen demand for better public services or facilitating coalition building among reform supporters inside and outside government. As aid providers stepped up their work in conflict-afflicted and fragile states, they began trying to understand and directly address the relationship between the political underpinnings of conflict and grave socioeconomic challenges.

The development practitioners most closely involved in establishing these new ways of thinking and acting politically consider this wave of change an overdue revolution in development aid. They see it as a chance to finally reverse the original sin of narrowly technocratic approaches to development and arrive at an integrated economic and political conception of what development is and how it can be achieved. Yet the new embrace of politics remains very much an uphill struggle. Many developmentalists continue to doubt the value of the move toward politics, viewing it as an analytically weak leap into a jungle of potential complications and distractions. They hope it is just one more fad in the long chain of transient enthusiasms that have marked the path of development aid, bound to fade away if they simply wait it out. Others see some value in a politics perspective but remain concerned about aid becoming "too political" and instinctively try to set limits on how far political thinking and action penetrate the core areas of development work. Many people in aid-receiving societies, both inside and outside of government, resist the idea that development aid should become more political, believing that donors have no right to involve themselves in domestic political issues and that political approaches are excuses for unwanted interventions rooted in ulterior motivations. Other actors in developing countries, especially civic activists trying to push their governments to reform, sometimes appreciate political frankness and engagement by outside aid groups. Yet they worry that donors may often be acting politically without a sufficiently deep understanding of the political complexities of the local scene.

As a result of these divided views, many of the new ideas about more political thinking and action have been only partially accepted within major aid organizations. Openly political aid programs such as democracy assistance efforts are usually funded with much smaller sums than more traditional areas of aid aimed at furthering economic growth or making progress in social sectors such as health. Political programs mostly operate in isolation from the still dominant socioeconomic agendas, remaining niche efforts in organizations focused primarily on other things. Attempts to introduce more political analysis into traditional areas of development work still face skepticism around the practical value of such studies. Many practitioners believe that the resources these efforts require and the hackles they sometimes raise with host country governments are not worth the benefit to aid providers. More political methods for facilitating socio-economic change remain only tentative experiments for which broader institutional acceptance is still far off. The growing pressure within aid circles to strictly define and measure results, as well as the long-standing bureaucratic constraints on flexible and innovative programming, cuts against more political approaches. In short, it is by no means clear whether a political revolution in development aid is really under way, or if it is, whether it will carry the day.

IT'S ALREADY POLITICAL

The unfolding wave of attention to politics in aid provokes a certain frustration or even snappishness in some observers. Development aid, they forcefully insist, *is inescapably, inevitably highly political, and always has been.* From the very beginnings of aid through to the present day, they point out, donors have regularly used foreign aid for manifestly political purposes: to shore up shaky allies, to reward friendly governments for useful cooperation on security issues, to win over unfriendly leaders, to gain access or influence in countries where they lack other ties, or just to show the flag generally. Although the end of the Cold War took away the anticommunist imperative of Western aid, geostrategic motives continue to drive much of foreign assistance. U.S. aid relationships with Afghanistan, Egypt, Iraq, Israel, and Pakistan, for example—some of the largest aid programs in the world—all aim at furthering U.S. diplomatic and security interests. And the United States is hardly the only donor to use aid for a range of purposes beyond reducing human misery. One does not have to look hard at the aid programs of France, Japan, the United Kingdom, or other major donors to see multiple motivations at work, often quite different from simply promoting socioeconomic development.

Furthermore, these observers point out, even when aid is designed and delivered primarily to foster socioeconomic development, it inevitably has political effects on recipient countries. Helping a government deliver better socioeconomic outcomes to its citizens will bolster that government's political standing. As a result, if aid is channeled to authoritarian governments, it can lend legitimacy to repressive regimes. Aid that flows directly to executive branch ministries and bypasses other parts of government, such as the legislative branch, may have the effect of increasing the centralization of the political system and weakening democratic checks and balances. Large aid flows to weak states can undermine those governments' accountability to their citizens as senior officials worry more about pleasing donors than serving their own constituencies. If multiple donors operate in a country in an uncoordinated fashion, as they often do, they can contribute to the fragmentation of the policy process and even of the governing institutions themselves by pursuing inconsistent agendas and placing competing demands on government agencies.

Those highlighting the inevitably political nature of aid also tend to disagree with the idea that it is possible to draw a clear line between socioeconomic and political issues. Reforms to expand access to healthcare, shift resources among educational priorities, or revise the tax code are about socioeconomic goods and outcomes. Yet they also involve political choices and values. As the divisive debate over healthcare reform in the United States highlights so vividly, socioeconomic issues are often the source of fundamental political divisions and debates. Additionally, while aid providers often talk about market reforms in politically neutral terms as maximizing economic goods or rationalizing state authority, market approaches grow out of a broader ideological framework with deeply embedded political values and norms. They involve basic choices about the proper role of the state in society and the balance between individual and collective interests. When development agencies use their financial leverage to push such reforms on developing country governments, they are promoting an inherently political agenda and imposing on the sovereignty of recipient states.

Those observers who react to the new wave of interest in politics in aid by highlighting the inevitably political nature of assistance tend to do so as part of a larger negative assessment of the development aid enterprise. They criticize major donors for using aid to advance geostrategic or other national interests rather than to benefit poor people around the world. They believe that aid providers tend to ignore the political side effects of socioeconomic aid and that these effects frequently corrode local accountability or democracy generally. They disagree with the market-centric paradigm underlying so much aid of the past several decades and feel that market reforms should be treated as a contestable choice, not an objective good. Whether or not one agrees with the overall political thrust of these criticisms, the fact remains that aid is unquestionably, inevitably political in these important ways. And it is also true that mainstream aid providers have all too often tried to deny or play down these political characteristics, insisting on technocratic neutrality even when acting in a highly political manner.

NEW WAYS OF BEING POLITICAL

But the movement since the 1990s is about making aid political in different ways than those inescapably political dimensions outlined just above. When enthusiasts of this new movement talk about the importance of aid providers "being political" or "working politically," they are not talking about prioritizing geostrategic motives or hiding political objectives under the cover of putatively neutral economic models. Rather they are referring to *efforts by development aid actors intentionally and openly to think and act politically for the purpose of making aid more effective in fostering development.* Aid providers are engaging in a diverse, growing array of efforts to work more politically. For the purposes of the analysis in this book, we divide the new politics agenda into two main halves: the pursuit of political goals and the use of politically smart methods.

Pursuing political goals: This is about using aid to advance explicitly political goals—which aid organizations usually frame at a general level as better governance (though as will be discussed later on, some aid providers have tried to cling to apolitical understandings of governance), democratic governance, or democracy itself. They adopt political goals for either instrumental reasons (the belief that certain political systems will help achieve improved socioeconomic outcomes) or for intrinsic reasons (the belief that certain political values are goods in their own right and should be promoted as separate objectives or as part of a unified political-economic conception of development), or more often for both instrumental and intrinsic reasons at once.

Using politically smart methods: This is about moving away from the dream of developmental change as a mechanical process in which supplying technocratic inputs to developing country governments will produce desirable socioeconomic outcomes. It requires recognizing that developmental change is an amalgam of complex, inherently political processes in which multiple contending actors assert their interests in diverse societal arenas, trying to reconcile them into shared positive outcomes. To be effective in helping advance development, aid actors need to operate from a genuine understanding of the political realities of the local context, engage with a diverse array of relevant actors both inside and outside the government, and insert aid strategically and subtly as a facilitating element in local processes of change.

These two dimensions of aid "being political" sometimes naturally go together and reinforce each other. For example, if aid actors take on the political goal of improving the prospects for free and fair elections in a

---

BOX 1.1   THE MULTIPLE MEANINGS OF "BEING POLITICAL" IN DEVELOPMENT AID

INESCAPABLE POLITICAL ELEMENTS

Aid is used to serve political purposes other than development, such as to reward friendly governments or win over new allies.

Aid has inevitable political consequences in recipient countries. Even if focused narrowly on economic goals, aid can bolster a government's standing with its citizens, skew accountability relationships, empower some sociopolitical groups over others, and much else.

Socioeconomic development goals involve contested political choices. All areas of social and economic change, whether tax policy, healthcare reform, or social safety nets, raise fundamental political issues such as the appropriate size of government, burden sharing, and fairness of distribution.

THE NEW POLITICS AGENDA

Aid should pursue political goals, such as advancing democratic governance within recipient countries, either as a means to promote socioeconomic development or as valuable objectives in their own right.

Aid should employ politically smart methods, moving away from technocratic approaches to analyze local political contexts, engage a diverse range of actors in recipient societies, and proactively facilitate processes of change within developing countries.

country run by a semiauthoritarian regime with a history of manipulating elections, they will clearly need incisive political methods—such as supporting an emergent coalition of assertive citizen groups mobilizing against electoral fraud—if they wish to make any difference. Similarly, a development actor that starts using more political methods may find itself gravitating toward more political goals. If, for instance, an aid organization carries out a political economy analysis of the chronic underdistribution of food to a particular region within a country and it reveals that systemic political marginalization of the ethnic minority concentrated in that region is the root cause of the problem, it may conclude that the most useful aid response is to try to directly address the underlying political problem rather than simply to provide more food.

But movement toward more political methods and more political goals do not necessarily go together. Programs with clearly political goals can and often are conducted using technocratic methods that do not reflect a deep understanding of the political context or any real attempt to facilitate locally driven processes of change. An aid provider may try to strengthen a poorly functioning parliament, for example, by offering training on how to write legislation when in fact the problem has much deeper roots relating to a fragmented and unrepresentative political party system. At the same time, highly political methods, such as supporting reform coalitions that directly intervene in the design and implementation of government policies, can be applied to programs animated by apolitical goals, such as the reduction of tuberculosis.

This separability of political methods and goals is, as we will see later on, important. Many advocates of more political approaches to development aid push for the adoption of both political goals and methods, believing that the two dimensions work hand in hand. Others start with a strong focus on methods and contend that a more nuanced political understanding of how developmental change occurs in specific settings actually points to uncertainty about the value of such preset political goals as democracy or citizen participation. In other words, for some scholars and practitioners, using more political methods actually means questioning some of the most common political goals.

The many meanings of "working politically" in aid cause considerable confusion. Discussions of the topic within the development aid community are often sidetracked by definitional chaos and an inability to agree on terms. Sometimes the observation that a development agency is "being political" is intended as a criticism, for example to highlight that aid is being used to curry favor with a diplomatically helpful but politically repugnant regime. Other times the same term is used as praise, to compliment an aid organization for intelligently navigating the complex local politics of a particular setting to win support for developmental reforms. Sometimes "being political" refers to intended actions on the part of aid providers, other times to the unintended consequences of aid. Sometimes it is about what aid is trying to accomplish, other times about how aid programs are operating.

Given this multiplicity of meanings and the surrounding confusion relating to the use of the word "political" with reference to assistance programs, it might be tempting to give up on the term altogether and find other ways to talk about changes in the goals and methods of development aid over recent decades. Yet hydra-headed as it is, the term "political" does capture crucial ideas that are worth preserving, above all a focus on contestation and cooperation among diverse societal actors with differing interests and power. Some definitions of politics take a limited view, stressing only activities within the formal domain of the state. We align with those writers and thinkers who subscribe to a broader view that encompasses the assertion of interests and the distribution of power throughout societies. Adrian Leftwich, for example, usefully reaches widely, defining politics as:

> all the processes of conflict, cooperation and negotiation in taking decisions about how resources are to be owned, used, produced and distributed. Inevitably, the contours of politics are framed by the inherited institutional environment (both formal and informal), by the political culture and by the differing degrees *and forms* of power, which participants bring to the process, and by their interests and their ideologies.[1]

Even though it is impossible to reach universal agreement on the precise meaning and limits of politics, for better or worse the word "political" is how these important challenges and changes in aid are framed and debated by development practitioners and observers.

THE AIM OF THE BOOK

This book seeks to explain and assess the unfolding movement in development aid to think and act more politically. We aim to clarify what these changes consist of, why they are occurring, and what their implications are for aid providers and recipients alike. The title gives away at least part of our conclusion—the revolution is not complete. But it leaves open many questions that we believe deserve close attention and that we try to answer, including how far mainstream aid providers have come in integrating political goals and methods into their work, why they have met with resistance, and whether this agenda is likely to continue moving forward or instead stagnate or retreat.

We believe that adopting political methods and goals aimed at making aid more effective is a valuable trend. The movement to renovate development aid by fully taking onboard political thinking and action is crucial to the future of the endeavor. A whole series of larger contextual factors— such as the relative decline of aid as a proportion of available international capital, the rise of new challengers to Western political and economic influence in the world, and ever tighter budgets in donor countries—are increasing the long-standing pressure on development aid to overcome uncertainty and outright skepticism about the overall value of the enterprise. It is therefore well past time to move past the chronic shortcomings of narrow technocratic approaches that fit poorly with local contexts or merely prolong the life of noxious regimes.

Of course, working more politically in aid is no panacea. Aid does have a crucial technical dimension, relating to both knowledge and resources— aspects that political approaches can supplement but not replace. There is little value in politically savvy approaches to implement socioeconomic programs if the programs themselves are poorly conceived and technically inappropriate. A certain degree of political awareness is important for all aid programs, but this is far from an exact science and political perspectives can certainly lead to errors alongside insights. Attempts to integrate aid programs into local political processes may run different risks than operating in more purely technocratic ways. We attempt to highlight the problems and challenges involved in more political approaches even as we identify their advantages and utility. But our aim is more than just explanation and assessment of this trend. We wish to focus attention on why aid providers are struggling to move forward on political goals and methods and how they can make further progress.

Our account proceeds in three parts. In chapter 2, we go back to the early decades of aid to trace the origins of the apolitical cast of modern development assistance. We identify the various sources of the technocratic outlook and examine why it held up for more than thirty years despite significant changes in development theories as well as some incisive early critical voices calling attention to the serious shortcomings of apolitical approaches.

The second section, comprising chapters 3, 4, and 5, takes the story forward from the opening to politics in the early 1990s through the resulting changes in the rest of that decade and the next. These were complicated years for development aid. A profusion of changes rocked the enterprise—changes in the overall geostrategic context, the direction of politics in the developing world, the international consensus on what development is and how it occurs, the pace of economic life, and the degree of freedom that external actors had to work across borders on economic and political issues. We attempt to identify why the door to politics opened, how aid providers sought to pass through that door, and what happened when they did. Chapter 3 covers the 1990s. Chapters 4 and 5 examine the first decade of the millennium, with chapter 4 focusing on the evolution of goals and chapter 5 focusing on methods.

In the third section, which spans chapters 6, 7, and 8, we identify and take the measure of a renewed push on politics in aid that emerged at the end of the first decade of the 2000s and continues today, a second wind to the changes that started in the early 1990s. Chapter 6 looks at the cutting edge of efforts to make aid methods politically smart, as well as the question of why such efforts have been so slow in coming over the past fifty years. Chapter 7 assesses the relative lack of change in the place of political goals in recent years and the causes of the only partial integration of these goals into the aid enterprise, highlighting the deeply unresolved debate among development researchers over whether democratic governance generates better socioeconomic outcomes. Chapter 8 probes the ongoing efforts of some aid organizations to integrate political perspectives, actions, and goals into traditional socioeconomic areas such as health, education, and agriculture as well as the resistance and pushback they have faced.

Finally, chapter 9 reviews the overall story from the 1960s to the present. It examines how current international trends are complicating efforts to advance the politics agenda and how aid providers can nevertheless move forward.

Some Caveats

We note here several brief clarifications and caveats. First, we refer throughout the text to the "mainstream aid community," a term that is obviously difficult to delimit with precision. We are referring to those organizations that fund, oversee, and carry out the official development aid of the Organisation for Economic Co-operation and Development (OECD) donor governments. We also include in that term bilateral aid agencies and those foreign ministries that now engage in aid work (an increasing trend, as we discuss), and the main multilateral aid actors such as the World Bank, the aid institutions of the European Commission, and the United Nations Development Programme (UNDP). To avoid overly frequent repetition, we use multiple terms to refer to the organizations making up this community, including "aid providers," "aid organizations," "aid agencies," and "donors," even though these terms are not necessarily precisely interchangeable under different interpretations. In particular we use the term "donors" broadly even though some institutions in the mainstream aid community, such as the World Bank, are not technically donor organizations. In talking about the people who populate this community, we refer largely interchangeably to "aid practitioners," "developmentalists," "development practitioners," and other similar terms, though again these terms do not have precisely delimited referents.

We try to cover many parts of the mainstream aid community but inevitably our reach is only partial across what has become a vast array of organizations and is shaped to some extent by how much information is available on the practices and programming of particular donors, which varies considerably among aid actors. We draw most heavily from the work of U.S., British, Canadian, European Union, and Northern European aid organizations, and the World Bank and UNDP. We do not focus on the work of private assistance organizations, like some of the major U.S. foundations or large UK charitable groups, though we recognize they are vital aid actors too. Despite this limited reach, we nevertheless believe that the issues we highlight are similar enough across most organizations that the overall narrative is broadly relevant to all parts of the mainstream aid community.

Second, we draw often upon official policy documents and declarations of aid organizations, but we do so with full awareness that what such organizations say on paper or in speeches by senior officials is not always an accurate guide to what they do in practice or what people at those organizations believe in private. We consider attention to such documents and declarations useful as one part of the larger effort to capture the evolution of donor orthodoxies over time. We strive as often as possible to incorporate analysis and examples of aid in practice, going behind the words to the deeds, based both on reports and evaluations of specific programmatic activities, many formal interviews and informal conversations with aid practitioners about their work, and multi-donor workshops hosted by Carnegie and other research institutions

Third, we present the evolution of thinking and action on the part of the international aid community in terms of a sequence or evolution of different stages over time. We do so despite the fact that aid actors do not move neatly in unison. An approach or outlook that becomes widespread within the community at a certain time may well have been tried earlier by one or more aid organizations. Or it may not be taken up by some actors until much later. Nevertheless, we believe that the stages we present are accurate enough to be analytically viable and that such frameworks of chronological stages are crucial to understanding the complicated evolution of the role of politics in international development aid as it has unfolded over the past fifty years.

THE ORIGINAL
FRAMEWORK:
1960s–1980s

CHAPTER 2

APOLITICAL ROOTS

INTRODUCTION

The idea that politics matter for development appears self-evident today, so much so that it is difficult to believe that development practitioners did not make the issue central to the aid endeavor from the start. Yet practitioners currently pushing their organizations to take politics into account usually find that they must struggle to overturn deeply entrenched organizational habits of avoiding politics or pretending to be apolitical. The new politics proponents tend not to locate the origin of these patterns very precisely. They assume the roots lie in the formative years of modern development aid, the 1950s and 1960s, although the 1970s and 1980s are suspect as well.

The early history of development aid is a well-known story, at least with regard to the major theories of and approaches to economic development: the 1960s dream of fostering state-led "economic takeoff" in the developing countries; the consequent shift in the 1970s toward explicit attention to poverty reduction and other basic needs alongside or sometimes in place of a focus on economic growth; and the rapid rise in the 1980s of the market-led model of economic development based on a core set of structural adjustment policies such as economic liberalization, privatization, and deregulation.

Much less familiar, however, is the place of politics as a goal or method of development work during those years. Some parts of that story are well known, such as the early hopeful belief that rapid economic development in poor countries would naturally lead to their political development, an essential part of what Samuel Huntington nicknamed and then devastatingly critiqued in his landmark 1968 book, *Political Order in Changing Societies*, as the development credo that "all good things go together."[1] Also familiar are the strictures Western aid providers imposed on developing countries in the 1980s to shrink their states as part of structural adjustment processes. Yet the larger picture of the place of politics in development assistance during the rise and fall of the initial orthodoxies has not been drawn.

To that end, this chapter addresses a number of core questions: Where did political goals fit within the evolving development theories and approaches? How politically informed were development methods? How did aid providers respond to the inevitable political obstacles and frustrations that arose as development aid unfolded? More broadly, why did an apolitical outlook gain such a strong and lasting grip on development aid in those early decades?

FORMATIVE YEARS

The modern development aid endeavor originated with an optimistic postwar vision of economic progress. The success of the Marshall Plan in Western Europe demonstrated how an infusion of resources could turn around devastated economies. Western officials hoped that similar assistance could help the decolonizing states of Africa, Asia, and the Middle East as well as Latin American countries escape from poverty. Additionally, the rapid pace of technological change in developed countries appeared to open up unlimited potential to transform individual lives. In 1949 U.S. President Harry Truman—decrying the misery in which more than half the world lived—boldly declared that

> for the first time in history, humanity possesses the knowledge and skill to relieve suffering of these people…our imponderable resources in technical knowledge are constantly growing and are inexhaustible. I believe that we should make available to peace-loving peoples the benefits of our store of technical knowledge in order to help them realize their aspirations for a better life.[2]

This call, known as Point Four of Truman's inaugural address, laid the foundation for U.S. development assistance abroad and reflected the optimistic hope at the time that new technologies could solve the problem of poverty.

By the early 1960s, development assistance had become an institutionalized enterprise. Major new development organizations were founded, including the United States Agency for International Development (USAID), the UK's Ministry of Overseas Development, and the World Bank's International Development Association. The emergent development aid community started with a fairly clear set of ideas about how aid could contribute to economic growth, which it viewed as the central driver of development. Aid would supply timely, well-targeted injections of capital to help developing country governments build power plants, roads, education systems, and other physical and social infrastructural foundations of economic modernization. Aid would also transfer to developing country counterparts the technical knowledge necessary for economic development, the know-how vital to fields like civil engineering, agriculture, and medicine. And aid would assist with what USAID and other new aid organizations termed "institution building"—helping recently decolonized states in the developing world build state institutions, especially those relating to key areas of economic management.

Indirect Political Goals

The immediate goals of development aid in this formative period were economic. But political goals were also clearly present. The United States viewed foreign assistance as a crucial tool to check the spread of leftist governments in the developing world. Many U.S. and other Western policymakers accepted the common policy maxim of those years that poverty was the root cause of leftist rebellions in developing countries. Fostering economic development, it followed, was a way to fight communism.

President John F. Kennedy and his foreign policy team hoped that aid would not just head off leftist takeovers in the Third World but also help multiply democracy there. In 1961 Kennedy described the fundamental task of foreign aid as helping to "make a historical demonstration that in the twentieth century, as in the nineteenth—in the southern half of the globe as in the north—economic growth and political democracy can develop hand in hand."[3] The belief that economic development would lead to political development (which was assumed to be the achievement of Western-style democratic systems) was a cardinal tenet of the modernization paradigm that underlay early development work. It drew from the influential work of Seymour Martin Lipset, who argued in 1959 that increased industrialization, urbanization, education, a stronger middle class, a denser civil society, greater equality, and other socioeconomic dimensions of modernization would create domestic social conditions supportive of democracy.[4]

This view of interconnected economic and political development made the Western, and particularly the American, historical experience (or at least mythologized versions of it) a guide for the developing world. It was part of what Robert Packenham chronicled in his classic book on development aid of the 1960s, *Liberal America and the Third World*, as the attempted application of "the American liberal experience" onto the developing world. This entailed the projection of a whole set of appealing but often misguided assumptions about how development would occur and how it could be aided, including "all good things go together" as well as "change and development are easy" and "radicalism and revolution are bad."[5]

Political goals were thus clearly present in development assistance in the early 1960s, but they were seen mainly as indirect goals that would follow from the achievement of more immediate economic ones. A partial exception to this was Kennedy's Alliance for Progress, launched in 1961 to further both democracy and social development in Latin America. The Alliance had explicit political goals and some politically controversial elements—such as land reform—but its main aim was to strengthen hemispheric ties as a way of fighting communism. This more directly pro-democratic approach lost steam when numerous Latin American governments regressed to dictatorial rule during the 1960s, shutting down the earlier hope for a widely democratic hemisphere.

Economic Development Theories

In their attempts to promote economic growth in developing countries, developmentalists drew on theories of the time that relied on a linear view of economic modernization. Their thinking about economic growth was heavily influenced by theories developed to explain the economies of industrialized countries. Prominent among these were the Harrod-Domar model, which posited that growth depended on investment levels, and the Solow model, which added the component of technological progress.[6] Extrapolating these ideas to the developing world, developmentalists saw economic growth as likely to result from increases in capital investment and technology. Drawing from similar ideas, Walt Whitman Rostow, in his influential 1960 book *The Stages of Economic Growth*, presented five stages of growth depicting the transition from a traditional to a high mass-consumption society. Economic "take-off" required changes in education and skills, productive technological development in key sectors, increased savings and investment, and the emergence of modern manufacturing.[7] Six years later, Hollis Chenery and Alan Strout also presented economic development as a series of phases and argued that developing countries faced growth bottlenecks due to deficiencies in skills, savings, and foreign exchange.[8] Strout at the time was chief of policy at USAID, and Chenery would go on to become vice president for development policy at the World Bank. This focus on the importance of increased investment and technological development provided a strong justification for foreign aid, which was well equipped to provide exactly those inputs.

Where did politics fit into this view of economic growth? Interestingly, Rostow gave it a central role. He wrote in *The Stages of Economic Growth* that "the building of an effective centralized national state—on the basis of coalitions touched with a new nationalism, in opposition to the traditional landed regional interests, the colonial power, or both . . . was, almost universally, a necessary condition for take-off" and that take-off in Britain and its former colonies was prompted not only by technological accumulation but also by "the emergence to political power of a group prepared to regard the modernization of the economy as serious, high-order political business."[9] Rostow later wrote *Politics and the Stages of Growth* in 1971 to elaborate his ideas on political development. These insights, however, were not as easily applicable to development practice as Rostow's writings on economic drivers, and they had much less influence on policy.

This is not to say that mainstream economic development theory discounted the role of government. On the contrary, it viewed government as a central driver of development. But it did not conceive of state-building processes and government behavior *politically*. Chenery and Strout, for example, emphasized the importance of domestic policies to prospects for growth but saw these conditions in technical and universal terms. They wrote that a "country maintaining high standards—say a marginal savings rate of .25 and a marginal capital-output ratio of less than 3.3—could safely be allotted whatever amount of aid it requested in the knowledge that the larger the amount of aid utilized, the higher would be its growth rate, and the more rapid its approach to self-sufficiency."[10] In other words, a government able to encourage savings and capital productivity would by definition use aid resources effectively.

Underlying this faith in proper policies was a strong belief in these years that aid-receiving governments were committed to developing their countries, and were not focused primarily on advancing the private interests of new ruling elites. In this view, aid was about *helping governmental counterparts do what they really wanted to do.* Anthony Downs had already observed in 1957 this general outlook among economists of his time: in their effort to move toward scientific analysis, economists paid little attention to political economy and thus "make policy prescriptions which assume governments should maximize welfare. But there is little point in advising governments to do so... unless there is some reason to believe that they will."[11]

This assumption of governmental good intentions was especially strong among developmentalists and was very much a product of the hopeful outlook of the early post-decolonization period and of the idealism of many members of the new aid community. As Christopher Adam and Stefan Dercon explain, Western development thinking focused on designing optimal interventions to address market failures, viewing the government as "a benevolent *deus ex machina,* disembodied from its social, historical, and political context that had fully internalized all relevant conflicts of interest."[12] As will be discussed further ahead, coming to terms with the weakness of that assumption has proven to be a long, angst-ridden process for the development community.

Technical Temptations

The Western-centric and largely apolitical orientation of development theory was replicated at the level of aid practice. Focusing exclusively on the technical aspects of development problems was an attractive option, seemingly so much simpler than complex issues of political intrusions on economic processes. This temptation of the technical also grew out of the considerable inexperience of many people within the new aid community and the instinctive reflex when confronted with dauntingly diverse and different foreign realities to project their own domestic experiences outward. The aid landscape was soon populated by projects attempting full-scale transfers of Western models, navigated by visiting Western experts with little knowledge of local contexts, often carried out on hurried time frames and with little buy-in by local counterparts. These methods were fueled by the strong American faith of these years in technology as a solution to all social and economic problems, whether at home or abroad. As David Lindauer and Lant Pritchett note, the "emphasis on accumulation did not exclude human capital; it just took the same approach to education as it did to steel. Large investments, spearheaded by the government, were required to create a labor force for industrialization."[13]

Aid providers could have conceived the institution-building assistance they got under way in those years as a form of political aid alongside the economic and social development programs. But they designed and implemented it too in an apolitical cast. They concentrated on the goal of promoting basic state competency to carry out economic and social development functions.[14] One of the most prominent areas of USAID's institution-building work in the 1960s, for example, focused on agricultural universities and sought to foster the indigenous expertise necessary to underpin a country's agricultural development. These programs were carried out by staff from American land grant colleges who rarely had experience in developing countries and worked to set up universities abroad on the model of their home institutions.[15] Donor-sponsored institution-building programs were set up in democracies and non-democracies alike—with the narrow technical definition of a good institution (that is, an efficient, competent one) potentially compatible with the state institutions of any kind of political system short of absolute despotism. And these programs do not appear to have reflected considered political understanding: aid providers approached institution building as a mechanistic process of transferring the needed management skills and organizational knowledge by applying blueprints from the West across diverse Third World contexts. Just as the right road-surfacing material would vanquish the problem of crumbling transportation infrastructure, a good dose of organizational management training, it was thought, would be sufficient to solve the problems of ministerial fecklessness in troubled Third World states.

This technocratic approach toward transforming developing country systems through better education extended from economic domains such as agriculture to the more obviously political area of law. Legal assistance made up a relatively small part of aid in the 1960s, but it gained a place in the U.S. development community when prominent U.S. lawyers and legal scholars began going abroad under the auspices of "law and development" programs. These programs sent U.S. legal experts to teach in developing countries and brought foreign students to the United States for legal studies. As James Gardner has described, this movement operated under the assumption that a stronger legal profession in developing countries, one that questioned "antiquated" legal systems and adopted the U.S. activist lawyer model, could contribute significantly to a country's development and strengthen its democracy.[16] Law and development proponents proposed to reform legal education in the Third World by replacing lecture and memorization with the case study and Socratic methods, and they promoted a new professional model emphasizing the instrumental use of law for social ends.[17]

U.S. legal "missionaries" carried out their efforts with scant attention to the sociopolitical context of target countries. They went abroad with U.S. legal models in their briefcases and attempted to apply them in legal cultures they knew only superficially, with little systematic regard for the role and interests of the state and lawyers in those societies.[18] David Trubek and Marc Galanter noted at the time that this movement was instead rooted in a series of fuzzy liberal assumptions. These included the view that state control furthered individual welfare and was exercised through law, that the legal profession did or could represent the public interest, that courts could provide justice for the poor, and that social behavior could be modified by changing the rules.[19] Gardner further explained that the movement's focus on reforming legal education was meant to encourage law students to become social actors, but it emphasized a technocratic case study method that did not encourage the examination of social context or offer any ethical guidance as to how the law should be used.[20] In keeping with the optimism of the times, law and development practitioners assumed that Third World countries were moving naturally toward greater political and economic development and that a new generation of lawyers would use their skills to advance developmental social change.

POLITICAL DISAPPOINTMENT

As the 1960s advanced, the hoped for knock-on political effects of development aid did not appear. Economic growth in developing countries did not automatically lead to the widespread social transformations—such as increased equality and a larger, more educated middle class—that modernization theorists saw as the preconditions of democracy. As Huntington so ably captured in *Political Order in Changing Societies*, what economic development did occur in developing countries often brought with it not democratization but heightened political conflict, violence, and repression. Far from marching in lockstep with economic progress, democracy significantly retreated in the second half of the 1960s—Latin America suffered various military takeovers, many initially pluralistic systems in sub-Saharan Africa sank into repressive one-party states, and democracy remained absent in most of Asia (with the large exception of India) and the Middle East. Policymakers' dreams of a simple path from economic growth to democratization thus faded in the harsh light of contrary realities.

For the development community, working in authoritarian contexts became the norm, a norm that ended up prevailing for more than twenty years. This reality reinforced the temptation of the technical that had by then become part of the bedrock of development work. To ensure their continued welcome in a largely nondemocratic developing world, aid organizations needed to avoid being political. That is to say, they could not talk politics, study the politics of the places they worked, work with politically sensitive nongovernmental actors, or attempt to change political systems. Moreover, for some sizable share of developmentalists, working closely with authoritarian governments was not a necessary evil but in fact the preferred option. In light of the instability that had marked many newly democratic developing countries in the first half of the 1960s, many aid providers came to believe that a firm hand, which often meant in practice a repressive, dictatorial hand, was the best bet for development. Autocratic leaders would be more stable than shaky democratic ones, better able to concentrate and exert the needed power to make the tough decisions necessary for development and to eschew short-term gains for the sake of long-term progress. The impressive economic growth led by dictatorships in Brazil and South Korea in the late 1960s seemed to reinforce that instinct. Reviewing the history of the World Bank's work in those years, Devesh Kapur, John Lewis, and Richard Webb note this outlook, writing that "authoritarian governments, less preoccupied by political survival and possessed of longer planning horizons and more freedom to impose technocratic agendas, were often at home with the Bank's traditional policy and lending preferences: stabilization and production-oriented investments."[21]

A Short-Lived Political Turn

In the United States, a loosely organized scattering of politicians, policy-makers, and aid practitioners pushed back against aid's accommodation to authoritarianism in the second half of the 1960s, advocating making political development an explicit rather than implicit part of U.S. foreign assistance. One of the strongest advocates of such an approach was Congressman Donald Fraser, who criticized the assumption that economic assistance would result in democratic progress as having "led us into blind alleys." He argued instead that "there is increasing evidence that the major shortcoming in the developing nations lies in their political and social structures. Until we address ourselves to this reality, little progress will be made."[22] Fraser, with the support of like-minded representatives, pushed for the passage of what became known as Title IX, a 1966 amendment to the U.S. Foreign Assistance Act that mandated that "emphasis shall be placed on assuring maximum participation in the task of economic development on the part of the people of the developing countries, through the encouragement of democratic private and local governmental institutions."[23]

Supporters of this new emphasis on participation—Title IX's proxy term for more open political engagement—were divided over how to implement it. Some called for a direct approach—directly supporting political organizations like political parties and parliaments. Others preferred not to risk rocking the overall aid boat too much politically and pushed for an indirect approach, contending, as Packenham explained, "that aid should focus not so much on explicitly political variables as on nonpolitical variables which in turn affected the political system."[24] The indirect approach won out. USAID Administrator William Gaud told Congress in 1968 that "the objectives of Title IX must be at the core of our development assistance. We have not tried to design a specific package of projects labeled Title IX. Instead we are trying to build Title IX objectives into the design and implementation process of the A.I.D. program."[25]

This ambitious promise of integrating political aid into the larger development assistance enterprise (which foreshadowed current efforts to integrate political goals and methods into socioeconomic areas of assistance, discussed in chapter 8) fell short in practice. Title IX led to a wave of studies of what a greater focus on participation might mean and some pilot efforts to make aid programs more participatory. USAID also supported various training programs for community leaders in developing countries and projects to assist local institutional development, often in sectors with direct relevance to economic development, such as farmers' cooperatives.[26] But on the whole there was no systemic change in the basic apolitical thrust of U.S. foreign assistance. Packenham notes that resistance within the mainstream U.S. development community toward more attention to politics was too great.

The U.S. policy community had adjusted to living with undemocratic governments in developing countries and was ready to support conservative authoritarians when it felt the alternative was takeover by communist or radical forces.[27] The realities of the Cold War meant that making and keeping friends within developing country governments was usually deemed more important than promoting democratic values. Moreover, even if the United States or other major donor actors had the political will to assist democracy in developing countries, many practitioners and policymakers doubted the feasibility of doing so through either aid or arm-twisting. Foreshadowing future challenges in democracy promotion, a USAID report to Congress in 1967 stated that the agency could neither export American democratic institutions nor "attempt to manufacture unique institutional solutions to host-country problems, and simply expect them to take root upon our insistence."[28]

Apolitical Methods

The accumulated disappointments with aid did not just spark thinking in the late 1960s about incorporating political goals into assistance. They also raised the idea of using more political methods. As technocratically conceived development programs began to bounce off often unreceptive foreign realities, some aid practitioners place the blame on the lack of organized political thinking and understanding at the operational level. This was especially clear in the institution-building domain. Reviews of early institution-building work underscored the need for greater understanding of the process of institutional development and the limitations of external experts coming in with narrowly focused technical solutions based on Western experiences.[29] As one writer noted, "little active thought was given to institution-building as a process—a complex and difficult one at that—or the possibilities and means of consciously influencing this process."[30]

This general problem was evident in reviews of the agricultural university institution-building efforts described earlier, which praised some of the efforts but noted significant limitations arising from the poor fit between technical capabilities and complex realities. One 1968 evaluation of USAID's program observed that "we have no thorough studies of the factors responsible for the development of the quite different types of land grant colleges which occur in the U.S.," much less how such institutions would develop in foreign countries, and "team members have only rarely been selected on the basis of demonstrated skills in institution building at home."[31] A later World Bank retrospective study found that its agricultural research programs sometimes had unrealistic expectations about how much domestic support would be available to sustain institutions. The World Bank, it said, "has been more successful in supporting development of physical facilities than in improving the planning and management of the research program and application of its results."[32]

The law and development movement was subject to particularly harsh criticism by the end of the decade, sometimes coming from its original architects and proponents. The U.S.-centric nature of law and development programs and their lack of attention to local conditions and needs led recipients to reject many of these efforts, particularly the call to change the model of legal education. The movement may have had more of an impact in promoting a new professional model of lawyers as engaged and assertive social actors, but here it encountered unexpected consequences.[33] With authoritarianism on the rise in the developing world, many law and development practitioners came to realize that neither the state nor the legal profession would automatically promote the general social welfare. As James Gardner observed, "the movement that was launched to train the 'architects of democracy' trained instead the legal technocrats of one or another military dictatorship, corporatist state, or privileged elite."[34]

Some analysts and practitioners extended the criticism of apolitical aid methods beyond institution-building programs and legal reform to all areas of assistance. Writing in 1967, Albert Hirschman argued that sociopolitical context plays a central role in the success of development projects and that aid planners face a basic dilemma: they should either take the sociopolitical context in which they are working as a given and adjust their project design and expectations accordingly ("trait-taking") or decide that their project requires transforming sociopolitical conditions ("trait-making") and acknowledge the difficulties of doing so. Yet this dilemma was rarely explicitly addressed in planning processes, leading many projects to fail due to unanticipated sociopolitical obstacles such as corruption or lack of political support.[35]

This ignorance of sociopolitical contexts in development planning was detrimental to project effectiveness but nevertheless appears to have had some logic. Hirschman observed that since development projects are complicated and unpredictable, to gain funding and support development planners tend to overestimate likely project benefits or present their projects either as following an established model that has worked well in other contexts (pseudo-imitation) or as an innovative and comprehensive project that will address all relevant issues (pseudo-comprehensive).[36] Hardheaded political analysis would likely undermine the rationale for high expectations, easy replicability or the ability to control all factors, raising difficult questions about the feasibility of meeting development goals.

Some development agencies did acknowledge the importance of gaining a better understanding of local contexts and began to hire social scientists to work on their projects. Yet power remained in the hands of those considered to be technical experts, usually economists or socioeconomic sector specialists. A sharply written article by Ian Hamnett in 1970, entitled "A Social Scientist Among Technicians," lamented the lack of political understanding in aid interventions using terms highly similar to laments coming from some aid practitioners today. Hamnett noted that social scientists were "regarded as a luxury or even prestige item" in development work. Their role, he said, was unfortunately confined to supporting technical experts by assessing what attitudes local people had toward development projects, how these people could be induced to accept technical development goals, and which goals might have to be abandoned as unworkable given local resistance.[37] In fulfilling this role, social scientists helped development planners deal with the dilemma Hirschman had articulated between trait-taking and trait-making in project design. Yet, as Hamnett noted, this was a highly limited incorporation of political thinking; technicians continued to drive the agenda.[38]

These early critics also pointed out how the absolute faith in technocratic solutions to development problems prevented serious consideration of the political consequences of aid. Hamnett observed that "decisions that were made on engineering or accounting grounds were not regarded as involving 'policy': they counted as 'objective' recommendations" and while development experts were wary of getting involved in anything "political," "where matters of 'technical rationality' were involved, the engineering experts would happily make recommendations of a fairly radical kind without any discomfort: for instance, to nationalise all water rights."[39] Hirschman sounded a similar note, explaining that "the technician's dictatorial ambition is often strangely combined with his disclaimer of responsibility for the ultimate decision which he shrugs off as having been influenced by 'political' factors."[40] This was the logical extension of the temptation of the technical and part of what made it such an appealing, but also dangerous, idea. Technocratic solutions were viewed not only as capable of solving the problems of the developing world, but also as unproblematic and objective recommendations. Since social and political factors were not considered an essential part of the development equation, the consequences of technical interventions in these areas were neglected. Yet the initial expressions of concern about the shortcomings of apolitical methods in these early years were lone voices, prescient but unable to gain much traction in an aid community already attached to apolitical methods and dominated by staff who saw themselves as technocrats.

THE SHIFT TO BASIC NEEDS

By the early 1970s, doubts about the ability of development aid to produce economic growth in recipient countries permeated Western policy circles. Moreover, even where aid appeared to be contributing to growth, the gains were not trickling down and improving the lives of poor people as much as aid providers had hoped, and developing country governments did not always appear to have the best interests of the poor at heart.[41] As a result, the aid community shifted gears, adopting a greater emphasis on poverty reduction alongside or sometimes in place of economic growth. Some aid providers formulated the challenge of reducing poverty in terms of a "basic human needs" strategy.

Definitions of basic needs differed, ranging from narrowly focused economic criteria to broader conceptions that cut across various social concerns or even political rights. A fierce, polarizing debate—an early phase of the growth vs. poverty reduction debate that has riven development economics for two generations—over the wisdom of the shift preoccupied many parts of the development community in those years. Growth proponents worried that shifting attention to poverty reduction would mean embracing economic redistribution and giving up on growth altogether. Advocates of a poverty focus accused growth proponents of callousness toward the suffering of the poor and of being stuck in a discredited paradigm. After he took up the presidency of the World Bank in 1968, Robert McNamara tried to bridge this divide. He embraced the cause of poverty reduction but insisted it could be pursued without forsaking growth, promoting instead the idea of "redistribution with growth."[42]

Challenging Western Models

The emergence of this new, or at least modified, development orthodoxy took place in a larger context of ideological ferment and argument over relations between the West and the Third World. The hopes of the early 1960s for mutually productive, positive relations between the West and developing countries in the South had dissipated. Angry accusations from many poor countries of Western political domination and economic exploitation multiplied. In response to Western lamentations about persistent poverty and rising inequality within poor countries, developing country governments pushed back, contending that the root problem was inequality *among* nations and structural obstacles at the international level that were keeping poor countries poor. The 1974 UN General Assembly resolution calling for a New International Economic Order—one that would feature state sovereignty, the right of developing countries to determine their own economic policies and control their own resources, and greater assistance to developing countries—formalized that view.[43]

Development aid thus had to navigate roiling political waters in those years. But the aid community did not respond with political goals in the sense of trying to achieve positive political change in developing countries through aid. The 1960s hope that fostering economic development would lead to political development had largely eroded. Authoritarianism dominated most of the developing world. The United States and its Cold War allies were focused in the developing world on maintaining the friendships they had—no matter that most were of the tyrannical rather than democratic type—rather than on trying to foster democratic change. Aid was a tool for reinforcing such friendships, not for trying to change friends.

Moreover, in at least parts of the development community critical views surfaced about the value of Western democracies as a model for Third World countries. Fidel Castro's early success in improving the living standards of many ordinary Cubans featured prominently in debates over ideal models of economic and political development for other developing countries. Questioning of Western models gained particular traction in the health sector, where some pointed to innovations such as Chinese barefoot doctors and Indian rural healthcare as a better solution to the needs of the poor than imported systems based on costly modern hospitals and highly trained doctors.[44] These views evolved into a global movement around primary healthcare, capped by the 1978 International Conference on Primary Health Care at Alma-Ata. The Alma-Ata declaration called for a comprehensive approach to healthcare based on priority treatment of common diseases and access to essential drugs as well as to health education, nutrition, and basic sanitation. It also declared that governments were responsible for the health of their people and that the people had a right and duty to participate in healthcare planning and implementation, introducing the issues of political rights and responsibilities into the healthcare debate.[45]

Within this divisive international context, basic human needs and poverty reduction acquired political associations, and some developmentalists saw them as political goals. For many on the left, no progress on poverty was possible without transforming exploitative economic and political power relations. This interpretation led some conservatives to regard the basic needs concept as dangerously political, believing that it sought to create new rights and implied radical economic redistribution.[46] Yet in practice basic needs never rose to the level of a political goal for development agencies. The questioning of Western models and criticism of the international order coming from developing countries did not fully penetrate aid agencies. The mainstream aid organizations that adopted the basic human needs agenda, such as USAID and the Canadian International Development Agency (CIDA), hewed to a more narrow interpretation of it as serving basic economic needs through health, education, agricultural support, and other programs targeted at the poor.[47] The UK government did not talk much about basic needs, saying it was not convinced they were compatible with growth.[48] The World Bank explored but did not fully embrace basic human needs terminology, in part out of fear of its radical implications. The Bank also resisted pressure to take human rights into account in its programs, saying they could conflict with economic goals.[49]

Development agencies did sometimes embrace participation as part of a poverty reduction approach, but participation usually fell short of being a goal in itself. The participation components of mainstream poverty programs were often instrumental means of securing the cooperation and contribution of poor people to donor or government development plans rather than a mechanism for popular liberation. The poor were rarely viewed as empowered actors able to claim their rights to government services.

Influencing Developing Country Policy

The modified development orthodoxy of the 1970s did confront aid providers with some of the challenges of crafting more politically informed methods. But it did not end up producing any systematic response to those challenges. Concentrating more directly on the task of poverty reduction led development agencies to try to influence the policies of recipient governments in a wide range of areas, especially relating to agriculture, health, and education. The World Bank played a particularly important role in such externally based policy advocacy. McNamara felt that it could have more impact on poverty reduction through policy influence and advice than through direct lending, implying a wider, deeper involvement in the policy processes of developing countries.[50] Accounts of the World Bank and, to a lesser extent, other development organizations in those years note the efforts of aid providers to weigh in with host country governments on socioeconomic decisionmaking processes. These accounts also highlight the limits of donors' attempted policy influence, such as the Bank's inability to overcome the political resistance it encountered trying to persuade the Brazilian government to give greater attention to equity.[51]

This engagement in trying to influence policy processes in developing countries—and the frustration that often accompanied it—produced an impetus in certain parts of the aid community to think more politically. More specifically, it prompted some development actors to consider carrying out more systematic political analysis of the local contexts where they were operating. At the World Bank, for example, some "Country Program Papers" (which were introduced in the late 1960s and served as the basis for high-level discussion of country loan programs) started explicitly considering the politics of borrowing governments.[52] Some of the Bank's country reviews also looked at political issues, such as a 1973 review of the roots of inequality in the Philippines.[53] A World Bank book written in 1981 on the basic human needs agenda highlighted a lack of will on the part of many developing country governments to implement poverty reduction policies. It recommended that aid providers give greater attention to understanding why developing country elites act as they do and how such elites could be incentivized to support poverty reduction policies. Prefiguring what today is a key operating assumption among proponents of greater attention to politics in development, it suggested that government policy in developing countries be seen as "one of the dependent variables that can be shaped and improved by the other variables of the social system, especially by reformist coalitions."[54]

Yet this emergent impulse in the 1970s for aid providers to start being more political by engaging in political analysis and thinking about how policy processes might be politically supported turned out to be only a tentative knock at the door of politics. The habits of technocratic approaches, and of standardized practices often poorly suited to local contexts, already ran deep. Mainstream aid organizations did not develop systematic new efforts to adopt more politically smart operations. A report in 1978 by the Overseas Development Institute observed that advocates of the basic human needs approach sometimes demanded a whole series of pro-poor policy changes from governments, underestimating domestic opposition to that agenda and failing to take seriously the challenge of finding ways to mobilize support for needed reforms.[55] At the same time, donors' propensity to dictate unrealistic policy solutions coexisted with a lack of serious commitment to follow through on their demands. Bilateral donors were generally more concerned with maintaining their diplomatic relationships with Third World governments, while the World Bank was undergoing a major push to increase the overall volume of its lending. Most incentives within aid agencies were to get money out the door, not to get caught up in troublesome policy debates. Recipient country governments often responded to what pressure did exist to enact pro-poor policies with protests that such efforts constituted unacceptable interference in their domestic politics.[56]

Political thinking was even less present at the project level. Significant percentages of development spending continued to go to traditional economic programs. To the extent that agencies developed basic needs or poverty-focused projects, such efforts remained technocratic in design and implementation.[57] As was the case in the 1960s, the apolitical tendency made itself felt especially strongly in programs relating to institutional reform. A World Bank review of its institutional development work from this period observed that little could be learned from the projects under review because the World Bank lacked a conceptual framework to guide its work in this area and noted that the "state of the art" of institutional development had a number of shortcomings. These included proceeding in a top-down fashion often poorly suited to local contexts, inappropriately applying quantitative techniques, and failing to link cultural and political patterns with organizational and managerial issues.[58] It observed particular problems in Bank work in the social sectors due to insufficient attention to local culture, but, revealing the continued technocratic bias of the time, also noted that work in technical and financial sectors is easier because processes that require high technology will be the same everywhere and "the modernizing effects of industry and technology are sufficiently powerful to overcome cultural traits."[59]

Rural Development and "The Anti-Politics Machine"

The dominance of exclusively technical approaches to social problems was evident in one of the most prominent, popular forms of pro-poor programming of the decade: "integrated rural development projects." These interventions aimed at improving small farm productivity by providing farmers in defined geographic areas with a variety of integrated social and economic services managed through a single project. They were driven by high hopes of finally addressing the multidimensional nature of poverty. But by the end of the decade, the model was widely considered a failure.[60] Retrospective evaluations of integrated rural development efforts by U.S. and UK aid agencies as well as the World Bank found them weakened by the sorts of shortcomings characteristic of programs that fail to take politics into account: a dependence on blueprint designs not well adapted to the needs of local communities, unreasonable expectations and time frames, difficulty reaching those famers most in need of assistance (including in some cases interventions that disproportionately benefited wealthy farmers who were better able than poor farmers to position themselves to receive assistance), the creation of unsustainable management institutions within the recipient countries that failed to integrate with existing domestic structures, and a general failure to take into account the broader social and policy context.[61] One 1987 evaluation concluded with calls for more attention to differences in social status and power among program participants and to the political commitment of the host government.[62]

A similar type of rural development program formed the basis for James Ferguson's *The Anti-Politics Machine,* a sharp critique of the apolitical nature of development assistance. Based on fieldwork in Lesotho in 1982–1983, Ferguson recounts how a World Bank and CIDA agricultural project systematically ignored Lesotho's sociopolitical context—including the fact that the economy was primarily centered around income from migrant laborers working in South Africa, the role and value of livestock to the community, and the political interests of the ruling party. The project recommended a focus on increasing agricultural productivity through a government-administered program to improve the quality of livestock and provide other services to small farmers. These solutions were ill-suited to the context, and the project failed to reach its development objectives. But that does not mean it had no effects. The project was co-opted by the ruling party and helped contribute to an expansion of bureaucratic state power. Despite these political consequences, the "technical" nature of this and similar initiatives elsewhere allowed their advocates to present them as a neutral good.[63]

In making this critique, Ferguson does not subscribe to the radical views of development that see the apparently apolitical nature of development as a facade that aid providers use to camouflage their efforts to impose exploitative capitalism on the developing world. He does, however, argue that ignorance of sociopolitical context serves a purpose for development actors. Development consultants tend to include only what is "useful" in their analyses, thus emphasizing areas where development actors have control, such as agricultural productivity, over areas where they do not, such as Lesotho's dependence on South Africa. Echoing Hirschman's critique of the "pseudo-imitation" project model, Ferguson also points out that presenting Lesotho as a typical least-developed country allowed the World Bank and others to justify recycling interventions they had used elsewhere.[64]

THE RISE OF THE MARKET MODEL

The market-led model of development, or neoliberal model, took hold in the development community with remarkable speed and force in the first half of the 1980s. It grew out of the accumulated discrediting of the earlier state-led model of development, the debt crisis in Latin America and elsewhere, and the rise of Reaganism and Thatcherism in the West. Out were attempts to persuade developing country governments to spend more on services to the poor. Getting developing country governments to cut spending and adopt stabilization and structural adjustment programs suddenly became the order of the day for major actors in the development community. Although this new development orthodoxy upended significant parts of the earlier approach—especially the prior emphasis on the state as the locomotive of development—it did not, at least in its first phase that unfolded across the 1980s, reverse the basic apolitical mindset of the development community. In fact, it largely reinforced this mindset in new ways.

The market model prioritized investment and trade over aid as key external factors for development. But aid did nonetheless have a role—providing financing and advice to help facilitate structural adjustment. Policy reform took center stage, coinciding with the rise of the international financial institutions as the driving intellectual force within the development community. This trend was marked in part by the highly influential 1981 World Bank report *Accelerated Development in Sub-Saharan Africa: An Agenda for Action*, known as the Berg report, which argued that diminishing the role of the state and achieving key domestic policy reforms were central to African development.[65] These ideas were enthusiastically adopted by the Reagan administration, which made policy dialogue and reform, institutional development (with a focus on decentralization and privatization), technology transfer, and private sector development the four pillars of its aid policy.[66]

The new orthodoxy radiated the confident belief that the solution to the problem of development was finally at hand. Development practitioners not only recognized the importance of domestic economic policies, but they also had a definitive answer to what the appropriate policies should be. Aid would help developing country governments understand that answer and put it into practice. These policies included trade liberalization, reliance on markets, and minimizing the role of government.[67] Anne Krueger, an architect of World Bank policy in the 1980s, also argued that there was general agreement around a number of additional policy lessons: countries needed appropriate exchange rates, effective incentive structures, high domestic savings, responsible fiscal and monetary policies, and human capital.[68] This new focus on "getting the policies right" (or perhaps more accurately, getting developing country governments to get the policies right) led to the wide use in the 1980s of policy-based lending and other forms of policy-related aid conditionality.

Host Country Policymaking

The new market orthodoxy led the development community more deeply into efforts to influence host country policymaking. Yet the mainstream aid providers operated from the idea that the market model was a purely economic model, not a quest for certain political outcomes. As long as host country governments put the "right" economic policies in place, any type of political system would do. Behind closed doors this political agnosticism gave way to the familiar belief of some developmentalists that authoritarian governments were better suited than democratic ones in the developing world to carry out the tough tasks necessary for structural adjustment, above all imposing fiscal austerity and sticking with it in the face of angry public reactions. The "Asian Tiger" model of development was highly influential in those years, and the strong hand and stable character of those governments, as well as their perceived market orientation, were an intrinsic part of that model for many of its advocates.[69]

The market model brought up inevitable questions about the role of the state. Aid providers presented their emphasis on the need for developing country governments to shrink their public sectors and to decrease economic regulation as a neutral technical recommendation. But it was in part intended to respond to a political problem that aid providers were increasingly giving attention to—the fact that previous state-led aid programs had fallen victim to state predation. The solution, however, was to minimize politics rather than engage with them. The smaller the state, the less predation could occur. Critics on the left saw moves to shrink the state as the incorporation of a political model into the overall development model—what these critics called "the neoliberal state," a weakened political state inclined to favor the interests of foreign investors and unwilling or unable to protect the interests of the poor. Conservatives did not have a monopoly on skepticism of the state, however. Some on the left also saw developing country states as part of the problem because their governments represented ruling class interests at the expense of popular welfare.[70] Aid to such states would thus be unlikely to benefit the poor.

As much as they tried to present their recommendations in apolitical terms, Western enthusiasts of the market model for developing countries could not escape the domestic politics of the countries in question. They needed some way to persuade recipient governments to adopt their preferred policies. At first Western governments hoped they could avoid these problems by letting the International Monetary Fund (IMF) and the World Bank take a lead in policy negotiations, believing they would appear as politically neutral, technically driven actors.[71] These institutions, however, quickly confronted the limits of their technical credibility as a persuasive force in the face of strong domestic resistance. Their reaction was to look for political methods but construe them in narrow, instrumental terms, that is, how could they find ways to avoid or overcome local opposition to market reforms? And their initial, quite blunt attempt to answer this question was to exert pressure on aid-receiving governments to adopt structural adjustment programs by making aid conditional on such reforms.

Pressure alone largely proved a study in frustration, however, and provoked within many developing countries a strong backlash against international donors. Structural adjustment programs tended to impose immediate costs on influential social groups while promising benefits that were mostly long term. Even authoritarian governments were sometimes unable or unwilling to impose these policies on their populations. What Western developmentalists presented as a rational economic model with self-evident legitimacy was debated fiercely within developing countries (and, of course, within at least some parts of the Western policy and scholarly worlds as well) as a deeply political set of choices raising fundamental issues about equity, fairness, and other sensitive issues.

Popular discontent led governments to cancel, renegotiate, or just not follow through on their structural adjustment commitments. In Peru, for example, the highly unpopular austerity measures imposed by IMF conditionality in the early 1980s contributed to the electoral defeat of the incumbent political party and the 1985 presidential victory of Alan Garcia, who once in office cut ties with the IMF and attempted to implement heterodox economic reform. In Zambia, efforts to liberalize prices and increase business efficiency led to rising prices and unemployment, hurting the urban working class. Strikes, rioting, and other protests became increasingly widespread. In 1987, after nearly a decade of IMF adjustment programs, the government canceled its relations with the Fund and backtracked on reforms.[72] Jeffrey Hawkins argued in 1991 that the Zambia program failed "because the reforms attacked the economic heart of the developmentalist political economic model without creating a basis of political support for a new regime" and that the IMF "must be willing to include politics in the reform equation."[73]

Political Glimmers

These experiences led some developmentalists to look beyond the blunt instrument of conditionality for other ways to understand and address the political obstacles to market reforms. The idea of carrying out political analyses to better understand the presence or absence of local political will to reform gained new attention at the World Bank and other aid organizations. Joan Nelson, for example, made the case in 1984 for more donor political analysis. Trying to deflect economists' concerns about the possible political sensitivities of such analysis, she argued that "anticipating political reactions and adjusting one's own action accordingly is not tantamount to intervention ... failure to do so, in fact, is irresponsible."[74] She proposed a framework for political analysis based on assessing the commitment of political leaders, the capacity of governments to implement programs, and the likely responses of important societal groups, as well as some techniques for addressing political obstacles and building societal support.[75] But as in the 1970s, the idea did not gain momentum within an aid community mired in the habit of avoiding unpleasant local political truths. Philip Ndegwa, a former Kenyan official, notes that, "in the early years of structural adjustment, the World Bank was rather naïve and unrealistic," trying to impose harsh conditions in short time frames without taking into account economic and political complexities.[76] In 1986 Robert Berg wrote that donors were insufficiently sensitive to the national political and administrative features of the places where they worked.[77] Similar strong calls for more attention to the politics of policy reform were still being heard at the end of the decade.[78]

Awareness of political constraints did lead to some efforts to affirmatively build political support for donor policies in recipient countries rather than simply apply pressure. The World Bank dabbled with the idea of trying to help aid-receiving countries build a broader societal consensus for structural adjustment programs through dialogue and targeted social programs. As Carol Lancaster recounts, the World Bank conducted a study of African perceptions of its work in 1983 that revealed criticism of arrogant Bank behavior and lack of knowledge of local realities among its staff. The organization responded with efforts to reach out to influential Africans, incorporate more African staff and advisers, and strengthen allies in recipient governments through workshops and seminars to develop reform programs that would be based on a wider societal consensus.[79]

Yet these efforts ended up amounting to little because they were not accompanied by a serious willingness to adjust economic prescriptions to local needs and demands. Claude Ake articulated the persistent frustration among many critics of the World Bank and the IMF when he argued in 1991 that officials of the international financial institutions "think that political variables can simply be treated as an engineering problem and 'factored in' to improve the effectiveness of their structural adjustment programs, and thus that they can avoid changing their overall approach to development" and "in every case, they were quite content to settle the issues with the president of the client country or his economics or finance minister. Having done so, they constantly urged the necessity of political will to carry out the program—a euphemism for its coercive imposition."[80]

The focus on growth and adjustment in the 1980s did not eliminate project assistance to social sectors, but this aid became if anything more apolitical. The language of "basic human needs" became that of "human resources" or "human capital," concepts easier to fit within economic growth models and less politically threatening. Donor aid for education, women, rural areas, and other social priorities was justified as supporting productive sectors essential to the economy and likely to be underfinanced by the free market.[81] Some voices, including CIDA President Marcel Massé early in the decade, called for greater attention to sociological factors in these programs and the inclusion of social scientists in development planning, but most agencies continued to fall short in this area.[82] Robert Berg noted in 1986 that, "since the on-board strength of social scientists in donor and recipient governmental organizations is low to non-existent, a turnaround in the mediocre social results of aided activities is not apt to come soon."[83]

New Focus on Institutions

The donor community also gave attention to helping strengthen domestic institutions, but this assistance was very much shaped by the ideological current of the times. It focused on government institutions that would carry out structural adjustment reforms or in some cases were important to human resource development, and it added an emphasis on the role of nongovernmental organizations. In the 1960s donors had cast such efforts as "institution building"; in the 1980s they stressed instead the concept of "institutional development." The difference was in helping create state institutions where they barely existed (the task in the 1960s) versus helping strengthen institutions that were already in place.[84] The World Bank set up a Public Sector Management Unit in 1983 and began to pursue comprehensive public sector reform in various regions, especially sub-Saharan Africa. USAID also engaged in a wave of institutional development work. Reflecting the general anti-state feelings of the time, its policy guidance emphasized the importance of working with private actors to deliver development outcomes and linking USAID institutional support to measures that help the private sector.[85]

While donors made some attempts to learn the lessons of past failed efforts at aiding developing country institutions, this new wave ended up being plagued by the same tendency to underestimate the underlying political complexities of such work and proceed from simplistic technocratic approaches based on the attempted transfer of Western blueprints. USAID's 1983 policy paper on institutional development, for example, emphasized the need to adapt institutions to local realities. Over the course of the decade the agency did experiment with some more iterative, process-focused approaches to programming, but these were limited by the need to establish targets in advance and provide clear accountability for project activities.[86] Various donor-sponsored reviews of institutional development work throughout the 1980s echoed depressingly familiar criticisms. USAID evaluations in 1982 and 1991 emphasized very similar points: the success of institutional development programs relies heavily on support from host government policymakers as well as realistic project plans, and such programs need to pay attention to the political influence and capacity of their counterparts rather than just their technical skills.[87]

Reviews of the World Bank's work pointed to similarly inadequate attention to political factors underlying institutional dysfunction, poorly executed, expatriate-dominated technical assistance carried out within overly short time frames and reliant on blueprint approaches, insufficient focus on institutionalization, and a lack of understanding of host government commitment and incentives.[88] An official evaluation of World Bank lending looking back at the 1970s and 1980s highlighted the central importance of institutional strength to program effectiveness but observed that "in many of the countries that most need it, there is rather little evidence of lasting achievement in institutional development through Bank-supported operations" and stressed the need for more institutional analysis to understand cultural values, political systems, and the motivations of key actors.[89] Beatrice Buyck pointed to a number of factors that contributed to these shortcomings in Bank work on institutional development, including high staff turnover, incentives to get projects out quickly and de-emphasize analysis of intangible factors that could threaten project approval, discomfort among technically trained Bank staff with political analysis and questioning of government motives, lack of institutional or staff knowledge on what works in public sector management, and the complex and unpredictable nature of institutional development processes.[90]

EARLY POLITICAL AID

In the 1980s, two Western powers, the United States and Germany, began providing openly political aid to the developing world in an effort to help countries democratize. In Germany this was carried out by the German *Stiftungen*, the political foundations affiliated with the main German political parties, such as the Konrad Adenauer Foundation and the Friedrich Ebert Foundation. After helping Spain and Portugal with their transitions to democracy in the 1970s, these foundations turned their attention to Latin America in the 1980s, extending support to political parties and civic activists taking part in the region's widening movement away from repressive military rule. In the United States, the Reagan administration decided to make democracy support a prominent part of its foreign policy framework, arguing that actively aiding freedom abroad was a crucial element of the Cold War struggle to check Soviet influence in the developing world. A supportive Congress funded the establishment of the National Endowment for Democracy in 1983. The endowment and its four core grantee organizations that were established soon after (representing the two main U.S. political parties as well as organized labor and the business community) started operating in many countries to support free and fair elections, political party development, independent labor unions, democracy activists, and other pro-democratic actors. Democracy aid gained a toehold at

USAID in the second half of the 1980s. An office for democracy strengthening opened in the agency's Latin America bureau to fund programs around the region intended to strengthen judicial systems and to support election administration and election monitoring, human rights activists, and democratic civic education. USAID's Asia and Near East bureau also conducted some democratic institution-building activities, mainly around legal reform and promoting awareness of civil and political rights.[91]

This new arena of explicitly political aid operated largely separately from the development aid community. In fact, the two communities regarded each other with wariness or even open suspicion. Developmentalists were skeptical that democracy aid would amount to anything more than organized efforts to manipulate foreign political outcomes for narrow national self-interest. And they feared that such activities would contaminate development aid by association in the eyes of host country governments and societies. Democracy aid providers, in turn, were skeptical of the world of development aid. They regarded such aid as usually slow, bureaucratic, and too cozy with repressive rulers. They were primarily concerned with political change, not economic growth or other traditional priorities of the development aid community. Even though USAID did open its door to democracy aid (largely through pressure from the State Department), it was at first only a small opening. Most people at the agency kept their distance from such work, and as Thomas Carothers notes in his review of the early years of democracy assistance at USAID, "AID sees itself as an economic development organization, not a political development one … political development assistance requires a deeply sophisticated understanding of the process of political change in diverse foreign cultures. AID lacks such political capabilities and has shown no interest in acquiring them."[92]

Though small and largely separate from the world of development aid, this new field of democracy aid was a noteworthy addition to the overall landscape of international assistance. It represented the start of a very different kind of assistance—aid that is specifically and openly political both in its goal and in the type of institutions with which it works. It embodied the direct approach to political work that USAID briefly considered in the late 1960s but ultimately avoided. As analyzed in subsequent chapters, it grew significantly in size and scope during the following two decades and began to build some bridges to the socioeconomic development community.

CONCLUSION

The practice of development assistance in its early decades was not isolated from politics. Development practitioners inevitably had to grapple with political realities in different ways. The aid community shied away, however, from adopting explicitly political goals, initially hoping that socioeconomic assistance would have follow-on positive political effects, but then largely giving up on that hope as Third World politics took a strongly authoritarian turn. The temptation of the technical strongly shaped the methods of development aid, with aid providers hoping they could resolve development challenges through technical best practices without having to involve themselves too deeply in messy local political realities. This apolitical approach grew out of the theories of economic development that dominated the early years of development aid.

Even as the initial orthodoxy of state-led development adopted a partial focus on basic human needs in the 1970s and then gave way to the surging new market orthodoxy of the 1980s, apolitical thinking about economic change continued to hold sway. Aid providers for the most part believed that economic development could occur under any type of political regime and that autocratic governance was compatible with each of the major development orthodoxies. The larger international political context of the Cold War reinforced the apolitical pattern in both the goals and methods of aid. Although the aid endeavor as a whole was very much tied to overarching geopolitical objectives, developmentalists on the ground wanted to steer clear of "playing politics" in order to gain credibility with host governments and aid-receiving societies. Moreover, the structures of the new business of international aid, dominated by the outlook of rationalistic economic planning, quickly took on forms and habits that worked against politically informed methods. While development economists in each of the decades, especially the 1980s, were eager to provide policy advice to developing country counterparts, aid practitioners did not systematically confront the domestic political factors behind government policy choices or how to deal with a lack of government commitment to their preferred policies.

Across the decades a growing set of incisive critics—Hirschman, Packenham, Hamnett, Ferguson, Buyck, and others—pointed out a number of similar factors that tended to discourage significant political analysis in development planning. Projects were more likely to be approved and funded if they appeared to be safe bets replicating initiatives that had worked elsewhere. And the internal pressure at aid organizations was to allocate funds with as little delay as possible. Sociopolitical analyses were likely to bring up more questions and complications than clear answers and could hinder project approval. Development agencies were also staffed largely by technical experts such as economists, engineers, agronomists, and others who tended to be uncomfortable with and unequipped for political analysis. They may have complained behind closed doors about political obstacles to their work, but they usually did not feel they could or should explicitly address them in program planning. Government partners were assumed to be trustworthy because their cooperation was necessary for project implementation. To the extent that aid providers carried out political analysis, it was usually narrowly targeted to produce operational guidance useful to specific projects rather than to explore the larger validity of program strategy.

Practitioners frustrated by programs that performed poorly did start to call for greater attention to sociopolitical contexts, more research on processes of institutional change, and efforts to build local political support for donor priorities. Critics pointed out the serious political consequences that putatively apolitical projects produced in developing countries, especially with regard to fortifying already overcentralized power structures. Yet these concerns generally did not reach the top levels of aid organizations or result in significant institutional responses to take politics more seriously within development planning—the deep early roots of the apolitical approach overrode their voices. By the end of the 1980s, however, aid organizations did begin to rethink some of their beliefs about the role of politics in the development process. This reconsideration, combined with the sudden reordering of the international political landscape in the 1990s, opened the door, at least partly, to politics. How and why the door opened is the subject of the next chapter.

BREAKING THE
POLITICAL TABOO:
1990s–2000s

CHAPTER 3

THE DOOR OPENS TO POLITICS

INTRODUCTION

After decades of avoiding talking about or acting on political issues, in the early 1990s mainstream aid organizations suddenly changed tack. They began repeatedly emphasizing a close connection between political and economic development, and publicly committing themselves to achieving political goals in the developing world. They held out these new goals, which some framed as improving developing country governance and others as fostering democracy, as being both intrinsically worthwhile and also instrumentally valuable for achieving socioeconomic progress in the places they worked.

Why after thirty years of a deeply entrenched apolitical approach did the mainstream development community abruptly shift gears and put politics (at least rhetorically) at the core of its agenda? To what extent did this new agenda at the level of stated commitments translate into more political approaches in practice? Were the changes more about pursuing political ends or employing more political methods? Answering these questions takes us deeply into the 1990s, a time of profound changes in the international context for development aid, and also brings us into the first decade of the new century. This chapter covers the 1990s while the next two follow the story into the subsequent decade.

NEW POLITICAL GOALS

Public commitments by major aid providers to political goals mushroomed in the 1990s. In 1991 USAID elaborated a new agency policy that explicitly tied democracy and governance to the agency's overall development mission, asserting that "political development is central to sustained economic and social development" and that arbitrary or unresponsive governments retard economic growth.[1] CIDA included political sustainability as one of five pillars of the Canadian aid organization's 1991 framework for sustainable development.[2] In the same year, the Swedish International Development Cooperation Agency (Sida) published official guidelines for "making government work" programs.[3] The World Bank published a major report in 1992 on governance and development, the product of a sizable task force on the topic, stating in clear terms that "good governance is central to creating and sustaining an environment which fosters strong and equitable development, and it is an essential complement to sound economic policies."[4] In 1993 the UK's Overseas Development Administration made "promotion of good government" a priority objective of foreign aid, and Norway's Ministry of Foreign Affairs released a strategy on "Support for Democratic Development."[5]

The Development Assistance Committee (DAC) of the Organisation for Economic Co-operation and Development, which often helps define and articulate consensus positions among major donors, expressed this new agenda in a 1993 policy document through a series of statements about the importance of certain types of political development for socioeconomic progress. It stated that "DAC Members believe that sustainable development requires a positive interaction between economic and political progress. This connection is so fundamental that participatory development and good governance must be *central concerns* in the allocation and design of development assistance" (emphasis added).[6]

These and other policy declarations highlighted a new but soon familiar set of elements that aid providers deemed helpful or even essential to development: democracy, good governance, state reform, institution building, accountability, the rule of law, anticorruption, transparency, participation, and human rights. These constituted a complicated mix of issues, distinct in some ways from one another yet overlapping substantially in others.

They made up a common swirl of politically related "good things" that each major aid organization drew from in its own ways. To the extent that aid agencies attempted to order this swirl, they usually divided it into three overarching categories: democracy, governance, and human rights. Some announced an intention to address all three categories; others emphasized only one or two. They attempted to draw these lines even though some of the component concepts, such as accountability and the rule of law, cut across all three categories, rendering any clear division analytically blurred.

This emergent set of critical elements for development did not in and of itself represent a new development orthodoxy. Instead, it was a supplement to the reigning market orthodoxy. Mainstream aid organizations still embraced the market model as the necessary driver of economic growth. But they now held that for this model to be fully effective it had to be combined with a generous helping of at least some of these other good things. Thus the development world shifted in those years to a kind of "market plus" or "markets but also …" model.

Looking back at this surge of new thinking and talk about development in the early 1990s, it is striking how much it put politics on the table. Some parts of the new list of priorities, like democracy, were much more explicitly political than others. But all of them concerned how governments function and how they relate to their citizens, and all more or less shared an underlying set of politically normative values about these processes. The door to politics had quite suddenly, but also quite clearly, opened for the development community.

SOURCES OF THE BREAKTHROUGH

As is usually the case with changed thinking about development models, when mainstream aid organizations began talking about the importance of pairing economic and political development, they presented the changed agenda as a self-evident, timeless truth, offering little explanation of where it came from and not acknowledging that until very recently a quite different but also apparently eternal verity had prevailed.

The newly expanded agenda had multiple sources. Above all, two quite different causal lines were at work: first, an important internal evolution in thinking within the development community about the market model, an evolution provoked by disappointments in attempting to spread it in the 1980s; and second, the changed context for development work brought about by the transformation of international politics. These two sets of changes were in some ways complementary but also sparked divisions beneath the surface of the apparent new policy consensus. The first trend translated primarily into a focus on effective institutions, while the second led to the introduction of democracy and human rights as aid priorities.

The Rediscovery of the State

The evolution of the market model reflected a gradual realization on the part of most development agencies that not only the "right" economic policies but also well-functioning state institutions are crucial for successful development. As aid organizations seized by the neoliberal orthodoxy of the 1980s pushed developing country governments to carry out structural adjustment and related market reform policies, they encountered not just resistance from power holders worried about protecting vested economic interests and anger from average citizens over austerity drives, but also a basic problem of state capacity. The weak states prevalent in the developing world were poorly prepared for designing, enacting, and above all implementing the many technically complex, administratively demanding policy measures that the market model required, from setting up privatization programs and reforming financial systems to establishing effective foreign investment regimes and revising tax systems. As a 1990 World Bank evaluation examining lending over the previous two decades argued, "an inadequate level of institutional development has played a central role in determining the performance of most unsatisfactory operations."[7]

This practical experience dovetailed with changing views of the market among economic theorists and especially the rise of the New Institutional Economics, which had significant influence in aid circles. Douglass North and other leading proponents of the New Institutional Economics argued that the prevailing market theories of the 1980s neglected the central importance of transaction costs in undermining economic efficiency. Economic models that assume rational actors with perfect information cannot adequately deal with a messy economic reality marked by uncertainty and mistrust. A market economy thus requires coherent institutions to protect property rights, enforce contracts, and fulfill other public functions. Such stable "rules of the game" drive economic performance.[8] These ideas were translated (not necessarily accurately) by aid officials into a broad imperative to strengthen state institutions in developing countries, moving beyond a focus on institutional development related to structural adjustment reforms toward a more expansive attempt to improve economic management generally.

Thus aid providers that had been pushing hard for developing countries to *shrink* their states—to reduce bloated public sectors and reduce state intervention in the economy—started shifting gears. Embracing the idea that these countries needed to have *effective* states, they began exploring how development aid could help them reach that goal. As Tony Killick argued in 1989, encouraging developing country governments to work through market mechanisms should not always imply reducing the overall role of the state but rather changing *how* it operates and recognizing that the amount of state intervention needed to address market failures will vary in different contexts.[9] Or as the 1998 study *Assessing Aid* put it, with regard to government, "less is not necessarily better, but 'better is better.'"[10]

This "rediscovery of the state" on the part of market reform enthusiasts connected up with a somewhat parallel line of thinking that had been quietly gaining force in the development community for some time. This was the view that weak governance generally—not related specifically to implementing the market reform agenda but concerning the capability of government institutions across the board in many developing countries—lay at the root of persistent underdevelopment. Frustrated with the record of African development efforts, a group of Africa specialists at the World Bank put forward this thinking in a landmark report published in 1989. *Sub-Saharan Africa: From Crisis to Sustainable Growth* contended that "underlying the litany of Africa's development problems is a crisis of governance."[11] Even though some of these developmentalists pushing for attention to governance were not ardent adherents of the market model, they recognized the natural convergence of their proposed focus on governance and the market enthusiasts' new concern over state effectiveness.

Thus the two lines of thinking joined up in the early 1990s as a broad push for attention to governance, institution building, state reform, the rule of law, and other associated concepts. The World Bank articulated this new view in its 1991 World Development Report, which espoused the value of markets but stated that "in defining and protecting property rights, providing effective legal, judicial, and regulatory systems, improving the efficiency of the civil service, and protecting the environment, *the state forms the very core of development*" (emphasis added).[12] The 1997 World Development Report on *The State in a Changing World* elaborated on the central importance of effective states for sustainable development.[13]

Anticorruption became another strong driver of attention to governance issues in the 1990s, especially in the second half of the decade. Donors wanted to ensure that their assistance was not diverted for corrupt purposes, particularly given increased public skepticism within donor countries about foreign aid. They found it difficult to maintain clean internal finances when their programs were operating in environments of pervasive corruption. This concern—combined with research that pointed to corruption as a constraint on development and the new space for public scrutiny of corruption in countries moving away from authoritarian rule—led to donor interest in measures to reduce corruption within aid-receiving countries as well as within donor programs themselves.[14] This movement gained considerable momentum in 1996 when World Bank President James Wolfensohn promised to fight "the cancer of corruption" through support to governmental and international anticorruption efforts, leading to the World Bank's first anticorruption strategy in 1997.[15] In 1997 the UN General Assembly called for UN action to combat corruption, and the UNDP, the UK Department for International Development (DFID), and other donors subsequently pledged additional actions to fight corruption as part of their governance work.[16]

A Changed International Political Landscape

This evolution in development thinking regarding governance and the state was driven by its own logic deriving from evolving economic theories and on-the-ground experience of aid providers. Largely coincidentally, but very importantly, it emerged at a time of tectonic changes in the international political context. These changes gave a broader push to making politics part of the aid agenda, going beyond governance efforts to democracy and human rights, and opening up space within many developing countries for attempts to address such issues through assistance.

One of the contextual changes, of course, was the global spread of democracy. The wave of authoritarian collapse and attempted democratic transitions that accelerated dramatically in the late 1980s and early 1990s in Latin America, Central and Eastern Europe, the former Soviet Union, sub-Saharan Africa, and Asia was the most intensive period of democratizing change in the developing world since the final major wave of decolonization in the 1950s and 1960s. Western governments saw this movement toward democracy as favorable to their economic and security interests and also good for the citizens of the countries in question. They thus sought to support it. Of course, they continued to maintain friendships with a number of "friendly tyrants," such as pro-Western Arab autocrats, who were useful on key economic and security fronts. And their level of commitment to supporting potential democratic transitions certainly varied.

Nevertheless, most major Western states made democracy support a part of their redefined strategic role in the new post–Cold War context. They adopted an array of methods to support this goal, including pro-democratic diplomacy and the promotion of democratic norms within multilateral institutions. They also greatly multiplied the number of aid programs specifically designed to foster and advance democratization. While the initial democracy aid efforts of the 1980s had primarily operated from specialized political foundations, the increased high-level interest in such aid during the 1990s led at least some Western governments to push their bilateral aid agencies to add democracy building to their portfolios.

The democratic wave also changed the place of human rights in development work. It brought about much greater consensus on human rights internationally, and specifically within the developing world, as well as more explicit linkages between human rights advocacy and development work. The 1993 World Conference on Human Rights in Vienna reflected this new consensus, announcing that "democracy, development and respect for human rights and fundamental freedoms are interdependent and mutually reinforcing" and calling for their promotion throughout the world.[17] The Vienna Declaration also reaffirmed a "right to development" as an integral part of human rights, declaring individuals as the central subjects of development and saying that development efforts should respect all human rights.[18]

In addition, Western human rights advocates found themselves in a different stance vis-à-vis many developing countries. Gone were dozens of authoritarian regimes that adamantly opposed the international human rights community. In their place were fledgling democratic governments. While these governments were certainly far from perfect in their human rights performance, their human rights problems were often a result of poor state capacity (such as weak legal systems) rather than malign intentions. Thus *aiding* these governments to protect human rights, instead of "naming and shaming" them on human rights deficiencies, became an important avenue of work for the human rights community, further adding to the new, more political mix of development priorities.

The widened international embrace of democracy and human rights affected the normative environment for all development actors, even those who did not explicitly adopt democracy and human rights as goals. The political relativism of previous decades fell away, making it harder for developing country governments to mount resistance to such norms on any principled grounds (as Cuba, for example, had long done). In addition, the opening up of space for citizen activism in many developing countries created the corresponding expectation that development programs would allow space for popular participation and at least not do anything to undermine human rights.

Despite the World Bank's previous skepticism about the developmental value of democracy and political rights, for example, the 1991 World Development Report made a point of stating that "political and civil liberties are not, contrary to a once-popular view, inconsistent with economic growth" and declared "patently false" the argument that only authoritarian governments can make the hard choices necessary for development.[19] Many development programs continued to be top-down and politically exclusive, but advocacy NGOs and citizen groups increasingly monitored projects and pressured development actors to do more to respect human rights.

Another major element of the changed international context—the end of the Cold War—also contributed to the opened door on politics in development. The global superpower rivalry had put pressure on the West (and also the Soviet Union) to use development aid for geostrategic purposes—as a tool to win over and maintain allies in the developing world. But the end of that contest freed aid to be more political in a developmental sense.

Western governments did of course continue to use aid in some cases to facilitate relations with certain developing country governments for various economic and strategic reasons. But they now felt less obliged to back many governments (no longer wary that they would turn to the Soviet Union) and could pressure them on political practices when they felt such practices were hurting development.

Western leaders were also confident that liberal democracy had won the global battle of ideas and should be encouraged in less free societies. Reflecting this sentiment, in 1990, senior policymakers in the United States, Great Britain, and France all announced that they would direct more foreign aid to countries making democratic progress.[20] These pledges were unevenly applied, but a wave of democratic conditionality soon emerged in Western aid to Africa, with donors using assistance as a lever to try to induce African governments to hold free and fair elections and make other domestic political changes. More generally, the end of the Cold War lifted the concern that had long prevailed in parts of the development community that any sign of paying attention to politics would be associated with the geostrategic contest for political influence in the developing world. Talking openly about political issues, conducting political analysis, and even thinking about how to engage politically started to seem like possible elements of development work.

EXPANDING THE DEVELOPMENT AGENDA

How did this opening up of the development agenda to politics translate over the course of the 1990s into changed aid practice? With respect to development agencies making political change a direct goal of assistance, we see a divided picture, one that reflects the dual drivers of the opening to politics. Some mainstream aid organizations adopted an explicit political preference, adding democracy support as a goal. Others were more cautious, focusing on the narrower issue of state effectiveness and making governance a priority area. Concerns over development effectiveness blended, at times uncomfortably, with the new emphasis on simultaneous political and economic development. The more general concept of participation also gained greater prominence, a further product of the times, sometimes as part of political development strategies and other times as a more inclusive way to bolster socioeconomic development effectiveness.

The Uncertain Embrace of Democracy

Over the course of the 1990s, a number of aid organizations, including USAID, CIDA, and Sida, added democracy to their core agenda. These agencies developed programs across the full spectrum of what quickly became a standard template of democracy aid—support for free and fair elections, political party development, constitutional reform, parliamentary strengthening, judicial and other legal institutional reform, local government strengthening, advocacy NGOs, independent media support, and democratic civic education. Although the specialized democracy aid organizations, such as the National Endowment for Democracy and the U.S. political party institutes, usually attracted the most attention as the public face of this rapidly growing field, the role of bilateral aid organizations quickly became much larger. USAID was by far the biggest funder of democracy aid in the world in the 1990s, devoting more than ten times the resources to such work as the National Endowment for Democracy (although USAID democracy programs only amounted to approximately 5 percent of overall U.S. development assistance in those years).[21]

These aid organizations supported democracy as an intrinsic value. But they also connected it to socioeconomic goals, with the DAC setting out the basic instrumental argument that "there is a vital connection between open, democratic and accountable systems of governance and respect for human rights, and the ability to achieve sustained economic and social development."[22] USAID sounded a similar note in 1994, arguing that "democratization is an essential part of sustainable development because it facilitates the protection of human rights, informed participation, and public sector accountability. USAID's success in the other core areas of sustainable development is inextricably related to democratization and good governance."[23] CIDA called democracy, good governance, and human rights integral to its developmental purpose and said that they create the social framework within which development efforts can be effective.[24]

The prevailing weight of scholarship in those years on the relationship of political systems to development outcomes pointed to a different view—that while politics matter for economic outcomes, democracies do not perform better economically than nondemocracies and there is no clear connection between regime type and economic growth.[25] But this new credo about the necessary tie between political development and economic development adopted by some aid agencies was not built from the bottom up, that is, from evidence to policy. It emerged essentially whole cloth in the exuberant, triumphalist spirit of the early 1990s—when both liberal democracy and market economics appeared to be the clear winners in the global ideological contest of previous decades. It was a kind of axiomatic conclusion in which correlation and cause blurred: almost all of the most economically successful countries were democracies, most long-established democracies were relatively wealthy, and so the conclusion—that democracy is good for development—was plausible enough for Western political leaders and senior policymakers looking to formulate broad agendas that would meet with easy public acceptance.

Development agencies did sometimes acknowledge that the link between democracy and development was not simple or direct. But given their newfound intrinsic commitment to democracy and human rights, there appeared to be sufficient cause to promote all these values together and present them as part of a unified vision for sustainable development. In short, the optimistic context of the time produced a reprise among at least some Western policymakers and aid specialists of the conviction that had emerged in the equally optimistic early 1960s: that in economic and political development, "all good things go together."

Mainstream aid organizations did put forward some specific propositions fleshing out the argument for the developmental value of democracy. They asserted, for example, that political accountability feedback mechanisms common in democracies tend to produce economic policymaking more attuned to the interests of the public. They further argued that the political openness of democracy allows for better scrutiny of economic actions by the government and more space for citizens to pursue free-market activities. But these assertions were rooted less in empirical studies than in commonsense observation that seemed logical but was not actually proven. Democracy advocates within mainstream aid organizations pointed to some evidence that most exceptionally bad economic performers were autocratic and often cited Amartya Sen's work on the socioeconomic importance of democracy, particularly his finding that famines do not occur in democracies. Those specific propositions, however, formed only a narrow basis for a prodevelopmental rationale for supporting democracy; they did not address how democracy would lead to positive and sustained development progress.[26] As will be discussed in chapter 7, figuring out whether this largely axiomatic embrace of the tie between democracy and development holds up to sustained research scrutiny has turned out to be a major source of complexity and contention in development circles.

In addition to official pronouncements linking democracy and economic development, some aid organizations made policy commitments to integrate democracy and respect for human rights throughout their development work. USAID devoted a section of its 1991 policy agenda to integrating democracy concerns across its programs. It expanded on this commitment in its 1994 *Strategies for Sustainable Development,* pledging to develop integrated country strategies that consider social, economic, political, and cultural factors together and minimize stovepiping among different sectors of aid.[27] CIDA in 1996 and Sida in 1997 made similar promises to integrate democracy, human rights, and governance concerns across their organizations and at all levels of program planning.[28]

Yet underneath such declarations, belief within development agencies in the importance of political change for socioeconomic development and commitment to the integration of political and economic concerns was highly uneven.[29] The mix of intrinsic and instrumental justifications for democracy sounded good at a rhetorical level, but the implications of this vision for specific programs were often unclear. Many of the practitioners who dominated aid agencies—the macroeconomists and technical sectoral specialists in such areas as basic infrastructure and health—doubted the validity of what they saw as a political fad being imposed from above. Even if they accepted that democracy was an intrinsically good thing and perhaps even a valuable contributor to overall development progress, they were unconvinced that attention to democracy was required for the success of their projects or that their programs should somehow support democratic development in addition to achieving more efficient agriculture, better schools, and other key priorities. Furthermore, their concern about antagonizing recipient governments and getting caught up in local political controversies intensified in the 1990s as democracy support efforts mushroomed. The end of the Cold War may have made it easier for donors to challenge recipient governments without suffering diplomatic consequences, but the success of individual aid projects still relied significantly on good relations with the host government.

Moreover, aid agencies did not put in place the organizational changes needed to support the full integration of democracy and rights perspectives into their traditional areas of socioeconomic focus. Some set up only weak structures to implement democracy aid. A 2008 review of CIDA's democracy and governance programming, for instance, praised the agency's 1996 human rights, democracy, and governance policy but painted a picture of institutional neglect since then. It noted that CIDA did not develop policy leadership or coordination around democracy and governance assistance and did not hire a cadre of specialized staff able to carry out this work.[30]

Others did much more to build up internal capacity on political aid but did so by building specialized structures concentrated on democracy and human rights support rather than crosscutting ones able to influence other sector programs. As a result, democracy programs operated mostly apart from socioeconomic programs, run from separate offices or bureaus, usually by practitioners belonging to a new cadre or professional specialization different from the traditional socioeconomic ones. At USAID, democracy support gained a strong institutional place in the 1990s, a significant step up from the nascent institutional structures accompanying the early wave of political aid in the 1980s. These changes were spearheaded by then Administrator Brian Atwood, who himself came from the democracy promotion community (having previously served as president of the National Democratic Institute for International Affairs). But democracy work remained a separate sector built into country programs through stand-alone strategic objectives, rarely well integrated with other USAID programs and still often resisted by mission directors rooted in old ways.

This division was clear in USAID's extensive efforts in the 1990s to promote market reform and democratization in Russia and other countries in the former Soviet bloc. While USAID presented economic and political liberalization as complementary goals, its aid programs in these areas worked independently and sometimes at cross-purposes. Democracy supporters entered Russia to work on electoral reform, political party training, civil society and media development, and the rule of law, including strengthening checks and balances in the political system.[31] Simultaneously, ever more numerous Western economic consultants arrived as part of a much larger and better funded economic aid program to press for the privatization of state enterprises and other rapid market reforms. These economic initiatives sometimes sanctioned or even encouraged reform by executive decree when parliamentary support was not forthcoming. USAID's Office of Democracy for Russia expressed concern that the reliance on decrees could undermine democratic processes in the country, but it had little influence on the economic reform programs.[32] The U.S.-aided privatization program ended up having even broader negative effects on the development of Russian democracy, contributing to the creation of a class of superwealthy "oligarchs" who began to exercise dominant political influence and power within a country still marked by weak rule of law.

Sticking to Governance

While some development agencies acted on the political development ideas of the early 1990s by adopting democracy as a goal, others stayed away from explicitly political objectives and limited themselves to adding governance to their core agenda. These organizations drew on the World Bank's politically neutral definition of governance as "the manner in which power is exercised in the management of a country's economic and social resources for development."[33] The main British government aid organization of the time, the Overseas Development Administration, preferred this approach. In an October 1993 policy statement, it highlighted various features of good governance associated with democratic systems but stopped short of embracing democracy, noting that "multiparty democracy in principle offers the best way of ensuring legitimacy. In some countries, however, a multiparty system may be either impractical or unsustainable at least in the short term."[34]

Although governance work involves institutions, processes, and values that could all be considered political, the World Bank and other aid organizations created boundaries between politics and governance aid. The World Bank was especially wary of politics given the explicit prohibition within its Articles of Agreement against interfering in the domestic politics of member states or making decisions based on the political character of loan recipients.[35] The Bank articulated the political limits of its governance work in its landmark 1992 report on governance and development, noting that governance work is compatible with this prohibition on political interference "if it is addressed in terms of having good order and discipline in the management of a country's resources." The report then highlighted four key dimensions of acceptable governance work for the World Bank: "public sector management, accountability, the legal framework for development, and information and transparency."[36]

The inclusion of governance within the development agenda was more a product of painful experience with failure and the rediscovery of the state than changing international political norms. Governance advocates were usually unconvinced that lack of democracy was the main constraint on development. They wanted to focus on the aspects of governance they considered central to economic progress, such as state economic management, and believed they could make substantial headway in these areas without getting involved in controversial debates around political values. Some thought that democracy was actually likely to undermine efficient economic management by placing new redistributive demands on the state and that democracy aid providers paid too little attention to state capacity. This was often a valid criticism, though donors that had adopted democracy as an objective also added governance work as part of the new political focus, seeing governance either as a subset of democracy programming or a supplement to it. When USAID, for example, set up a new unit within the agency dedicated to political aid, it was called the "Center for Democracy and Governance."

Most governance practitioners initially addressed those institutions they saw as the least political and most important to effective public financial management and a well-regulated market. They also defined desirable governance narrowly in apolitical terms of efficiency and competence and emphasized issues such as financial accountability, transparency in budget management, civil service reform, and the legal regulation of the market.[37] These aspects of governance appeared to have a clear connection to development results. David Dollar and Lant Pritchett argued in *Assessing Aid*, for example, that sound economic management—defined as good policies as well as rule of law, quality public bureaucracy, and low corruption—is so essential to development effectiveness that it would likely be counterproductive to give funding to governments that lacked these qualities.[38]

Reflecting the continued strength of the market model, development actors also promoted efforts to deconcentrate state power through decentralization and privatization of state enterprises.

Over the course of the 1990s, the World Bank and other mainstream aid organizations somewhat broadened their initially narrow, technocratic approach to governance. As the rediscovery of the state gained force, they widened the range of state institutions targeted, extending beyond the circumscribed domain of economic management agencies to a wider mix including judiciaries, parliaments, provincial and local governments, and others. Very importantly, they broadened their thinking about what constitutes the core of effective governance, going beyond their initial emphasis on efficiency and competence to include more politically normative elements relating to how government institutions treat ordinary citizens. Thus the governance agenda started emphasizing accountability and inclusion, which mixed with the broader idea of participation as a useful way of building greater public buy-in to market-oriented assistance.

As the concept of governance widened, governance practitioners sought to avoid charges of political interference by stressing the strictly instrumental nature of their work for sustained economic development. Unlike democracy aid enthusiasts, governance providers saw themselves as working squarely within the socioeconomic development realm. Yet this argument was not persuasive to critics within and outside development agencies who saw the Western aid community now pushing Western liberal political values as the solution to development based on political hubris rather than strict evidence. As Mick Moore argued in a critique of the 1992 World Bank report on governance and development, the Bank did not take a very empirical approach to deciding what kind of governance would be good for development. It did not look at which developing countries had made the most progress in the last twenty to thirty years to identify what sort of governance these countries had. Such an approach would have pointed to the Asian Tigers—Hong Kong, Singapore, South Korea, and Taiwan—and their autocratic governance, which was at odds with the liberal-pluralist vision of good government that development actors had relatively suddenly decided was indispensable.[39]

Like democracy supporters, governance advocates faced challenges in mainstreaming agency-wide commitments to governance work within operational programs. While governance was more closely tied to socio-economic development effectiveness than democracy support, many sector experts remained unconvinced that addressing governance was essential for the success of their programs. The UK Department for International Development, or DFID (which replaced the Overseas Development Administration in 1997), made progress in institutionalizing a governance focus throughout its work, creating a cadre of government and institutions advisers in the second half of the 1990s who provided advice on organizational and institutional development to programs in country offices. Yet even at DFID governance only slowly gained a place within the socio-economic sectors. The World Bank also attempted to mainstream attention to governance, and a survey of thirty-seven country strategies from 1998 to 1999 found that 78 percent mentioned governance and anticorruption, though attention to governance was uneven within programs.[40]

A Renewed Focus on Participation

Alongside the new interest in democracy and governance, aid organizations in the 1990s increased their attention to fostering participation in development, not just as part of governance, but throughout the development agenda. Public participation was by no means a new issue in development work. It had been a preoccupation of aid efforts as far back as the 1950s. But the changing international context of the 1990s—the increased space in many developing countries for citizen initiatives and the multiplication of both transnational and local NGOs as important development actors—helped significantly raise the place of participation in mainstream development rhetoric and practice.[41] Both multilateral agencies and bilateral donors, as well as the OECD's DAC, declared new commitments to strengthening participatory development. UNDP's 1993 Human Development Report, for example, proclaimed that "people's participation is becoming the central issue of our time" and "the implications of widespread participation are profound—embracing every aspect of development."[42]

It is easy to see why citizen participation was and continues to be an appealing concept for donors. It responded both to the changing global political environment and to hardheaded concerns about program effectiveness. Supporters made the case that participation was both intrinsically valuable as a way to empower poor people and instrumentally useful for achieving better development outcomes. At the same time, the concept of participation was vague enough to allow development actors to interpret it as they saw fit and did not commit them to specific political objectives. Even some authoritarian governments talked of a commitment to greater participation and showed a willingness to host programs encouraging participatory development.

While increasing the appeal of participation, its nebulous nature complicated efforts to define or mainstream it as an objective. Some development actors explicitly tied participatory development to political processes and democracy and human rights objectives. UN agencies and some other aid actors drew on human rights language to present participation as a right, implying that donors had certain obligations to promote it.[43] Others conceived of participation much more narrowly as public consultation in development planning.[44] This sometimes meant small-scale meetings to explain projects to local people, and sometimes more extensive efforts to involve beneficiaries and NGOs in creating donor country strategies.

The clearest instrumental case for participation came from empirical studies that showed a connection between increased beneficiary participation and better project performance.[45] Dollar and Pritchett praised participatory approaches to development as an important way to improve development effectiveness, arguing that "the top-down, technocratic approach to project design and service delivery has not worked in areas critical for development—rural water supply, primary education, natural resource management, and many more."[46] These studies, however, hewed to the more narrow interpretation of participation within specific donor programs rather than broad popular participation in society. Even this limited conception of participation was met with skepticism by some development practitioners who doubted that public consultations were worth the resources and time they required.[47]

TECHNOCRATIC PERSISTENCE

The opening up of the development agenda to politics, whether indirectly under the rubric of participation or governance or more directly through a focus on democracy and rights, produced many new types of assistance programs, but surprisingly little change, at least in the first decade, in the apolitical methods that had long dominated the assistance world. Aid practitioners continued to rely heavily on the replication of Western best practices as a solution to even the most tricky political development challenges and assumed that recipient countries would be willing to undertake recommended reforms. The temptation of the technical still held sway, serving as a kind of methodological safety blanket for aid providers thrust into the challenging position of having to move quickly to develop programs in new areas.

In Democracy Aid

As democracy aid mushroomed in the 1990s, it was natural to expect that such programs would adopt highly political methods, given the explicitly political objectives of such work. This seemed especially likely since many people working on democracy programs were newcomers to the assistance world. They often came from the domain of domestic political work, such as campaign consulting, and wanted democracy aid to operate very differently from what they saw as the overly bureaucratic and cautious realm of socioeconomic aid.

Yet interestingly, at least in its first major phase from the mid-1980s through the 1990s, democracy assistance was strongly marked by the same technocratic methods as socioeconomic assistance. This was partly due to organizational constraints. The fact that many democracy aid programs were funded and overseen by large development agencies forced them to adapt to the bureaucratic requirements of official aid planning and performance monitoring, constraining their ability to implement the kind of flexible and politically challenging programs that some practitioners wanted. But technocratic instincts on the part of the new wave of democracy aid personnel also played a role. As the new community of democracy aid providers set out to build up this emergent area of assistance, they often gravitated toward the familiar aid approach of institutional modeling: settle on a template of key institutional features necessary for democracy, diagnose how a country in political transition measures up to that template, and then carry out training programs and other knowledge transfers to help the counterpart institutions become like those in established democracies.

This approach underplayed wider, deeper considerations about how political change actually occurs and how external aid providers can best facilitate it. It often failed to take into account the underlying interests of the local counterparts, assuming instead that an intrinsic forward reform dynamic would naturally drive positive democratic change.

Thus, for example, aid programs designed to strengthen parliaments focused on such formalistic attributes as procedural rules, provision of equipment, and establishment of information services, rather than zeroing in on the underlying problems of the incentives of parliamentarians vis-à-vis their constituents, the role of money in politics, and other structural features weakening political representation. Media strengthening programs labored mightily to train journalists to improve their level of professionalism and give them knowledge of investigative reporting. Yet these programs often gave scant attention to the ownership structures that determined whether media organizations were willing to scrutinize power holders. Political party assistance offered endless training seminars to political party activists based on a set idea of how parties should function in a democracy without addressing the hard fact of deep resistance to reform among the leaders of those parties. This resistance frequently undermined knowledge-based efforts to transform the behavior of party activists.

Writing in 1999 about this first generation of democracy aid programs, Thomas Carothers highlighted what he called "the missing link of power" in these efforts:

> Much too often, aid to reshape institutions in transitional societies is a self-contained effort, disconnected from the society in which the institutions are rooted—the structures of power, authority, interest, hierarchies, loyalties, and traditions that make up the dense weave of sociopolitical life. ... Aid providers treat political change in a pseudoscientific manner as a clinical process to be guided by manuals, technical seminars, and flowcharts. ... The truth that politics involves harshly competing interests, bitter power struggles, and fundamentally conflicting values—not to mention greed, stupidity, and hatred—is downplayed until it asserts itself, unwanted, at some later stage. Democracy projects often fail

then, their formal frameworks splintered when they smash up against the obdurate foundations of the local scene.[48]

In Governance Aid

The initial tide of aid interventions aimed at supporting improved governance embodied similarly apolitical methods. Following the broader pattern of work on structural adjustment, some aid organizations sought to promote better governance in developing countries by making aid conditional on certain institutional reforms. Attempts at imposing governance conditionality proved disappointing, however, as donors realized that (as with structural adjustment conditions) governance conditions were too difficult to enforce and that sustainable improvements required domestic support for change.[49]

In addition to experimenting with conditionality, donors built up an array of governance programs. Yet despite the lessons of institutional development efforts of decades past on the importance of understanding institutional change as a complex political process, their methods in these programs followed a familiar line—providing technical assistance to host country counterpart institutions in the hope or belief that better knowledge and skills would transform bad governance practices into good ones. They made little effort to investigate the causes of bad governance in any probing way and then to design assistance interventions to address the causes. To the extent that they analyzed state institutions, they focused on the functioning of formal structures. It is striking, for example, how the 1992 World Bank report on governance and development at least briefly discussed the causes of weak governance, highlighting "a high degree of concentration of political power."[50] Yet when it turned to concrete lines of action, it highlighted skills training carried out in cooperation with host governments and other conventional types of technical assistance.[51] As Catherine Weaver observed, the World Bank needed to justify its governance objectives in economic terms in order to gain internal legitimacy for the agenda, but this led to an apolitical view of the problem that precluded "the perceived need to hire more social scientists and to develop the policy tools and skill sets necessary to address the *political* economy of governance reform."[52]

Aid providers moving into rule of law work in the 1990s, an important part of the new governance domain, responded to the dauntingly difficult question of how societies long afflicted by a very weak hold of law can change course with narrowly focused judicial programs to train judges, provide better courtroom equipment, and upgrade case management systems. The first generation of donor-sponsored anticorruption programs avoided the murky political roots of most corrupt practices, concentrating on technocratic approaches such as the formation of governmental anticorruption commissions and training programs on financial control practices.

The early governance programs proceeded from the idea of inculcating or fostering "best practices" in selected state institutions of developing countries. Aid providers largely drew these best practices from the experience of their own state institutions. Although development practitioners typically insisted they were not attempting any simplistic application of Western blueprints to the developing world, the basic idea of trying to transfer knowledge to reproduce Western-inspired institutional endpoints was manifest. This approach was problematic not only in contexts where elites lacked interest in donor goals but also in those where political leaders were relatively committed to furthering development. In the former case, technocratic institutional support assumed and relied on a level of government support that did not exist and failed to address entrenched opposition to change. Yet even when power holders did want to improve governance and promote broad-based economic development, they usually found donor programs badly suited to their needs and overly prescriptive. A surprisingly direct line could be traced from these governance programs back to the discredited institution-building programs of the 1960s that had so often failed due to a lack of political understanding of the root causes of governance deficiencies and an absence of creative context-specific solutions.

One difference was considerable attention in the 1990s to finding and backing "champions of reform" in counterpart institutions. This emphasis reflected at least some recognition of the accumulated experience of seemingly well-designed institutional reforms bouncing off their targets because of lack of commitment at the top. But it also followed from the familiar technocratic impulse to assume that resistance to well-designed programs merely required finding influential supporters rather than rethinking the wisdom of the project. Unfortunately for donors, their "champions" were not always as committed to the agenda as they seemed. Developing country governments were generally not very enthusiastic about the governance agenda but were sometimes willing to accept governance programs as a way to appear reform-minded and gain access to other aid funds. Even committed "champions" often proved disappointing when development practitioners learned they were simply not powerful enough to overcome structural and other obstacles to change.[53]

Some governance programs did depart from the standard capacity building of state institutions model to engage in more politically informed work. USAID, for example, funded an innovative project in the 1990s, "Implementing Policy Change," that attempted to look seriously at the political complexities underlying policy reform. It emphasized stakeholder analysis and the importance of involving key players and building consensus around a policy rather than assuming that once reforms became law they would automatically go into effect. This program worked on a varied group of projects in forty countries, ranging from attempting to improve communication within the Zambian cabinet to supporting national business associations in West Africa and helping them lobby their governments.[54]

Governance practitioners also started recognizing the productive role civil society could play in pressing for improved governance. Domestically driven experiences within developing countries, such as the Porto Alegre participatory budgeting process in Brazil in the early 1990s and the creation of citizen report cards on public services in Bangalore in 1993, gained widespread attention as innovative ways to improve governance by engaging citizens in the process and sparked donor support for similar experiments elsewhere.[55] Many aid programs, for example, sought to support local anti-corruption NGOs and build civil society and media capacity to monitor corruption.[56] But these sorts of efforts remained a minority within the broader context of top-down governance assistance. They also often mimicked the apolitical approach directed at state institutions—taking an uncritical view of civil society as a community of rational and altruistic community actors who simply needed more training and resources.

The apolitical approach of governance aid to what was, at root, a naturally political area met with a punishing and largely accurate volley of criticism from both external observers and donors' own assessments. These criticisms flagged various facets of the problem of politics, or perhaps more accurately, the continuing problem of apoliticalness, converging around several major points:

- Governance was added to the donor agenda in order to sustain the market consensus rather than challenge it. It did not constitute a serious rethinking of aid objectives or a willingness to take social and political factors as seriously as economic calculations.[57] As a result, donors downplayed the political nature of governance and attempted to separate out the rational aspects of governance associated with technical knowledge from the irrational political parts.[58]

- Mainstream aid organizations usually attempted to work closely with and support the main state institutions in aid-receiving countries and shied away from seriously challenging them. Yet the governance problems being addressed were often rooted in the core power structures in a country. A built-in contradiction therefore existed within most governance work, rendering it superficial and ineffective.

- Governance aid treated governance as a product of state institutions rather than as the result of complex relational processes between a wide range of societal actors and forces. As a result, its theory of change—that knowledge transfers and other technocratic efforts to modify governing institutions from the top down would produce better governance—was often undermined by the realities of entrenched power structures resistant to real change.[59] Reviews of public sector management projects found a lack of attention to the process of institutional development and to the fact that key actors sometimes did not have an incentive to support well-functioning formal institutions.[60] As Adrian Leftwich argued, "an independent and competent administration is not simply a product of 'institution building' or improved training, but of *politics*. And if the politics do not give rise to the kind of state which can generate, sustain and protect an effective and independent capacity for governance, then there will be no positive developmental consequences."[61]

- Governance aid operated from an Anglo-American model of governance, both in terms of the way governing institutions function and the roles they should play. Such a model was not necessarily a good fit for other, very different societies, nor a good developmental path given the differences in starting points and legacies.[62] What aid providers presented as objective governance "best practices" were in fact highly political options that should be and often were contested within developing countries.

- Donors lacked the level of context awareness and political sophistication required to move beyond institutional blueprints to design more effective interventions.[63]

In Participatory Development

The rise of participation as an element of the expanded development agenda of the 1990s was about both goals and methods. The only way to achieve the goal of participatory development was to have people participate in development projects, which had natural connections to more political methods— especially involving a wider range of actors in programs. Yet even in this domain the temptation of the technical reigned. Aid providers usually pursued participation in ways that downplayed its political dimensions, unless these efforts were explicitly tied to a democracy-building program.

While donors articulated both intrinsic and instrumental justifications for increased participation, in practice the instrumental view usually prevailed. Assistance actors tended to interpret participation to mean increasing recipient participation within donor planning processes in order to win community support for development projects and gain information from local people on their needs and the feasibility of proposed projects.[64] One of the most visible operational manifestations of this participation focus was the move toward participatory poverty assessments and participatory rural appraisals. These studies were meant to complement quantitative poverty measures by consulting poor people and other stakeholders, thus making programs more responsive to the multidimensional nature of poverty.[65] They were sometimes funded by bilateral donors and fed into World Bank planning processes. The share of World Bank poverty assessments with a participatory component rose from about 20 percent in 1994 to around 50 percent in 1996–1998.[66] These overall numbers included studies that differed considerably in their scope and level of participation, with some focusing on the local level and others taking into account national planning processes.[67] Donors also supported participation by funding local NGOs and attempting to build the capacity of poor communities. These types of activities encompassed a similarly wide range of interpretations of participation, from funding NGOs as service providers and policy advocates to building the capacity of communities to take over and monitor services themselves.

This opening of development programs to participation appears to have had some positive effects in enhancing the awareness of aid providers of local contexts and the causal relationship between exclusion and poor governance and persistent poverty. Participatory poverty assessments and other participatory analyses sometimes contributed to giving poor people more of a voice in development planning and raising their expectations for responsiveness from authorities.[68] Certain participatory studies went beyond perceptions of poverty to look at how ordinary people interacted with government and community organizations, examining deeper issues of power and state-society relations.[69] Yet, reflecting the vagueness of the concept, participation was incorporated unevenly and often superficially across projects.

Some observers asserted that donor efforts to increase participation exemplified a continuing unwillingness of aid organizations to face the implications of a real embrace of politics—they limited participation to narrow circles of technocratic, "tame" civil society groups, didn't include political opposition parties, and seemed more intent on getting a "participatory" rubber stamp to donor agendas late in the planning process than genuinely opening up priority-setting processes to fundamental debate and choice. Attributing local resistance to their aid projects to ignorance and lack of information, some aid providers saw participatory processes as a way of changing the minds of local citizens rather than actually listening to their concerns and doing something different as a result.[70] Certain critics asserted that participatory approaches were actively disempowering to the poor because they sought to shift the burden for planning and implementing development projects to poor communities, along with the blame for failures.[71]

Critics also charged that even well-meaning participatory development projects operated under a false belief that the poor could be empowered through such methods as public consultation rather than through deeper processes of mobilization and struggle. Development projects often failed to take into account how power relations within recipient communities would affect the ability of marginalized groups to participate, neglecting within-community inequality and assuming that poor people had the needed capacity to become effective participants in consultation processes.[72] Programs also usually focused on local-level participation within the context of specific development projects rather than the broader policy and power structures that have a greater impact on poverty.[73]

To the extent that development practitioners did try to look at broader structures, they had difficulty dealing with government opposition to their efforts to promote participation, either through NGO funding or participatory processes. A 1998 World Bank report acknowledged that "unfortunately, the laws of many developing countries either do not provide adequately for NGOs or are aimed at their control and repression," but the organization's response to this insight was to put together a handbook of good and bad practices for NGO laws and provide technical assistance to governments that wished to improve their laws.[74] This attitude was similarly applied to winning over local government support for participation. Sophisticated analyses of forms of participation, the importance of context-specificity and local analysis, and the likelihood of political opposition were followed by rather simplistic recommendations to convince government officials of the developmental usefulness of community participation through field visits, pilot studies, training on how to work with communities, and other knowledge transfers.[75] These recommendations reflected the options that aid practitioners saw as both feasible and within their mandates but were unlikely to do much to win over government officials who saw substantial community participation in decisionmaking as a threat to their own power.

THE CASE OF DECENTRALIZATION AND LOCAL GOVERNMENT ASSISTANCE

The boundaries between democracy, governance, and participation programs were somewhat artificial, with certain projects carrying out largely the same activities under different labels because they were implemented by different development agencies or different departments within the same agency. Some real programmatic differences did exist, of course. A governance program would not entail political party support, for example, while democracy assistance was unlikely to focus on improving top-down public financial management. Many participatory programs focused on improving the effectiveness of socioeconomic development projects and not on contributing to institutional change to strengthen either governance or democracy. But there were also areas where these approaches overlapped. One notable example was the significant increase in efforts over the course of the 1990s to support decentralization, or sometimes democratic decentralization, within developing countries. These programs usually combined elements of strengthening both governance and democratic participation, and they provided some opportunities to more seriously consider the politics of development. Yet they, too, fell victim to many of the apolitical shortcomings outlined in the sections above.

Donors already had some experience with decentralization. Aid to local governments and local service delivery was a familiar part of the development tool kit reaching back decades. The main difference was that in the 1990s many countries moved toward political decentralization, devolving political power and representation to subnational governments, rather than the more common administrative and fiscal decentralization of previous decades. In some countries this push to decentralize was part of a broader movement toward democratization, though decentralization also occurred in authoritarian contexts. Past efforts at decentralization aid had not been very effective, but proponents of decentralization in the 1990s argued that democratic decentralization would be more successful because it included such elements as accountability, participation, and empowerment.[76] The United States, the United Kingdom, UNDP, the World Bank, and other aid providers stepped up work related to decentralization, sometimes framing it as part of larger democracy support efforts.[77]

Like other popular concepts in development, the rise of decentralization became associated with a wide range of hopes and objectives. Proponents pointed to the potential for decentralization to bring government closer to the people and increase transparency and responsiveness, reduce ethnic conflict, create local revenue sources, improve public service delivery, improve local government capacity, develop future leaders, increase central government support to local areas, help disadvantaged groups, gather information on local needs, promote local bottom-up development planning, and much else.[78] These reflected democracy, governance, and participation goals as well as concerns with privatization and reducing the role of the state. But most of these hopes were not based on empirical analysis of whether decentralization was in fact likely to bring about any of these good things. Many aid practitioners and donor agencies thus remained skeptical that decentralization was good for development.

In most countries, donors were following rather than driving country moves toward decentralization. Domestic political leaders had their own reasons to decentralize, and donors came in afterward to provide support. In cases where donors did identify decentralization as a major obstacle to development and tried to lead the government, as USAID, the World Bank, the European Union, and other donors did in Romania in the 1990s, they usually faced substantial government resistance.[79] This should not have been surprising: decentralization is a highly political decision with far-reaching implications for the balance of power in a society. Leaders are unlikely to embark upon it unless they believe it will serve their interests.

Apolitical Models and Methods

Even when domestic leaders were committed to decentralization in principle, donors faced numerous challenges in attempting to influence *how* the process would occur. They offered technical advice and best-practice models of which institutional arrangements would work best, paying less attention to whether domestic leaders shared their idea of what the "best" outcome would be. As one study noted, donors thought "decentralization would be defined in normatively state-of-the-art legal frameworks. It would then be implemented according to these frameworks, but only if national politicians and bureaucrats were sufficiently enlightened and committed to decentralization."[80] But almost as much as the initial decision to decentralize, the details of how decentralization will be implemented and how levels of government will share power bring up serious political conflicts. They are thus unlikely to reflect purely technical considerations of which arrangements will best promote socioeconomic and democratic goals.

A review of USAID programs in this area observed some level of bureaucratic and political resistance to decentralization in all its case studies.[81] A World Bank evaluation of its decentralization work found that the organization had some success in improving public financial management of local government and setting up legal frameworks for fiscal transfers but that it fell short in other areas such as influencing the division of responsibilities among levels of government. The report found that there was little consideration of the possible opposition of interest groups and public officials and that a "weak understanding of political economy factors and associated risks led to overly ambitious objectives that often limited development effectiveness."[82] The same evaluation cited a survey of partner agencies finding complaints that "Bank staff are 'politically naïve' and do not have a historical perspective essential in this area."[83]

In addition to offering policy advice on the overall framework for decentralization, donors sought to assist newly empowered local governments take on their added responsibilities and promote participation at the local level. These efforts provided some opportunities to address limitations in other types of governance, democracy, and participatory aid. Since donors could not assist all local governments, they had more room to support only the localities where they believed there was serious political will for reform. Democracy programs at the local level were confronted with low-capacity local governance and had to pay attention to the linkage between traditional governance issues such as public administration and service delivery and their core concerns with accountability and representation.[84] Participation efforts within decentralization programs were linked to local institutions rather than carried out in isolation of domestic structures.

Yet decentralization programs also replicated the limitations of aid in other areas of democracy, governance, and participation. They often failed to recognize how local-level power relations would affect democracy and development goals. Harry Blair observes that the appeal of decentralization lay in the idea of a clear linear chain between decentralization, greater representation for underrepresented groups, empowerment of these groups, and concrete socioeconomic benefits and poverty reduction.[85] In reality, however, there is no reason to expect that decentralization will lead to greater empowerment of marginalized groups. Local elites are just as dominant and exclusive as national elites, if not more so, and women and minorities are not likely to benefit from decentralization unless there is a specific effort to empower them (or, as Blair points out, unless minorities are geographically concentrated).[86] On the contrary, richer communities and better-off people within poor communities are usually better positioned to take advantage of the opportunities created by decentralization.[87] Additionally, local ethnic, religious, and other divisions are likely to impede cooperative behavior around public goods provision.[88]

Improved government responsiveness also did not come automatically with decentralization. Local governments were usually administratively weak and did not have a clear comparative advantage in service delivery. Nor were they necessarily more accountable than national governments. Efforts to promote participation through community consultations were not effective when leaders felt free to ignore the feedback they received.[89] Local government programs did spark multiple experiments with ways to make local governments more accountable and responsive to citizens. Drawing on the success of the Bangalore public service report card and other social accountability experiments, the World Bank and other aid organizations funded a program in Ethiopia in 1996 to strengthen civil society oversight over local governments and providers of basic services.[90] USAID decentralization programs promoted a range of accountability mechanisms, including elections and party assistance, civil society aid, media aid, public meetings, formal grievance procedures and opinion surveys.

Yet an evaluation found that these mechanisms were effective only when used in combination with each other and their success was context-dependent.[91] An extensive World Bank review of experiences with decentralization and participation similarly found that democratic decentralization can sometimes facilitate accountability—and credible elections work better than the more informal consultative mechanisms of stand-alone participatory programs—but devolving power to the local level can also open up more opportunities for clientelism. Local governments thus need to be constrained by a broader framework of functioning accountability mechanisms, including an effective central state, in order to fulfill the good governance hopes of decentralization proponents.[92]

Decentralization and local government programs brought development practitioners into closer contact with local-level governance issues and helped build linkages among governance, democracy, and participation programs. The smaller scale allowed for various efforts to bring citizens closer to the state and experiment with accountability mechanisms. But experience with decentralization also revealed the shallowness of assumptions about the cooperative nature of local communities, the greater responsiveness and effectiveness of lower levels of government, and the rational character of decentralization processes.

CONCLUSION

The early 1990s were an exhilarating time in international affairs, profoundly colored by a feeling of victory and optimism that animated Western policy-makers with a sense of affirmation about how all countries should be run, politically as well as economically. It was a time of the breaking down of walls, both politically between different parts of the world and intellectually across different policy domains, producing new interconnections and fusions not just in development work but also in many other areas. These years appeared to usher in a fundamental opening of the development agenda to a whole series of politically related ideas and practices, significantly leavening the previously apolitical market model.

In this apparently transformative period, however, the actual place of politics in development work changed less than many initially expected. Although senior Western politicians and policymakers spoke often in those years about a natural connection between economic and political objectives in development work, this potential synthesis took hold only very partially in development practice. Political goals were presented as both intrinsic objectives and instrumental means to advance socioeconomic development, but major parts of the mainstream aid community held back from embracing either of these rationales. Some aid organizations did incorporate an explicit political goal—democracy—into their agenda. But in translating this policy goal into action, they established political aid as a relatively separate domain, apart from other, much larger socioeconomic undertakings. Others tried to address political issues without admitting to political objectives, shielding themselves behind seemingly technocratic ideas of governance. Whatever position development agencies officially adopted, many of their staff preferred to stay focused on reducing poverty or facilitating economic growth as their overarching raison d'être and were not entirely convinced that political change was necessary to achieve these ends.

Although replete with political concepts and possibilities, the expanded development orthodoxy made little dent across the 1990s on the long-standing apolitical methods of development work, below the level of overall goals. Even the new domain of democracy aid, although openly political in intent, often proceeded in technocratic ways. The first wave of governance programs reproduced the apolitical impulses of decades past, sometimes giving them new life by spreading them into sectors where aid providers had not previously worked. Efforts to step up participation in development followed a similar pattern. In democracy, governance, and participatory work, development actors were repeatedly frustrated by the basic dilemma that their proposed reforms required local commitment but often threatened the power of important domestic actors. These hard realities of power are not easily addressed even with careful analysis, but they were frequently ignored in planning processes. Yet despite this hesitant early motion, donor adoption both of political objectives and methods continued and expanded in the first decade of the new century, as chronicled in the next two chapters.

CHAPTER 4

ADVANCING POLITICAL GOALS

INTRODUCTION

The 1990s embrace of political goals in development assistance contributed to a changing aid landscape in the following decade. Donors' initial tendency to frame their pursuit of strengthening governance in developing countries as a technical undertaking gave way to more openly political conceptions of the task. In addition, more aid providers went beyond governance goals to embrace democracy itself as a core objective. Growing concern with what donors came to label as "fragile states" further raised attention to political issues on the development agenda, with Western policymakers coming to see weak states as not just a developmental concern but also as a security threat. By the end of the decade, the aid community was spending in the neighborhood of $10 billion annually on political aid programs, directing at least some political aid to every aid-receiving country. And some aid providers were trying to encourage positive political changes in aid-receiving countries by practicing some degree of political selectivity in decisions about where to channel their assistance.

Yet at the same time, the donor pursuit of political goals encountered significant limits. Both in their use of political selectivity and political programming, aid providers only partially translated their stated political intentions into consistent deeds. Moreover, in stepping up their political work, they encountered hard questions and serious doubts from both governmental and nongovernmental actors in developing countries about the legitimacy and value of such programs. This chapter examines both the progress and the challenges of efforts by development practitioners to define and achieve political goals alongside their more traditional socio-economic ones. The next chapter traces the parallel evolution toward more politically informed assistance methods.

AN APPEALING HALFWAY HOUSE

By the early years of the 2000s almost all mainstream aid organizations had adopted at least some political goals. Strengthening governance in aid-receiving countries was on essentially every development agency's list of priorities. Those that had embraced governance goals in the 1990s moved ahead to elaborate operational policy guidance for governance programming. Those that had only tentatively approached the topic before, such as the European Union, released governance policies in the first half of the 2000s. Not only did more donors embrace the goal of strengthening governance, but they also broadened their conception of what constitutes good governance. Moving further away from the early narrow focus on state efficiency and competence, they steadily gave greater emphasis to governance principles relating to the interests and roles of *citizens* in governance processes. They highlighted participation, accountability, inclusion, and transparency (and, less consistently, representation and responsiveness) as desirable governance features. Some of these elements had formed part of original more managerial governance programs of the early 1990s. Aid actors in those years highlighted the value of increasing the accountability of bureaucratic functionaries to their superiors, for instance. But donors now built on the scattered bottom-up efforts of the 1990s to stress more consistently the importance of accountability as a downward obligation of state institutions to their citizens. Doing so introduced a significantly greater political dimension to governance work.

A Political Prefix

This expanded list of desirable governance features—especially participation, accountability, inclusion, and transparency—became something of a standard litany in the assistance world. Many aid providers viewed them as intrinsically democratic principles and began labeling their larger goal as support for *democratic* governance. UNDP, for example, started highlighting the goal of democratic governance in its policy statements early in the decade and later described its work in this area as fostering inclusive participation, strengthening responsive governing institutions, and grounding governance in international principles.[1] The European Commission's development policy also took on a commitment to advancing democratic governance, which it defines as including human rights, democratization processes, the rule of law, transparent and accountable government, and effective institutions.[2] Other donors, such as Japan and Australia, do not explicitly refer to "democratic governance" but include democracy and human rights within their governance frameworks.[3] Séverine Bellina et al. argue that adding the prefix "democratic" to governance allowed or encouraged aid agencies to move beyond purely economic conceptions of governance to recognize its political character and consider issues of power and legitimacy vis-à-vis host country governments.[4]

The fact that many democracies actually exhibit quite poor governance in a number of respects is an uncomfortable reality for the "democratic governance" formulation. If pressed on this issue, proponents of the democratic governance line argue that when democracies do not exhibit good governance (that is, when they govern incompetently, unaccountably, and untransparently), it is because they are not doing well as democracies—in other words, that well-functioning democracies tend to embody the core desirable governance characteristics.

Donors' widespread adoption across the last decade of the goal of fostering democratic governance represents a convenient halfway house on the path to a potentially more fully political posture. It is some distance down the political road, past the initial way station of just plain "governance." But in most cases it is still safely short of a direct commitment to fostering democracy as a regime type. UNDP, for example, under the leadership of Mark Malloch-Brown in the early 2000s, pushed for a widened set of political goals. China, Russia, and some other member states resisted embracing democracy support per se, viewing such a move as an inappropriate and politically loaded diversion from UNDP's core development mission. Settling on "democratic governance" as a programmatic priority was the compromise solution.

If one asks representatives of a mainstream aid organization that touts democratic governance as a priority whether their agency seeks to foster democracy in other countries, that person is likely to insist that their position is not as political as that. The distinction they draw is usually between trying to change other countries' political *systems* (too political) and trying to advance certain political *values* in the operation of the existing system (acceptably political). The European Commission, for example, says that "there is no particular institutional model for democratic governance, which simply affirms the rights of all citizens on the road to sustainable development."[5]

Democracy Itself

Some mainstream aid organizations went beyond democratic governance to embrace democracy as a stated goal. USAID was the first large governmental aid agency to do so, in the early 1990s. Over the course of that decade it was joined by the aid agencies or foreign ministries of Canada, Denmark, Germany, and Sweden. In practice, a great deal of overlap exists between the programs that aid organizations sponsor to support *democratic governance* and the programs that other agencies carry out to support *democracy*. For example, an undertaking to help village mayors reach out to and work more effectively with their constituents could just as easily be a democratic governance program as a democracy program. The same is true for numerous other aid interventions in this general area, whether it is helping citizens gain greater access to courts, promoting transparent budgeting, or training journalists in investigative reporting.

Sometimes a programmatic boundary between democratic governance and democracy is identifiable, particularly in how assertive development programs are willing to be toward host country governments. The emphasis on improving democratic governance processes implies that development agencies are working in partnership with recipient governments. UNDP, for example, works only at the invitation of developing country governments. France, whose foreign ministry also expresses a commitment to supporting democratic governance rather than democracy, stresses that its aid should not be judged by its ability to impose universal standards but rather "by its ability to provide each partner with specific experience and expertise to enable them to develop their own policies."[6] In contrast, more assertive democracy support programs sometimes go around unresponsive authoritarian governments to support openly oppositional actors (see the discussion of donor approaches to Zimbabwe later in this chapter). Democratic governance portfolios also tend to stay clear of elements of the typical democracy aid portfolio that donors see as highly political—above all, elections assistance and political party support. Yet this boundary does not always hold. UNDP has engaged in substantial programming on both elections and political party development despite its adherence to the goal of democratic governance; at the same time, some bilateral donors that explicitly support democracy nevertheless avoid party work.[7]

Just Governance

While the goal of democratic governance became common in the Western aid community during the last decade, some mainstream aid organizations still refrained from attaching any political prefix to "governance." The multilateral development banks that are formally prohibited from engagement in politics—the World Bank, Asian Development Bank, and African Development Bank—stuck to supporting governance, without "democratic" or other prefixes attached to it.[8] Nevertheless, their governance programs tend to stress many of the same principles that inform the democratic governance work (or the democracy work) of other aid organizations. The World Bank in particular significantly elevated and expanded its governance work with the launch of its 2007 governance and anticorruption (GAC) strategy, which stressed the importance of accountability, transparency, and participation.[9] It is sometimes hard to see much difference between the World Bank's non-prefixed governance programming and that of the agencies that embrace democratic language, at least with regard to basic programmatic content (the fact that the World Bank operates mostly through project lending rather than grants and other forms of direct support does, of course, lead to differences in methods).

DFID is a difficult case to categorize in this regard. It was a leader in adopting governance as a developmental priority but has gone back and forth in general statements of institutional policy about whether to put "democratic" in front of governance and to make a general commitment to support democracy.[10] It has based its definition of good governance on state capability, responsiveness, and accountability and its policy statements acknowledge that "elections and democracy are an important part of the equation," but not the only part.[11] In recent years DFID has carried out programs labeled "strengthening democracy" that consist of projects similar to those sponsored by organizations that make supporting democracy a clear overall organizational priority.

Enter the Foreign Ministries

As the donor embrace of political goals widened, the range of Western governmental actors involved in political assistance followed suit. In particular, Western foreign ministries started becoming direct providers of political aid. In Canada, France, Germany, the United Kingdom, and the United States, for example, foreign ministries opened up specific funding lines for democracy and governance assistance. Sometimes (as in France) these lines replaced substantial parts of the engagement by the country's aid agency in this domain. In most of the others, foreign ministry funding operates as a new source of assistance in parallel to the work of the aid agency. Sometimes such funding lines are large, in the many tens or even hundreds of millions of dollars per year, as in Germany and the United States; in other cases, as in Canada, they are relatively modest.

In some northern European countries, such as Denmark, the Netherlands, and Norway, foreign ministries became involved in political assistance as part of a much larger organizational rearrangement of development assistance: the transfer of responsibility for most or all development assistance from aid agencies to foreign ministries, with the aid agencies either being folded into the foreign ministries and losing any separate identity or being largely reduced to technical advisory organizations.

The growing involvement of foreign ministries in the aid business has had diverse consequences for political assistance. On the one hand, foreign ministries are less prone than traditional development agencies to operate from a conception of development as being about only socioeconomic goals and technocratic interventions. Foreign ministries instinctively view assistance as a tool that should serve the country's larger foreign policy interests, rather than only a developmental interest, and thus see political aid as a natural part of such an undertaking. On the other hand, however, this also means that political programming is more closely related to the overall bilateral relationship between the donor and the aid-receiving government. Where no other strong interests are present, foreign ministries may be willing to be more assertive than aid agencies in pursuing democratization and other political goals. But if the recipient government is an important ally, the foreign ministry staff may be more hesitant than development aid practitioners to support politically challenging programs. They can also be sensitive about aid practitioners conducting political analysis or seeking to work in political ways, feeling that *they* are the natural authority within the government on political issues abroad and that development actors should not intrude on their turf.

A further complication comes from the fact that some foreign ministry personnel assigned to work on aid programs lack aid experience and training. They may be less inclined than development specialists to think about how assistance must enter the fabric of the local contexts to be effective and to understand the long-term nature of developmental change. Thus some of the political methods aimed at making aid an effective contributor to developmental processes (as discussed in chapters 5 and 6) have been taken up more slowly at foreign ministries than at aid agencies. In short, the engagement of foreign ministries in political aid has produced the minor paradox of aid that is sometimes more openly political in goals but less politically smart in methods.[12]

THE FRAGILE STATES AGENDA

Adding to the overall movement across the last decade toward a greater adoption of political goals was the rise of the fragile states agenda—the heightened emphasis by major development organizations on aiding countries they viewed as having especially weak states. The fragile states agenda emerged in part from donors' recognition that though directing aid to good performers may be good policy in terms of aid effectiveness, following this approach exclusively would leave many countries experiencing acute problems without much external help. The extraordinarily extensive human suffering in states experiencing devastating conflict or state collapse, such as the Democratic Republic of Congo, called for a more effective response.

The changed international security environment for the West after the terrorist attacks on the United States of September 11, 2001, intensified this new attention to seriously troubled states. Suddenly collapsed states or states functioning so poorly as to leave parts of their territory ungoverned appeared not just as generators of large-scale humanitarian crises but as breeding grounds for violent political extremists with the potential to threaten international security. As the World Bank warned in 2002 after establishing a special task force on what it called "Low Income Countries Under Stress" (a precursor to the fragile states designation):

> aid does not work well in these environments because governments lack the capacity or inclination to use finance effectively for poverty reduction. Yet neglect of such countries perpetuates poverty in some of the world's poorest countries and may contribute to the collapse of the state, with adverse regional and even global consequences.[13]

Thus across the decade many major Western aid organizations stepped up work targeting fragile states. Afghanistan (after the ouster of the Taliban) and Iraq (after the ouster of Saddam Hussein) became enormous aid endeavors, soaking up billions of aid dollars in broad-ranging efforts to support simultaneous economic and political reconstruction. Beyond those two exceptionally high-profile cases, many other troubled states also rose on the list of donor priorities.

Definitions of "fragile states" or "state fragility" vary somewhat among aid groups. DFID, for example, in 2005 defined fragile states as "those where the government cannot or will not deliver core functions to the majority of its people, including the poor."[14] In the same year USAID offered a two-tiered definition, distinguishing between "vulnerable" states with questionable legitimacy that are unable to adequately provide for their populations and "crisis" states where violent conflict is a great risk or where the government lacks control over its territory, is unable or unwilling to provide vital services, or has weak or nonexistent legitimacy.[15] The OECD Development Assistance Committee similarly defined fragile states in 2011 as "those that have weak capacity to carry out basic functions of governing their population and territory, and lack the ability to develop mutually constructive and reinforcing relations with society."[16]

Drawing a sharp line between states that do not do a very good job of providing for their citizens (which is true of essentially all aid-receiving countries) and states that do such a poor job that they merit the designation "fragile" is obviously not easy. Different aid agencies have developed different criteria for assessing fragility, with varying outcomes. DFID, for example, came up with a list of forty-six fragile states based on World Bank Country Policy and Institutional Assessment scores from 2004–2005, but it included some countries—such as Ethiopia—which the Bank itself did not consider fragile.[17]

Fragility is often linked to conflict. Many countries that major aid organizations designate as fragile are either in the midst of civil or inter-state conflict, just coming out of conflict, or on the verge of entering into conflict. At the same time, developing countries plagued by chronic civil conflict are usually not considered fragile states if their basic state institutions function at a reasonable level. Colombia falls into that category. But not all fragile states are conflict-affected. In its 2005 list of fragile states, for example, DFID included many countries under category headings not relating to conflict, including "unable/unwilling" (such as Uzbekistan), "gradual reform with occasional setbacks" (such as Cameroon), or "arrested development" (such as Guyana).[18]

In fragile states, politics is—essentially by definition—a central element of the overall developmental challenge. For donors to simply attend to social and economic needs without giving significant attention to the basic functioning of core political institutions makes no sense. Donors thus have to integrate political goals—usually formulated as trying to help establish or fix basic institutions of governance or sometimes much more broadly as democratic peacebuilding and state building—into the task of relieving socioeconomic hardship. As a DFID study asserted in 2005, "weak institutions are the central driver of state fragility."[19] The 2011 World Development Report, *Conflict, Security, and Development*, greatly raised the profile of this issue within the mainstream development community. Its central message was that "strengthening legitimate institutions and governance to provide citizen security, justice, and jobs is crucial to break cycles of violence."[20]

The fragile states agenda also highlights the importance of paying attention to the unintended political effects of donor assistance. While all aid has political consequences in recipient countries, the heavy influx of donor funds in fragile contexts tends to be particularly disruptive. The disproportionate influence of external aid on the economy and the weakness of state institutions mean that many social services are delivered directly by donors, often through NGOs and parallel implementing structures not well integrated with either the government or the work of other external actors. Development programs that are insufficiently sensitive to the local context can also contribute to drivers of conflict. Reflecting these concerns, in 2007 the OECD's DAC countries agreed to a set of ten "Fragile States Principles" to guide engagement in fragile contexts. These include starting from the local context, focusing on state building as the central objective, recognizing the links among political, security, and development objectives, and ensuring that aid activities do no harm.[21]

Grappling with how to address the core challenges involved in seriously troubled states has thus forced aid practitioners to think more politically. In the second half of the last decade, DFID elaborated the concept of achieving political settlements as a key objective. It defined a political settlement as "the expression of a common understanding, usually forged between elites, about how power is organised and exercised" and held inclusive settlements to be crucial to peaceful societies and effective, legitimate states.[22] USAID introduced conflict assessments to help it understand the political roots of state failure and identify responses that can contribute to rather than undermine peacebuilding and state building. Many other donors developed their own conflict assessment tools. Throughout the aid community, the fragile states agenda has translated into a greater focus on the interrelationship between political and socioeconomic failures and the need for integrated political-economic responses.

RIGHTS, POLITICS, AND THE MEANING OF DEVELOPMENT

Aid organizations' widespread adoption of political goals across the last two decades had multiple motivational roots. It almost always reflected an instrumental outlook: the belief that certain political practices and processes will help developing countries achieve sustained socioeconomic success. This was an especially pressing imperative in fragile and conflict-affected states. Sometimes political goals also grew out of an intrinsic rationale: the conviction that certain political practices and processes are moral goods in and of themselves that deserve to be pursued alongside poverty reduction and other socioeconomic goals. As seen in chapter 3, these two rationales for political aid were frequently paired but arose from distinct historical trends: the instrumental justification emerged from the accumulated frustrations of development work in the 1970s and 1980s, while the intrinsic justification reflected the outburst of democratic enthusiasm surrounding the end of the Cold War and the spread of democratic transitions in the developing world.

Generally, those aid providers hewing to less political formulations of governance (like the multilateral development banks) emphasize the instrumental rationale. For example, since the World Bank by mandate can consider only economic factors, it cannot rely on the intrinsic argument for accountability, transparency, and other good governance attributes. DFID is not so constrained but nevertheless consistently stresses the instrumental value of all its governance policies, presenting even human rights as primarily a means toward poverty reduction rather than an end in themselves.[23] Those emphasizing democratic governance, or democracy itself, like USAID and many northern European donors, supplement their adherence to the instrumental rationale with stated commitments to the intrinsic rationale, highlighting political values such as freedom of expression and religion and the right to political participation and representation as good things in and of themselves.

Expanding the Idea of Development

Some development practitioners seek to take the intrinsic rationale further, to move beyond conceiving of democratic governance or democracy as valuable goals *alongside* socioeconomic development to view such political conditions as *inextricably part* of development itself. They draw inspiration from the work of Amartya Sen, who advocates conceiving of development in terms of maximizing the capabilities of individuals to achieve things they value rather than maximizing economic growth or per capita income. This view includes enhancing political as well as social and economic freedoms. Sen argued in his 1999 book *Development as Freedom* that "viewing development in terms of expanding substantive freedoms directs attention to the ends that make development important, rather than merely to some of the means that, inter alia, play a prominent part in the process."[24]

In the late 1990s and early 2000s this integrated political-economic view of development gained some traction in mainstream development agencies. UNDP was an early advocate of Sen's approach, producing an annual Human Development Report starting in 1990 to draw attention to the multidimensional nature of development. But its conception of human development was primarily a reaction to the reductionist focus on economic growth as a measure of development rather than an attempt to include political values. Its Human Development Index thus focuses on health, education, and living standards, presenting a multidimensional socioeconomic indicator of development but not an integrated political and socioeconomic measure. Other donors sought to build politics more explicitly into conceptions of development. In 2001 the OECD DAC released guidelines on poverty reduction that defined poverty in terms of not just economic and human deprivation (measured by indicators such as income, material well-being, and education) but also political and sociocultural deprivation (including concepts like human rights, political voice, empowerment, and dignity).[25] Sida, the Swedish International Development Cooperation Agency, took a similar view in 2002, declaring that "the essence of poverty is not only lack of material resources but also lack of power and choice. A litmus test of if an intervention decreases poverty could thus be if the effect is that poor people have increased scope to decide over their lives."[26]

Another effort to take the intrinsic rationale further toward an integration of political and economic concerns came through a push by some aid organizations to adopt a rights-based approach to development in which aid providers would seek to make the promotion of human rights—broadly defined to include both political and civil rights as well as economic, social, and cultural rights—a fundamental part of their approach. The rights-based approach to development is similar to the capabilities approach but relies more explicitly on international human rights frameworks. There is no clear consensus on what a rights-based approach implies, but at its fullest it means conceiving of development goals as human rights and human rights as constitutive of development.[27] Proponents highlight the fact that the Universal Declaration of Human Rights and the two major international covenants on rights from the 1960s cover civil and political rights as well as economic, social, and cultural rights. Some make reference to the "right to development" that emerged in multilateral human rights forums in previous decades. They view these international human rights agreements as providing international legitimacy for an integrated view of political and socioeconomic goals. Some also feel that these agreements can be interpreted as giving legal force to donor involvement in recipients' domestic politics. As a DFID policy statement noted in 2000, "development involves a process of political struggle over priorities and access to resources. Official donor agencies have found this difficult and challenging. A human rights perspective on development reveals these competing claims and legitimises excluded peoples' efforts to strengthen their voice in the political process."[28]

Given its close association with international human rights agreements, the United Nations has been the most prominent advocate of a rights-based approach to development work. In 1997 Secretary General Kofi Annan called for the integration of human rights into all UN activities. The following year UNDP released a policy pledging to "develop a human rights approach to sustainable human development programming, thereby ensuring that human rights will be mainstreamed in its activities and not relegated only to specific human rights projects" and said such a "human rights approach to poverty alleviation will emphasize empowerment, participation and nondiscrimination and address vulnerability, marginalization and exclusion."[29] In 2000, DFID committed itself to a human rights-based approach, focusing on promoting participation, inclusion, and strengthening the ability of states to fulfill their human rights obligations.[30] Other donors such as Sida adopted a human rights-based approach and linked it to the capabilities approach. Sida emphasized what it terms a "rights perspective," which it views as "a broader concept than the more commonly accepted definition of HRBA [human rights-based approach], as it also includes democracy."[31]

Falling Short

Both Sen's capabilities approach and the rights-based approach are appealing for advocates of greater attention to normative political values in development work because they seem to remove the need to rely on the instrumental case for political goals as contributing to socioeconomic outcomes. On the capabilities side, if economic growth and other indicators such as literacy and infant mortality are primarily important as a means of improving people's lives, why should other sources of well-being such as civil and political freedoms be valued any less? On the rights side, if development agencies commit to furthering human rights, why wouldn't civil and political rights—internationally recognized as inalienable rights—deserve equal consideration with social and economic rights? Moreover, both approaches are grounded in universally appealing ideas about improving individual lives.

Yet neither of the approaches was able to gain widespread acceptance across the decade, even within the agencies that were initially their strongest proponents. At DFID, for example, attention to the rights-based approach, at least framed as such, faded in the second half of the decade. At Sida, declarations of commitment to the rights-based approach have continued at the level of overall policy positioning but actual incorporation of a rights-based approach into Sida's programs has been a slow and uneven process. Some proponents of this agenda within Sida feel that it is a continuing struggle to achieve the operational adoption of a human rights-based approach throughout the agency.[32]

Most aid providers preferred to stick to socioeconomic conceptions of development, whether rooted primarily in economic growth, poverty reduction, or a wider set of socioeconomic elements, including health, education, and other public services. They did so in part out of practicality. Maximizing a broad range of human capabilities is an appealing concept, but it is hard to define these capabilities in practice or weigh which ones should get priority. Human rights-based approaches bring up the same issues of how to translate broad commitments into practice and also introduce additional worries around legal obligations. If international human rights frameworks give donors the legitimacy to promote human rights in developing countries, do they also imply a duty to do so?

More important, most developmentalists were just not convinced that civil and political rights are an integral part of the definition of development. Even UNDP's policy statement on its human rights approach noted that the agency would focus primarily on economic, social, and cultural rights, given that those were closest to its developmental mission, implying that it did not consider civil and political rights as equally integral to development.[33] Thus as most aid agencies added political goals to their agendas during the decade, they did so mainly on the bases noted earlier—either as an instrumental element serving socioeconomic development, or as a distinct goal worth pursuing alongside but separate from socioeconomic objectives.

The 2000 UN General Assembly Millennium Declaration reflected this separation between political and socioeconomic goals. It named freedom as one of the fundamental values essential to international relations and urged member states to promote democracy and strengthen the rule of law and all human rights. Yet it reserved its concrete commitments for traditional socioeconomic issues. The quantitative targets it set out for achievement by 2015 (which with some changes formed the basis for the Millennium Development Goals, or MDGs) included poverty, hunger, safe drinking water, universal primary education, and health—they did not include governance, democracy, or political and civil rights.

The Millennium Development Goals became the driving objectives of most mainstream aid organizations and the yardstick by which they still measure their development success, solidifying the preeminence of socioeconomic concerns within the development community. The European Commission's governance policy, for example, notes that "while governance and capacity building should indeed be high on the development cooperation agenda, poverty reduction and the other MDGs remain the overriding objectives of EU development policy. . . . Good governance, though a complementary objective, is basically *a means towards the ends represented by these priority objectives*" (emphasis added).[34]

The rights-based and capabilities views have not entirely disappeared, and most aid organizations embrace some elements of both approaches as important for their development work. The most influential include a focus on putting individuals at the center of development strategies and an emphasis on the principles of empowerment, participation, and inclusion.[35] But the effort to introduce intrinsic political values into the core of the operational idea of development has largely fallen short, and political goals are usually considered as separate and often secondary priorities. It is instructive in this regard that even the strongest proponents of the intrinsic value of political goals also usually try to make the instrumental case that democracy and political rights contribute to socioeconomic development.

As will be discussed in chapter 7, there is currently some renewed push to enhance the place of intrinsic goals within development aid, but the instrumental case for political goals has remained shaky in the eyes of many developmentalists.

ATTEMPTS AT AID SELECTIVITY

Though the intrinsic case for political goals did not win full acceptance within the development community, by the end of the 2000s the pattern of widespread adoption of political objectives by mainstream aid organizations was clear. Whether they formulated it in terms of governance, democratic governance, or democracy, donors pledged to pursue broad political goals. But what have these stated policies meant in practice?

One way of converting words to deeds on the political aid front is through aid selectivity. This entails aid providers directing more aid to those developing country governments that demonstrate political behavior that accords with donor desires (whether with regard to governance or to democracy generally) and less to those that do not. Sometimes aid selectivity operates just from an instrumentalist socioeconomic perspective, focusing on a narrow definition of governance and invoking the rationale that without good economic management, aid dollars will likely be wasted.[36] It follows the idea that aid effectiveness requires channeling assistance to those governments most likely to use it well. In other cases, however, selectivity is based on democratic performance rather than just on effective governance and is tied more to an intrinsic political rationale—the desire to avoid aiding repressive regimes and to encourage developing country governments to uphold democratic norms. Across the last decade, many mainstream aid organizations indicated publicly and privately that they were stepping up the use of aid selectivity to advance their goal of helping positively affect the political development of aid-receiving countries.

Rising attention to selectivity during the last decade reflected increased recognition of the shortcomings of aid conditionality in the 1980s and 1990s. Donors had made extensive use of both economic and political conditionality in those years. Initially they did so mostly to create pressure for structural adjustment reforms. In the 1990s, as democracy spread in the developing world, donors tried to use conditionality to push countries in a democratic direction, such as withholding aid in some African countries in response to governments' refusal to hold free and fair elections. But they encountered significant limits in spurring sustainable economic or political reforms through such means. In the case of democratic conditionality, recipient governments usually found ways to appease donor demands without substantially changing their core political practices or structures. Many embraced some trappings of democracy, such as elections and parliaments, but maintained autocratic control. A study by Gordon Crawford of 29 cases of political conditionality in the 1990s pointed to a lack of donor commitment to seriously enforce democratic conditions as a major additional reason for this failure. He argued that "when *any* other foreign policy goal comes into conflict with the promotion of human rights and democracy, then it is the latter that is abandoned."[37]

Faced with this disappointing record, some people within aid circles raised the idea that positive selectivity could be a more promising means to encourage good governance. Rather than strong-arming autocratic governments to reform by cutting off aid—requiring a degree of donor commitment and recipient government responsiveness that rarely exists—development agencies should instead pick partners that are already moving down a positive political path. Instead of searching for "champions of reform" within particular countries to press forward donor priorities, they should select partners based on whether their governments as a whole can be considered reform champions.

Weak Practice

Political selectivity is an attractive idea but in practice has been applied only weakly. In a 2008 report on aid practices by a large range of donors, William Easterly and Tobias Pfutze found that 80 percent of bilateral and multilateral development assistance goes to countries judged by Freedom House as "unfree" or "partly free," with unfree countries receiving 33 percent of aid. They also found that donors were not adjusting funding levels in response to political changes in recipient countries.[38] A similar study by Daniel Kaufmann and Veronika Penciakova concluded that selectivity actually *decreased* across the last decade, with an increasing share of aid going to countries with high levels of corruption and poor governance.[39]

Despite frequent stated intentions in the last decade to advance political goals, aid providers (especially bilateral aid organizations that necessarily conform to the foreign policy priorities of national governments) continue funding countries that perform poorly on democratic governance. There are several reasons for this. In fragile and conflict-affected states, humanitarian and security concerns can be so pressing that donors provide significant aid no matter how bad the local political conditions. Sometimes aid providers believe that the recipient government is committed to socioeconomic progress despite serious democracy or governance problems and thus is worth supporting in socioeconomic areas. In still other cases larger economic and strategic interests override the stated desire to support democratic governance and lead donors to fund friendly governments with atrocious political records. U.S. foreign assistance throughout the last decade continued to concentrate significantly on countries of special geopolitical importance to the United States, such as Afghanistan, Iraq, Pakistan, Egypt, and Jordan, despite their serious governance and democracy shortcomings.[40] Britain, France, and other major European aid actors also shape aid programs to support larger economic and strategic interests, such as sometimes favoring former colonies with questionable democratic records.

In recent years some donors have sharply reduced the number of their aid recipients, providing an opportunity for greater use of selectivity in deciding which countries will continue to receive aid. Even here, however, governance is generally a weak selection criterion. The Netherlands, for example, announced in 2010 a reduction in the number of aid partners from thirty-three to fewer than sixteen, but its selection criteria focused on the added value of Dutch aid in those countries rather than the quality of their governance.[41] Canada moved to focus 80 percent of its assistance on twenty countries, but its selection criteria are similarly vague on governance, focusing on a potential recipient's "real needs, their capacity to benefit from aid, and their alignment with Canadian foreign policy priorities."[42] Canada's priority countries range widely in quality of governance, including Afghanistan, Haiti, Ukraine, and Vietnam as well as more stable and democratic countries like Colombia, Ghana, and Peru. Sweden did put explicit emphasis on democratic performance as it transitioned in the second half of the decade from 67 aid recipients to 33. It included democratic governance and human rights as factors in its selection process alongside other criteria such as poverty levels and Swedish added value.[43] It phased out most development aid to some longtime Swedish aid partners, such as Vietnam, with democracy concerns sometimes weighing significantly in those decisions.[44] Democracy nevertheless had to compete with other criteria, like economic need, and Sida has maintained aid relationships with Uganda, Rwanda, and other authoritarian states while cutting assistance to more democratic partners such as Namibia and South Africa.

Special Structures

While promoting democracy and governance plays only a very secondary role in determining overall aid allocations, donors have created some special funds that make governance a criterion to access extra money. The most prominent of these is the Millennium Challenge Corporation (MCC), which the United States created in 2004 to provide extra assistance to countries demonstrating "good governance, economic freedom, and investments in their citizens," based primarily on their performance on a variety of externally based indicators such as the Freedom House ratings and World Bank governance indicators. Although the MCC's two primary goals are poverty reduction and economic growth, it includes democracy, rule of law, and effective governance criteria in its eligibility determinations.

In a few cases, MCC programs have been suspended when aid recipients failed to maintain high scores on governance criteria. For example, the MCC placed a hold on Malawi's $350 million compact in July 2011 and then formally suspended it in March 2012 following political violence and concerns about Malawi's commitment to good governance under then-President Bingu wa Mutharika. The suspension was lifted in June 2012 after the newly elected president, Joyce Banda, implemented a series of democratic and economic reforms.[45] Thanks to its emphasis on good policy performance, Sheila Herrling and Steve Radelet credit the MCC with promoting a significant "MCC Effect" by incentivizing potential recipients to introduce important policy reforms in order to meet eligibility criteria.[46] However, despite its successes, the impact of the MCC approach on the development aid sector has so far been limited. In 2012, the MCC had a budget of $898 million, a significant amount but small compared with the combined USAID and State Department aid budget of over $30 billion.[47]

Its competitive selection model based on third-party criteria has not been copied by other major donor agencies as of yet. And although the MCC is based on a commitment to distribute grants independently from U.S. foreign policy objectives by using transparent and independent indicators, its Board of Directors still has considerable discretion in its allocation decisions. The Board can decide not to award a compact to eligible countries or in some cases give aid even to technically non-eligible countries.[48] Georgia, for example, was awarded a compact in 2004 despite falling short on control of corruption and other "ruling justly" indicators, stirring suspicion that the decision was motivated more by Georgia's strategic importance than its quality of governance.[49]

The European Union included democracy and human rights conditions in its 2000 Cotonou Agreement with African, Caribbean, and Pacific countries and in 2006 announced a "governance incentive tranche" for these countries intended to reward governance progress with extra money. The tranche consists of one-twelfth of the 2008–2013 European Development Fund, or about 2.7 billion euros.[50] Yet, as Nadia Molenaers and Leen Nijs demonstrate, in practice there is a weak correlation between governance performance and funding. The value of the tranche ranges from only 10 to 30 percent, with 90 percent of countries receiving 20 to 25 percent and even the lowest performing getting 10 percent just for submitting a plan.[51] The tranche also represented only a small percentage of total aid and in almost all cases less than 0.5 percent of the recipient country's GNP, limiting its power to serve as a real incentive for governance improvements.[52]

The most significant use of selectivity is usually in *how* aid is distributed rather than *how much* is allocated, specifically whether developing country governments are eligible for direct budget support. Donors see budget support as an attractive carrot for developing country governments willing to consider governance reforms. They also recognize that when directed to undemocratic governments, this form of assistance is more likely than other forms to strengthen such governments. This is true both because the money flows directly to the executive branch, often bypassing parliaments and other domestic political actors, and because the recipient governments have considerable flexibility in how to use it.[53]

As will be discussed in chapter 7, some donors have recently introduced new selection procedures to try to ensure that budget support does not undermine democratic accountability in developing countries. Yet as Anna Lekvall explains, development practitioners are sometimes reluctant to withhold budget support even from repressive regimes. This is in part because they believe that direct assistance provides them with more opportunities to engage aid-receiving governments in constructive dialogues on democracy and human rights issues. But these policy dialogues, in her view, are usually toothless; donors list their concerns about various political shortcomings, government ministers promise to address them, and nothing changes in practice.[54] When aid providers get sufficiently frustrated, they have few options except to resort to the familiar conditionality tool of aid cutoffs. In the same year that the MCC suspended its compact with Malawi over governance concerns, for example, the UK, World Bank, European Union, African Development Bank, and other donors also suspended budget support to the country.[55] Yet these cases are relatively rare, and even direct support is usually shut off only in extreme cases of democratic or governance retreat.

Selectivity and conditionality allow donors to establish some redlines of undemocratic activity they are unwilling to tolerate and has resulted in some new money for high-performing developing countries. But overall these measures have fallen short of any major shift in using aid to support or stimulate improved political performance. Limits in the commitment of donors to their stated governance and democracy objectives undercut movement toward making such goals a major selection criterion. Additionally, selectivity and conditionality are both blunt instruments for fostering political change and have trouble distinguishing among differential governmental political performance beyond general categories like "poor," "average," and "high performing."

THE EXTENT AND LIMITS OF POLITICAL AID

The more extensive and important way that aid providers have acted on their widening embrace of political goals is through direct political aid—that is to say, aid programs designed to support political change (very broadly understood here to include efforts to strengthen governance, democratic governance, or democracy). As discussed in chapter 3, political aid includes a wide array of programs roughly falling into three general baskets:

(1) support for the reform of state institutions, including executive branch ministries, legislatures, judiciaries and other legal institutions, and regional and local governments; (2) aid for civil society development, especially to NGOs working on public interest issues such as human rights, women's issues, and anticorruption, but also other parts of civil society including independent media, unions, business associations, civic education groups, and others; and (3) support for core democratic political processes, above all free and fair elections and political party development.

The OECD estimates that combined government and civil society aid from DAC countries exceeded $10 billion annually by the late 2000s, amounting to about 10 percent of overall DAC assistance.[56] U.S. assistance represented about half of this total, with European aid making up most of the other half. UNDP was spending over $1 billion annually on democratic governance work by the end of the decade.[57] The World Bank and other multilateral development banks also devoted significant resources to governance work.[58] Given that most aid programs relating to democracy and governance are not very cost-intensive (compared with some other types of aid that involve large transfers of cash or material goods), this funding has produced a very large range of activities reaching numerous governmental and nongovernmental institutions in more than 100 countries around the world.

A Lesser Priority

Although political aid is now part of the overall portfolio of almost all mainstream aid organizations, it remains a lesser priority relative to socioeconomic aid, as reflected in basic budget numbers. Precise measurement of aid flows in different categories is always elusive given the complexities and diversity of systems at different aid organizations for labeling and accounting for aid flows. Very roughly speaking, however, the share of funds devoted to political aid at most major aid organizations is 5 to 15 percent. In other words, political aid is significant but it is greatly outweighed by socioeconomic programming. A few major aid providers do spend a markedly higher share of their resources on political aid. Democratic governance is the largest sector of aid programming at UNDP, for instance, making up nearly 40 percent of its budget in 2009.[59] And Sida and AusAID, the

Australian Agency for International Development, allocate approximately one-quarter of their assistance to governance and civil society work.[60] But such cases are exceptions.

Additionally, aid spending on democracy and governance has often been concentrated on a relatively small number of high-priority countries. The result is that many developing countries receive quite limited amounts of such aid, which do not reach the kind of critical mass of activities that can make a difference to a recipient country's overall political direction. For example, during the second half of the last decade, the U.S. government devoted such a sizable share of its democracy and government spending to just two countries—Iraq and Afghanistan—that many other countries struggling with serious governance issues received only small amounts: in fiscal year 2011, when the United States spent $597 million for democracy and governance aid in Afghanistan and $229.5 million in Iraq, it spent only $0.1 million on Côte d'Ivoire, $0.4 million on Malawi, and $2.3 million on Tanzania.[61]

Furthermore, although all of the aid within this very broad category of programs seeking to strengthen democracy, democratic governance, or governance can be considered political, in practice significant parts of it consist of highly technocratic programs that are political only in a very narrow sense of the term. Spending on programs in areas such as public financial management, local government capacity building, and legal institutional strengthening usually greatly outweighs spending on programs focused on political party development, election observation, and politically assertive NGOs. For example, in 2009 the two largest sectors of democracy and governance programming—public sector administration and legal and judicial development—each made up nearly 30 percent of total DAC aid in this area. By contrast, aid to democratic participation and civil society constituted 13 percent, aid to media made up 2 percent, and aid to parties and legislatures just 1 percent.[62]

This emphasis on aid to governing institutions is clear in most aid-receiving countries, and especially in those where donors are friendly with recipient governments and hesitant to push them politically in any way. To cite just one of many possible examples, Egypt was one of the largest recipients of U.S. democracy and governance aid from the mid-1990s to the early 2000s. Being closely aligned with the undemocratic government of the country, the U.S. government directed much of this assistance to technocratic governance programs—such as supporting a new case management system in the courts and greater administrative decentralization of certain central state functions—that consumed significant aid dollars without putting any political pressure on President Hosni Mubarak's regime. In other words, just as within the overall pool of assistance socioeconomic programs greatly outweigh their political counterparts, within the pool of political assistance, the less political programs usually outweigh the more political ones.

VARIED STRATEGIES OF POLITICAL AID

As outlined at the start of the previous section, political aid ranges across a wide landscape of program areas. The overall orientation of such aid in any particular country varies depending on the local political conditions and the interests of the aid providers. These overall orientations could be called strategies, but that might imply a greater coherence and coordination of action than usually exists. Individual aid providers do develop strategies for their political aid in specific countries but rarely work together to develop a coherent donor strategy. Joint "donor baskets" emerge in some places around common concerns such as an important transitional election in a country coming out of conflict. But these are usually limited in programmatic scope and in time, and attract the participation of only some aid providers.

Although not formally strategies, the overall orientations or emphases of external political aid in different countries do follow certain patterns and take on characteristic configurations. To give a very basic flavor of how political aid has taken shape in specific cases, we present here country case overviews in four types of settings:

1. Countries that are at least somewhat politically open and pluralistic and that appear to be trying to move ahead on democracy or democratic governance, even though they may well be struggling with elements of political stagnation or decay.

2. Countries whose governments routinely violate democratic norms and are not moving forward democratically but do appear (at least to some outside observers) to be committed to socioeconomic development and to be achieving some progress in that domain.

3. Countries whose governments are both undemocratic and developmental failures.

4. Countries embroiled in civil conflict.

This is just a simple categorical framework used here only to organize some illustrative cases, not intended to be of any lasting analytic value. It is not tied to the fragile states framework, which is much broader (typical donor lists of fragile states encompass countries that would fit in all four of the above categories).

Trying to Be Democratic

In aid-receiving countries that have made some progress toward democratic governance and whose governments appear to be trying to go further in that direction, aid providers usually work fairly widely across most parts of the overall political aid portfolio, emphasizing areas of assistance that match specific phases of the country's unfolding political life. Donors operate from the assumption that aid programs across the three main categories of political assistance noted above will reinforce each other. For example, they tend to believe that the reform of state institutions will give independent civil society organizations more effective partners with which to work, that strengthening civil society will help stimulate and assist state reform, that better elections will inject greater accountability into state institutions, and so forth. Aid providers intend their broad-ranging political assistance to complement and reinforce what is usually a much larger set of socioeconomic aid programs operating across multiple sectors.

Indonesia is one such example. Since the fall of President Suharto during the economic crisis of 1998, major Western aid providers have sought to help consolidate Indonesia's democratic transition as part of their broader backing for Indonesian development. Supporting Indonesia's democratic path appeals to Western aid providers as a chance to help the country bring its political development better in line with its significant economic progress. It is also considered a way to support a positive example of the possibility and value of democracy in a large Muslim country. With post-Suharto Indonesia making progress broadly across the democracy-building agenda, Western political aid has been similarly diverse. Aid programs have evolved in parallel with the evolution of Indonesia's political development. For example, after 1998 a small surge of assistance supported the initial burst of constitutional and other legal reforms, as well as the country's first several rounds of free and fair elections. As the Indonesian government then sought to implement its far-reaching decentralization program, donors followed suit, offering substantial aid for that purpose. As corruption concerns gained public attention, Western donors stepped up anticorruption assistance, and so on.

Given the positive view that most Western governments have of the Indonesian government's domestic political intentions, most political aid is carried out in open, friendly partnership with the government. Since the middle years of the last decade, political aid, while still supporting some activities on the civil society side, has most strongly emphasized different facets of governance—support for public sector reform, rule-of-law work including many anticorruption programs, and considerable ongoing support for decentralization through capacity building with relevant government bodies. The European Commission's program on "Good Governance in the Indonesian Judiciary" provided training and other support for Indonesian judges as well as legal aid to the poor, and added to other EC efforts to support reforms in Indonesia's Attorney General's Office and the national police. The German government funds a program on "Decentralization as a Contribution to Good Governance" that helps key national ministries work out the needed technical elements of administrative and fiscal decentralization and supports capacity-building of local governments. The World Bank's major development policy loans support institutional reforms related to improved public financial management. USAID funds a wide range of programs in related areas, including support for the Supreme Court and the Attorney General's Office, local governments, political parties, and civil society organizations.

Not Democratic but Possibly Developmental

Very different dynamics prevail in aid-receiving countries that have strong authoritarian political tendencies but whose governments are perceived by at least some outside observers as having a serious commitment to and some success in socioeconomic development. Ethiopia, Rwanda, Uganda, and Vietnam are examples, although many other countries, including

Kazakhstan, Uzbekistan, and both Tunisia and Egypt before the fall of their leaders in 2011, exhibit this configuration at least to some degree. In contrast to the other categories of cases discussed here, in this group of countries aid providers confront a significant tension between their socioeconomic goals and the goal of advancing democratic governance or democracy. In such cases most aid providers downplay political aid and concentrate on socioeconomic assistance. They base this approach on the conviction that the possibility of making significant progress in lifting people out of poverty is worth the risk of bolstering the domestic popularity and legitimacy of a politically noxious government. Usually only a few major donors, if any, are willing to withhold socioeconomic aid to the government or support any sharper-edged political aid.

To the extent that donors provide political aid, it is usually technocratic assistance that tries to partner with rather than challenge the government. Typically these are programs on public sector reform, rule-of-law development, and local government strengthening that aim at circumscribed institutional improvements such as greater administrative coherence and competency and do not touch on such sensitive political issues as the political independence of the institutions or the overall political balance of power.

Ethiopia is a paradigmatic case. During the last decade, the Ethiopian government led by Prime Minister Meles Zenawi (who died in August 2012) made important social and economic strides, reducing poverty as well as improving health, education, and other basic socioeconomic goods. Yet Zenawi's government was also intolerant of opposition, cracking down harshly on opposition forces at various junctures, and limiting space for open expression and other basic political and civil rights. As the 2011–2015 USAID country strategy for Ethiopia notes, this situation has put the international aid community in a bind:.

> The donor community is torn between the competing objectives of engaging with and assisting Ethiopia as a high profile example of poverty and vulnerability to famine, and addressing the major challenges and constraints to democratic space, human rights abuses, and severe restrictions on civil society and constitutionally guaranteed freedoms of speech, association and access to information. The GOE

[Government of Ethiopia] does not make this any easier, wavering between seductive and sophisticated rhetoric on development and economic topics on the one hand, and political repression, state dominance over the economy, and outright downplaying of humanitarian emergencies on the other hand. Added to this double-edged sword is the GOE's extreme sensitivity to any direct or even implied criticism, and its willingness to actively punish the criticizer, including members of the international community.[63]

Torn though the donor community is emotionally, in real terms it was highly supportive of the Ethiopian government across the last decade. International development aid to Ethiopia doubled from 2004 to 2008, totaling $3.3 billion in 2008, despite the country's increasing authoritarianism.[64] This aid has focused on core socioeconomic areas, especially food security, health, and education. In their country strategies, most major donors have downplayed political concerns, preferring to emphasize other issues. For example, the European Commission's 2008–2013 strategy for Ethiopia was quite positive about the prospects for the gradual development of a democratic society and political system in the country, saying that all political actors recognize "the importance and necessity of establishing an inclusive political process which offers a place and voice for all Ethiopian political forces."[65]

The major donors did pursue some political aid programs, but mostly of a politically unchallenging nature, usually focused on public sector reform, administrative elements of decentralization, budget management, or similar issues. Aid actors have provided some support to politically engaged civil society groups, including democracy and human rights organizations, but have not pushed back strongly against new Ethiopian government restrictions on foreign funding of such groups. This overall supportive stance can be partly attributed to Ethiopia's foreign policy cooperation with major Western donor governments on important international security issues such as combating Islamist extremists in Somalia. But it also reflects strong feelings among many aid practitioners that the Ethiopian government is committed to poverty reduction. The Swedish government is a leading exception in this regard. Sida ended its budgetary support to Ethiopia due to the government's lack of respect for democratic principles and has tried to work primarily outside of government channels. Yet even Sida notes that "supporting democratic development in Ethiopia is a tough balancing act."[66]

Neither Democratic nor Developmental

The international aid community takes a more assertive political approach in poor countries where the government is clearly undermining both socioeconomic development and democratic politics and no countervailing interests induce Western governments to stay on friendly terms. In such cases aid providers usually get involved on the socioeconomic side only via the nongovernmental sector, avoiding channeling aid through the government, except if necessary for humanitarian purposes. On the political side they may mount programs that challenge the government fairly directly. If they are allowed to work in the country, they will do so by supporting independent civil society activists, independent media, and opposition political parties. If they are shut out of the country, as was the case, for example, with Burma for many years, they may support political and civic activists in exile and offshore independent media. This political assistance usually operates as part of a broader diplomatic strategy of criticism and isolation of the government.

Zimbabwe is a highly visible case of a developing country whose government is committed neither to development nor democratic governance, and where Western donors have no countervailing interests causing them to try to stay on good terms with the regime. President Robert Mugabe has been leading his country on a catastrophic economic path and governing in a harshly undemocratic fashion for decades. Mugabe agreed to a two-party coalition government after contested elections in 2008 but has nevertheless continued to hold the main levers of power. Western donor governments have reacted to this dismal governing record with considerable antagonism. They do give some aid to the country. DAC donors provided $634.5 million in net bilateral flows to Zimbabwe in 2010.[67] But they have directed most of that aid through multilateral or local nongovernmental channels rather than to the government.

At least some major donors have attempted to use political aid to foster democratic change in Zimbabwe. Over the past ten years, for example, Sida and USAID have given significant support for independent media development, election monitoring, NGO development, and other forms of civil society activity that aim to foster greater political pluralism and openness. Some of this pro-democratic political aid is formally nonpartisan. But relations between the Swedish and U.S. governments on the one hand and the Zimbabwean government on the other are antagonistic enough that in some cases the assistance is fairly clearly pro-oppositional. For some time during the last decade, for example, USAID funded political training programs that concentrated attention on Zimbabwe's opposition parties. A 2007 report on the U.S. aid programs in the country noted that "it is doubtful that pro-democracy forces would have had the wherewithal to continue to organize opposition to the regime in the face of such a brutal assault in the absence of the medical and legal safety net provided by USG [U.S. government] funding."[68]

Other major donors prefer less open political assistance. DFID, for example, highly cognizant of President Mugabe's tendency to brand local political or civil society activists as agents of a hostile British government, noted in a 2009 report that "in the tense political environment [of Zimbabwe], DFID is unable to provide any direct support for democratisation activities, including activities by NGOs." The report further noted that in place of such direct DFID support, the Foreign and Commonwealth Office was providing grants to Zimbabwean NGOs for activities that included "maintaining democratic spaces, regional advocacy, media, access to justice and local governance support" but "UK support is not publicised, for fear of compromising the grantees."[69]

Conflict-Affected

In developing countries embroiled in civil conflict, donors face yet another set of challenges. Where major Western governments support the government, significant aid usually flows as an integral part of the overall Western policy stance. Socioeconomic assistance attempts to help the government cope with the consequences of conflict and meet citizens' basic needs. On the political side, aid seeks to help fortify the basic governance capacity of the state at all levels. Rule-of-law programs to build a functioning capacity for peaceful dispute resolution are often an important element of this aid package. If transitional elections are on the agenda, the international community is usually willing to invest quite substantially to help make sure the elections come off credibly. If a country has settled a conflict and is immersed in post-conflict reconstruction efforts, external political aid will target issues such as political reconciliation, demilitarization, and establishing rebalanced civil-military relations. Donors are currently engaged in significant such efforts in Afghanistan, the Democratic Republic of Congo, Iraq, and other conflict-torn countries.

Afghanistan has been a consuming case of conflict-related aid for major Western donors since the U.S.-led ouster of the Taliban in late 2001. They have contributed enormous amounts of funds to the larger project of first helping the new Afghan government take political control of the country and then supporting it in what has turned into an unexpectedly protracted and problematic fight against a resurgent Taliban. They have given aid across the many categories of political assistance, including for elections, political party development, constitutional reform, NGO development, independent media, women's rights, public sector reform, legislative assistance, local government strengthening, and rule-of-law building.

By far the greatest thrust of Western political aid has gone to help establish and make functional basic governing institutions in the country, at the national, provincial, and village levels. Even a cursory review of the range of donor-supported efforts in this domain over the last decade produces a remarkably long list of such undertakings. All of the major donors operating in the country, including the United States, the United Kingdom, Germany, the European Commission, the United Nations, the Netherlands, Sweden, Canada, Italy, and Denmark, have contributed to core governance work. They have made rule-of-law development a major part of their assistance, trying to build up the police, judiciary, prosecutors' offices, and other legal institutions.

These programs have sought to strengthen the government as well as to reshape it in basic ways. Elections assistance, especially around the 2009 elections, aimed both to help the government pull off the elections under extremely difficult conditions and to try to encourage or pressure the government to improve its respect for basic principles of good electoral behavior. Donors have also tried to support efforts to combat the overwhelming levels of corruption that define post-Taliban Afghan politics, despite evidence that key governmental "allies" in that fight are integral players in the corruption machine. This dualistic approach has not worked out in practice, meeting deep resistance from the Afghan government and resulting in an uncomfortable partnership marked by steadily accumulating frustration, antagonism, and conflict in both directions.[70]

REACTIONS BY RECIPIENTS

As aid providers have broadened their embrace of political goals within the many limits and constraints discussed above, how have aid-receiving countries reacted?

Authoritarian and semiauthoritarian governments in the developing world naturally feel direct conflicts between the increased donor attention to democratic governance or democracy and their own political intentions and values. Such governments do sometimes accept or even welcome governance aid when it appears focused on helping build state capacity as long as it is pursued in ways that do not challenge the governments' overall grip on power. But they bridle at and sometimes actively push back against the more political side of the new aid agenda, especially support for independent civil society organizations, political party development, and election monitoring. President Mugabe in Zimbabwe, for example, drove out many Western NGOs from his country, accusing them of political subversion. In 2004, Zimbabwe's parliament prohibited local NGOs from receiving any outside support. Ethiopia expelled the U.S. party institutes from the country prior to its 2005 elections and in 2009 passed highly restrictive NGO legislation limiting foreign funding for human rights and advocacy groups. Writing in 2006, Thomas Carothers warned that, "after two decades of the steady expansion of democracy-building programs around the world, a growing number of governments are starting to crack down on such activities within their borders."[71] At the same time, as noted above, donors often have reasons for not pressing a political agenda very hard in undemocratic countries, whether out of deference to countervailing interests such as access to oil or cooperation on counterterrorism or out of a willingness to downplay pointed political aid when signs of commitment to socioeconomic development appear present.

But even developing country governments committed to democratic governance or democracy tend to be skeptical about or resistant to the donor embrace of political goals. This reflects several overarching beliefs held by many in developing countries (and in developed countries as well):

- That it is inappropriate for donor governments to try to influence the political life of aid-receiving countries—that the aid relationship is supposed to be about socioeconomic cooperation, not political engagement.

- That aid providers are fatally inconsistent and hypocritical in their pursuit of political goals, punishing one government for falling short on democracy while embracing an even less democratic government on the basis of other interests, and using political aid as a lever for strategic purposes, such as gaining influence, persecuting disliked leaders, or supporting useful friends, that are very different than the stated ones.

- That the causal connection between donors' stated political goals and what is actually needed to achieve socioeconomic progress is not well established.

- That the political agenda represents a further aggravation of the problem of donor overload on recipient governments—yet more requests, expectations, and demands on governments already facing serious capacity constraints.

These doubts and suspicions about the donor pursuit of democratic governance and democracy often extend even to the less directly political side of the political agenda, that is, to governance work. The donor awakening to governance in the 1990s provoked many negative reactions in developing countries along the lines of the four points outlined above, reactions that did not ease up much as donors broadened their governance conception to emphasize participation, transparency, and accountability. The donor emphasis on anticorruption as a central element of the governance focus has proved a particular sore point. Developing country elites deeply resent the frequent talk of pervasive corruption in their countries and often believe that donors wield the anticorruption ax largely to embarrass or weaken them.

Still, the widespread negativity within developing countries about the donor push on politics is neither uniform nor always a significant barrier to such work. Despite doubts on the side of recipient country governments, countless political aid programs go on all around the developing world. Underneath the rhetorically charged negativity, developing country governments in many cases have found value in political aid programs. They often want help making their courts more efficient, their parliaments more effective, their elections more organized, their local governments more capable, and much else—as long as they feel they have some control and ownership over the process. Moreover, outside of governments, at least some civil society actors in developing countries are happy that aid providers are investing in public interest NGOs, independent media, labor unions, women's organizations, community activist groups, and many other parts of the nongovernmental side. They also appreciate donor efforts to advance reforms of state institutions and push on corruption. Restrictive NGO laws prohibiting or sharply limiting foreign funding have large impact precisely because external funding is often the only lifeline for domestic human rights or democracy groups. Thus, the overall picture is quite complex, combining generalized skepticism and suspicion with receptivity among some actors to parts of the increased political thrust of development aid. But to the extent that donors have achieved a certain degree of consensus among themselves about the value of adopting political goals, that consensus does not extend widely among their partners within developing countries.

Some developing countries have advocated steps to enhance cooperation between donors and recipients in pursuing political goals. Fragile states have been particularly active in this regard. Despite the recognition in principle by aid providers of the interrelated nature of political and socioeconomic development in fragile contexts and the likelihood of serious unintended consequences of aid programs in these places, they have fallen short of putting these insights into practice. A 2011 DAC review of donor application of its Fragile States Principles found that donors were off-track in most areas, noting in particular that "development partners do not systematically ensure that their interventions are context- and conflict-sensitive, nor do they monitor the unintended consequences of their support to statebuilding."[72] The familiar problem of the overload of donor demands on recipient governments is particularly problematic in fragile contexts. Responding to frustrations with the current state of international aid in their countries, leaders of fragile and conflict-affected states created the g7+ group in 2010 to advocate for improved assistance practice. The group, now numbering 19 states, has proposed a "New Deal" on aid to fragile states calling for the common pursuit of state-building goals, including "legitimate politics," but also for greater coordination of aid with a leadership role for the domestic government and a single national plan to transition out of fragility.[73] This document has won the plaudits of major aid actors, including the UN, European Union, World Bank, the United States, and the United Kingdom.

CONCLUSION

By the end of the last decade, most major aid organizations had adopted and were actively pursuing political goals, whether formulated in terms of a broad conception of governance that incorporated various politically normative elements, or in terms of democracy itself. They funded programs specifically devoted to supporting political change in all parts of the developing world, whether directly with governments, or indirectly with political parties, civil society organizations, or other nongovernmental groups. And some attempted to apply a degree of political selectivity in their aid to encourage positive political progress and punish backsliding. As donors became increasingly involved in fragile and conflict-affected states, they confronted more directly the problem of how to help support the establishment of basic political settlements and foundational state building. Any visitor to the international aid community who was up to date until the late 1980s, but then disappeared for twenty years before returning, would likely be quite struck by how much political goals had come to figure in official aid policy in the intervening years.

Yet at the same time, the shift toward more political aid is often less than initially meets the eye. The overall spending on political aid remains for most donors a minor share of aid spending generally. In many countries out of the international limelight it translates into only fairly modest sets of activities. The substance of political aid varies substantially across not only donors but probably more significantly across country contexts. Many of what are formally presented as politically related aid programs remain quite technocratic in spirit and practice, such as the extensive programs focused on public sector reform. Particularly when working in countries with friendly governments, donors often shy away from programs that address basic power relations. Considerable skepticism and resistance from many aid-receiving countries about the donor pursuit of political goals has complicated and constrained aid providers. In chapter 9 we take up more broadly the underlying question of the assertiveness of aid, in effect, how far assistance programs can or do go in challenging power structures in developing countries.

Finally, although political aid has increased considerably in amount and geographic reach, major aid organizations continue to treat it as something of a niche topic—maintaining separate departments or groups focused on such programs, as though politics were just one more specialized sector, like health or water, rather than a lens through which all developmental change must be understood and approached. Many politics specialists within the major aid agencies feel that they constantly have to struggle for resources and attention within larger organizations that remain dominated by economists and other traditional developmentalists who see the political side of aid as a sideshow. As discussed in chapter 8, the integration of political perspectives and approaches into socioeconomic areas of aid has been slow in coming and is only now starting to get taken up seriously by most major aid providers, more than twenty years after the initial opening to politics.

Alongside the movement on goals during the last decade, important movement toward more political methods also occurred, affecting both socioeconomic and political aid. The next chapter examines that story.

CHAPTER 5

TOWARD POLITICALLY INFORMED METHODS

INTRODUCTION

As mainstream aid organizations adopted increasingly political goals across the last decade, their operational methods evolved in at least somewhat parallel fashion. Their pursuit of governance, democratic governance, or democracy, especially with a growing emphasis on state-citizen relational values such as participation, accountability, transparency, and inclusiveness, affected not just *what* they were trying to achieve but also *how* they hoped to produce change. Development actors realized that to attain these goals, they needed to seek deeper understanding of the local political contexts where they worked, to broaden the range of actors with which they partnered, and to sharpen their efforts to facilitate transformative processes of change. In short, they needed to adopt more politically smart methods.

Different aid providers experimented with their own ways of putting these ideas into practice. As with the evolution of more political goals, the movement on methods is a story of partial and often inconsistent change, with donors struggling to find a comfortable balance between the conflicting imperatives to "take politics into account" but not to be "too political." The overall movement was extensive during the last decade, producing a minor ocean of new activities, one much too large to chart in every last detail. But it is marked by several major lines of work, which we highlight in this chapter:

- Efforts to multiply and scale up participation in development planning and programming;
- The opening up of governance assistance to the "demand side";
- The rise of political economy analysis; and
- The evolution of democracy aid away from the temptation of the technical.

These moves prompted assistance providers to be more political in their methods. Yet they faced familiar shortcomings concerning the real level of capacity and commitment within the aid community to engage much more deeply and systematically with complex, often highly problematic local political realities.

ELEVATING PARTICIPATORY DEVELOPMENT

The broad impetus that emerged in the 1990s to make development more participatory grew more ambitious as aid entered the following decade. Aid providers looked to citizen participation to address a number of significant development challenges, including project efficiency as well as the newly prominent issues of country ownership and empowering the poor.

National Participation and the Poverty Reduction Strategy Papers

One element of this thrust was more participatory development planning at the national level. The "rediscovery of the state" of the 1990s had, among other things, prompted greater attention to national-level development planning processes. The backlash against structural adjustment conditionality, as well as substantial new research findings on the importance of recipient commitment to development plans for aid effectiveness, also led donors to look for ways to build national support for their work.[1] Expanding participatory processes from the local to the national level was a logical response.

Donors thus scaled up participation in their assessments. The stand-alone participatory poverty assessments of the 1990s continued, but rather than focusing only on poor people's experience with poverty at the local level, some second- and third-generation analyses paid more attention to national and sector-wide issues and tried to influence national policy.[2] This broader focus allowed for greater examination of the influence of power relations and national politics on development outcomes. In preparation for the 2000/2001 World Development Report, the World Bank carried out its most ambitious participatory study of poverty, "Voices of the Poor." The study brought together participatory analyses of poverty issues from fifty countries and highlighted the ways in which powerlessness among the poor perpetuates poverty.[3] It helped point the World Development Report to an emphasis on empowering the poor as one of three key aspects of a poverty reduction strategy, alongside promoting opportunity and enhancing security.[4]

Donors also sought to facilitate national-level participatory planning processes. A 2000 DFID policy paper noted that participation in development had been too concentrated at the level of community projects without feeding into national policy and budget formation processes.[5] The European Union's 2000 Cotonou Agreement institutionalized the participation of civil society in EU development policy, and in 2002 the European Commission said that non-state actors were evolving from being mainly providers of services to becoming advocates who could contribute to policy discussions and enhance country ownership of the development process.[6]

The most ambitious attempt to involve non-state actors in national development planning came through the Poverty Reduction Strategy Papers (PRSPs), launched by the World Bank and the International Monetary Fund in 1999 as part of the Highly Indebted Poor Countries (HIPC) Initiative. The HIPC Initiative linked debt relief for poor countries to greater governmental commitments to poverty reduction and the creation of a participatory poverty reduction plan. Donors hoped that including a participatory dimension in these planning processes would help empower the poor and create a broad national consensus around development policy.[7] This was seen as a paradigm shift for the notoriously exclusive international financial institutions, a move from negotiating loans with a relatively small group of actors in the executive branch behind closed doors to directly engaging societies. DFID, UNDP, and other donors supported the PRSP process and said they would use the poverty reduction papers to help guide their development programming.[8] Reflecting on the adoption of PRSPs, David Booth wrote in 2005 that "1999 was the occasion when this accumulated wisdom [about participation] seemed to many people to be ripe for 'scaling up' to national policymaking. This was also a culminating moment in the long flirtation between the big official agencies and development NGOs, for whom the inclusion of 'civil society' is a litmus test of sound policymaking."[9] Numerous Poverty Reduction Strategy Papers were carried out in the early 2000s, especially in Africa, with thirty-three interim PRSPs and nine final PRSPs already completed by the end of 2001.[10] The process differed somewhat among countries, but in most cases the finance or planning ministry drafted a three-year poverty reduction strategy and then sought feedback from selected civil society groups.[11]

Critical Views

The participatory element of these processes represented a step forward in terms of widening the relationship among development agencies, aid-receiving governments, and recipient societies. PRSPs responded to several of the criticisms of early participatory efforts in the 1990s, notably the previous decades' focus on local-level participation in relatively small development projects disconnected from more influential national processes. They also recognized the national government's role and responsibility in poverty reduction. It soon became clear, however, that PRSPs would not meet the high hopes surrounding their launch. A rapidly emerging critical line of analysis and research on these exercises, including official donor reviews, pointed to significant limitations relating to the incompleteness or truncated character of their opening to politics:

- PRSPs failed to sufficiently take into account local realities. They proceeded from the usually flawed assumptions that sufficient political space existed in a country to allow for meaningful participation on important issues of national development and that the power balance between the government and civil society was sufficiently even to allow for balanced negotiation of interests.[12]

- Civil society actors taking part in PRSPs were often chosen by the host governments and were not representative of the society as a whole. They were generally from urban areas and could rarely speak directly for the poor.[13]

- PRSPs were frequently dominated by the usual development planners within government—notably finance ministries—and largely excluded such important political actors as opposition parties and parliaments. They were poorly integrated with local political processes, meaning that a PRSP could be negotiated and agreed upon shortly before a national election brought in a new government with a new set of priorities.[14]

- Most PRSPs limited societal participation in the planning process to information sharing rather than real collaboration between civil society actors and the government. The actual drafting of PRSPs still occurred behind closed governmental doors. Moreover, the World Bank and the IMF showed little inclination to compromise on macroeconomic policy goals no matter what feedback they received from civil society. According to a World Bank review, most PRSPs ended up looking very similar despite the great diversity of the specific national contexts. There was little accountability to ensure that civil society input was taken seriously.[15] Some outside critics thus argued that the PRSP process was intended more to legitimize and expand the role of international financial institutions within poor countries and allow autocratic governments to appear participatory than to facilitate real debate about appropriate economic models and poverty reduction strategies.[16]

At their core, PRSPs represented a technocratic response to the idea of more participatory, politically contextualized development planning. They attempted to address deep-seated issues such as a lack of popular voice in government through an externally imposed and sanitized consultation process that did not explicitly address the sources of disempowerment. They were not based on in-depth analysis of the interests of governmental and other actors in different reforms and instead assumed that governments would respond positively to citizen inputs.[17] As David Booth noted, the "implicit theory about political change that underlay the concept and its operationalisation has been proven naïve."[18]

Community-Managed Development

The increased attention to national participatory processes did not displace local-level participatory development programs. Assistance actors continued to be strongly attracted to the potential of local participatory programs, which provide opportunities to directly engage poor communities and give citizens more power over development outcomes. Conscious of the criticisms of previous attempts at information sharing and consultation as superficial, some donors increasingly moved in the late 1990s and early 2000s toward what they called "community-driven" or "community-managed" development.[19] The driving idea behind these programs was that rather than vague consultation sessions, or rubber stamping of donor plans, community members would have some direct control over development planning and resource allocation. This concept was already common within many developing countries. A number of Latin American governments, for example, set up social investment funds in the late 1980s and 1990s, giving communities the opportunity to propose small-scale infrastructure projects, apply for funding, and take responsibility for implementation.[20]

As with PRSPs, high ambitions accompanied these community-managed programs. Ghazala Mansuri and Vijayendra Rao describe the programs as having "the explicit objective of reversing power relations in a way that creates agency and voice for poor people. ... This is expected to make development funds more responsive to their needs, improve the targeting of poverty programs, make government more responsive, improve the delivery of public goods and services, and strengthen the capabilities of citizens to undertake self-initiated development activities."[21] In short, community-driven development would help achieve nearly all the major aspects of the broadened donor agenda—to empower the poor, improve governance, and fight poverty—all by transforming power relations.

Community-driven development programs nevertheless manifested many of the same apolitical characteristics as the local participatory programs of the 1990s and the integrated rural development programs of the 1970s. Donors often continued to see local communities as homogenous, harmonious entities that would automatically work in the collective interest and did not pay sufficient attention to inequalities within communities and the possibility of elite capture of development resources.[22] Some programs set up parallel implementing structures that were not well harmonized with local governments even if they were endorsed by national governments. Program planners saw such structures as necessary to improve efficiency and prevent local governments from misusing development resources, but the trade-off came in reduced linkages with domestic political processes. Additionally, the focus on the local level, while presenting some advantages, reduced the scale of the problems these programs could address. In an extensive recent review of nearly 500 studies on participatory development and decentralization efforts, Mansuri and Rao point to many of these shortcomings and note that despite some progress over time "inflexible institutional rules that do not internalize the complexity inherent in engaging with civic-led development remain, and insufficient emphasis continues to be placed on the importance of context. Unless these conditions improve, participatory development projects will continue to struggle to make a difference."[23]

The potential and continued challenges of community-managed development programs are illustrated by one of the most prominent early efforts in this area, the World Bank's extensive Kecamatan Development Program (KDP) in Indonesia. KDP was implemented in three phases from 1998 to 2008, costing $1.3 billion and reaching nearly half of Indonesia's villages.[24] The program was driven by social development specialists within the World Bank who wanted to get beyond narrow cost-benefit analyses and introduce ethnography and social analysis into development planning.[25] It was based on a study of local-level institutions in the late 1990s that highlighted the problem of poor people's lack of access to local decisionmaking. Hoping to increase local-level participation and accountability for development results, the World Bank set up a system in which communities could apply for competitive grants to undertake infrastructure projects.[26] It attempted to avoid corruption and what one Bank case study termed "misguided government takeovers" by using consultants to implement the program and sidestepping local governments in the initial phases, though it later tried to integrate them into the process.[27]

The Bank considered KDP innovative and successful and made it a model for similar programs in other countries. KDP entailed a more serious effort than most community development programs to adapt its design to local context and may have helped legitimize the use of ethnography within the Bank as an important aspect of development planning.[28] Evaluations of its impact found mixed results: some indicated positive effects on the empowerment of women and other marginalized groups, on efficient use of resources, and on conflict resolution while others pointed to limited success in reducing corruption through citizen monitoring and few gains in social cohesion.[29] Given its broad reach and long timeframe, results obviously varied in different places.

KDP also met with sharp criticism. Tania Murray Li, for example, argues that the ethnographic analyses adopted an apolitical lens, focusing on issues amenable to a technical solution, such as the lack of participatory processes, rather than more significant structural causes of poverty such as land rights. She and others further fault the World Bank for taking a narrow approach to increasing citizen participation, allowing voice only within the processes set up by the program and limiting the available development choices to small-scale infrastructure projects.[30] KDP could thus help communities build a new bridge and give citizens greater ownership over that bridge, but it was less good at addressing the deeper sources of poverty and inequality. Its proponents countered that even small steps toward giving marginalized citizens a greater voice in development could create higher expectations and empower societal groups to demand more from donors and their governments in the future.

Partial Progress

Both the PRSPs and community-driven development projects constituted constructive reactions to some of the shortcomings of previous participatory development efforts and represented an advance in taking politics into account. It is easy to see how a program like KDP based on extensive social studies and substantial room for recipient input was more effective than the rural development program James Ferguson observed in Lesotho in the early 1980s, which systematically misdiagnosed the structural features of the economy and the needs of individuals. KDP may not have fundamentally transformed social relations, but it at least brought useful infrastructure to people in need of it and proved empowering to at least some of them. PRSPs have not delivered the broadly owned development plans with significant input from the poor that many hoped for, but they have provided some useful opportunities for civil society to participate in development planning and in some places raised citizens' expectations about their right to be consulted. The core idea behind the PRSP processes— that national development priorities should be set through an inclusive process—has become widely accepted as good practice. The major OECD DAC international aid effectiveness conferences in 2005 in Paris, 2008 in Accra, and 2011 in Busan all called for inclusive country-owned processes of development planning, and a 2011 evaluation of the application of the OECD DAC's Paris Principles found that about half of the countries reviewed had strengthened the consultative and participatory nature of their development strategies since 2005.[31]

Participatory approaches have thus become a standard part of donor good practice, but attempts to expand their scope and application have also highlighted their significant limitations. Donor-sponsored participatory processes can go only so far in enabling poor people to challenge power relations and confront the fundamental constraints they face in escaping poverty, particularly if aid actors do not want to antagonize host governments. Development agencies still struggle to come to terms with the deeply political nature of participation and empowerment, in large part because acknowledging it would bring up uncomfortable questions about the possibility of remaining a neutral technical actor in such processes. Many participatory programs are set up on the assumption, and in some respects the requirement, that "the poor" and "civil society" have relatively coherent and unified views that they will be given room to express within defined participatory spaces. Such programs often operate from the expectation that power holders will be responsive to citizen input and do not fully take into account their potentially diverging interests and potential to disrupt the process. The participatory spaces often operate parallel to domestic political processes. That these programs do not deliver all the results their proponents hope for should not be surprising. Citizens in developed democracies may value the opportunity to participate in town hall meetings and have some say over the construction of a new school, for example, but few would say that such forums fundamentally transform their life prospects or role in society.

FOSTERING DEMAND FOR GOOD GOVERNANCE

The rise of participatory methods in overall development assistance contributed to a wider evolution of governance assistance toward more political methods. Aid providers expanded their initial top-down orientation to strengthening government institutions to build in a bottom-up dimension, or what some aid organizations called "the demand side" of governance.[32] This stream shares many characteristics with the participatory programs discussed above, including a concern with aid effectiveness and empowerment. Yet in contrast to some participatory efforts that bypassed local institutions in favor of parallel donor mechanisms, demand-side work is specifically aimed at improving recipient country governance and thus makes domestic institutions its target.

Origins

These efforts grew naturally out of the expansion of donor definitions of good governance to include principles involving the relationship between state and society, such as participation, accountability, and inclusiveness. They were also fueled by the accumulated frustration that donors experienced in their attempts to help strengthen state institutions in the 1990s—their frequent encounters with the discouraging reality that many power holders in poor countries benefit from and thus seek to maintain existing arrangements of governance, no matter how developmentally dysfunctional. The resulting donor attention to what aid practitioners framed as the need to find or nurture "political will" for reform on the part of governments led them to the idea of fostering greater demand for improved governance from citizens. Since ordinary citizens are the ones who pay the highest price for poor governance, donors assumed they would have a strong interest in pressing for reforms. Some positive experiments in the 1990s around participatory budgeting and citizen monitoring of public services reinforced this idea.

Movement toward demand-side governance work reflected not only the accumulation of experience within aid circles but also important changes in developing countries themselves. A host of factors came together after the early 1990s—especially the collapse of authoritarian rule in many places and the spread of new communications technologies—to unleash enormous civil society growth in places where governments had traditionally occupied most of the organized sociopolitical space. Citizens in many countries began to demand a greater say in how they were governed. Some governments moved to proactively open up spaces for a more deliberative approach to democracy, promising access to information, participatory budgeting, and other mechanisms for citizen involvement.[33] Given all this, it was only natural for the aid community to begin to shift gears and try to respond to the interests and aspirations of the many new actors and forces on the nongovernmental side.

Within the much smaller ambit of aid focused specifically on democracy support, supporting civil society had crystallized earlier, already back in the late 1980s and early 1990s, as a key element of bolstering democratic activists willing to challenge entrenched power structures. Civil society aid grew quickly within democracy promotion circles in the 1990s, supporting civic activists engaged in advocacy for greater political freedom or more rapid political reform. These individuals usually worked in public interest NGOs such as human rights groups.[34] Such assistance was not much focused on socioeconomic issues and existed somewhat separately from the domain of traditional development aid.

In the second half of the 1990s, mainstream aid organizations began raising the civil society issue in the domain of governance and socioeconomic work, framing it in terms of need for attention to the demand side of governance. The OECD DAC Ad Hoc Group on Participatory Development, for example, concluded in 1997 that "technocratic approaches to institutional change and legal reform fail without effective local demand for change, expressed through local constituencies and locally-based skills for building grassroots and national participation."[35] DFID in 2000 sounded a similar note, saying that "the concept of participation is shifting from beneficiary participation in state-delivered programmes to an understanding of participation as a means of holding the state accountable."[36] In one of the most influential arguments for demand-side work, the 2004 World Development Report, *Making Services Work for Poor People*, presented social accountability as a means to improve public service delivery. It suggested that citizens could hold service providers accountable through direct means as well as indirectly by pushing the state to pressure service providers to perform better.[37]

As with participatory programs more broadly, demand-side initiatives thus reflect both instrumental concerns around improved program effectiveness and the increased attention to empowerment, inclusion, and other political values arising out of the expanded good governance agenda.

Anuradha Joshi points out that these two drivers reflect very different intellectual origins: the first seeks to apply market mechanisms to the public sector by stressing accountability to consumers and consumer choice, while the second is a rights-based approach concerned with deepening democracy and citizenship.[38] Yet—as is often the case when instrumental and intrinsic approaches coexist—aid organizations usually give primary emphasis to the instrumental case. This has been particularly true since the 2004 World Development Report. The market view fits more comfortably with economic thinking within donor agencies and provides an opportunity to talk about political processes in seemingly safe terms. The very use of the economistic term "demand side" to describe what is in fact a very political concept underlines the economic orientation of such programs. Yet both views have some force within donor agencies, and many development practitioners believe strongly in the inherent value of participation and empowerment even if they stress the instrumental case in efforts to gain support for their programs.

The Demand-Side "Tool Kit"

By the middle of the 2000s most major donors included bottom-up approaches as a central part of their governance strategies.[39] Such programs encompass a diverse sea of activities but converge around some common patterns and forms. They generally utilize nongovernmental organizations as their main organizational partner or vehicle. These NGOs vary in their substantive focus (from broad socioeconomic goals to narrow technical issues) and level of organization (national, regional, or community-based), but at least in the early wave of such work they were usually elite-led organizations lacking a wide grassroots base. The donor tendency to concentrate on NGOs within the much wider array of organizations that make up civil society in developing countries—which includes religious organizations, trade unions, professional associations, ethnic organizations, cultural groups, social movements, or others—is a much documented and analyzed tendency in development aid.[40] It reflects the appeal of NGOs as groups focused on (or willing to focus on) the sorts of governance reforms that donors care about, the relative newness of these organizations and their lack of ties to problematic past power structures or events, and their ability to function as competent aid recipients that can meet the bureaucratic demands of development agencies by producing coherent budgets, work plans, and activity reports. They fit well with the donor desire to work more politically without being "too political." Unlike social movements or trade unions, they appear to have local legitimacy to engage on political issues without being associated with a particular ideological agenda. And they allow aid providers to partner with local actors without surrendering too much control over program objectives and methods.

The substantive focus of these demand-side programs also varies but follows certain major lines, such as anticorruption, women's rights, legal reform, budgeting, and other areas having to do with governmental competence and honesty. They make use of what has quickly become a familiar "tool kit" of demand-side work, including:

- public access to information;

- participatory budgeting;

- citizen monitoring of public service provision or of other governmental activity;

- public interest advocacy campaigns for policy reform;

- capacity building for citizen activists and journalists on governance issues; and

- rights awareness and other civic education efforts.

Donors have implemented these programs in multiple regions and levels of government. A very small, merely illustrative sampling of what has become an enormous array of such programs includes: the World Bank assisted the implementation of access to information laws in Bangladesh and Nicaragua and piloted citizen report cards in Ethiopia and Mozambique; AusAID fostered community involvement in holding governments accountable for service delivery in East Timor and the Philippines; USAID partnered with Procurement Watch Inc. in pushing for procurement reform in the Philippines; DFID funded a civil society organization advocating for land rights for the poor in Bangladesh; and Sweden and Norway supported the Sri Lankan Press Institute in its efforts to train journalists and advance freedom of the press.[41]

Some development practitioners outside the governance sector also embraced the demand-side perspective. Social development specialists in particular often saw such strategies as a useful tool to further their sector goals by encouraging increased funding for their social priorities and improving government effectiveness in these areas. Bottom-up approaches to improving public service delivery became especially popular, particularly after the 2004 World Development Report. Tools such as citizen report cards were regarded as a method through which greater accountability to citizens could bring clear improvements in services with direct links to poverty reduction.

Given the multiplicity of funding lines in this area and the lack of clear programmatic boundaries, it is impossible to estimate the spending levels devoted to demand-side governance work. But spending on these types of programs unquestionably increased substantially. Overall official development assistance spending by DAC members on the components of government and civil society aid that are most tied to demand-side processes—democratic participation and civil society, legislatures and political parties, media, human rights, and women's organizations—increased from about $500 million in the mid-1990s to more than $3 billion in 2010.[42] At DFID, for example, civil society was the fastest-growing area of governance aid in 2004–2009, increasing 84 percent during that period.[43] This was alongside a 50 percent growth in overall (both governance- and non-governance-related) DFID civil society funding between 1997 and 2006.[44] Within this overall trend of increased attention to the demand side, individual development agencies came from different starting points. USAID, for example, had already accumulated significant experience in this domain through its early civil society assistance relating to democracy goals and felt it could transfer such learning to bottom-up approaches in the socioeconomic field.[45] The World Bank provided important intellectual leadership for demand-side work but found such programs a poor fit with its loan model and had to rely on special trust fund support for most of its operational work in this area.[46]

This rebalancing of governance assistance to include substantial attention to the citizen side represents significant movement toward more politically smart methods. It has greatly expanded the range of actors with which aid organizations work, deepening their reach in recipient countries. Even more importantly, such aid at least proceeds from a potentially more realistic conception of how governance change is likely to come about. It moves beyond the overly reductive notion embodied in top-down governance work that injections of new technical knowledge or additions of hardware will transform governing institutions. It assumes that governance change will most likely come about through a political process—the assertion and resolution of multiple competing interests relating to the exercise of state power.

Successes and Limitations

Demand-side initiatives have been associated with some notable successes. Civil society groups that have focused on participatory budgeting and budget transparency have pushed governments in some places to increase the proportion of their budgets devoted to education, health care, and other social sectors and have used expenditure tracking to help ensure that these funds are not lost to corruption.[47] Budget groups in India, Mexico, South Africa, and Uganda also played a significant role in helping legislators learn more about the budget process and better hold government ministers to account.[48] In multiple studies in India, citizen report cards and complaint procedures have been found to improve the responsiveness of public officials and the quality of public services. In some Indian states, these report cards and procedures are codified into law.[49] Participation in civil society groups in Bangladesh, Brazil, Mexico, and elsewhere has also helped poor and marginalized individuals learn about their legal rights and feel empowered to assert them.[50]

Yet this positive movement away from the temptation of the technical toward more political methods represents only partial progress. An essential limitation remains in the basic conception of process at the heart of the demand-side approach—the assumption that a relatively narrow band of civil society organizations representing usually moderate points of view and employing moderate methods for achieving change will be able to make a significant dent in entrenched structures and patterns of power in societies that are typically marked by profound inequalities and a weak tradition of government responsiveness. In other words, although the addition of the demand side represents the embrace of at least somewhat more political processes of governance change, it still often proceeds from a constrained, even simplistic, conception of political process. As these programs unfolded over the course of the 2000s, these limits became apparent alongside their successes, attracting critical attention from outside scholars and analysts of development aid as well as evaluative undertakings within aid organizations themselves.

Several outside studies and major evaluations in the late 2000s found some positive results of demand-side work with regard to greater citizen participation in and awareness of development issues, but less impact on the core donor priorities of poverty reduction and institutional change.[51] They further noted uneven outcomes across different contexts, with some approaches working well in certain places but falling short in others. Significantly, these reviews pointed to a failure to engage with several layers of political complexity and reality:

- The issues that donor-supported civil society actors treat as objectively desirable reform items are in fact parts of larger political agendas competing with other alternatives for priority in the country—the focus on putatively universal principles such as inclusiveness and accountability hides the reality of basic ideological choice and contest. Societal actors necessarily operate in an environment of competition and conflict without clear lines between what is "reform" and what is "anti-reform" and in which there is no simple duality of citizens versus the state. The appealing image of altruistic civil society actors fighting for the interests of the poor against entrenched elite actors often obscures more nuanced battles of interests and ideas. Development agencies frequently lack understanding of how their agendas fit into these domestic political debates and power struggles and are reluctant to acknowledge the contested nature of their goals.[52]

- Civil society groups are not neutral partners but rather actors with their own interests, social connections, histories, and shortcomings. Some do not seek to advance the public interest (assuming that that is even a coherent concept), but instead work on behalf of the private interests of particular groups and individuals. Others may have laudable goals but lack the capacity and connections to productively further these objectives. In particular, many of the larger NGOs in developing countries are run by elites who may be public spirited but cannot claim to fully represent the views of those living in poverty. Aid providers often choose which actors to support based more on convenience or perceived shared values than on rigorous analysis of which organization would be the most effective partner in particular contexts.[53]

- Demand-side aid tends to reach only a very limited range of organizations, ones whose values and structures align closely with aid organizations, excluding large numbers of organizations which might be more representative and politically powerful. That in effect narrows the political range of contestation rather than broadens it. The methods of activism that civil society aid organizations support are a truncated set of the overall range of possible methods. They exclude more challenging tactics such as mass mobilization, civil disobedience, strikes, and other forms of open protest.[54]

- Donor funding actively skews the incentives and priorities of civil society groups, reducing their domestic legitimacy and their ability to represent local views. The tendency to rely on short-term project funding exacerbates this problem by forcing NGOs to constantly adapt their activities to shifting donor priorities.[55] To the extent that aid actors support civil society groups with strong grassroots connections, their funding can cause these organizations to become increasingly responsive to the preferences and needs of donors at the expense of accountability to their grassroots members. Nicola Banks and David Hulme thus argue that donor support depoliticizes civil society organizations by encouraging them to adopt moderate positions and professionalize themselves rather than build deeper linkages with social movements.[56]

- Many societies do not offer the kind of political enabling environment necessary for bottom-up contestation to significantly influence power holders and contribute to improved governance. Increased citizen awareness of poor governance is unlikely to lead to reforms if power holders do not suffer negative consequences from ignoring complaints.[57] A review by Rosie McGee and John Gaventa, for example, found "little evidence of impact" of transparency and accountability initiatives in non-democratic settings.[58]

Assessing the Advances

The quantity and types of aid that development agencies provide in their demand-side work often pale before the challenges outlined above. These programs usually focus on building the capacity of specific actors to engage in formal processes of dialogue with power holders; they do not always ask whether such processes are the most effective means of state-society bargaining. They have trouble helping societal actors address core political economy obstacles to social accountability such as unequal power relations within society and between the government and citizens.[59]

Where programs are successful, evaluations often point to favorable political factors. A review of civil society engagement in Uganda and South Africa by Mark Robinson and Steven Friedman, for example, found that civil society organizations that succeeded in facilitating policy reforms relied on good technical knowledge as well as the policy advocacy skills, relationships with government officials, and perceived legitimacy necessary to leverage their technical assets into policy impact.[60] Other reviews point to the advantages of multiple bottom-up strategies, linking engagement in formal spaces or civil society advocacy with broader social mobilization and coalition-building efforts.[61] Successful bottom-up advocacy also relies on a positive enabling environment, relating not just to sufficient political space for civil society to operate but also the capacity of government to respond to citizen demands. McGee and Gaventa conclude that critical to the success of transparency and accountability initiatives are "political will and a political environment that favours a balanced supply- and demand-side approach to accountability."[62] This observation indicates an important limitation to the demand-side approach: the driving idea behind the move to bottom-up approaches is that such programs can help build political will where it does not exist. But at least a minimal degree of support from government is necessary for demand-side approaches to work.

By the late 2000s it was quite evident that existing bottom-up approaches to governance were far from a silver bullet to confronting the persistent challenge of lack of political will and that they needed some significant rethinking and refining. But it was equally clear that the opening to the citizen side of governance represented a major breakthrough in development thinking and practice. The field of development aid is often swayed in both its goals and methods by swinging pendulums. Movement in one direction appears as fundamental progress until the pendulum hurtles back in reverse. In this case, however, the expansion of governance work to include bottom-up approaches is unlikely to end up as just a temporary movement that will disappear in a swing back to an exclusive emphasis on top-down change. It has opened up governance work to much greater possibilities and accomplishments. It remains the most natural response to the problem of building broad political support for developmental reform. And a changing global context is increasingly making demand-side work an imperative. Greater pluralism in many developing countries as well as advances in communications technology are making it much harder for governments and donors alike to shield their programs from citizen scrutiny. This is the case even in undemocratic contexts. As discussed in the next chapter, some aid practitioners are trying to take citizen-based approaches further as part of a renewed push on the politics agenda generally.

SEARCHING FOR POLITICAL UNDERSTANDING

The early frustrations aid providers experienced as they took up governance work in the 1990s did more than prompt movement toward bottom-up approaches. These difficult experiences also provoked recognition among at least some practitioners of the need for much better understanding of the political contexts in which they were working. As aid actors attempted to assist new institutions and a wide range of social actors, they faced obvious knowledge gaps and frequent blockages on what appeared to them to be self-evidently valuable governance reforms. The mixed initial experience with civil society assistance and demand-side approaches only reinforced the importance of more sophisticated political knowledge. And given that their work on governance aimed to advance socioeconomic development generally, the new interest in better understanding local realities extended to broader questions about how and why positive socioeconomic change might come about at all.

The importance of greater local political knowledge became particularly evident and urgent as development agencies rapidly increased their work in conflict-affected states. As seen in chapter 4, in countries fractured by serious civil conflict, development practitioners quickly realized that they could not achieve sustainable development results without coming to grips with political realities. This meant understanding how power is distributed, the grievances of particular groups, and how to make progress toward political settlements. Conflict countries represented extreme cases, but the issues they raised around state fragility, social grievances, and the potentially negative unintended consequences of foreign assistance resonated throughout development work.

New Analytic Tools

A number of major aid organizations thus began to develop new analytic tools to provide deeper understanding of the core political dynamics of countries where they worked. Most of these early tools were specifically designed to guide governance or conflict strategies rather than inform socioeconomic development programs generally. The World Bank in 1999 launched "Institutional and Governance Reviews" to assess the performance of partner country institutions and determine the political feasibility of reforms.[63] USAID in 2000 released a democratic governance assessment tool to inform its democracy and governance strategies. This tool urged attention to democratic shortcomings in recipient countries and also to how the "political game" is played in each of those societies.[64] For conflict contexts, in the early 2000s major development actors devised conflict assessment tools to guide practitioners in analyzing the sources and dynamics of conflict in developing countries—looking at social, political, economic, security, and external forces—and their implications for development programs.[65] These analyses were usually designed to identify potential as well as active conflicts and were thus applied even in some relatively peaceful contexts.

A further set of tools took a broader approach, attempting to assess and understand the politics of a wide range of development challenges. DFID built on the foundation of a pathbreaking set of papers by Sue Unsworth on understanding the political dynamics of socioeconomic change by establishing in 2002 a series of "Drivers of Change" studies of various countries, mostly in sub-Saharan Africa and Asia. Sida launched a series of "Power Analyses" in 2003, starting with Ethiopia, where a review of past programming had found disappointing results on key Sida development goals from 1996 to 2001 despite significant Swedish assistance.[66] The World Bank built on its more narrowly focused institutional and governance reviews to start carrying out wider political economy analyses in some places.[67] As the decade progressed, other organizations joined the trend, including the Netherlands Ministry of Foreign Affairs—which carried out more than 30 country-level political analyses from 2007 to 2009 within the framework of "Strategic Governance and Corruption Assessments" (SGACA)—and the Norwegian Agency for Development Cooperation (Norad).[68]

These assessment tools had different official names but mostly converged under the general moniker of "political economy analyses." This became the preferred term because these analyses focused on the interactions between political conditions and economic issues, and also because "political *economy* analysis" seemed less likely than "political analysis" to raise hackles within development institutions hesitant about sounding too political.[69] A description of political economy analysis in a World Bank how-to note captures the common ground of these different tools:

> Political economy is the study of both politics and economics, and specifically the interactions between them. It focuses on power and resources, how they are distributed and contested in different country and sector contexts, and the resulting implications for development outcomes. PE analysis involves more than a review of institutional and governance arrangements: it also considers the underlying interests, incentives, rents/rent distribution, historical legacies, prior experiences with reforms, social trends, and how all of these factors affect or impede change.[70]

Common Elements

Political economy analyses overlapped significantly with elements of governance analysis and conflict assessments but went further in examining how political factors affect socioeconomic development work. Unlike governance assessments, which usually looked at a limited set of core governance institutions in a country and measured them against good governance standards, and conflict assessments, which focused on conflict risks, political economy studies were designed to inform interventions in any sector.[71] Most of the first wave of these analyses were country studies, wide-reaching efforts to gain a comprehensive picture of a country's developmental dynamics. They usually proceeded through an analytic framework consisting of the following main elements:[72]

- *Structural or foundational factors:* What historical, geographic, social, economic, and political conditions have shaped the country's development? What are the sources of state authority (or lack thereof), and how autonomous is the country in relation to international actors? What are the primary areas of economic activity? Which groups hold political and economic power, and how did they acquire it? What are the most important social and ideological cleavages?

- *Formal and informal institutions:* What rules and institutional arrangements—formal and informal—bear most significantly on the country's development? What institutions (state or non-state) hold the most power? Are these institutions considered legitimate? What type of engagement exists between state and society? Where does political contestation primarily occur? How transparent are formal and informal institutions, and how do they interact with each other? How do patronage systems operate?

- *Actors:* Who are the key government, societal, and external players influencing development processes? What are their interests and incentives? How do they make decisions? Who holds power? How do they use it? Who are the likely winners and losers of reform? Who has the ability to block reform? How do these actors relate to each other?

- *Processes:* How has developmental change occurred in the past? How do the structural, institutional, and stakeholder variables interact and constrain each other? What relevant changes are in progress? Are any major socioeconomic trends or pressures likely to change the rules of the game in the future? What are the most salient political issues today?

- *Implications for donors:* What are the primary constraints on development? What are the entry points for change? What are the likely risks? Who are potential supporters of reform, and what capacity do they have to contribute to change? Is it possible to accommodate the interests of powerful players within a program for pro-poor change? Where

is reform not feasible? Where is it desirable to work within the current
political context and power holders and where is it necessary to try to
expand the existing space for reform?

Development agencies varied somewhat in how they addressed these
topics in their assessment tools. Many conducted stand-alone stakeholder
analyses concentrated on relevant actors and their interests. Such studies
are a quick and useful way to map who supports or opposes certain priorities and their relative power. They can inform *how* to implement specific
programs or policies, though they usually do not capture the larger development challenges and political structures that can guide decisions on
what development priorities should be. For example, a stakeholder analysis
might help aid actors determine the feasibility of passing local-level budget
transparency requirements but not tell them whether budget transparency
responds to a clear need on the ground or if it is likely to be an effective
tool for empowering the poor. Full political economy analyses go beyond
stakeholder analysis, but early studies tended to focus on surveying the
relevant structures, institutions, and actors while paying less explicit attention to how change occurs or operational implications for development
programs. Donors increasingly incorporated the last two elements as they
refined their frameworks.

How Useful for Programs?

Despite the varied national contexts, political economy studies usually
highlighted the same few basic issues—the ubiquity and power of patronage
systems in the developing world and the negative incentives for most power
holders there to carry out governance reforms that aid providers typically recommend. They also underlined the poor functionality of major
governing institutions in these countries and the devastating effects of this
reality on development efforts. These and other similarly general conclusions were rarely news for those familiar with the countries in question.
Some aid practitioners and persons in aid-receiving countries accordingly
saw them as expensive, time-consuming affirmations of the obvious.

But having such conclusions set forth in official assessments did help open
up conversations within aid organizations, putting on the table unpleasant
political realities that were otherwise avoided. As a review commissioned by

the OECD Development Assistance Committee Network on Governance in 2005 concluded, "almost all donors emphasised that, although the analysis had not told them anything very new, it had served to structure their thinking, to make implicit knowledge explicit, to give them a shared language and basis for discussion of the political and institutional context and its impact on development, and to legitimise this discourse."[73] Reading through a lessons learned paper by the Netherlands Ministry of Foreign Affairs on its experience with its SGACA assessments, for example, both the obviousness and the bluntness of some of the lessons are striking. Among them: "patron-client networks are a fact" and "the Netherlands does not expect religion to play a direct role in politics. However, the SGACAs present a very different picture."[74]

These analyses were not, however, as helpful in opening up more frank and productive conversations about such issues *between* aid organizations and recipient governments. Unsurprisingly given the negative reactions to the governance agenda outlined in the previous chapter, the governments whose countries were studied in these exercises generally did not like aid organizations commissioning probing analyses of how institutions actually worked in their societies, given that such studies usually highlighted patronage, corruption, and other institutional flaws. They objected both in principle to the idea of such studies and often in practice to the specific findings.[75] Their sensitivity and resistance provoked debates within aid organizations about whether such studies might harm donor-recipient relations. Aid organizations became cautious about sharing the studies with host country counterparts and often with fellow aid organizations, or even within their own organizations.

Country studies were also not as helpful as their proponents initially hoped in leading to different, and better, aid programs. One common criticism was that their findings were either too general or too wide-ranging across the whole panorama of the country's developmental landscape to be useful as a guide for designing new assistance interventions.[76] The comprehensive focus of political economy analyses was an advantage in some ways over conflict or governance assessments, but it also made these studies more difficult to translate into practice. Another complaint was that the studies were good at bringing to light the many obstacles to change but not in showing how to address them. They thus functioned more as depressants than stimulants for aid practitioners. The Dutch 2010 review of experience with political economy analyses came down hard in this regard, concluding that its SGACAs were "of limited practical use" and that "the SGACA process should not be repeated," although it recognized that "an analysis of the political context, preferably demand-driven and country-specific, is needed in one form or another."[77] The World Bank's 2011 evaluation of its governance and anticorruption program echoed similar complaints, saying that "the operational benefits of free-standing PEA [political economy analysis] reports were often limited by an overly academic orientation, uneven methodological rigor, and a lack of consistency between recommended actions and prevailing interpretations of the Bank's Articles of Agreement."[78] But it, too, urged better, rather than less, analysis.

The 2005 DAC review of initial donor experiences with political economy analysis was somewhat more positive, finding that these studies "led to changes in country plans and programmes, but only up to a point."[79] It concluded that in Bangladesh, political economy analyses encouraged DFID to enhance its engagement with political processes and a broad range of stakeholders, the World Bank to pay more attention to corruption and institutional reform in its sector programs, and Sida to close out a local governance program that was being blocked by local power structures and instead consider exploring ways to negotiate with elites to advance the interests of the poor.[80] A large-scale DFID political economy analysis of Nigeria in 2003 helped DFID shift gears somewhat, explicitly challenging a number of common assumptions such as that "'democracy' creates political space for pro-poor change," "'champions of change' will drive reform," and "lack of capacity is the problem."[81] It prompted DFID to realistically assess its limited influence in the country and look for new ways to support change in the face of deep structural challenges relating to a lack of accountability of state to society and the pernicious effects of oil dependence.[82]

In other words, this first generation of political economy analyses for the most part were useful to improve understanding, open up internal conversations, and flag some awkward issues for attention. To the limited extent they affected development programming, their primary influence was in steering aid organizations away from areas likely to be unproductive. They had less effect on the actual focus and substance of aid programming. As examined in the next chapter, however, they paved the ground for a subsequent, more focused line of political economy analyses that is proving useful in shaping operations.

MAKING POLITICAL AID MORE POLITICAL

As discussed in chapter 3, democracy assistance was pursued through surprisingly apolitical methods in its early years. But in the last decade, democracy aid underwent its own evolution toward more political methods. These moves sometimes overlapped with the evolution of socioeconomic aid (especially given that governance assistance in many agencies straddles the development and democracy domains) and sometimes proceeded separately from it. As in socioeconomic aid, the increasing use of political methods in democracy work was driven by the frustration practitioners experienced when assistance efforts failed to gain traction due to a lack of local impetus for change.

The surge of democracy aid in the 1990s was rooted in the idea of a forward political reform dynamic in countries that had experienced authoritarian collapse. This dynamic presumably included institutional development, a stronger and more active role for civil society, and elections that were more free and fair. This was a natural assumption in the heady days of democracy's global spread. But as countries moved beyond the initial optimistic phase of post-authoritarian politics into the hard slog of consolidating democracy, it became increasingly apparent in many places that the reform dynamic had dissipated. Some countries ended up spinning their wheels politically, alternating power between contending elites but not deepening democracy. Others drifted into semiauthoritarian rule that embodied the forms of democracy but not its substance.[83] In these and other cases, conventional democracy programs had trouble gaining traction. Democracy aid providers responded by looking for ways to directly spark positive reforms.

As in development work, the first step for many democracy practitioners was to come to terms with the fact that every element of democratic consolidation is more about working out conflicting political interests than achieving technical improvements in formal structures. As Greg Power observed with regard to parliamentary programs, donors too often assumed "that given the right structure, rules, skills and resources politicians will inevitably behave in a way that ensures an effective parliamentary democracy. Yet, in every parliament around the world there is a gap between the formal powers that the institution has to hold government to account, and the willingness or ability of politicians to use that power."[84]

To influence political institutions, democracy supporters needed a much more sophisticated understanding of the underlying causes behind democratic deficiencies and potential avenues for change. There was less effort within the democracy community to develop formal political economy analyses as a guide to programming, though democracy programming within aid agencies benefited from democracy and governance assessments and other similar tools.[85] Democracy support organizations took various more informal measures to increase political understanding among their staff. Some sought to gain contextual political knowledge by implementing their programs in closer cooperation with country nationals, either by hiring local staff or using local partners. A majority of the staff of the National Democratic Institute, for example, now consists of non-U.S. nationals.[86] Many also adopted more realistic theories and expectations of change in response to on-the-ground experiences and political science literature.

Some of the resulting programmatic adjustments came on the governance side of the democracy aid realm and basically followed the line described in the previous section about giving greater attention to the demand side. Thus, many democracy programs focused on parliamentary strengthening moved away from an earlier focus on training parliamentarians on how to draft laws, read a budget, or form committees and moved toward efforts to stimulate productive engagement between citizens and their representatives.[87] Rule-of-law aid programs shifted from their initial principal emphasis on technocratic measures like judicial training or modernizing court facilities toward initiatives to increase the legal empowerment of disadvantaged groups and expand legal access.[88]

Changes also took place in other types of democracy programs, such as those focused on core political processes. Some elections assistance moved beyond the early efforts to bolster the technical capacity of electoral commissions toward approaches that would avoid legitimating skillful semiauthoritarians intent on using elections to validate their rule. This included refusing to engage in technical assistance in some cases and focusing on alternative approaches such as parallel vote counts and empowering domestic observers. Political party aid providers started to face the fact that many of the party leaders with whom they worked actively resisted most recommended reforms as a threat to their power. Consequently, they started trying alternatives to conventional training programs, looking more carefully within parties to identify and strengthen potential agents of internal party change, and also engaging more broadly beyond specific parties to support efforts to modify the legal and financial structure shaping dysfunctional party systems.[89]

In short, a general pattern emerged of democracy aid becoming more political in its methods—reaching a wider range of actors, making use of more sophisticated assessments of local political realities, and trying harder to foster processes of change originating from dynamic interactions of contending interests and forces. Yet although this was a trend in many parts of the democracy aid community, the issue of "how political to be" nevertheless proved divisive.

Some democracy aid providers, especially in the United States, reacted to the proliferation of semiauthoritarian regimes by becoming more politically assertive and challenging. They felt that as these regimes became notably skillful at manipulating democratic forms and deceiving international audiences about their political intentions, it was important to push harder on them for real change. In some cases, like Russia, this meant assisting politically outspoken human rights groups and activists or other civil society actors interested in challenging the regime politically. In some places where strongman leaders were attempting to use elections to legitimate their rule, aid providers made politically strategic use of assistance to help mobilize civil forces and opposition parties to press hard for free and fair elections. This included assistance for an interrelated set of activities that put pressure on the regime to hold a clean election and respect the results, including support for get-out-the-vote campaigns, domestic election monitoring groups, independent media, and opposition political parties.[90] When such assistance efforts were carried out in places where "electoral revolutions" occurred, most notably Georgia, Serbia, and Ukraine, they attracted considerable international attention.[91] They caused some government officials and other people in different parts of the world to start seeing Western democracy aid as the sharp edge of a political sword that they believed the U.S. government and some of its allies wielded to undercut regimes they disliked.

For other parts of the democracy aid community, especially in Europe and international institutions, these more politically challenging forms of democracy aid were a step too far in the political direction. These aid providers were willing to acknowledge the need to grasp the realities of local contexts and be politically smart in their operations. But they were not willing to be so politically assertive.

As a result, a divide of sorts opened up in the overall set of organizations involved in democracy aid: some gravitated toward openly political approaches, while others preferred a less political, more "developmental" approach.[92] The latter group argued that democratization is a complex and iterative process and that outside actors should focus on supporting the long-term social and political conditions for democracy rather than confronting power structures head-on in hopes of catalytic change. This divide echoed the debates in the United States in the 1960s around direct versus indirect political assistance. It also corresponded roughly to the division in the democracy aid community between organizations that pursue democracy out of an intrinsic belief in its value, with relatively little focus on socioeconomic dimensions, and those that have arrived at democracy aid more as an extension of socioeconomic assistance (usually through governance work) and see its instrumental, pro-development rationale as being as important as its core raison d'être.

CONCLUSION

Aid providers made important advances toward more political methods during the first decade of the new century. Building on the increased space opened up by their extensive adoption of political goals and responding to the vexing challenges of trying to make progress on governance and other political areas, they began conducting political analyses, widening the scope of actors with whom they worked, fostering greater citizen participation, and looking for ways to stimulate local demand for reform. Democracy aid specialists also moved away from technical methods toward more politically informed engagement.

This represented notable progress, but it was only a preliminary effort to move the aid industry away from the technocratic methods that have produced so many programs ill-adapted to local contexts and devoid of a realistic theory of change. Aid providers experimenting with new methods often took halting steps—they had trouble making good use of their own political analyses, underestimated how difficult it would be to influence deeply rooted and dysfunctional power structures, and continued to think in terms of trying to manage or even control political processes in developing countries rather than learning how to work with or inside them. The focus on demand and supply for reform downplayed the contested nature of reform goals and led some aid providers to assume that politics operated much like a market. Nevertheless, these initial steps opened doors and minds toward refining political methods. The next chapter explores the current state of efforts to take this movement further and institutionalize politically smart development programming.

THE WAY FORWARD

CHAPTER 6

POLITICALLY SMART DEVELOPMENT AID?

INTRODUCTION

The opening of the door to politics in the early 1990s proved groundbreaking. Over the course of that decade and the next, the international aid community traveled some distance toward thinking and acting more politically. Most major aid organizations adopted some explicitly political goals alongside their traditional socioeconomic ones. In parallel, they moved partly away from the temptation of the technical to pursue more political methods. Yet despite these changes, it is striking that in the late years of the last decade and continuing through to the present, a chorus of voices emerged among aid practitioners and development scholars calling on the aid community to further step up its efforts to embrace politics. They started organizing conferences on "Politics into Practice," writing articles and reports with titles like "What's Politics Got to Do With It?," pushing their bosses within aid organizations to declare publicly that "politics matters," launching innovative initiatives that embody political thinking in new ways, and working to mainstream political methods into a wider range of assistance programming.[1]

This renewed push on politics is still unfolding. It represents the current frontier of the larger evolution toward taking politics seriously in development aid. Though still in progress, this renewed push is far enough along that some questions about it can be addressed: What does it consist of in practice? Why has it come about? Is it an elaboration of the earlier opening to politics that started in the 1990s or something different? How much further is it taking development aid toward political goals and methods?

So far, the renewed push appears to be aimed primarily at going further on methods. This chapter outlines the current state of thinking about operating politically at the level of methods, tracing how some practitioners are building on the gains of the last decade to pursue political methods more deeply and widely. It highlights three core lines of such work:

- Developing more practical political economy tools and making wider use of such analysis in program planning;

- Refining bottom-up strategies and attempting to bridge the divide between state-centered and citizen-oriented approaches to governance support; and

- Mounting direct efforts to stimulate political processes of developmental change.

What this renewed push may mean for a further embrace of political goals is another important question, one that has much to do with the ongoing research debate over the relationship between political institutions and socioeconomic progress. The next chapter takes on that topic.

AN EMERGING CONSENSUS ON METHODS

Aid providers started pursuing more political methods over the past two decades in somewhat improvisational, or even haphazard fashion, usually in response to specific frustrations on the ground. They reacted to the perceived need to build greater in-country legitimacy and ownership of often unpopular market-reform measures by adopting more participatory approaches. They opened up governance assistance to bottom-up approaches in large part due to the lack of progress generated by top-down methods. They began carrying out political economy analyses to figure out why some programs were not working and where they could find better entry points for progress. While these efforts added up to significantly more political modes of operating, they were not driven by a coherent embrace of the importance of politics to development work.

Does this piecemeal adoption of political methods undermine their potential? Development scholars and practitioners at the forefront of the politics agenda argue that it does, that taking politics seriously in development is, or at least should be, more than the sum of disparate political strands. As seen in previous chapters, aid practitioners can work in governance and other political areas without being politically informed or politically engaged. Even work that appears to draw on political thinking may well reflect a technician's view of politics, with mechanistic efforts to engineer incentives and impose best practices for citizen-state relations. Or as scholars at the Centre for the Future State note about major aid organizations in their important study *An Upside Down View of Governance*, "their instinctive response is to 'manage' the local politics rather than see them as integral to finding a way forward."[2]

For proponents of more political approaches, working politically is less about doing *more* things—entering more political areas, working on demand-side efforts—than about doing things *differently*. It is about recognizing that developmental change at every step, in every sector, at every level, is an inherently political process. The key to more effective assistance is to conceive of aid interventions as integral parts of productive sociopolitical processes that produce positive developmental change. In other words, politics is an approach rather than a sector.

THE NEW COMMON WISDOM

Some development experts have been making this argument for years or even decades, but their once lonely voices have multiplied and started to gain greater traction. A number of research programs, many donor-funded, have made the politics of development their central focus and are aimed at fostering more comprehensive political thinking among mainstream aid actors.[3] These include the Africa Politics and Power Programme at the Overseas Development Institute, the Centre for the Future State and the Development Research Centre on Citizenship, Participation, and Accountability at the Institute of Development Studies, the Developmental Leadership Program, and the Effective States and Inclusive Development Research Centre at the University of Manchester. In addition, at least some aid agencies have carried out significant internal studies about the politics of development in preparation for issuing new policy statements and operational guidance. Researchers and development practitioners have come together repeatedly in recent years to review the evolution of governance work and more broadly the place of politics in the development agenda.[4] In short, a small but influential community of people working in or around the assistance community is now offering incisive ideas about how to take politics seriously in development aid. They do not constitute a unified movement but do converge around some core recommendations, which include:

- *Assume that development is a political process.* The role of politics is apparent in support for democratic governance or democracy, but politics affects all areas of development and no sector can afford to ignore political realities such as power dynamics or ideological conflicts. Whether development in any specific country advances or retreats is usually substantially due to political factors. Just as importantly, development assistance has significant political consequences in recipient societies that need to be better understood and explicitly factored into planning and evaluation processes.

- *Start from local political context.* Development practitioners should seek to understand the political context not only to anticipate likely obstacles to pre-formed plans but also as the basis for developing their strategies in the first place. Program designs should grow out of the specific constraints and opportunities of the recipient country and should consider structural and institutional factors in addition to the interests of key actors. This does not mean that programs will necessarily be focused on changing recipient country dynamics; a better understanding of the context may point to the need to address international dimensions of problems such as state corruption.

- *Focus on function rather than form.* Development programs should concentrate on what institutional arrangements can deliver development outcomes in specific contexts rather than trying to import model institutions or textbook rules. This means thinking about goals in terms of best fit rather than best practice. It also requires recognizing the important role that informal institutions and relationships play in development and looking for ways to engage with such institutions.

- *Work flexibly to facilitate processes of change.* International aid continues to provide valuable technical inputs to developing countries, but resources and technical advice are most useful if they fit into positive processes of change within recipient societies. Aid must therefore be more about the facilitation of process than the attempted reproduction of preset endpoints. These development processes, as noted above, are inherently political. Moreover, developmental change is rarely linear, and programs need to be adaptable not only to initial contextual circumstances but also to changes and unforeseen obstacles along the way.

- *Think of programs within broader political systems.* Practitioners should understand the specific political factors of direct relevance to the projects they support as well as how their efforts fit into the broader political context. Recognizing that the larger political context is rarely entirely static, they should understand and try to work constructively on the relationship between the particular developmental changes that aid seeks to facilitate and related trends in the overall political environment. One vital concept, particularly in fragile state contexts, is gearing development programs toward positively influencing the underlying political settlement in partner countries.[5]

- *Link aid to an informed theory of political change.* Much of the push on politics centers around more context-specific programming, but a fine-grained understanding of the local political situation is of limited use without a sense of how change is likely to occur. While the development community has sophisticated economic growth models, it lacks a similar understanding of the drivers of institutional and political transformation. This is partly due to the complexity of processes of political change, but just as importantly to the low investment in political research and staff expertise in politics within development agencies. Several research programs are attempting to build up knowledge to fill this gap and have come up with sometimes contradictory findings, as will be outlined in the following chapter.

These recommendations are all about politics, yet they reflect a relentlessly pragmatic approach to development, one that focuses intensely on how developmental change can be facilitated. They do not point to specific political goals. They could be just as useful to an agricultural development program as to a democracy program. Despite the continuing fear on the part of economists within mainstream aid organizations about the hazards of "being political," *the central result of being more political in methods is not zealotry about ideological goals but greater realism about what aid can achieve and how it can do so.* Although embracing political goals encourages taking politics on board as a method, much can unquestionably be done to adopt politically smarter methods without shifting to openly political goals. Reflecting this fact, it is notable that among the major aid organizations, DFID and the World Bank have gone especially far in putting into practice the above recommendations about methods despite being among the least explicitly normative about political goals.

Policy Uptake

The emerging common wisdom on the importance of political methods is making its way into official policy statements at multiple aid organizations. DFID has been a visible advocate of more attention to politics, through both its policy statements and support for research. In 2006 then Secretary of State for International Development Hilary Benn declared that "making progress is about making politics work," and DFID subsequently released a White Paper that stressed the importance of politics, including the need to understand political dynamics in developing countries.[6] Its 2009 White Paper pushed further—highlighting the need to work politically in fragile states as well as the importance of political economy analysis more generally—and pledging that "the UK will increasingly put politics at the heart of its action."[7] Elements of the emerging consensus on political methods outlined above have featured prominently in sector policy statements and official publications.[8]

Other development actors have been less explicit than DFID about politics in their agency-wide policy statements, but they repeatedly highlight elements of political methods in their governance strategies and guidance documents. The World Bank's 2012 governance and anticorruption strategy discusses the importance of political economy analysis and attention to governance across development work, as well as the need to address both formal and informal rules of the game, move from best practice to good fit and problem-based approaches, engage flexibly on processes, and improve knowledge about and evaluation of institutional change.[9] It gave significantly greater attention to these issues than the Bank's 2007 governance and anticorruption strategy. AusAID's 2011 governance strategy similarly stresses the importance of political analysis and emphasizes that "supporting governance reforms is not a purely technical matter. The quality of leadership and the ability of citizens to effectively engage with their government impact greatly on development outcomes. This is a political process, and statebuilding is an endogenous process."[10]

The trend has also gained traction among multilateral actors. UNDP's 2012 Institutional and Context Analysis tool notes that "there is increasing recognition among development practitioners that technical solutions, however ably formulated, are not enough to achieve the intended result. Political processes, informal institutions, and power relations all play vital roles in the success or failure of development interventions" and "development requires a change in power relations and/or incentive systems."[11] The European Commission's aid arm, EuropeAid, has released a series of reference documents on specific topics that take political insights significantly on board.[12] The OECD DAC's governance network also emphasizes politically smart methods in pushing its members to rethink their governance work, exemplified by its reports on political analysis and in particular its recent stream of work around domestic accountability.[13]

On the whole, this new consensus on political methods has gained significant ground but remains a tentative advance. Within most aid organizations it is pushed by a relatively small group of practitioners with enough influence over policy to spark some changes in rhetoric and in individual programs but insufficient numbers to constitute a broad cultural shift within the aid bureaucracy. The broad recommendations are usually accepted in principle. Not many practitioners openly argue that it is unimportant to think about politics in development, that local contexts are already well enough understood, that Western institutional best practices should be exported whole cloth to developing countries, that process is of secondary importance, that programs can function in isolation of the larger political context, or that more knowledge about how political change occurs would not be helpful. Many would even assume that these various principles are now part of standard operations. Yet in fact, translating this new consensus into systematic practice is still very much a work in progress. Progress has been made in gaining better political understanding, widening efforts on the demand side, and finding new ways to directly stimulate processes of developmental change. Yet structural obstacles with how aid is delivered persist, as do technocratic mindsets.

PRACTICAL POLITICAL ANALYSIS

Efforts to move toward politically smarter programming naturally begin with better political understanding. Although the first wave of country-level political economy studies carried out by major aid organizations in the last decade were not always easily applicable to practice, the underlying conviction that more effective aid requires better political understanding did not go away. If anything, it has grown stronger. Practitioners trying to work seriously in the governance domain inevitably feel a need for in-depth knowledge of the complex institutions and processes at stake. And while governance programs helped open the door to politics, many socioeconomic sector specialists similarly recognize that better political information and insight are important to their work. Moreover, although the large-scale, country-level analyses encountered some problems and pushback from in-country staff, development agencies also undertook many smaller-scale, project-specific stakeholder analyses that incorporated some features of political economy analyses and often proved useful.

More Focused

As a result, mainstream aid organizations are both expanding and rethinking their use of political economy analysis. The thrust of this move is toward more focused studies, moving from the country level to sector-level or problem-focused approaches. They are also paying more explicit attention to the implications of the findings for assistance programming and putting greater emphasis on working closely with in-country staff to ensure uptake. Sector-level analyses examine the political economy issues related to potential change in specific areas of concern, such as health or education, or toward a particular institution or set of institutions, such as a national civil service or a judicial system. They apply the broad political economy methodology outlined in chapter 5—looking at structural factors, formal and informal institutions, actors, processes of change, and operational implications—to provide an understanding of how the sector operates, the main drivers of and obstacles to change, and potential openings for developmental reform. Problem-driven analyses take a similar form but focus on a particular development challenge rather than a specific area of programming. Thus a sector-level analysis could pose the question "how does the water sector operate in country x?" while a problem-driven analysis may ask "what is a politically feasible way to increase access to potable water in country x?"[14]

The advantage of a narrower focus is, of course, the greater level of specificity it allows. Rather than saying that the governance of an entire country is plagued by patronage—a finding that may be both obvious and difficult to make use of in any specific program—the analysis can identify how the patronage system works in the ministry with most control over the particular development issue at hand. Such an analysis can also offer guidance on whether the program should try to maneuver around problems caused by patronage, or whether it needs to face them head-on in order to achieve its goals. The corresponding disadvantage is that such studies may leave out some elements of the larger context that impinge on the sector or problem and affect potential reform efforts. An analysis too focused on the operation of the water sector, for example, could neglect to assess the overall stability of the government and its likelihood to survive long enough to implement reforms.

Given development agencies' limited resources for carrying out analyses, they have to balance the value of specificity against the utility of analyses general enough to be relevant to more than one project. Some political economy analyses thus combine an overview of the overall national political economy of development with more specific sections on particular sectors or problems. In many countries, practitioners can also draw on substantial literature on country-level political economy. Here the challenge is more to educate staff on what information already exists than to conduct new studies. It is likely more useful to invest in an analysis of the use of oil revenue in a particular Nigerian state, for example, than to write another general overview of Nigerian politics. DFID Nigeria has thus followed up its country-level 2003 Drivers of Change study with more specific analyses of each of its focus states as well as political economy training for its in-country staff examining specific sectors and case studies.[15]

Building Capacity

Several major development agencies have moved in recent years to scale up their capacity to conduct targeted political economy studies:

- The World Bank is making the mainstreaming of political economy analysis across all its projects a major feature of its governance and anti-corruption agenda.[16] It has opened up discussion of a problem-driven approach, releasing a guide to problem-driven political economy analysis in 2009 as well as a shorter how-to note in 2011, and has influenced other donors to move in this direction.[17] A team of specialists at the World Bank carries out trainings for staff on the use of political economy analyses and provides support to those who wish to carry out analyses.

- DFID also continues to be a leader in this area and has built on its experience with Drivers of Change to develop a more flexible framework that can be adapted to specific country and program needs. It released a how-to note in 2009 to introduce practitioners to the various levels of analysis, existing political economy tools, and possible uses of analysis in practice.[18]

- EuropeAid is emphasizing a sector-level approach, and has released its own framework, "Analysing and Addressing Governance in Sector Operations," providing detailed guidance on diagnosing and addressing governance problems in different socioeconomic domains.[19]

- UNDP recently released guidance for its staff on how to conduct "Institutional and Context Analysis" to assist with both country- and project-level strategic planning, noting that "we lack a tool that can provide the kind of insider knowledge of the interests of national and other actors, and that can be the difference between a programme's success or failure. ... Consequently, many projects fail."[20]

- AusAID does not have its own political economy tool, but its governance strategy calls for "a systematic approach to political economy analysis" to guide its work.[21]

The World Bank, DFID, the European Commission, UNDP, and other donors interested in political economy analysis have proactively attempted to share experiences on political economy analysis both within their own staffs and with each other and the wider development aid community.[22]

In addition to new stand-alone political economy analysis tools, some donors have attempted to incorporate political economy elements into other existing analytic frameworks. Governance assessments, which became common in the last decade, have in at least some cases evolved from early technically focused checklist reviews of state institutions to more probing, political economy–style analyses of the hows and whys of governance in particular settings. As will be discussed in more detail later in the chapter, UNDP has taken the political nature of such assessments a step further by pioneering a participatory governance assessment methodology. In this approach, a diverse group of governmental and civil society actors within the aid-receiving country takes primary responsibility for carrying out a governance assessment. The intention is that the process of carrying out such an assessment, together with the conversations it generates, will stimulate useful dialogue and cooperation among varied sociopolitical actors around improved governance.[23]

Although USAID was a pioneer in the use of governance assessments and other analytic tools such as stakeholder analysis and conflict analysis, it has moved only recently to widen its use of political economy analysis in socioeconomic areas of assistance. Its democracy and governance assessment framework includes significant political economy elements but is conducted only every few years in any given country and has uneven influence on socioeconomic sector planning. A few USAID country missions have conducted or are conducting political economy analyses, but this is largely at their own initiative with minimal central guidance. A working group within the agency recently reviewed the issue. Guidance on political economy analyses was subsequently posted on an internal agency website, and some efforts are being made within the agency to raise attention to the topic and to support interested country staff.

Tracking Uptake

As the use of political economy analysis moves away from large, visible country studies to smaller-scale, more diverse efforts, tracking the frequency of use across donors becomes impossible. Equally elusive is attempting to ascertain in any systematic way how such analyses are affecting programming. But some encouraging evidence exists. A 2011 World Bank review, for example, found a correlation between the depth of institutional analysis—particularly attention to informal institutions and demand-side objectives—and project responsiveness to local governance realities.[24] A recent survey of public sector staff at the World Bank further found that 84 percent believe political economy analysis is important to the institution's work.[25] AusAID's review of its governance work found that the highest-performing programs shared a few common characteristics, including a deep understanding of the nature of local leadership and the political, social, and cultural context as well as early attention to monitoring and evaluation and gender equity issues.[26]

In addition to these broad surveys, specific case studies and anecdotal evidence from interviews and conversations with practitioners indicate that the new generation of political economy analyses are being used more widely and are affecting what aid practitioners do (and what they often choose not to do) in particular settings. The World Bank's Zambia office has described how a number of sectoral-level political economy studies it carried out helped it shift strategy and gain traction on reforms it had previously pushed without success. For example, an analysis of the energy sector found that past recommendations to increase energy tariffs—which in Zambia were lower than the cost of generating electricity—had failed because of political opposition from powerful urban sectors that would be hurt by higher energy prices. As a result, the World Bank changed its approach: instead of stressing the importance of tariff increases as a means of achieving greater economic efficiency, it began emphasizing reforms that would increase access to energy in rural areas, where only 3 percent of the population had electricity. This argument helped build political support for measures to improve the fiscal situation of the energy company, including tariff increases, and allow it to reach more customers.[27]

Some political economy analyses highlight the need for deeper changes in strategy. DFID Nepal, for example, conducted a set of sector-level studies in areas it considered critical to growth and in need of a strategic rethink, including agriculture, power, health, and police. As Stephen Jones explains, the study of the police force in Nepal highlighted a number of challenges, including political interference, corruption and patronage, and a lack of police accountability. Past donor programs to address these issues were thwarted in part because of "the political leadership at any given time which has been unwilling to relinquish direct control of the police and the ability to influence staffing and other decisions."[28] The analysis underscored Nepal's move to federalism as a potentially important opening to increase police independence. As a result, DFID substantially revised its program design to emphasize stakeholder involvement and focus on the opportunities created by federalism.[29] The police and other sector studies in Nepal provided no magic bullets, but they did allow DFID to approach development problems with a more realistic view of the challenges and most promising entry points.

Where political economy analysis has been helpful in influencing programs, practitioners usually cite a number of similar success factors. Some of these involve the quality of the analysis itself, including ensuring that studies are well-timed to feed into country and program planning processes, are carried out by a team with knowledge of both the local politics and aid programs, draw on diverse sources of information, and contain clear, operational recommendations. But the key factor in turning good analysis into changed programming is the level of support and interest in the analysis among those who are supposed to apply it, particularly the head of office and sector team leaders. It is thus critical that there be a good relationship and frequent interaction between the people conducting the analysis and operational staff. This allows analysts to better communicate their findings and also helps ensure that the study responds to operational concerns and existing staff knowledge.[30]

As with the earlier broader analyses, the most important role political economy studies sometimes play is in introducing political issues and reality checks into staff discussions and helping orient development practitioners new to the country's political context. For that to occur, it is crucial that analyses are embraced by the country office and incorporated into normal operations. For example, in 2012 a USAID mission director in Africa whose country office had recently carried out a political economy study wrote in a message back to headquarters about the utility of the analysis:

> Because of the predisposition by many officers to place unqualified confidence in technical solutions, we insist that newcomers read the analysis as part of their briefing materials. I really can't emphasize this point enough. The organization is full of people who think technical solutions are a silver bullet for development challenges that are embedded in all manner of political/economic relations, social organization

and cultural norms. ... We need to learn how to make these important structures work for development results, rather than against them. That is where the value of such analyses most lies—they can give us insights into this process. It has informed our strategies for trying to move forward agricultural reforms, governance improvements in the health sector and educational reforms.[31]

Recognizing the importance of in-country staff support, guidance documents now devote more attention to how analysts should work with practitioners on the ground in addition to what questions they should address. Yet structural challenges to making wider use of political economy analysis nevertheless remain, as discussed later in this chapter.

While political economy analysis is a central element of the move by aid organizations to improve contextual understanding, development practitioners also, of course, often rely on less formal means of gaining political insight. Locally hired staff, for instance, can be a vital source of political knowledge, and some aid organizations are starting to make better use of such capacities as part of the larger push on political understanding. Governance or public affairs specialists within country offices also sometimes play a wider role in serving as political consultants for other sectors in addition to implementing their own programs. DFID has made extensive use of its governance advisers for this purpose. USAID, in contrast, does not give its democracy and governance specialists a clear mandate to advise other sectors. Some country directors are particularly politically savvy and play a crucial role in guiding their staff to take politics more into account. These country-based efforts to increase political understanding are usually even more dependent than are political economy analyses on the interest and support of country team leadership, which varies widely across country offices. But such methods can nevertheless play a powerful role in inserting political thinking into the day-to-day work of development aid.

RETHINKING BOTTOM-UP APPROACHES

As discussed in the last chapter, a natural donor response in the second half of the 1990s and the early 2000s to governance programs failing because of a lack of high-level commitment to reform was an increase in efforts to foster demand for reform from below. Yet the initial wave of such programs encountered significant limits in their conception of political change and their adaptation to local political realities. This has led aid practitioners committed to this line of work to regroup and reflect on how to do better. Their conclusions broadly echo the general principles of working more politically, as outlined in the first section of this chapter, but apply them specifically to the challenges of bottom-up governance. Toward the late 2000s major aid organizations put forward these ideas in policy frameworks, which, though worded in different ways, are strikingly similar in their core elements.

They started with the imperative to improve political understanding specifically relating to demand-side actors and the context in which such actors operate. A 2010 overview study of assistance to civil society organizations (CSOs) noted that "donors see that this increased focus on supporting and strengthening southern civil society requires a more contextually nuanced understanding of the social and political landscape of recipient countries."[32] UNDP's 2009 civil society strategy articulated a common vision in aid circles about the need to go beyond simplistic views of NGOs as avatars of the demand side: "there is a growing realization that civil society is no magic bullet and that 'CSOs' often have uneven capacities and unspecified mandates. While civil society is accepted as a development partner, the euphoria of the 1990s has given way to more critical and realistic perceptions."[33] Following from that view is the felt need for greater knowledge of the interests and the power of potential civil society partners. Practitioners also need to understand how other standard demand-side methodologies, such as citizen report cards, are affected by and interact with the political context. DFID, the European Commission, Norad, Sida, UNDP, the World Bank, and others have thus called for more political economy analyses (or similar studies of political context) to guide their demand-side programs and particularly the selection of societal partners.[34]

Guiding Principles

Beyond better political understanding, donor policy statements tend to emphasize a similar set of guiding principles to renovate the demand-side approach, including:

Aid organizations need to work with a wider range of partners to help facilitate state-society relations. Internalizing the criticism that they too narrowly translated the concept of civil society into Western-oriented NGOs, major aid organizations at the forefront of demand-side work now emphasize the need to embrace a wider interpretation of civil society and to work with more representative and powerful social actors. Norad casts this revised perspective in terms of increasing engagement with traditional institutions and leaders, social movements, and political alliances working to achieve just development. It has also said Norwegian aid would base its funding to NGOs more than before on "these partners' ability to strengthen local partners with firm links with the grass roots, local networks and alliances stretching both horizontally and upwards towards the national level in the recipient country."[35] The European Commission calls for a recognition of the diversity of civil society and the need to "move beyond the usual civil society 'suspects.'"[36]

The push is also to include other state institutions, offering a much more varied landscape rather than one primarily defined by government on the one side and the nongovernmental sector on the other. For example, the World Bank's 2012 governance and anticorruption strategy defines the demand side as including "the institutional arrangements that facilitate constructive engagement between the state and non-state actors, such as citizens and the private sector, as well as non-state institutions of accountability, such as parliaments and ombudsmen, information commissions, anti-corruption agencies, supreme audit agencies, the judiciary and other justice institutions, as well as other third party monitoring mechanisms."[37]

Aid organizations should move beyond thinking of governance supply and demand as separate poles and instead stimulate productive processes of state-society inter-relations. The push here is to move fully beyond the earlier economistic assumption that more assertive demand-side actors will automatically translate into a greater supply of good governance from the state. Instead, governance should be viewed as a fluid set of interrelationships among diverse institutions spanning many parts of society. By extension, aid actors will need to engage on multiple levels and in multiple ways to effectively influence citizen-state relations. Development agencies have taken this imperative on board to varying degrees:

- Some maintain the supply-demand dichotomy but call for more attention to ensuring that states have the capacity to respond to citizen demand. UNDP's 2009 civil strategy, for example, encourages working "*on 'both sides* of the citizen-state equation' to facilitate accountability" (emphasis added).[38]

- The European Commission's 2011 reference document on engaging with non-state actors attempts to go further, calling for efforts to deepen knowledge about relations between state and society rather than strengthening non-state actors on the one hand and building state capacity on the other.[39]

- AusAID's governance strategy notes that while Australia has a history of supporting demand-side programs, "research suggests that this work go further because treating demand and supply approaches separately is unlikely to be successful. Positive change is only likely if it is led by local people using broad and powerful enough coalitions that span government and civil society."[40]

- The World Bank's 2012 governance and anticorruption strategy similarly remarks that growth in the demand side of governance has been the biggest change in governance work since 2007 but notes that "while there has been good progress to date in some aspects of this agenda, its overall impact has been limited by the absence of an *integrated view* of how to systematically support and identify opportunities for a stronger and more strategic engagement... bringing the state and the citizen more closely together" (emphasis added).[41]

Some donors also explicitly acknowledge that processes of citizen-state interaction vary considerably among countries and can take nontraditional forms. DFID 2011's review of its governance work, for instance, calls for "focusing more on informal institutions and informal linkages between citizens, officials, and politicians to achieve governance outcomes."[42] Sweden's 2009 civil society strategy stresses that "civil society actors organise and mobilise themselves in different ways depending on the context in which they work, with regard to factors such as geography, history, cultural tradition and political situation. Civil society organisations interact continuously and in complex forms with the state, local authorities and the market. This interaction involves cooperation, but also competition for social, economic, political and cultural power."[43]

Aid should strengthen (and not undermine) broader domestic systems of accountability. Development agencies have called for improved accountability since the beginning of their work on governance. Assistance providers initially focused on increasing accountability within bureaucracies to improve public sector management and the use of aid resources. Early demand-side efforts expanded this conception and worked to promote accountability processes around specific ends—such as mobilizing popular pressure around educational quality.

The natural next step of these efforts is to recognize the importance of situating demand-side programs within an effort to build more general political accountability of states to their citizens on all issues. The EC's 2011 reference document on engaging with non-state actors, for example, calls for practitioners to "consider domestic accountability as a 'system' that ought to be supported in the long-term and less through isolated, donor-driven actions."[44] Donors are increasingly interested in researching what types of domestic processes are most important for building state accountability, leading some scholars and practitioners to push for a greater focus on the role of taxation.[45] In the face of criticism that foreign aid makes governments more responsive to donors than to their own people, development agencies have begun to look more seriously at how their overall assistance—not just in the governance domain but in all sectors—affects the ability of citizens to hold their states accountable.

Aid organizations need to give greater attention to supporting positive enabling environments for demand-side activities. Once accountability is recognized as a multifaceted process of interaction between state and societal actors, it is not a large jump to acknowledge that bottom-up efforts to improve governance require a positive legal framework and adequate political space to enable societal actors to make demands and pressure the state to respond. Citizen report cards or budget transparency do not work well if individuals have no right to free expression. This theme was present in the initial wave of demand-side work but is now receiving more attention. The continued pushback by some governments, manifested in growing restrictions on foreign funding for domestic civil society, has brought the issue into much sharper relief. A 2012 European Commission consultation paper on civil society strategy thus devotes a section to "responding to the challenges related to a shrinking legal and regulatory space for CSO action."[46] The World Bank's 2009 guidance note on multi-stakeholder engagement says that "good practice in this context would include helping to remove barriers for CSOs to operate and ... recommending, for instance, that government regulations regarding CSOs are transparent, clearly prescribed in law and, in their design or application, do not favor any partisan political interest, or impose undue barriers to entry."[47] The international aid effectiveness conferences in Accra in 2008 and Busan in 2011 also mentioned the importance of providing an enabling environment for civil society actors, and Sida, USAID, and other donors are actively working on this issue.

The growing acceptance of these various policy recommendations regarding how to implement demand-side work more effectively is reflected in a major recent report from the OECD DAC, the product of a two-year stream of work on domestic accountability by the DAC's governance network, which touches on all of these themes and calls for "much more politically informed, smarter aid" within an "accountability systems" approach.[48]

But What Changes in Practice?

It is striking how much most mainstream aid organizations are willing to embrace (at least in principle) what are quite political elements of taking bottom-up approaches forward. Development agencies are stating their intention to delve analytically into the political interests and actions of a wide range of local actors, to work directly with politically engaged local organizations well beyond the usual set of donor-favored technocratic NGOs, to find ways to put unhappy citizens into more systematic, forceful contact with power holders, and to help widen or at least preserve the available political space for the assertion of citizens' interests.

It is too early to tell how far in practice this stated commitment to take demand-side work further will go. Most aid actors can point to certain programs that have taken a more integrated view of citizen-state relations and applied other insights about effective bottom-up work. Demand-side practitioners have not abandoned the standard tool kit of interventions, such as public access to information and civil society capacity building. But some have shifted from believing these will automatically result in more responsive states to seeing them as strategic entry points to begin a struggle for greater accountability. They have also sought to harness the power of new information and communication technologies to reach out to a much wider range of citizens. Innovative efforts on information transparency have shown the value of pairing efforts to push for public information on government budgets with proactive moves to mobilize citizens around the findings, build civil society monitoring capacity, reach out to the media, and both lobby and offer capacity building to government officials to respond.[49] These combined efforts grapple with the complex and political nature of citizen-state relations and are more likely to be effective than any one intervention in isolation. The following section describes some specific efforts to work politically to influence developmental processes, many of which entail engaging actors across the state-society divide.

Despite these signs of progress, a continuing gap remains between these recommended good practices and the bulk of existing aid programming. The intellectual convergence around politically smart demand-side programming confronts hard operational realities. For example, while Western-oriented NGOs have limitations as development partners, they are more likely than grassroots social movements to have the legal status, budgetary expertise, and financial reporting capacity needed to handle grants from donors. To the extent that donors can reach nontraditional groups, a strong danger remains that outside funding will distort the incentives and local accountability of these organizations. In most places donors will remain wary of jumping into divisive social conflicts such as land rights struggles by embracing highly politicized citizen groups, even if those organizations are more influential players than more technocratic legal reform groups.

Even when development agencies recognize that a problematic enabling environment is constraining civil society activism in a particular country, they may not want to antagonize the host government by pushing hard on the issue of permitting civil society organizations to receive foreign funding or operate freely. The DAC report mentioned above underlines that applying the various guiding principles for better demand-side work more widely "will require some step changes in donor approaches, suggesting the need for different roles, new forms of assistance, adjustments to funding modalities and new approaches to risk and results management...but changing policy and practice remains difficult, and needs to proceed cautiously where the evidence base remains patchy."[50]

Individual aid organization policy documents provide some guidance on how to change practice, but they are short on specific operational instructions or promises of structural changes in how aid is delivered. In contrast to the earlier shift from top-down governance work to demand-side work, which opened up entire new areas of programming and funding, the imperative to approach citizen-state relations more politically is mainly about implementing existing initiatives in a more strategic and coordinated fashion. Some of this can come in the form of new operational tools—such as requirements for political economy analysis to accompany programs—but much of it is about improving the political capacity of staff and their space to implement flexible programs and reach out to multiple and nontraditional actors. Some development actors, including DFID, the European Commission, UNDP, and the World Bank, devote attention in their policy statements and guidance documents to the need to build up such capacity and knowledge. But they present the commitment as a plan for the future rather than a statement about existing reforms. As will be discussed later in this chapter, there has been insufficient effort to grapple with the basic inconsistencies between current aid delivery systems and the requirements of more politically smart approaches.

INNOVATIONS ON PROCESS

Technocratic approaches to assistance embody a lack of interest in process. They assume that developmental change follows essentially automatically once the necessary inputs—such as capital or technology—are supplied. A cardinal element of working more politically is paying greater attention to how change occurs. It implies a direct focus on stimulating or facilitating processes of developmental change within recipient societies. It works from the assumption that such processes will necessarily involve political issues of power and conflicting interests.

The embrace of bottom-up work represented an initial foray into process-focused aid. Moving from stand-alone demand-side programming to integrated approaches that seek to reshape citizen-state relations is a further step. Various recent or ongoing programs take up a process focus in multiple ways, not confined to bottom-up governance. A sampling of such efforts is presented here, not intended as a comprehensive list, but as illustrations of moves to transform political insights into changed programming.

Applied Research on Leadership and Agency

A process-focused approach to development naturally highlights the role of the domestic actors driving these processes of change. Development scholars and practitioners are moving beyond simplistic early ideas about reform champions—which emphasized finding someone in government to push donor-supported changes—to think more deeply about why key actors choose to support developmental change, what constraints they work under, and how to foster pro-developmental leadership. The Developmental Leadership Program (DLP), a development policy research consortium led by the British development scholar Adrian Leftwich, emphasizes the critical role that leaders, elites, and coalitions play in the politics of development. It concentrates on the centrality of leadership in developmental change—not political leadership per se, but leadership at any level or from any part of society—out of the conviction that development aid organizations have failed to give sufficient attention to the role of individuals in shaping effective institutions and promoting developmental change. Through its papers and studies, and direct work within aid organizations (particularly with its primary funder, AusAID), DLP seeks to advance understanding and application of this core idea and a related set of operational principles, which include the imperative to take advantage of critical junctures for change, the need to address collective action problems, the importance of coalitions, the useful role of intermediary organizations that allow aid actors to be more political, the need to base developmental change on locally driven processes, and the need to artfully blend political process work with technical inputs and an understanding of underlying structures.[51]

The Africa Power and Politics Programme similarly stresses the importance of understanding how different development actors relate to and work with each other. In the program's final synthesis report, David Booth urges donors to move from a principal-agent perspective to a collective action approach, arguing that "governance challenges in Africa are not fundamentally about one set of people getting another set of people to behave better" and that the focus should instead be on "a more sophisticated interpretation that emphasises the overcoming of problems of coordination, credibility and collective action among sets of actors with complex interlocking interests."[52]

Political Counseling for Power Holders

Some assistance efforts seek to provide what is essentially political counseling for power holders on how to carry out reforms. These efforts differ from the older model of placing external technical advisers in aid-receiving governments. These political counselors are not there to supply technical input for the design of new policies. They aim to help power holders with the *how* as much as the *what* of change. For example, the Communication for Governance and Accountability Program (CommGAP) of the World Bank, which ran from 2006 to 2011 and still organizes some training programs, worked to help officials in developing countries better understand and manage the political dynamics of reform processes—how to build political will within the leadership for reform, to extend the coalitions to other stakeholders and win bureaucratic buy-in, and to activate public opinion in favor of reforms. It has done so through the lens of communication methods, which has served as a way for the politically cautious World Bank to talk about issues of political process with developing country counterparts. In 2011 CommGAP published *People, Politics, and Change,* a training manual for domestic actors within and outside of government as well as development practitioners, with guidance on how to handle various stages of the reform process, from conducting initial political economy analyses to coalition building and managing conflict among stakeholders.[53]

The Africa Governance Initiative (AGI), founded by Tony Blair, provides in-country political support to selected African governments (which have recently included Guinea, Liberia, Rwanda, Sierra Leone, and South Sudan) at their request to help them carry out reform efforts. Its model is based on finding leaders who they believe are reformers and helping them govern more effectively. AGI offers direct consultations between Tony Blair and the political leaders of these countries and embeds political advisory teams directly around developing country leaders, with the specific charge of building domestic capacity to understand and effectively manage the politics of reform. Its efforts have ranged from working with the cabinet secretariat in Rwanda to improve the effectiveness of cabinet decisionmaking processes, to supporting the design, donor coordination, and implementation of free healthcare for young children and pregnant women in Sierra Leone, to working with the Liberian National Investment Commission to create an investor guide to the country and assist with other measures to attract foreign investment.[54]

Building Reform Coalitions

Political counseling efforts necessarily assume a cooperative relationship between aid providers and developing country leaders. Other development interventions try to stimulate reform in the face of low commitment at the top by supporting reform coalitions that bring together actors from across different lines. The Asia Foundation, for example, has undertaken a series of projects in the Philippines, Indonesia, and elsewhere to help generate specific reforms by supporting the identification, organization, and activation of informal change coalitions. These coalitions link up actors with a direct interest in reform, from within government as well as nongovernmental organizations, business, unions, and other sectors. The projects proceed from the assumption that reforms are deeply political processes, that such processes are of unpredictable length and shape, that reform coalitions are best organized by local "developmental entrepreneurs" with a talent for and interest in doing so, and that through artful use of local intermediary organizations, external actors can play an active role in helping to identify key reform areas and get such coalitions operating.

The Asia Foundation has applied these general principles to encourage reforms in both governance and economic policy. In Indonesia, with DFID funding, it supported local civil society organizations in 38 districts to push for improved governance and public services at the local level. It placed special emphasis on pairing technically focused NGOs with politically influential Muslim mass-based organizations and encouraging the Muslim organizations to get more involved in budget monitoring and other governance issues. Civil society partners had significant flexibility to adapt to local political realities and thus both processes and outcomes varied among districts. In one district with a pro-reform mayor, for example, the NGO PATTIRO worked as part of the mayor's advisory team to help the local government implement a poverty alleviation plan. In another district where the mayor was not supportive of reform, the same NGO conducted stakeholder analysis and found allies within the bureaucracy, parliament, Muslim organizations, the media, and among other key actors to push through pro-poor legislation and build political support for improving fiscal management and oversight.[55]

In the Philippines, the Asia Foundation, with USAID support, adopted a similarly process-focused approach in tackling the quite different challenge of national economic policy reform.[56] It supported coalitions working for reforms on issues ranging from civil aviation to water privatization to property rights. One important initiative centered around reducing domestic shipping costs by changing regulations to allow shipping on trucks that drive on and off boats (known as roll-on/roll-off) instead of on cargo containers, which incur significant handling costs. This reform had long been presented as a good technical solution but was thwarted by the Port Authority, labor unions, and other powerful actors, which received revenue from cargo handling and opposed a change in the status quo. The Asia Foundation supported a local reform proponent, who identified other actors with an interest in lowering shipping costs, such as the Department of Agriculture and business associations, and built a reform coalition. The coalition zeroed in on a critical political juncture around the presidential election and used it to pressure the president to sign an executive order establishing a roll-on/roll-off policy.[57]

DFID has pursued a similar but somewhat more formal approach to helping form and back mixed reform coalitions on a wide range of issues. In Nigeria, for example, DFID followed up its major Drivers of Change study that highlighted the lack of reform incentives among many power holders with a "Coalitions for Change" program that sought to advance reform through new coalitions uniting active stakeholders. DFID funded the establishment of a Nigerian management team that helped set up issue-based coalitions of government, media, civil society, and other actors around challenges such as disability rights, constitutional reform, water management, extractive industry accountability, and public spending monitoring. DFID created a similar program in Burma in the late 2000s, known as "Pyoe Pin" or "Green Shoots." In the authoritarian, reform-deficient environment of Burma at the time, the program identified a mix of social and economic areas possibly susceptible to a reform push—from the rice market chain to HIV/AIDS—and helped establish coalitions to work for change in each of these areas. The objective of the program is not just to promote better policies but also the broader strengthening of civil society and social capital in the country.[58]

The work of these coalitions is thoroughly political—starting with analyses of the political landscape for reform, moving to the banding together of interested actors and devising the most effective tactics for persuading or pressing the relevant officials, mobilizing public opinion when necessary, adjusting coalitions as interests shift, and seizing political moments of opportunity or lying low at times when reform possibilities are dormant. DFID, USAID, and other donors fostering such coalitions usually try to stay one step removed politically by working through intermediary groups (in the Philippines, the Asia Foundation; in Burma, the British Council). But in taking the challenge of process seriously, they are inevitably cutting much closer to the political bone.

Political Dialogues for Developmental Change

Sponsoring political dialogue processes among contending national political actors is a common methodology among external actors aiming to promote conflict resolution and peacebuilding. Some aid groups are trying to employ such dialogues outside of conflict contexts to facilitate socioeconomic development. As with coalition building, this proceeds from the recognition that lasting reform is likely to require broad political support from a variety of actors. UNDP's Political Analysis and Prospective Scenarios Project (PAPEP) initiative, piloted by its Latin America division, has helped frame and facilitate dialogue among national political actors to promote consensus around the changes needed for developmental progress. PAPEP operates from the idea that problematic political interactions at the national level—especially confrontation and a breakdown in political consensus—adversely affect the ability of governments to effectively address core developmental challenges. It seeks to employ political analysis to diagnose potential reform scenarios, map likely outcomes and challenges, analyze the political feasibility and impact of various policy options, and use these findings to facilitate dialogue processes among key stakeholders on productive paths forward. In Paraguay, for instance, PAPEP conducted a study of public administration reform and organized discussions of its findings with government officials, opposition parties, civil society, and the private sector. This helped increase the public visibility of the issue and provided momentum to the public administration secretary in pressing the president and cabinet as well as the opposition to support gradual reform.[59] PAPEP's dialogue efforts have developmental as well as democratic goals, which in UNDP's view are intrinsically interrelated.

Justice as Process

As aid organizations moved significantly into rule-of-law assistance over the last two decades, they proceeded through the same evolutionary sequence as other areas of governance work: after spending some years on top-down approaches (trying to reform judiciaries and other formal legal institutions through technical assistance) but frequently encountering a lack of will or interest in change, they began pursuing bottom-up approaches to try to create demand for legal reform, under the rubrics of legal empowerment and legal access. The Justice for the Poor Program at the World Bank, largely funded by an AusAID trust fund, seeks to take that evolution still further, defining the goal of justice work not in terms of bolstering supply or demand per se but as a relational process of helping create "equitable spaces of social contestation."[60]

The program is distinctive for its strong emphasis on research on the local context, its broad view of justice as an issue that extends beyond the formal justice sector, and its focus on legal pluralism, or the multiple institutional forms and sources of law. In Vanuatu, for example, the program became involved in the problem of land management, a major issue in the country because at the time of its independence all land was declared to be customary, meaning it reverted to indigenous owners and is governed by context-specific customary laws, complicating its use for economic purposes. The program has sought to stimulate public discussion around what was essentially a taboo subject and help build an advisory service that communities can use to negotiate effectively with potential land investors.

It has also consulted with other World Bank projects in Vanuatu and South Sudan to help them be more responsive to local realities and ensure that they support rather than undermine local justice processes.

Common Elements

These various initiatives are not ideal examples of politically informed and engaged programs—the diverse streams and emphases of the politics agenda mean that such examples do not exist—but they represent important attempts to take seriously the question of how to directly stimulate processes of developmental change. They cut across many domains, but share some key elements: (1) they make significant use of political analysis as a basis for action, though this is not always a formal written political economy analysis; (2) they often take a somewhat experimentalist approach, trying multiple lines of work at once to see which succeed and which don't, accepting differential outcomes as an inevitable part of a more flexible, locally driven approach; (3) they view the process of implementing the program as itself an important opportunity to build domestic capacity and developmental leadership; (4) they employ relatively more open-ended time frames—they try to operate on a long-term basis, to show staying power to local counterparts, yet at the same time they look to seize political junctures for change that may suddenly open up; (5) they usually benefit from flexible funding through such mechanisms as grants and trust funds and often work through an intermediary organization; and (6) they tend to be relatively small efforts in larger organizations, led by defined teams of proponents who are trying to create new operational approaches that they hope will be adopted more widely. They are small-scale crusades struggling to gain traction within their own agencies.

AGAINST THE GRAIN

The further movement toward more political methods described in this chapter is significant. When added to the changes that unfolded in the development community over the last decade, real progress toward more politically savvy aid programming is evident. Certainly the temptation of the technical no longer reigns unchallenged at major aid organizations, and there is greater recognition that technical and political approaches should complement each other. Many development agencies have made productive use of political economy analysis—whether at the country level or focused on particular sectors or problems—to understand the dynamics of the contexts in which they work. They have broadened the range of local actors with which they work far beyond the traditional executive branch counterparts who were the anchor of earlier technocratic approaches. They work directly with a wide range of governmental institutions as well as nongovernmental organizations and give more thought to how and why they should tailor their ties with specific actors to fit the challenges at hand. And some programs are trying to go beyond old assumptions about techno-cratic inputs and outputs to directly facilitate or stimulate change through flexible processes of sociopolitical contestation.

Still Struggling

How widely have political methods really been taken on board within the mainstream aid community? Unquestionably, a considerable amount of activity exists relating to political economy studies, demand-side work, new initiatives aimed at fostering changes in citizen-state relations, and other areas reflecting more political methods. Proponents of these approaches can now point to important examples of how working politically can lead to positive outcomes in each of these areas, something that was not true a decade ago.

Yet, talking with people within mainstream aid organizations who are especially interested in and committed to these issues, it is striking how much they feel they are still struggling to gain a secure foothold for their ideas within their own organizations. This is true even at those agencies that appear to have made the most progress in implementing the politics agenda and are seen as exemplars for others. Some of these practitioners ruefully note that while being more politically smart can be characterized as "working with the grain" in recipient societies, they feel they have to work *against* the grain of their own agencies to overcome powerful default modes and mindsets that favor traditional apolitical methods.[61] Having opened the door to carrying out political economy studies of recipient countries that raise sensitive issues about entrenched interests and perverse incentives, it is time, they argue, to turn those tools on mainstream aid organizations and come to terms with why being politically smart is so difficult for them.

Looking back over what is now more than fifty years of modern development assistance to date, it is indeed remarkable, and rather dispiriting, how long the road has been to becoming politically smart—or even minimally politically aware. All along the way, starting already in the 1960s with the thoughtful work of Albert Hirschman and others, observers and critics have again and again pointed out the same basic deficiencies resulting from apolitical methods. Evaluations of programs from the 1960s to the present offer earnest lists of lessons learned that repeat the same set of imperatives, including the need to proactively foster local commitment for reform, the importance of long-term, flexible program structures, the need for improved understanding of both local contexts and processes of institutional change, and the need to promote locally rooted processes of change rather than transferring blueprints. Box 6.1 highlights just one example, the repetition across decades of the insight that local commitment is important to reform success (emphases added).

Listening to a World Bank official enthusiastically report how the Bank is now for the first time formally analyzing the political dynamics of a large, troubled country where it has been working for decades, or a Swedish aid official note with pride that a political economy study of a poorly performing African country opened her colleagues' eyes to the fact that the country's entrenched patronage system was undercutting efforts for reform, or reading in a Dutch evaluation the finding that the interests of rulers in aid-receiving countries are not always the same as those of aid providers, it is hard not to slap one's forehead at the obviousness of such steps and insights and wonder how such progress can possibly have taken decades to achieve.

Institutional Obstacles

Some of the answer lies with the various misguided or overly simplistic theories of development that underlay development aid along the way. The belief on the part of development economists that some timely injections of capital or technical know-how, or the adoption of key market-friendly policy reforms would be enough to put impoverished countries on the road to prosperity encouraged reductionist ideas about aid approaches.

BOX 6.1   LESSONS NOT LEARNED: The Imperative of Local Commitment to Reform

- **1968:** A report on USAID's agricultural institution building notes that "building an effective agricultural institution involves not only erecting and equipping laboratories and libraries, developing a technically competent staff and adopting appropriate rules and regulations. Even more important...is the development of *a sense of institutional dedication* to resolving the important problems of agriculture, the evolution of customs and traditions which favor this dedication, and the formation of *a staff solidly committed to these goals and purpose.*"[1]

- **1980:** A World Bank study finds mixed success with institutional development (ID) in the work of the World Bank and other actors, saying that "the first and *most commonly suggested reason for success is political: borrowers' commitment* and support for ID objectives."[2]

- **1984:** A review of World Bank, IDB (Inter-American Development Bank), USAID, and CIDA aid programs found that among the most cited determinants of aid effectiveness was "thorough understanding and *firm commitment by host country agencies involved*" and that "achievement of such commitment may often require active participation in project planning."[3]

- **1991:** A World Bank paper on technical assistance for institutional development notes that "perhaps the most important prerequisite for successful ID-related TA *is serious commitment on the part of the borrower*" but "several factors tend to discourage systematic, explicit attention to the issue of government commitment in Bank work."[4]

- **2005:** A World Bank study on development lessons found that "perhaps the most important lesson of the 1990s is that technocratic responses to improve governance work only in very auspicious settings—where there is *committed leadership*, a broadly based coalition in support of reform, and sufficient capacity to carry the reform process forward."[5]

- **2010:** A book by the German Organisation for Technical Cooperation (GTZ) argues that "the belief that development processes can only be shaped according to the approaches of external actors and state actors; by their objectives, rules and practices, has proven to be a shortcoming...managing development cooperation successfully means having an understanding of the relevant networks of actors, and *involving them in the direction of management processes.*"[6]

---

1   Committee on Institutional Cooperation, *Building Institutions to Serve Agriculture: A Summary Report of the CIC-AID Rural Development Research Project* (Lafayette, Ind.: Purdue University, 1968), 9.

2   World Bank, "The World Bank and Institutional Development: Experience and Directions for Future Work" (Washington, D.C.: World Bank, Projects Advisory Staff, 1980), 2, 6.

3   C. S. Gulick, "Effectiveness of AID: Evaluation Findings of the World Bank, the Inter-American Bank, the Agency for International Development and the Canadian International Development Agency," draft, August 1984, 2.

4   Beatrice Buyck, "The Bank's Use of Technical Assistance for Institutional Development," Working Paper 578 (Washington, D.C.: World Bank, January 1991), 25.

5   World Bank, *Economic Growth in the 1990s: Learning from a Decade of Reform* (Washington, D.C.: World Bank, 2005), 302.

6   Sarah Frenken and Ulrich Müller (eds.), *Ownership and Political Steering in Developing Countries: Proceedings of International Conferences in London and Berlin* (Eschborn/Baden Baden: Deutsche Gesellschaft für Technische Zusammenarbeit and Nomos Publishers, 2010), 10–11.

Such theories reinforced the harmful but distressingly persistent idea that external actors can play a vital role in the socioeconomic transformation of other societies without actually getting very involved in those countries, that is to say, without understanding their local structures of power and interests, without tailoring aid specifically to local contexts, without focusing on how processes of positive change may actually come about and be reinforced, without working with many different actors throughout the society, and much else. While there has been significant progress in making discussions of politics less taboo within development agencies, apolitical mindsets have not disappeared. As one practitioner noted to us, "We don't get laughed out of the room anymore when we mention politics" but that is still a far cry from widespread acceptance that a fundamental shift in approach is required.

In addition to the technocratic theories that have guided the development enterprise, the politics agenda faces multiple obstacles arising out of the basic structures and mechanisms of aid. Operating more politically cuts against many fundamental areas of concern that have shaped how the aid community operates. These concerns include:

- *Cost*: Development agencies, perennially defensive in their own societies about the value of the aid enterprise, want to keep administrative costs low. Carrying out substantial analyses, customizing programs to local contexts rather than utilizing standardized models, hiring a wider range of governance specialists with new areas of skills and knowledge, and other elements of operating more politically all raise up-front costs. Advocates of political smart approaches point out that higher costs can save money down the road through better aid performance and leaner, more strategic programs, but they are still struggling to make the case.

- *Speed*: Aid organizations, also defensive about accusations of being slow-moving, are under pressure to get money out the door to justify their next year's budget requests and want aid to flow as quickly as possible. Being more political in methods, however, takes time due to more analysis, more flexible program time frames, and more interaction with local partners.[62]

- *Control*: Traditional aid mechanisms strive for high levels of control over aid funds to ensure that they are not misspent and that they serve donor interests. More political methods mean less control. They emphasize flexible and adaptive programming and usually shift greater responsibility to local actors for the use of aid. As aid reaches a wider range of actors, control diffuses accordingly.

- *Definiteness*: Assistance providers want to define the intended outcomes of their work as precisely as possible and show high rates of achieving such objectives. Being more political complicates the search for certainty. As programs focus more on adapting flexibly to local circumstances, defining expected outcomes becomes more complex than with traditional projects focused on vaccinations, road building, or textbook delivery. In addition, developing efforts to facilitate local processes of change through mixes of local coalitions, aid intermediaries, and other actors complicates issues of attribution or causality.

- *Uncontroversial*: Development agencies like to be seen as neutral providers of important social goods. They want aid to be uncontroversial in the places where it is carried out so that no particular project or program alienates the host government or others in the recipient society. They do not want to put at risk their reputations, the rest of the aid in that country, or their overall relationship with the host government. Being more political often means being more challenging of the host government, even if only in limited ways, and being more intrusive in the society overall. Host governments tend to be uncomfortable with donor political analysis, much less more political action. As such, the chance of controversy and adverse reactions is higher.

In short, the traditional mechanisms of mainstream aid are designed to keep costs low, move aid quickly, maintain a high degree of control, define specific outcomes, and be uncontroversial. Introducing more political methods means, at least potentially, higher administrative costs, slower disbursement, less control, less definite outcomes, and more controversy. To cite just one example, the Pyoe Pin ("Green Shoots") project in Burma described above relies on many such methods: it takes a very long-term

approach (the project is already in its second five-year phase), began operating without predefined issue areas (it spent substantial time initially
working locally to settle on issue priorities), engages expatriate and local
staff working side by side (and only expatriate staff who have lived in the
country for years and know it very well), blends its specific advocacy goals
with the broader, less tangible goal of achieving positive citizen-led change
in a context where such change long seemed almost impossible, operates
with considerable autonomy from directives from headquarters, and takes
on sensitive, sometimes controversial issues that respond to citizen rather
than host government preferences.

Difficulty of Change

It is important to remember that these are not new institutional obstacles. They are depressingly familiar. Writing in 1989, Derick Brinkerhoff
and Marcus Ingle described efforts to apply a flexible, iterative approach
to development programming but noted that "accountability requirements demanding advance determination of results to be produced and
controls during implementation offer few incentives to apply the process
model, despite the positive results emerging from situations where it has
been tried."[63] Two years later, Beatrice Buyck explained that the World
Bank's institutional development efforts had been hampered by inattention
to government commitment but that improving understanding was difficult because of "neglect of in-depth country knowledge and a poor institutional memory, both attributable in part to the frequent rotation of staff"
and "pressures to lend discourage analysis of intangibles that may threaten
a project's clean bill of health at appraisal... analyzing commitment is
conceptually difficult... and Bank staff with technical training may feel
uncomfortable in an area that essentially requires political understanding
and second guessing of a borrower's agents and motives."[64]

When asked why their organizations have been so slow to take seriously
the value of operating more politically, some practitioners point not just to
the problem of entrenched structures and mechanisms but also to a more
fundamental challenge: a lack of real accountability of personnel within
large aid organizations for longer-term aid results. With personnel usually

changing positions every two or three years, they note, they are rarely held to account for how programs or projects that they initiate actually perform over the medium to long term. All the incentives are on the side of getting programs or projects under way quickly, keeping administrative costs low, committing as large an amount of programming funds as possible, presenting persuasively rigorous frameworks of intended results, and ticking off some promising benchmark achievements in the first year or two. By the time it becomes known whether the aid intervention had meaningful, sustained results, the aid officials responsible for the intervention are long gone. Thus the interest of practitioners on the ground in different methods that entail near-term costs for long-term benefits of impact and sustainability is often low.

For now, the considerable evolution in donor recognition of the importance of politics has not translated into a concerted effort to address these internal organizational constraints to politically smarter programming. It is one thing to declare in a policy statement that development is an inherently political process or that aid programs should reach out to new actors; changing the basic mechanisms of assistance programming is much more difficult. To the extent that donors address internal issues in their policy statements, it is most often around building staff capacity to deal with political issues and working across sector boundaries to mainstream governance perspectives in socioeconomic programs, challenges that will be explored further in chapter 8. But there are few efforts to directly address the constraints posed by the pressure to minimize costs and controversy while maximizing speed, control, and definiteness. There are some tentative efforts to acknowledge the lack of fit between rigid procedures and political realities. The World Bank, for example, has indicated it will review its risk assessment framework to recognize that it must manage rather than seek to avoid all risk in its programs.[65] Aid practitioners committed to the politics agenda feel, however, that they are operating in a highly constrained organizational space that shows few signs of expanding.

The push to better accommodate political methods also fits uneasily with other internal reform efforts. Nearly every aid agency is putting renewed emphasis on the importance of improving monitoring and evaluation systems, but this is translating into many efforts to define and then measure intended results more precisely rather than developing more flexible, politically nuanced evaluation procedures. As will be discussed in chapter 9, this has created a major and still unmet challenge for the politics agenda.

Some aid providers are going further in seeking to promote institutional change. Under the leadership of Administrator Rajiv Shah, USAID in 2009 initiated an ambitious set of internal reforms, which is presented externally under the moniker of "USAID Forward." Although these reforms were not specifically conceived in terms of more politically smart development aid, some elements of them do open the door to a greater incorporation of politics. For example, the ongoing procurement reforms mean an increased share of U.S. assistance will go directly to recipient governments and to local NGOS and private sector organizations within aid-receiving countries. Providing more direct assistance to governments requires USAID to invest more in assessing the recipient government in question, under the rubric of mitigating public financial management and democratic accountability risks. But whether this will extend to a broader use of political economy tools remains to be seen. USAID Forward also includes a focus on building policy capacity within USAID, which means more investment in country-level strategic planning and sector-level project design. Again, this emphasis provides opportunities for greater use of political economy analysis, but it also requires training a cadre of staff to undertake or oversee such studies, and finding a place for it alongside other types of assessments (for example, sustainability, gender, environmental, conflict, constraints to growth, cost-benefit, and social soundness) that the agency is also suggesting be used for strategy development and project design.

CONCLUSION

The renewed push to replace long-standing technocratic methods of development aid with politically savvy programming is making some real progress. An emerging research and aid policy consensus holds that developmental change inevitably involves politics, that aid programs should grow out of the local context and focus on feasible rather than best-practice solutions, that technical assistance should feed into indigenous processes of change, that projects should think about their place within broader political systems, and that aid providers must focus closely on understanding how political and institutional change occurs. Aid agencies have increased their investments in political analysis and developed more useful analytic tools that have helped inform programs in the field. They are also acknowledging the complexity of attempts to influence citizen-state relations and experimenting with various innovative approaches to influence developmental processes. Yet these examples of progress are just that—examples that show how it is possible to put politically smart methods into practice. They still fall well short of a sea change in development programming. And structural and intellectual constraints limit the ability of their proponents to make further progress. A broader transformation of the aid industry toward widespread adoption of politically savvy methods therefore remains a distant prospect.

The painfully slow and still only partial adoption of more political methods—despite thoughtful practitioners and scholars having repeatedly pointed out across many decades the adverse consequences of clinging to technocratic, politically uninformed methods—is at least partially the result of aid organizations being unwilling to take on the challenge of renovating entrenched aid mechanisms and problematic organizational incentives. The next chapter returns to the state of political goals among aid providers, highlighting the interplay between some current attempts at going further and the continuing reality of an uncertain empirical case for the instrumental value of political goals for developmental progress.

CHAPTER 7

THE UNRESOLVED DEBATE ON POLITICAL GOALS

INTRODUCTION

What has the renewed push on politics in the development community meant for the pursuit of political goals? As analyzed in chapter 4, by the end of the last decade most mainstream aid organizations had adopted (at least formally) significant political goals, whether formulated in terms of governance or, more commonly, democratic governance or democracy. Even those that still held just to governance emphasized principles such as participation, inclusion, accountability, and transparency that overlapped substantially with the democratic governance agenda. Some agencies spoke of these principles explicitly as human rights principles. Most aid organizations grounded their adoption of political goals in both instrumental and intrinsic rationales: asserting that achieving these goals would contribute to better socioeconomic outcomes while also maintaining that no matter what the socioeconomic effects, such goals were valuable in and of themselves in their advancement of basic human dignity.

Yet although political goals gained a significant place in official donor policies, in practice they remained of secondary priority for the mainstream aid community relative to core socioeconomic objectives, above all poverty reduction. Most major aid organizations devoted the lion's share of their budgets to socioeconomic programming. They continued to downplay political goals when they perceived a conflict with socioeconomic objectives. Programming aimed at fostering democratic governance or democracy was usually not well integrated into socioeconomic programming. Despite publicly declaring a commitment to political goals, in private many senior aid officials continued to express concern that aid should not become "too political" or even political at all and tried to steer their organizations away from any assertive political stances vis-à-vis counterpart governments.

Given those limitations, it is natural to ask whether the renewed push by various practitioners and scholars to encourage the aid community to think and work more politically is translating into more active donor pursuit of political goals. Recent global events, above all the outbreak of political change in the Arab world, have at least raised this possibility. The process of rethinking international development goals after the 2015 target date for completion of the Millennium Development Goals (MDGs) has also opened up discussions around a greater possible place for human rights and democratic governance on the international development agenda. Yet these efforts continue to face considerable headwinds because of competing interests in donor countries, opposition from some developing countries, and continued empirical uncertainty about the instrumental value of democratic governance for socioeconomic development.

A PUSH FROM THE ARAB AWAKENING

The rapid collapse of long-standing autocratic governments in Tunisia, Egypt, and Libya in 2011 and the broader wave of citizen protest and political turmoil in the Arab world have vividly highlighted the dangers of focusing only on socioeconomic change while neglecting the political side of development. Tunisia and Egypt, the first two countries to witness major uprisings in the Arab Awakening, had over the course of the last decade successfully adopted at least some elements of the market model prescribed by the Western aid community. The World Bank and other aid providers had viewed Tunisia in particular as an Arab success story of market-oriented economic development.[1] Yet these rosy economic assessments neglected to fully consider that market reforms were taking place in contexts of rampant corruption and cronyism as well as frequent abuses of human dignity, feeding popular frustration against arrogant, unaccountable systems of centralized power.

The Arab Awakening sparked a new wave of affirmations in Western policy circles of the importance of matching a focus on economic development with attention to political reform. In April 2011 then World Bank President Robert Zoellick gave a speech on "A New Social Contract for Development" in which he urged a change of mindset in response to the Arab Awakening, calling for a focus on "what we missed; when we did not speak loudly enough; where we self-censored—citizens' voices, yes, but also our own.... Will this be 1848, 1968, 1979, or 1989? Or will it be 2011, the year we learned that civic participation matters to development, and that, in addition to regimes, something more has changed."[2] Coming from the head of a development organization traditionally reluctant to openly discuss politics or challenge host governments, the speech was striking.

USAID Administrator Rajiv Shah took a similarly self-reflective position in a June 2011 speech urging renewed commitment to merging development and democracy goals in the wake of the Arab Awakening. He acknowledged that USAID had sometimes worked too closely with dictatorial regimes in the Arab world and that "despite being the world's largest supporter of democracy, rights and governance assistance, we still act as though democracy and development are two different objectives," adding that "we should not wage decades-old debates about whether democracy or development should proceed first; about dignity before bread or bread before dignity. As the Arab Spring has reminded us, economic prosperity and political freedom must go hand in hand."[3]

The European Commission released a series of policy statements in response to the Arab Spring, including an "Agenda for Change" for EU development policy, which stated that "people-led movements in North Africa and the Middle East have highlighted that sound progress on the MDGs is essential, but not sufficient" and led to the conclusion that "the objectives of development, democracy, human rights, good governance and security are intertwined."[4] Speaking in Indonesia in 2012, UK Prime Minister David Cameron asserted that "the independence of the judiciary and the rule of law, the rights of individuals, free media and association, a proper place in society for the army, strong political parties and civil society... together make up a golden thread that can be found woven through successful countries and sustainable economies all over the world... the Arab Spring has shown that denying people their rights in the name of stability and security actually makes countries less stable in the end."[5]

These bold statements have been accompanied by some modest changes in aid policy. As part of its broader efforts on procurement reform and in response to a call by Shah to ensure that USAID will not "empower a government at the expense of its people," the agency is instituting a "democracy, human rights, and governance review" when it provides direct financial assistance to partner governments.[6] In addition to evaluating the quality of recipient government public financial management, USAID missions will have to assess whether the government is subject to democratic accountability mechanisms before direct support is approved. This review, however, will not establish specific democratic accountability thresholds for U.S. assistance and can be waived if necessary "to avoid impairment of foreign assistance objectives."[7] It is nevertheless a step toward ensuring that the agency at least formally considers how its assistance will affect democratic governance. The European Union has similarly added transparency and budget oversight components to its budget support eligibility criteria. The EU now requires that recipient governments make public relevant budget information or demonstrate progress toward more public disclosure in order to receive direct EU financing. The EU guidance also calls for supporting a participatory approach and systematically integrating oversight by legislatures, subnational authorities, and civil society organizations into budget support arrangements.[8]

In parallel fashion, though not explicitly driven by the events of the Arab Awakening, the Millennium Challenge Corporation strengthened its democracy criteria in 2011 by requiring that countries pass a minimum threshold score with regard to either political rights or civil liberties to qualify for compact assistance, rather than simply having to perform better than the median when ranked among peers.[9] The new system is meant to ensure that countries do not pass the political threshold simply because other countries are performing less well.

On the whole, however, there are no signs of any significant ongoing or planned changes in the relative priority that mainstream aid organizations give to political goals as a result of the Arab Awakening. There is some new attention among Western donors to supporting democratic change in those countries in the Middle East that appear to be moving in a somewhat democratic direction, above all Egypt and Tunisia. Western aid providers have increased political aid to those countries to support constitutional reform, elections, democratic governance reforms, independent civil society development, and other elements of potential democratic transitions. But the difficult political transitions in Egypt, Libya, and elsewhere in the aftermath of the uprisings have already provided plenty of space for skeptics of democracy as a development priority. In other parts of the region where autocrats still reign, such as in the various monarchies, old patterns of Western support for useful autocratic allies largely continue. Aid to Jordan and Morocco, for example, remains characterized by an emphasis on socioeconomic issues and a soft line on political reform. In the rest of the developing world, there is little sign that events in the Middle East and North Africa have produced any broader shift in the overall weight of political goals within aid programs.

MIXED DONOR INTERESTS

Why, despite the renewed policy commitments to democracy in the wake of the Arab Awakening, is there a continuing gap between words and deeds on this central issue? One important part of the answer lies in the broader framework of national interests in which aid inevitably operates, a subject already touched upon in chapter 4. Most of the donor governments that make up the mainstream aid community (whether acting through their own bilateral aid programs or through their contributions to multilateral aid institutions) profess a general interest in supporting democratic governance or democracy around the world, not just as part of their development policy, but as an overarching foreign policy goal. They do so out of the conviction that a more democratic world is, on the whole, a more favorable environment for established democracies like themselves.

Yet when put into practice, this policy stance encounters many constraints. The broad desire to support democracy is only one of several overarching Western interests, coexisting and sometimes clashing with those relating to promoting beneficial economic relations and productive security ties with other countries. Very generally speaking, when significant economic or security interests exist that point an established democracy, whether it is the United States, Great Britain, Germany or any other, to the need to get along with an undemocratic government, it will downplay its general interest in supporting democracy for the sake of maintaining that relationship. As the 2012 report of the Global Commission on Elections, Democracy, and Security put it, "Democracy assistance is usually an afterthought in development and security assistance," which "means that other donor agendas and interests often trump democracy assistance."[10] There is nothing startling in this; it is a well-known fact of international political life. It does not mean that the interest of major Western governments in supporting democracy in the world is meaningless, just that it is often outweighed by countervailing "hard" interests, whether for example the value of access to oil from Saudi Arabia, the United Arab Emirates, Kazakhstan, or Angola, access to natural gas or security cooperation from Russia, trade with China, or cooperation with Algeria and Ethiopia against Islamist extremism.

Thus while political aid has become part of the work of the development aid community—in service of the broad donor interest in development—it is nevertheless subject to the reality that donor governments do not always want to promote political change in specific developing countries. The result is an inevitable gap between stated aspiration and practical reality with regard to the application of political aid.

AFTER THE MILLENNIUM DEVELOPMENT GOALS

Despite the lack of any broad shift in the place of political goals in development aid in response to the Arab Awakening, the rapidly approaching 2015 end date of the Millennium Development Goals (MDGs) has opened up new discussions about the issue on the international stage. Over the last decade the MDGs helped galvanize international action around a concrete set of priorities—ending poverty and hunger, achieving universal primary education, promoting gender equality, reducing child mortality, improving maternal health, combating HIV/AIDS and other major diseases, ensuring environmental sustainability, and developing a global partnership for development. These goals gained unprecedented global attention and support in part because they were specific, measurable, and reflected uncontroversial development needs. Yet, as noted in chapter 4, the lack of explicit MDG targets on governance, democracy, or civil and political rights (except for one indicator on women's participation in parliament) reinforced the dominance of socioeconomic goals in development aid. Proponents of political goals hope to gain greater recognition of such priorities in a new framework, whether through explicit overarching human rights or democratic governance goals, more targeted formulations focused on selected governance principles, the integration of governance principles into socioeconomic goals, or some combination of these approaches.

These proponents believe that the case for inclusion of human rights or democratic governance—or both—in a successor framework is strong. Besides allowing for a broader concept of development and a greater focus on issues of equity, participation, and accountability, human rights obligations are already recognized in international agreements. The Millennium Declaration, on which the MDGs were based, included explicit references to human rights and democracy. Advocates of political goals thus feel that they missed an opportunity in 2000 to embed a rights-based or governance-focused approach in the international development agenda and are eager to promote such views in the post-2015 framework. They argue both that human freedom (whether defined as capabilities or rights) and democratic governance are goods in and of themselves, and that the absence of such elements in the MDGs undermined their developmental utility. Specifically, they note that the original targets gave insufficient attention to the underlying governance processes and structures in developing countries that were needed to produce the desired socioeconomic results. Moreover, the focus on aggregate targets in the MDGs neglected the problems of inequality within countries and the welfare of marginalized groups.[11]

Various influential UN bodies and international civil society organizations have called for greater attention to human rights in the post-2015 development framework. UN Secretary General Ban Ki-moon has stated that there should be more consideration of how to operationalize human rights in a post-2015 agenda and that "the instrumental value of the principles of equality, non-discrimination, participation and accountability for effective governance and more sustained and equitable development outcomes should be underscored."[12] The report of the UN System Task Team on the post-2015 UN Development Agenda suggested that the new framework be "based on the three fundamental principles of human rights, equality, and sustainability."[13] The UN Office of the High Commissioner for Human Rights (OHCHR) has further argued that a human rights focus is an international obligation as well as instrumentally valuable for development progress.[14] "Beyond 2015," a group bringing together 500 organizations from around the world, has declared that a framework based on human rights principles is a "must-have" for any new set of goals.[15] Save the Children has similarly stated that "human rights principles like universality, equality and inalienability must underpin everything that is agreed. And, unlike with the MDGs, these principles must be visible in the targets established."[16]

Taking a somewhat different approach, some prominent actors advocate for specific democratic governance or democracy goals. A 2012 UNDP discussion paper suggests that a global goal on democratic governance would be a way to recognize the fundamental role that democratic governance plays in prospects for sustainable development.[17] The clearest model for this would be Mongolia, which already voluntarily created a ninth MDG for itself on human rights and democratic governance. A major report by the Centre for International Governance Innovation (CIGI) and the Korea Development Institute (KDI) proposes eleven "Bellagio Goals"—developed through a series of working groups and consultation meetings—that would apply to developed as well as developing countries and include a goal on "empowering people to realize their civil and political rights."[18] The report of the Global Commission on Elections, Democracy, and Security chaired by Kofi Annan also calls for greater focus on political freedom and says that "the post-2015 framework should include specific programmes and goals for delivering elections with integrity, with an emphasis on inclusion, transparency, and accountability."[19] By including one stream on governance (organized by the UNDP and OHCHR) in a series of global and country consultations that it is holding on the post-2015 framework, the United Nations is acknowledging the importance of including governance in any future framework.[20]

Overarching human rights and democratic governance goals are likely to face the same core obstacles in 2015 that worked against their inclusion in 2000. Some detractors claim that measuring achievement of political targets is too difficult, for instance. Advocates of democratic governance or human rights goals stress that significant progress has been made since 2000 in creating indicators of progress in these areas and that even better measures could be devised if the international community committed resources to developing them. Mongolia already has a set of indicators for its democracy goal that could be adopted by other countries and the UNDP working paper suggests a number of further possible measurement approaches and potential country-specific targets.[21] The CIGI/KDI report also suggests possible measures.[22]

The larger challenges to explicit democratic governance or human rights targets are sovereignty concerns within developing countries and the lack of consensus that these political goals are legitimate development objectives. A democracy or governance goal would likely meet serious opposition from many developing countries as unacceptable political interference in their internal affairs.[23] Firm human rights commitments face the same challenges. In a report to the government of the Netherlands, the Advisory Council on International Affairs (AIV) notes that "although, in an ideal world, an explicit and globally endorsed human rights approach should be in force, the AIV sees this, as yet, as politically unfeasible in a post-2015 system" due to problems of enforceability and the unwillingness of many states to recognize development goals as rights.[24] In remarks to Parliament in November 2012, UK International Development Secretary Justine Greening warned that "no doubt there will be challenging discussions to have [on human rights] and there will be red lines they [some developing countries] won't go beyond."[25]

More Targeted Approaches

A potentially less controversial approach would be to include goals focused on selected elements of democratic governance and human rights frameworks that have clear relevance to socioeconomic development. One important stream of advocacy focuses on issues around the rule of law, citizen security, and state fragility. David Cameron has said that he will use his position as co-chair of the UN's High-level Panel on the Post-2015 Development Agenda to advocate for attention to the elements of his "golden thread" approach mentioned earlier, particularly the rule of law, the absence of conflict and corruption, and property rights and strong institutions.[26] George Soros and Fazle Hasan Abed (founder of the Bangladeshi development NGO BRAC) have called for post-2015 targets on universal legal identity, awareness of legal rights, and access to the formal justice system.[27]

While these issues are relevant to some degree for all developing countries, a particular push has come for more attention to justice and security issues in fragile states. Fragile and conflict-affected states have made the least progress toward achieving the current MDGs, with poorly functioning institutions widely accepted as a fundamental obstacle. Recognizing this challenge, the g7+ group of fragile and conflict-affected countries has advocated a set of Peacebuilding and Statebuilding Goals—which include security, justice, legitimate politics based on inclusive political settlements, economic foundations to generate employment and improve livelihoods, and capacity for revenue management and accountable service delivery—and is developing indicators for these goals.[28] As mentioned in chapter 4, this initiative has been well received by mainstream aid actors. The g7+ group wants these goals to help inform post-MDG discussions, and leaders of its member countries are prominently represented on the UN High-level Panel on the Post-2015 Development Agenda, including Liberian President Ellen Johnson Sirleaf, a co-chair of the panel, and Timor-Leste Finance Minister Emilia Pires, who heads the g7+.[29] International targets around the rule of law, security, and state fragility are also likely to be politically sensitive and could be opposed by some developing countries, but advocates believe they provide a clearer link with socioeconomic development than a general democratic governance goal.

Transparency and accountability could be another important entry point to insert governance and human rights into a post-2015 framework. These principles stress consensual elements and generally provoke fewer sovereignty objections than separate goals around a particular type of political system or concrete human rights obligations.[30] They also seem to promise clear developmental benefits. Proponents of such an approach point to the example of the Open Government Partnership (OGP) launched in 2011, a voluntary organization that has so far brought more than fifty governments together to make commitments to enhance transparency and citizen participation and open themselves up to internal and external monitoring.[31] The OGP has attracted participation by countries that are very sensitive about external meddling in their affairs, including Russia—though its commitments are still pending—as well as Azerbaijan, Jordan, and other undemocratic states.

Alternatively, rather than establishing stand-alone goals on citizen security, access to justice, or government transparency, these or other related issues could instead be integrated *within* socioeconomic development goals. Other governance and human rights principles such as participation, inclusion, and equity could also be incorporated in socioeconomic targets. A goal on public goods provision, for instance, could include references to equal access, local monitoring mechanisms, and other aspects of the bottom-up approaches to governance.[32] Some advocates believe that such an approach is preferable to stand-alone goals given that it would fit more comfortably with the currently weak consensus on political norms across the development community. Yet other proponents of inserting the political agenda into a post-2015 MDG successor framework believe it would be better to push hard for as long as possible in favor of at least some stand-alone goals relating to human rights and democratic governance, and that an integrated approach should be only a fallback option or an addition to stand-alone targets.

DO POLITICS MATTER FOR DEVELOPMENT?

While diverging national interests among Western donor countries and concerns about sovereignty have hindered the incorporation of political goals into the international development agenda, the most serious obstacle remains the fact that political goals are not fully accepted as a development priority. Most developmentalists acknowledge the desirability of liberal political values as good things in and of themselves for people in developing countries. But many still prefer that the development enterprise stay primarily, or even exclusively, focused on socioeconomic goals. In other words, despite the official evolution of aid policy since the 1990s regarding the addition of political goals, many developmentalists continue to believe that expanding the ambit of aid to cover political ends unhelpfully waters down and often complicates the core pursuit of socioeconomic progress (by directly thrusting aid organizations into the political fray in developing countries and putting at risk relations with host governments).

Moreover, the instrumental rationale for such goals—the proposition that democratic political governance is either generative of or necessary for sustained socioeconomic development—also remains a source of debate. Senior policymakers in the major donor governments embraced this rationale in the 1990s enthusiastically but also rather axiomatically. The empirical case for it was not well established at the time, but it was an appealing idea that embodied the optimism of the immediate post–Cold War period, renewing the old developmental assumption from the 1960s that all good things, political as well as economic, go together. Adherents of this view assumed that the empirical case for it would solidify over time and that further research would prove a positive causal connection. Yet the instrumental case for political goals is far from settled. An open, at times fierce, debate continues among development scholars over the determinants of socioeconomic progress and in particular whether democratic governance is indeed a key factor, with disagreements and uncertainty within the scholarly community reinforcing the skepticism of development officials wary of political entanglements. Given the importance of this continuing debate for the politics agenda, we review it here in some detail, highlighting the contending camps and the direction of the most recent research.

Despite the rapid rise of attention to governance in development aid over the past twenty years, some scholars are still skeptical of the idea that governance of any form is the key determinant of developmental success or failure. Instead, they emphasize structural factors within countries or the international system as the main drivers of economic conditions. Jared Diamond's widely read *Guns, Germs, and Steel*, for example, highlights the importance of environmental factors—such as how the original distribution of plants and animals in an area affected the potential for farming and thus for social specialization—as the most fundamental historic drivers of economic inequality among nations.[33] Jeffrey Sachs takes a similar approach to the present, arguing against the idea that political institutions or conditions explain Africa's economic woes. Although he acknowledges that economic development requires a minimum level of governance and political commitment, he sees no evidence that African countries fare worse in that regard than other countries if one controls for income. He points instead to a host of other factors, including disease, geography, natural resources, technology, and geopolitics, as key developmental determinants. Rather than focusing on the need for governance reforms, he therefore advocates a major increase in aid to developing countries, particularly in the form of investment in infrastructure, public services, and technology.[34] Sachs views institutions as important but sees governance patterns as more a result than a cause of development.

Abhijit Banerjee and Esther Duflo take a somewhat different approach, stressing instead the importance of good development policies. In their view, the problem within developing countries is often not vested political interests opposing the poor but deficient policy design. Good policies can be implemented in bad political environments—including those marked by corruption and flawed elections—and bad policies can arise from good political environments. Instead of trying to improve governance per se, or political systems more broadly, they argue that good (pro-developmental) policies can contribute to a better political economy environment and recommend focusing on incremental micro reforms in that direction.[35]

Yet while governance is undoubtedly not the only factor influencing a country's developmental prospects, a large body of research points to its centrally important role. In one influential study, for example, Daron Acemoglu, Simon Johnson, and James Robinson examined the effect of colonial experiences on development outcomes, arguing that there is a strong relationship between historic institutional formation and current income per capita, after controlling for latitude, climate, disease, and other factors.[36] Scholars have further pointed to paired examples of similarly situated countries with widely differing development outcomes—among them North and South Korea, Haiti and the Dominican Republic, East and West Germany, Zambia and Botswana—to illustrate the important effects of governance.[37] Referencing this debate, Francis Fukuyama asserts that "there has been a broad recognition among economists in recent years that 'institutions matter': poor countries are poor not because they lack resources, but because they lack effective political institutions."[38]

IN SUPPORT OF THE ORTHODOXY

While many development scholars believe that governance matters for development, sharp debates still rage among them about what *type* of governance is important. Three main camps exist: scholars who largely support the democratic governance orthodoxy, those who stress the importance of an active developmental state, and a third group that emphasizes multiple and context-specific governance paths to development.

One important line of research backs the official donor consensus on democratic governance, holding that key features of this model contribute to economic growth or other positive socioeconomic outcomes. Daniel Kaufmann and some of his then colleagues at the World Bank launched a prominent, influential line of empirical research in the second half of the 1990s that pointed to this conclusion. They found a positive causal relationship between countries' performance on a set of aggregate Worldwide Governance Indicators—which include voice and accountability, political stability and absence of violence, government effectiveness, regulatory quality, rule of law, and control of corruption—and their development performance as measured by per capita income, infant mortality, and literacy.[39] This work attracted numerous critics raising methodological and conceptual objections around the validity of the indicators and the possibility of controlling for sufficient other possible explanations to prove a causal impact of governance on development.[40] It has nevertheless gained widespread influence in the development community. Other researchers have added to the Kaufmann et al. research, taking it forward in different ways. For example, in a cross-country study of the relative weight of different factors bearing on development, William Easterly and Ross Levine use the Worldwide Governance Indicators as well as a property rights index to test the relationship between institutions and growth. They find that only through institutions do geographic endowments and economic policies affect GDP per capita.[41]

A subset of scholars in the good governance camp relies on similar statistical measures yet embraces a narrower and more economistic conception of governance, emphasizing the role of secure property rights, regulatory quality, and the rule of law as the main drivers of economic growth. Dani Rodrik, Arvind Subramanian, and Francesco Trebbi find that, based on a composite indicator of measures for property rights and the rule of law promulgated by Kaufmann et al., institutions trump such factors as geography and trade as the primary explanation for variations in income levels around the world.[42] Using data from political investment risk services, Stephen Knack and Philip Keefer also find that institutions that protect property rights—which they define to include factors such as contract enforceability, infrastructure quality, risk of expropriation, corruption of government, quality of bureaucracy, and rule of law—have a significant positive impact on growth and investment.[43] Robert Hall and Charles Jones use similar measures to argue that these same institutions and practices combined with free trade policies (or what they call "social infrastructure") play a key role in explaining variance in output per worker—a central driver of growth—across multiple countries.[44]

Several researchers have put forward a similar line of thinking on a broader historical canvas. In *Violence and Social Orders*, Douglass North, John Wallis, and Barry Weingast provide a conceptual framework to interpret economic history and its divergent outcomes, arguing that what they call "open access societies," which are characterized by impersonal governance, political and economic competition, and shared beliefs in equality and inclusion, are more successful at sustaining positive growth rates over a long period of time than are "limited access orders" or "natural states" where elites bend governing institutions to fit their personal interests and create economic rents.[45] Similarly, in their widely discussed book, *Why Nations Fail*, Daron Acemoglu and James Robinson conclude that nations succeed socioeconomically when they develop "inclusive" political and economic institutions and fail when they have "extractive" institutions that protect the interests of the elite against challenges from competitors.[46]

Researchers in the good governance camp usually stop short of arguing that democracy itself (rather than just certain elements of governance or democratic governance) fosters development. They draw the same line as do some aid organizations between democracy as a political system and democratic governance elements such as inclusion, accountability, and transparency. The core conclusions of the foundational work done by Adam Przeworski and Fernando Limongi in the early 1990s that found no significant link between political regime type (democratic versus nondemocratic) and average economic growth rates, are still widely cited in development circles as a reason not to give attention to democracy (even though the authors emphasized in subsequent writings that there is not a "shred of evidence that democracy need be sacrificed on the altar of development").[47] Moreover, some researchers highlight the developmental importance of governance elements related to state competence and coherence while rejecting the developmental value of specifically democratic practices such as elections. Paul Collier, for example, generally supports donor attention to governance, especially the rule of law. But in *Wars, Guns, and Votes*, he argues that elections are dangerous for development because of what he asserts is their tendency to provoke violent conflict in chronically poor and politically unstable countries (although his findings have been challenged by other cross-country studies).[48]

The Case for Democracy

Some scholars do make the case for the developmental value of democracy per se. In *The Democracy Advantage*, Morton Halperin, Joseph Siegle, and Michael Weinstein contend that democracies have realized consistently higher and more stable levels of economic growth and social welfare than autocracies during the past four decades. The connection between democracy and growth does not hold when they consider only low-income countries—which they attribute to the strong outlier effects of the East Asian Tiger economies—but the relationship between democracy and social welfare (measured by the Human Development Index and other social indicators) is positive at all income levels.[49]

Pippa Norris has sought to refine this argument by exploring the interrelationship between democracy and competent bureaucratic governance. Applying statistical controls for geographic, social, and cultural factors, she finds that—contrary to Halperin et al. and in line with Przeworski and Limongi—liberal democracy on its own does not significantly affect economic growth or social welfare indicators. But the combination of democratic government and a capable bureaucracy does have a significant positive impact on growth and social welfare. Bureaucratic democracies perform better than bureaucratic autocracies on average, and autocratic governments with weak states have the worst record.[50]

What Does This Mean for Practice?

North et al.'s "open access orders," Acemoglu and Robinson's "inclusive institutions," and other developmentally valuable political features highlighted by researchers emphasizing the importance of liberal political institutions sufficiently resemble basic elements of democratic governance that practitioners supportive of that agenda can point to these scholarly accounts for backing. They do so even though the writers in question tend to be cautious about extending their research conclusions to aid policy recommendations. Acemoglu and Robinson note that "attempts by international institutions to engineer economic growth by hectoring poor countries into adopting better policies and institutions are not successful because they do not take place in the context of an explanation of why bad policies and institutions are there in the first place."[51] The authors indicate that the development of some kind of centralized order, a degree of pluralism, an active civil society, and particularly a free media are likely to be key elements in the development of more inclusive institutions but stress that "many of these factors are historically predetermined and change only slowly."[52]

North et al. similarly caution that "the concepts of limited and open access in both economics and politics are subtle and multidimensional" and that "putting them into practice will require serious effort that is beyond the scope of this study."[53] They argue that simply transplanting institutions such as elections, property rights, deregulated markets, or even policies to provide more public goods will not benefit development as long as states are not yet transitioning to "open access societies." Such an approach could in fact be dangerous; restricted access in "natural states"—which they consider most developing countries to be—not only maximizes the incomes of elites but also helps the state control societal violence, thus fulfilling a useful role in fragile or divided states.[54] Rodrik and Subramanian also warn that the importance of certain institutional functions—such as the protection of property rights—does not imply particular institutional forms and that their findings may not provide much guidance for policymakers. Instead, they suggest that "desirable institutional arrangements have a large element of context specificity arising from differences in historical trajectories, geography, political economy, and other initial conditions."[55]

In sum, a number of significant research findings provide both statistical and historical evidence that democratic governance is useful to economic development. But they also caution that these effects rely on the complex interaction of a number of institutions and that in the absence of other enabling factors, one variable in isolation—such as elections or formal legal reforms—is unlikely to have a significant impact on growth. And this research stream does not provide much guidance on how a country can move from having an under-institutionalized state without rule of law or democratic accountability toward effective democratic governance. Moreover, as the following section outlines, a number of scholars have drawn attention to another model of effective developmental governance that departs significantly from the democratic governance orthodoxy.

THE DEVELOPMENTAL STATE ALTERNATIVE

A contending line of research agrees that a country's governance is a major determinant of its socioeconomic development but rejects the idea that the standard donor model of democratic governance is the answer. Focusing on the defining characteristics of developing countries that in recent decades have managed to achieve rapid growth, scholars embracing this view emphasize the advantages of "developmental states." Developmental states are defined by their capacity to effectively mobilize resources, a willingness to actively intervene in the process of national development, and an understanding of which policies are crucial for economic growth.

This view gained strength in the early 1990s due to a reinterpretation of the striking developmental success of what became known as "the Asian Tigers."[56] Originally seen by some as free market success stories, Hong Kong, Singapore, South Korea, and Taiwan did not follow Western good governance principles. They centralized power, steamrollered inclusiveness through harsh treatment of organized labor, and tolerated or cultivated significant levels of patronage. Yet they were also characterized by strong elite attachment to the importance of development, an autonomous and capable bureaucracy able to make and implement effective economic policies, and a high level of cooperation between state and market actors.[57] Proponents of the developmental state perspective find similar patterns of governance in China, Ethiopia, Rwanda, Vietnam, and many of the other fast-growing developing countries of recent years.

These cases have led some scholars to conclude that the key to rapid growth and economic transformation is not democratic governance but rather government commitment and capacity to invest national resources strategically in the service of national development.[58] Mushtaq Khan outlines this argument by distinguishing between "growth-enhancing" and "market-enhancing" aspects of governance. He sees the good governance agenda as being primarily about market-enhancing measures such as property rights, rule of law, anticorruption, and transparency, which maintain efficient markets and restrict the state. These governance objectives may be good things, but they are not necessarily feasible goals in developing countries or sufficient conditions for economic growth. Instead, developing country governments need to implement explicitly growth-enhancing measures, such as actively encouraging investment and the rapid acquisition of new technologies. In order to do so, they require certain key governance capabilities like the ability to monitor resource use and to withdraw support from actors who are not contributing to the economy—attributes that are not common in most developing country governments (or in many developed countries).[59] Peter Evans and James Rauch further underscore the role of bureaucratic authority in facilitating economic growth. Their cross-country research points to the importance of a bureaucracy's "Weberianness" (measured by such indicators as the degree to which the government employs meritocratic recruitment and offers long-term careers). They view their findings as support more for the developmental state model than for good governance reform, arguing that the East Asian developmental states were characterized by highly effective state bureaucracies.[60]

The Africa Power and Politics Programme at the Overseas Development Institute, led by David Booth, follows a similar line, emphasizing the importance of state capacity and cohesion and criticizing the donor fixation on democratic governance as ideologically rather than empirically based. Drawing on Khan, Booth argues that the conditions that facilitate effective functioning of market economies are very different from the more active state role needed to spur economic transformation in African countries.[61] Finding that the main barriers to growth in Africa are weak, fragmented, clientelistic political systems beset with collective action problems, the program points to the benefits of "developmental patrimonialism," a system of governance that, though patronage-based, effectively centralizes decisionmaking and rent seeking while also enforcing discipline in the political class. The program's research on service delivery in Malawi, Niger, Rwanda, and Uganda, for instance, finds that Rwanda demonstrates significantly better public goods provision than the other three cases, pointing to policy coherence, effective top-down performance discipline, and locally anchored institutions as key success factors.[62]

Wariness About Democracy

Adherents of the developmental state model tend to be wary of democracy in developing countries, at least for developmental purposes. They see the frequent fragmentation of political authority in fledgling democratic systems as cutting against the overarching importance of centralized, coherent state power and capacity. In his major comparative study of the role of the state in development, Atul Kohli compared South Korea's stunning economic success in the second half of the twentieth century with India's and Brazil's more middling performances and Nigeria's persistent developmental failures. He argues that pluralistic systems in poor countries struggle to reconcile their political need to respond to citizens' near-term interests with the broader goal of economic transformation. They thus end up hampered by fragmented authority structures, politicized bureaucracies, and other negative characteristics of such systems. Cohesive authoritarian regimes such as South Korea's in the 1950s and 1960s, meanwhile, are able to adopt a single-minded commitment to growth and mobilize society around that goal. Kohli thus contends that an "element of 'ruthlessness' or of coercion in its various forms has also been omnipresent in the most successful cases of rapid industrialization in the contemporary developing world," though he cautions that this does not mean that the costs of repression are worth the economic benefits.[63] Booth argues that democratic governments in Africa are generally not helpful for short-term or medium-term development because they are characterized more by competitive clientelism than substantive representation. Instead, "what poor developing countries really need are leaders who, as well as constructing sufficiently inclusive coalitions of support, are able to show that they can 'get things done.'"[64]

The case of China casts the divide between the democratic governance and developmental state schools into sharp relief. For proponents of the developmental state model, China's economic success is powerful, even game-changing evidence against the view that Western-style good governance is necessary for socioeconomic development. In their opinion, China embodies the central features of the developmental state model and some of its violations of standard good governance precepts are actually functional parts of its successful approach. For proponents of the developmental value of democratic governance, China is an awkward case. Their most common response is to argue about sustainability. China has indeed achieved remarkable economic growth, they acknowledge, but millions of its people are still living in poverty and the country faces growing concerns about inequality. Unless it becomes more law-based, politically inclusive, and accountable, its economic success will run aground, they say, due to accumulating citizen anger and alienation.[65] They also note that China's economic growth is overshadowed or at least darkly colored by its many developmental shortcomings, such as environmental degradation and labor abuse, which are directly related to its lack of political inclusiveness and accountability.

But How?

Yet even if one accepts that China and the East Asian Tigers are good development models, the larger challenge of this approach is that developmental states are both rare and difficult to promote. In sub-Saharan Africa, Booth identifies only Rwanda and Ethiopia as current developmental patrimonial states. As Khan and others point out, successful developmental states require a delicate balance of high state capacity—already a major challenge—with at least three critical factors: leadership commitment to development, government capacity to impose discipline and prevent corruption, and wise and selective economic policies. These characteristics are more the exception than the norm in authoritarian states.

Proponents of the developmental state model acknowledge that state capacity to promote development is not the same thing as the equally crucial leadership *commitment* to do so. A strong and unchallenged authoritarian state may be more capable of promoting economic transformation than a fragmented democratic state, but its leaders could just as easily choose to use their power to extract rents for themselves at the expense of the general welfare. As Timothy Besley observes, "No one really knows how to get a state to start recognizing and addressing the core needs of its population."[66] Examining the historic emergence of developmental states, many scholars point to the presence of an external threat as an important driver of pro-developmental policies.[67] Booth, for example, notes that developmental patrimonialism has arisen due to either the personal popularity of a wartime or national liberation leader or in response to large-scale internal violence or similar threats that solidified elite discipline (as in Rwanda and Ethiopia).[68] These are obviously not conditions that donors can or should promote. Moreover, even when overall leadership support for development exists, it remains extremely difficult to enforce discipline among powerful bureaucratic and private actors. Recent scandals in China, for example, have highlighted the challenge of preventing political elites from using their positions to benefit themselves and their families financially, despite a cohesive party structure with a high degree of commitment to economic progress.

Equally crucially, the developmental state model can only work well if the government in question is able to make good economic decisions and is conscious of its own limits. As James Scott argues in *Seeing Like a State*, an authoritarian state with a single-minded commitment to transformative development and few checks on its power can be a recipe for economic disaster. Ambitious top-down plans tend to fail because they fit poorly with complex informal social realities and neglect the importance of practical local knowledge.[69] The tragic experience of China's Great Leap Forward is the most jarring testament to the risks of such experiments. What allowed development states to work well in the East Asian cases, as Peter Evans argues, was not just high capacity and commitment but also the *selective* use of state intervention only where it was needed. Also valuable were close links with the private sector that gave bureaucratic actors information about what economic measures would be useful and allowed them to negotiate implementation.[70] These governments were able to both accumulate power and exercise self-restraint in their use of it.

Given that most authoritarian governments do not demonstrate unwavering commitment to inclusive development paired with judicious economic policies, some scholars have attempted to reconcile the developmental state and democratic governance approaches. Evans, for example, has argued that in the twenty-first century developmental states can no longer afford to rely only on their relationship with industrial elites; they need to be embedded more broadly in civil society, in large part because states are now expected to deliver a wide array of social welfare measures in addition to economic growth.[71] Gordon White has outlined a similar conception of a democratic developmental state, emphasizing the importance of accountable political elites who have strong capacity to implement socioeconomic programs as well as administrative autonomy and "inclusive embeddedness" in society.[72] These are not easy conditions to satisfy and require a bureaucracy powerful enough to deal with the fragmenting pressures of democratic politics. But they are not necessarily more difficult than the preconditions for building an autocratic developmental state, where the absence of bottom-up accountability creates constant pressure on the maintenance of elite discipline. Besley suggests, for example, that democratic accountability may help build the leadership commitment to development so critical for developmental states.[73] Norris's research on the interaction of democracy and bureaucratic governance points to a similar conclusion.[74] Richard Sandbrook et al. examine the cases of Chile, Costa Rica, Kerala, and Mauritius and find that significant socioeconomic progress has occurred in democratic developmental states and that this can create a virtuous cycle in which democracy encourages states to act developmentally and developmental success helps to consolidate democracy.[75]

The stream of research on developmental states is a significant challenge to the notion that liberal governance alone is a likely path to rapid economic progress for developing countries. It mounts what many aid practitioners find to be a persuasive case that donors should not try to insist on good governance reforms in places where a developmental state is functioning, because efforts to create more checks on state power or minimize the state role in the economy could undermine a successful interventionist development model. Yet, to an even greater degree than research on democratic governance, the developmental state approach provides little guidance on how to actively assist in the creation of developmentally effective governance structures where they do not currently exist.

MANY ROADS TO ROME

A loosely linked set of studies in the past decade has sought to define a pragmatic middle ground between the good governance and the developmental state camps. Scholars working in this vein accept that governance is usually a critical factor in development but do not believe that any one model of governance will necessarily produce the best socioeconomic outcomes for most countries or be feasible in most places. They subscribe instead to a multiple path philosophy, noting that very different governance systems have helped enable developmental progress in the past. Outsiders looking for governance answers in a poor country should therefore take a pragmatic, eclectic approach that focuses very closely on the particulars of the national context. Part of this outlook is the conviction that the effects of governance arrangements in different countries tend to be much more ambiguous and complex than either of the two standard approaches described above would suggest, with likely trade-offs between different features of a single governance model rather than clearly delineated good and bad practices.

Merilee Grindle's influential work on "good enough governance" focuses on the issue of feasibility. Concerned that donors armed with preset governance blueprints are overwhelming countries with unrealistic demands to achieve ideal types, she argues that in any given country aid providers should focus on those elements of governance most crucial to unblocking specific obstacles to economic development. She underlines that such an approach must be based on in-depth understanding of and adaptation to the local context and of the inevitable trade-offs among different development priorities.[76]

Dani Rodrik asserts that while governance is instrumentally (and intrinsically) important, no single set of governance arrangements will necessarily achieve good socioeconomic outcomes in all places. Instead, effective institutions can take many different forms. What works in governance will depend on local circumstances, and governance reforms are more likely to be feasible and helpful if they are targeted to address specific constraints to development progress rather than comprehensive reform of the political system.[77] Similarly, Francis Fukuyama and Brian Levy outline various possible approaches to governance reform. In a 2010 paper they present four main options: (1) a focus on state capacity building; (2) transformational governance change centered on democratic institutions and the rule of law; (3) "just enough governance" to address binding constraints on growth; and (4) bottom-up mobilization to demand democratic and development progress. In their view, aid actors should take a thoroughly pragmatic, differentiated approach to recommending and facilitating governance reforms, carefully analyzing a country's starting point, under-standing what processes are already inducing change, and following the least disruptive reform path to open space for economic progress.[78] In *The Origins of Political Order*, Fukuyama traces the development of political order from the earliest societies up to the modern age, examining how the institutional components of the modern state were gradually put in place. He highlights the very different governance paths and sequences that various countries have taken, contrasting, for example, China's process of state building without rule of law with the European development of rule of law and accountability before the creation of strong states. Drawing on this evidence, Fukuyama argues that the "factors driving the development of any given political institution are multiple, complex, and often depen-dent on accidental or contingent events."[79]

Some developmentalists place particular emphasis on an additional dimension of the multiple path outlook—informal institutions that operate alongside and in place of formal governance institutions. As Sue Unsworth, Mick Moore, and others at the Centre for the Future State argue in *An Upside Down View of Governance,* the crucial role of informal institutions in many socioeconomic processes of change undercuts the ability of aid actors to assert with confidence that any particular set of formal institu-tions or mechanisms is crucial to development. Recognizing the impor-tance of informal institutions should encourage aid actors to go much deeper in their efforts to understand local contexts and prioritize action in areas that they may actually be able to influence rather than in those that they believe a priori to be decisive.[80] David Booth, recognizing that developmental patrimonialism is unlikely to emerge in most places and is difficult to promote from the outside, has suggested a focus on identifying and supporting domestically driven problem-solving efforts. He notes that such initiatives often consist of hybrid combinations of local norms and modern state institutions.[81]

The multiple paths approach appears to provide a more nuanced, prac-tical way forward for development actors than either the democratic gov-ernance or developmental state models, yet it also struggles to provide easily applicable policy recommendations. Recognizing that countries can improve their governance in many different ways calls for greater humility in donor prescriptions and more attention to how external efforts to promote governance interact with and affect local institutions. But neither development scholars nor practitioners know enough about how governance change occurs or how incremental reforms add up to larger transformations to be able to say with the kind of certainty that donors want that a specific approach will work best in a particular context.

DIVERSITY BEHIND THE DOORS

The embrace by the mainstream aid community of political goals gained a sizable head of steam in the 1990s due to the newfound conviction that political factors were critical to economic success. Today there is considerable empirical support for that very general proposition and some consensus around basic elements of what constitute developmental politics, including the importance of an effective and technically competent state capable of delivering public goods and providing a secure environment for economic activity, functioning accountability mechanisms (whether democratic or top-down), and at least some degree of elite commitment to inclusive development. Yet this consensus does not extend to more specific prescriptions such as the proper limits of state power or the developmental value of liberal democracy.

Enough supportive research has emerged since to assure proponents of the democratic governance orthodoxy that it is a credo rooted in empirical truth. While contrary approaches exist, none is sufficiently internally coherent or widely enough applicable to deal the democratic governance perspective a fatal blow. And in any case, axiomatic approaches to public policy can survive a lack of empirical validation for many years, or even indefinitely, if they are intuitively appealing or politically useful. This is the case, for example, with the U.S. predilection to resort to economic sanctions when trying to bend the will of an uncooperative foreign government, despite a clear preponderance of research evidence that sanctions rarely achieve their intended objectives.

Moreover, the idea that "our" form of governance is the key for poor countries straining to become prosperous is powerfully attractive to Western politicians and senior policy officials who need to explain development policy to often doubtful or uninterested publics. Given public concern that aid may be wasted by corrupt recipient governments, the stress on the rule of law and anticorruption measures has a reassuring disciplinary quality, implying a greater degree of control than is often possible. It would not be an easy sell at home for Western aid agencies to say that they have decided to foster authoritarian governance, such as that practiced by China, or that corruption may actually not be a prohibitive obstacle to development. It would be even more difficult for Western politicians to fly a banner for development aid proclaiming that, despite a half-century of aid experience, experts still do not know what kinds of politics or governance are helpful for development in any particular situation and that they recommend experimenting with different approaches in different contexts.

Yet neither the initial head of steam nor the subsequent research favoring the good governance outlook has proved strong enough to overcome widespread doubt about this orthodoxy within major aid organizations. As described above, several major lines of thinking advanced by respected scholars take issue with the official policy consensus. Those who doubted the new democratic governance orthodoxy when it surged to the fore in the 1990s have considerable empirical support for continuing doubt. And though studies are multiplying and insights deepening, no consensus appears on the horizon.

The main lines of division have persisted for decades. One can easily trace the current debate over democratic governance versus developmental states back to the 1960s clash between proponents of the idea that "all good things go together" in development and those who argued that a strong hand is useful to get countries moving along the developmental road. Both sides have moderated somewhat since then. Proponents of "all good things" show greater realism about the economic and political challenges facing developing countries. Adherents of the developmental state model show less willingness than in earlier decades to endorse repressive governments and more recognition of the narrow conditions under which developmental states work well. But despite countless studies attempting to settle the argument one way or the other, the division of views has remained remarkably constant over fifty years.

What exists in aid circles is not a simple divergence between an official policy line and unofficial adherence to an alternative line. The situation is much more complex: behind the doors of mainstream aid organizations lies a strikingly wide range of views about the role of politics in development and

little consensus on the proper place for political goals within the development agenda. Some people genuinely believe, often ardently, in the official
line. But many others subscribe to quite different views. Taken together,
these form a whole ladder of viewpoints, with the descending rungs at an
increasing distance from the official line. Box 7.1 sets out the main rungs on
this ladder, embodying seven different points of view.

Aid organizations thus officially embrace a fairly standard set of political goals as part of their agenda and rhetoric but then implement them
partially and inconsistently in parallel to the partial and inconsistent belief
in the orthodoxy behind the doors. The variation of views within each
aid organization is high. In addition, many aid practitioners do not hold
strongly to any one position on the issue but are understandably unsure
and migrate from one view to another depending on the situation or the
moment. Others believe strongly in the intrinsic importance of political
goals even if they are unsure about their value for socioeconomic development. The overall weight of particular views varies within different organizations. Different internal cultures lean more one way or the other, but no
aid organization has achieved a clear consensus.

CONCLUSION

Mainstream development agencies have arrived at an uncomfortable but
seemingly stable middle ground on political goals. On the one hand, certain
principles of democratic governance have gained a durable place within
development work. For both intrinsic and instrumental reasons, donors are
very unlikely to either abandon governance altogether or return to a narrow
technocratic view of governance, giving up their commitment to participation, inclusion, transparency, and accountability. Western politicians and
senior policymakers will likely continue to proclaim the appealing idea
of a natural correspondence between democratic governance and developmental success. World events, most recently the Arab Awakening, continue
to provide compelling evidence of the perils of ignoring political factors in
favor of a sole focus on socioeconomic progress.

Yet on the other hand, the obstacles to translating these broad normative commitments into more active promotion of political goals within

BOX 7.1   THE INSTRUMENTAL CASE LADDER

1. Liberal democracy is crucial for sustained socioeconomic development.

2. Democratic governance, including not just competent states but also participation, accountability, transparency, and inclusiveness, is crucial for sustained socio-economic development, but democracy itself is not.

3. Only certain elements of democratic governance, above all the rule of law and property rights, are key to development.

4. Governance is crucial to development, but the patterns of governance that most reliably produce rapid economic growth are not democratic governance but developmental states characterized by strong, centralized state power and capacity and by a commitment to promote growth from above.

5. Governance is crucial to development, but no one model is necessarily best; multiple paths of governance have worked in different situations, and the best type of governance will depend greatly on the specifics of particular country situations.

6. Governance may be an important determinant of development, but outside actors are rarely able to significantly shape the country's governance and therefore should concentrate on other things that they can influence and that they know are important, especially developmental basics relating to economic growth, health, and food.

7. Governance is not as important a determinant of development as structural features; governance is largely a result of rather than a cause of development.

development policy and programs remain just as robust. The mixed interests of the main donor governments in supporting democratic governance or democracy in the developing world are a continuing reality. So, too, are the frequent objections on the recipient side to donors' political objectives. Moreover, it is unlikely that the lack of consensus among empirical researchers on the instrumental case for the developmental effects of democratic governance will suddenly evolve in such a way as to persuade skeptics to embrace it in practice. As the next chapter will explore, this tension has come to the fore as many mainstream development actors try to integrate attention to politics and governance more widely across socioeconomic programs.

THE INTEGRATION FRONTIER

INTRODUCTION

The renewed push on politics has led to significant progress in the use of political methods and some rethinking but limited change in the overall place of political goals in development aid. This political movement is also making itself felt in a further way, one that relates to both methods and goals, in the form of efforts within major aid organizations to mainstream political tools and approaches into what are often called traditional sectors of assistance, such as health, education, infrastructure, and agriculture. Aid providers usually refer to these efforts as governance integration, because they entail incorporating governance perspectives and principles into these other sectors. Proponents of this mainstreaming seek not just to influence aid policies and some specific programs but also to change the institutional structures and culture that undergird the long-standing view of governance as a stand-alone sector rather than a crosscutting lens on all development issues.

Such integration is a complex undertaking, one that at most organizations is only starting to gain traction but has potential for lasting significance. It raises two overarching questions. First, *what* should be integrated? Is the point of mainstreaming to insert political goals directly into socioeconomic sector programming, so that, for example, a health program is also explicitly aimed at furthering certain governance values, like participation and accountability? If so, is this about embedding an intrinsic commitment to such values throughout assistance or doing so on the basis of instrumental, aid effectiveness reasons? Or is integration primarily about methods rather than goals—injecting more political understanding and process-focused approaches into development programming? Second, *how* should mainstreaming be implemented? As we have seen earlier, it takes more than the head of an agency declaring that all programs will reflect certain governance values or that aid will be politically informed to ensure that such changes occur in practice. Integration proponents have to face the obstacles to the uptake of political methods and goals described in previous chapters, challenges that take particular forms when practitioners attempt to mainstream such approaches throughout aid.

The push to mainstream politics also raises important questions for the future of existing political work, both in advancing political goals and employing politically savvy methods. The opportunity to inject political values into new areas of aid is tempered by fears in some parts of the democracy and human rights assistance communities that their core priorities will be de-emphasized in favor of crosscutting support to socioeconomic objectives. On their end, advocates of greater use of political methods must grapple with how to mainstream political understanding without succumbing to superficiality. And integration efforts are not occurring in an intellectual vacuum—other movements gaining traction within the development community, notably the rising popularity of randomized control trials as a means of learning about what works in development, challenge some core elements of the renewed push on politics.

THE MAINSTREAMING IMPERATIVE

The new politics agenda is driven by a committed but diverse group of aid practitioners and development scholars who share a belief in the fundamental importance of greater attention to politics within development aid. They come at the issue from quite different perspectives and backgrounds, but many arrived at politics through experience with governance programs. Governance specialists are thus often the main proponents of integration within aid organizations. They feel that they have made progress in understanding governance and how it can be strengthened, and they want to spread their insights horizontally across the aid domain.

Governance practitioners tend to believe that governance improvements can contribute to better outcomes in every socioeconomic sector. They want sector specialists to take into account the political context, particularly the effectiveness and underlying dynamics of key host country institutions, when designing interventions. A primary education project that seeks to change the operation of schools but is not built on a clear understanding of the full range of structural and institutional constraints that affect schools—such as the capacity of the ministry of education to carry out reform plans—may generate some short-term gains but is unlikely to produce sustained benefits. Many governance advocates go further and argue that governance principles such as participation, transparency, inclusiveness, and accountability should apply across all sectors. Thus, for example, they might assert that decisions about the allocation of health resources in different regions of a country should be made in a participatory fashion and subsequent implementation of health services should be monitored by citizen groups. They hold that integrating governance in such ways is likely to improve the effectiveness of socioeconomic programs and ensure that all assistance is delivered in a way consistent with the political values of donors.

As with the broader question of how governance influences overall economic development, the evidence for positive effects of good governance reforms in specific sectors is still an unfolding and contested area. Good governance proponents usually contend that sufficient positive experiences exist in participatory budgeting, community monitoring, and other types of bottom-up efforts to back up their views. They also usually believe that the intrinsic rationale for governance principles like inclusion and participation is powerful and that these ideas should not be considered as just another programming tool that can be tossed aside in the face of insufficient proof of instrumental effectiveness.

While much of the push for integration comes from governance specialists, it is not a one-way process of governance practitioners pushing their agenda on other sectors. Many socioeconomic sector specialists have grappled with the negative impact of governance deficiencies and other political obstacles on the effectiveness of their work. As a result, some have become strong advocates for paying more attention to governance issues within their areas of expertise. They believe that knowledge can and

should also move in the other direction—that they can share their experiences with governance specialists who may lack knowledge of their sector,
thereby helping those specialists learn how governance bears on concrete
socioeconomic issues directly relevant to people's lives.

This evolution toward greater recognition of the importance of governance within traditional sectors is clear in the health domain. Aid programs
aimed at improving the health of people in poor countries have long epit-
omized the dream of technocratic solutions to development. Medicine
remains the ultimate technical intervention. Smallpox was eradicated not
through widespread improvements in governance but by teams of experts
vaccinating populations in developing countries, through coercion if necessary. Yet in the past decade significant movement has occurred within
the health community to think more seriously about how and why health
systems succeed or fail. A doctor may not need political analysis to know
what to prescribe for a child with malaria, but the broader challenge of
reducing malaria in a stricken country raises a whole series of questions
about institutional performance, the interests of health providers and
policymakers, and other governance issues. The rise of a governance perspective in the health domain is evident in the evolution of the massive U.S.
President's Emergency Plan for AIDS Relief (PEPFAR), which has moved
from a first phase focused on quickly getting treatment to millions of people
with HIV to a second phase focused on strengthening health systems and
sustainable country programs. In addition to pragmatic questions of health
system effectiveness, there is a strong current of thinking within the health
community that considers access to health a human right and wants to
incorporate rights-based approaches into health programs.

INTEGRATION POLICIES

Since the second half of the last decade, many major aid providers,
including USAID and CIDA, have started embracing governance integration at the level of official policy. The World Bank and particularly DFID
made mainstreaming a priority early in their governance work, but they,
too, are grappling with how to intensify and improve integration.

DFID has long connected its attention to governance with the aim of
mainstreaming politically informed methods across its development work

generally. As governance rose in prominence in UK aid in the second half of the 1990s, the newly established DFID created a cadre of "governance and institutions" advisers (now numbering over 100) who were placed in headquarters as well as within country offices to help make all programs more aware of governance issues. Since DFID embraced political economy analysis in the early 2000s, these advisers have played a central role in encouraging its wider application. The governance specialists also manage core programming around political governance program areas such as parliamentary strengthening and civil service reform. Unlike in some other agencies, DFID governance advisers do not have an explicit democracy mandate, though they do implement democracy and human rights programs in some places. In addition to governance advisers, other DFID employees such as conflict specialists and social development experts play important roles in encouraging crosscutting governance work in the field.

The World Bank has not developed a comparable cadre of governance experts but takes a similar view of governance as an inherently integrative area. Since the institution is constrained in its ability to advocate political goals for their own sake, it justifies attention to governance as directly useful for its socioeconomic work. Its 2007 governance and anticorruption strategy, for example, states that "the principal purpose of the [World Bank Group's] engagement on governance and anticorruption is to support poverty reduction" and calls for "incorporating concrete good governance and anticorruption objectives in sectoral programs, tailored to each sector's distinctive features and potential risks."[1] The World Bank's 2012 governance and anticorruption strategy points to the need for further movement in this area. The first pillar of the strategy, "Scaling Up and Systematizing Success," advocates systematic mainstreaming of governance elements such as "the use of political economy analysis, transparency, accountability, civil society participation, monitoring, and oversight."[2] Some of these elements, such as political economy analysis, are most associated with political methods, while accountability and civil society participation could be considered political goals in their own right as well as means to more effective programs.

USAID, in contrast to DFID and the World Bank, places political goals at the center of its official statements on integration. USAID's very first policy document on democracy and governance, issued in 1991, stated that "USAID can encourage the establishment of democratic values and practices, respect for basic human rights and lawful governance *across all sectors and the full range of its development programs* [emphasis added]. Over the long term, this indirect support may be more significant than specific projects that provide direct assistance to support democratic institutions."[3] Despite this stated intention, USAID ended up developing democracy and governance work largely as a stand-alone area. As mentioned in the last chapter, in the wake of the outbreak of political uprisings in the Arab world in 2011, USAID Administrator Rajiv Shah promised to do more to integrate democracy and good governance goals throughout the agency's programs. He stated in a speech that it was time to make progress on "breaking down the wall that has long existed between development practitioners and democracy, rights and governance experts" and argued that "without political reform, we're not helping to develop countries; we're delivering services, undermining our chances for long-term success."[4] Shah proposed some specific steps to put these commitments into practice, including the democratic accountability analysis described earlier as well as creating a second track of funding within the major presidential initiatives (on health, food security, and climate change) for democracy, rights, and governance programming. This policy movement has primarily been about democratic goals. As USAID officials have attempted to turn the administrator's speech into operational guidance, however, some have seen it as an opportunity to open up conversations about political understanding and to introduce more political analysis into sector planning.

Canada has moved to mainstream its governance work as part of a larger reorganization intended to streamline operations and focus on a smaller set of priority sectors. It has shifted from a large stand-alone governance sector to make governance a crosscutting theme across its programs. The Canadian government has set five thematic priorities for its development assistance: increasing food security, stimulating sustainable economic growth, securing the future of children and youth, advancing democracy, and ensuring security and stability. The official development agency, CIDA, focuses on the first three objectives (though it still maintains some democracy and security programming) and has adopted environmental sustainability, gender equality, and governance as crosscutting themes.[5] CIDA argues that governance is a crosscutting concern because it contributes to the success of other development objectives and "because all projects provide opportunities for promoting principles of good governance, such as participation, inclusion, equity, transparency, and accountability."[6]

Some agencies have sought to advance integration less through organizational change and more by encouraging the wide use of governance analysis. The Swiss Agency for Development and Cooperation (SDC) has chosen governance, alongside gender equality, as a "transversal" theme that it seeks to incorporate across all its programs. It distinguishes transversal governance integrated within socioeconomic sector programs from its continued work on core areas of governance such as decentralization and justice reform. SDC has released a guide to help operational staff take into account the five principles of accountability, transparency, nondiscrimination, participation, and efficiency throughout their work.[7] EuropeAid issued a guide to sector-level political economy analysis that similarly urges sector specialists to take account of governance in their work, making the case that democratic governance is critical to sustainable development and aid effectiveness in all sectors. The guide calls for attention to core governance issues of rules, interests, and power as well as the principles of participation, inclusion, transparency, and accountability.[8] Both these guides blend consideration of political goals and methods.

These various moves on integration at different donor agencies share some common elements. They are framed in terms of integrating governance, not politics per se, but emphasize the role of political analysis and understanding as an integral part of this effort. They all make the case that governance integration will help socioeconomic sectors as much as it will serve core governance goals. Not all directly embrace democracy, but they still emphasize the common good governance principles of participation, inclusion, transparency, and accountability.

INTEGRATION IN PRACTICE

Most development agencies remain at an early stage of integration, but they have already experimented with various efforts to transform their stated policies into changes in the field. Integration proponents have focused on increasing attention to governance and political economy issues in program planning and on building the capacity of staff working in socioeconomic sectors to consider and act on these issues. CIDA, for example, is considering requiring that every project include a governance analysis that examines participation, accountability, and other governance features on top of an existing policy that all projects examine their likely impact on human rights and conflict. Every project would be expected to address deficiencies that exist along these various lines.[9] SDC has created a detailed checklist of governance issues to consider in project planning and review processes.[10] USAID is developing guidance on how to incorporate democracy, human rights, and governance into country strategies.

The World Bank is trying to take a less prescriptive approach to how governance issues should be mainstreamed but has been among the most systematic in measuring whether governance elements appear in strategies. A 2011 review painted a mixed picture. It found that nearly all country strategies included some consideration of governance elements but that few included explicit discussion of smarter project design and less than a third of projects were deemed responsive to the demand side. The same review observed that 25 percent of World Bank projects used governance or political economy analysis "to a great extent," an increase from 15 percent before the release of its 2007 GAC strategy.[11] The World Bank has developed political economy analyses in the agriculture, energy, extractive industries, fiscal decentralization, health, social development, and water sectors as well as in more traditional governance domains.[12]

Including governance within planning processes is a key part of integration, but it is merely a first step. Sometimes it is only "integration light"—the relatively superficial adoption of some elements of participation, transparency, or other such values in a program, essentially just to check off a box in a guidance framework on integration. Ensuring that governance is substantively taken into account requires moving beyond just mentioning governance issues to adopting more concrete measures such as requiring specific governance objectives and including governance indicators within each program's results and evaluation frameworks. Just as importantly, integrating politics in a way that will genuinely improve the effectiveness of sector programs and advance broader governance goals requires that staff have the capacity to work on these complex issues within their programs.

Development agencies have thus focused on a number of tools to assist sector specialists in taking governance and political economy into account in their work, including how-to notes, training sessions, and providing resource people to whom sector staff can turn for advice. The World Bank has taken numerous steps in this direction, including incorporating governance issues into general staff trainings and producing how-to materials on governance integration. It has also established cross-sector communities of practice on elements of integration such as political economy analysis and demand for good governance and designated point persons on governance within some sectoral practice groups.

EuropeAid has adopted a similar approach focused on analysis and experience sharing. As noted above, it has put together a detailed guide to considering governance within sectors and also provides space for practitioners to share resources and ideas through communities of practice and its capacity4dev website.

DFID also offers governance trainings for sector staff and how-to notes on addressing specific governance challenges in socioeconomic sectors, but it stands out for its focus on placing governance advisers to work alongside sector experts on programs.[13] Pairing governance and sector specialists in the field is a promising approach as it allows for support on governance issues as they come up and also helps governance practitioners gain a better understanding of sector programs. However, most agencies do not have the critical mass of governance specialists needed to make this a realistic option for widespread integration. USAID is one of the few donors that does have a large cadre of governance experts within country offices and could theoretically adopt a similar model. USAID democracy and governance practitioners, however, have been primarily focused on implementing stand-alone democracy and governance programs and usually do not have the time or mandate to be cross-sectoral advisers. Democracy and governance staff have tried in recent years to cooperate more with other sectors but this is still not a well-institutionalized practice throughout the agency.

The USAID country program in Guinea provides one example of the potential for governance and sector staff to work closely together in pursuit of joint goals. Following fiscal constraints on the country mission as well as a 2005 fragile state assessment that pointed to governance as the main problem facing Guinea, USAID fused its work in the country into a single integrated program organized under a democratic governance rubric, staffed by governance practitioners as well as specialists in health, education, and agriculture. The program applied participatory practices as well as transparency and accountability mechanisms to a series of activities within socioeconomic sectors, such as community participation in advocating for more health funding from local governments. An evaluation of the program found positive impact on core democratic governance priorities like increased information sharing and public participation around local government budgets as well as socioeconomic outcomes such as increased use of health services.[14]

CHALLENGES OF INTEGRATION

As development agencies experiment with integration, they encounter all the barriers to uptake of both political goals and methods discussed in previous chapters as well as issues specifically associated with mainstreaming efforts. While at the rhetorical level development agencies usually present their work as part of an integrated whole, the reality is that staff are organized in sector silos with their own programs and usually do not have extensive opportunities to work with other departments. Elements of being politically smart such as political economy analysis, demand-side approaches, and process-focused programs have proved useful to programs in many different areas, from economic policy reform to health service delivery. Nevertheless, many socioeconomic sector specialists continue to see such activities as governance issues that lie apart from their central concerns. They can thus be less willing than governance specialists to invest in the administrative costs of conducting political analysis or other elements of more political programming, seeing these as "extras" not essential to their core mission. When integration entails direct cooperation between governance and socioeconomic specialists, tensions can also arise over how costs will be split between their respective departments.

Moreover, socioeconomic sector practitioners often expect more speed, control, definiteness, and lack of political controversy in aid interventions than do governance experts. Individual socioeconomic specialists interested in governance and willing to experiment with integrated programs remain accountable to their sector leadership and may feel pressure not to depart from accepted practice. While democracy and governance programs do try to generate "logframes" with precisely defined inputs, outputs, outcomes, and impacts, specialists in these areas also argue that the changes they seek to foster are inevitably long-term processes that are difficult to measure precisely. It is more difficult for health specialists to adjust from a focus on highly specific issues like providing vaccinations, where they can prove exactly how many people have been helped, to a more amorphous mission relating to improving institutional quality or other governance features. As described later in this chapter, this is particularly problematic in the context of the rising popularity of randomized control trials in development work.

Integrated programs face further challenges with how to measure and report their impact. Fully integrated programs need to demonstrate effects across both governance and socioeconomic sector objectives. In these cases it is often unclear how these results will be evaluated and what the relative weight of each factor should be in determining program success. For example, an agriculture program may seek to build state capacity to provide advisory services to farmers and help them make use of new technologies. Should the success of the program be measured based only on increases in farmer incomes? Or should there be specific measures relating to intermediary steps in the process such as policy reform, institutional strengthening, training programs, and uptake of new farming techniques? Will governance specialists be responsible for some results and agriculture experts responsible for others? These distinctions are significant because governance experts are usually very concerned with process questions (are policies developed in a participatory fashion? is the state providing equitable support?), while sector specialists may be more focused on their sector end-goal (what has been the impact on farmer livelihoods?).

Governance is also not the only issue that donors are trying to mainstream across their programming, and it has to compete for time and resources with other crosscutting themes. At USAID, for example, pursuing integrated approaches to development is one of the operational principles of the agency's 2011 Policy Framework, which calls for not just governance integration but also crosscutting approaches to climate change, integrated health, nutrition, and agriculture programs, and similar efforts in other sectors.[15] All USAID projects require analyses of gender, environment, and sustainability, while analyses around political economy and conflict issues are optional. At CIDA, as noted earlier, environmental sustainability and gender equality are also supposed to be integrated in all programs. Gender and environmental impact studies are a common requirement at other mainstream development agencies as well. In principle this is a good thing. Every development program should take into account potential synergies with other sector activities as well as the program's likely impact on gender equality, the environment, drivers of conflict, and other critical issues. In practice, however, sector staff can feel overwhelmed by all the elements they need to include within their program plans and the proliferation of analyses they are encouraged to undertake. Political economy analysis or explicit consideration of governance in their programs can seem like just another hoop through which they have to jump.

WINNING CROSS-SECTORAL SUPPORT

Where aid programs have successfully embodied an integrated governance approach, practitioners usually point to strong support from country office leadership and key sector staff as crucial facilitating conditions. Building such support among operational staff and convincing them that attention to politics will help rather than obstruct their programs is thus the central challenge of governance mainstreaming. Sector specialists are not going to make use of how-to notes and training or agree to side-by-side work with governance specialists unless they are persuaded of the importance of this agenda.

Governance integration proponents feel that they—more so than gender or environmental advocates—can make the case that their issues are central to aid effectiveness in all areas. And it is true that many sector specialists have responded to frustrations in their work—around corruption, weak institutions, or any other of the myriad governance issues within socioeconomic sectors—by actively seeking resources to help them address these challenges. Sector specialists who have made productive use of political economy analyses have also shared their experiences with colleagues, encouraging them to use similar tools. But other practitioners resist governance mainstreaming, often annoyed that people lacking substantial experience or expertise in their sectors are trying to tell them how to improve their work. Within organizations attempting governance integration, arguments sometimes flare between governance specialists and sector specialists, as summarized in Box 8.1.

BOX 8.1   ARGUMENTS OVER INTEGRATION

SECTOR SPECIALISTS:

- We are already well aware that state institutions have a major impact in our sectors and we've been taking institutional reform issues into account for decades, even if we have not used the term "governance."

- Fostering governance principles like participation is also old hat for us. What's new here?

- We are not convinced that reflexively applying high-minded principles like social accountability or inclusiveness will necessarily improve development outcomes—sometimes more inclusion can gum up the works, slowing down important decisions or derailing rational outcomes.

- Even if a focus on governance would help solve some problems, it may not be as cost-effective as other methods of assistance that are more direct delivery–oriented.

GOVERNANCE SPECIALISTS:

- Although some sector specialists certainly take serious account of governance issues, many do not—there is a need for greater consistency of application of these ideas.

- Of course inclusiveness, accountability, and other core governance values should not be applied reflexively, but governance specialists have accumulated considerable knowledge about how to apply them effectively, and sector experts could benefit from their experience.

- While direct delivery methods that avoid the complexity of taking politics into account sound appealing, neglecting the governance dimension has often led to unsustainable solutions.

- Evidence for the value of governance integration in traditional sectors will emerge if integration is fully pursued and then examined over time.

This argument over integration is complicated by debates over what "governance" means. Socioeconomic sector specialists tend to be more comfortable with the early, narrow definitions that emphasize effective institutional management. Many are skeptical of later, broadened conceptions of good governance that are peppered with normative political values. The World

Bank's governance and anticorruption strategy signals this problem, noting that "sectors that have taken a narrower, more management-oriented definition of governance have made less progress in recognizing how the use of a real governance lens can improve development effectiveness."[16] In this case a "real governance lens" is one that takes into account not just state capacity but also legitimacy, authority, and accountability.[17] As described above, policy statements by other donors tend to go even further in presenting what some would consider normative political goals—such as participation, inclusion, equity, and transparency—as necessary to improved sector outcomes. Yet, as we have seen, the evidence base is contested in this area, and not all sector specialists are convinced that the full good governance agenda is useful to them. Even among governance specialists, no clear consensus exists around what "real" consideration of governance entails. Some see participation and social accountability as essential elements of governance integration; others prefer a best-fit approach focused on whatever governance reforms will deliver particular development results.

Some socioeconomic sector specialists thus worry that what is touted to them as a means to help their programs' effectiveness is really a bureaucratic ploy to enlist their resources for the sake of a normative political agenda. If this agenda is pursued as not just governance but also democracy integration it meets even greater resistance. To many socioeconomic sector specialists, advancing democracy sounds like being asked to cross a political bridge that will only cause trouble. Thus, for example, they may be willing to discuss what level of participation is useful in a health project or a road project, but framing the question as how these programs can be pro-democratic is generally not well received. They are similarly hesitant about rights-based approaches to development, which seem to create new obligations and constraints beyond what is necessarily useful to their core sector goals.

This creates a dilemma for politics advocates, particularly proponents of democratic governance or human rights. Should they stick with emphasizing the elements of governance and political methods that have clear relevance for sector programs, such as improving the efficiency of service delivery systems and conducting stakeholder analyses to determine who supports and who opposes a particular reform? Or should they insist that sector specialists embrace the full good governance agenda replete with political values? From the point of view of political *methods*, letting sector specialists pick and choose which parts of governance are useful to them is a good idea as long as they apply the various elements effectively. Suppose for example that a political analysis examining an agriculture project indicates a need for better top-down accountability in the agriculture ministry but predicts that greater citizen participation will probably not make a difference in program effectiveness. In such a case focusing on increasing bureaucratic capacity may be perfectly justified as long as it addresses the problem in a politically smart fashion (and not just by creating a technical training for agriculture ministry officials). From a political *goals* perspective, however, increased citizen participation in agricultural decisions could be an end in itself. Moreover, simply strengthening the monitoring capacities of an authoritarian government's agriculture ministry with no attention to a greater role for citizens may have potentially harmful consequences for democracy. Aid organizations are reluctant to face this conflict head-on, instead continuing to proclaim that adhering to good governance values is also a means to more effective socioeconomic outcomes. Yet in practice they largely focus on responding to demand from socioeconomic sectors for what they find useful instead of insisting on full incorporation of political values.

THE FEAR OF WATERED-DOWN POLITICAL GOALS

Democracy and human rights advocates regard the advance of governance integration with mixed feelings. Most believe that more political thinking and engagement in the domain of socioeconomic development aid is a good thing. Yet they understandably fear the dilution of their political concerns, worried that integration will mean a watering down of political goals in favor of toothless principles like "foster greater participation" or even more technocratic visions of strengthening state effectiveness.

Some specialized democracy aid organizations have begun proactively giving attention to the socioeconomic impact of their work. They have done so in recognition of the fact that one cause of the relative stagnation of democracy's global advance toward the end of the 1990s was the failure of many new democracies to govern effectively and produce good socioeconomic results for their citizens. They thus began asking themselves whether and how their efforts to strengthen democratic institutions and processes could directly contribute to better socioeconomic results. The National Democratic Institute has a stream of work under the general heading of "Delivering on Democracy" intended to help answer these questions. In Haiti, for example, it supports local committees that bring together civic groups and citizens to work with local governments on socioeconomic issues ranging from health to education to reconstruction efforts.[18] The International Republican Institute has sought to use polling to help political parties in shaky democracies better understand the day-to-day socioeconomic concerns of their citizens and find ways to address them. The International Institute for Democracy and Electoral Assistance has established a Democracy and Development Programme, which among other things examines how local democratic processes and institutions can contribute to better service delivery.

Democracy advocates within mainstream development agencies as well as in specialized democracy aid organizations see the potential of integrative work but do not want it to become a substitute for their core programming. They insist that programs specifically focused on elections, parliaments, media, and other traditional areas of democracy support remain valuable and necessary even if they cannot be directly linked to socioeconomic results. Most mainstream aid agencies have not shown signs of cutting core democracy funding in favor of a shift to integrated programs, but moves like that of CIDA to de-emphasize its stand-alone governance programs in favor of mainstreaming are taken by some as worrying signs (though CIDA is maintaining some dedicated work around democracy and human rights). U.S. democracy promotion organizations have watched USAID's growing interest in integration with some wariness.

Human rights advocates also see the appeal of integration but are similarly worried about the dilution of their central principles. When applied at the project or program level, the human rights–based approach has significant similarities to governance integration. For example, when in the second half of the past decade Sida redesigned its assistance program in Kenya to fully incorporate human rights—a case Sida holds out as a leading example of its use of the human rights–based approach—this resemblance was evident. The Sida office first carried out a power analysis of the country's overall development landscape, highlighting the counterproductive effects of the entrenched patronage system. It followed that up with political economy studies of the various sectors in which Sida had been working. It redesigned its assistance efforts in each of the sectors to build in an emphasis on participation, inclusiveness, equality, and transparency. The country office pushed hard to engage the relevant Kenyan ministries in these sectoral discussions and also to include Kenyan human rights activists. The result was a significantly changed program. In the education sector, for instance, the program shifted from providing resources to schools to encouraging greater inclusion of socially marginalized groups in the education system.[19]

Proponents of the human rights–based approach nevertheless caution against equating it with governance mainstreaming. A full rights-based approach, they argue, is more than just including principles such as accountability as a way to improve governance and project effectiveness. It means helping citizens to claim their rights from duty bearers in government and assisting duty bearers to deliver on their obligations.[20] Designing a health program that allows beneficiaries to participate in decisions may be a good thing, but it cannot be considered rights-based if participation is presented as a privilege rather than a right or if beneficiaries are able to demand services only from the donor rather than from their government. As discussed in the previous chapter, this distinction underlies much of the concern with whether post-2015 international development goals will include explicit human rights and governance commitments or vaguer crosscutting principles (or neither).

Just as socioeconomic sector specialists fear that their resources will be redirected to serve political goals in the name of integration, democracy and human rights proponents worry that their core priorities will end up slipping behind socioeconomic objectives within their own programs. They know that they represent a relatively small part of overall assistance spending and occupy a fragile place within development agencies that are primarily concerned with other goals. Some thus express a natural inclination to protect what they have rather than open the floodgate of mainstreaming. Yet if integration is going to occur, they want a voice in the process. They hope to take advantage of what opportunities exist to embed their values within organizational cultures and bring mainstream aid practice more closely into alignment with the aid agencies' stated commitments to democracy and human rights. Just as important, they want to ensure that development programs are not doing harm in these areas. Pursuing integration in a politically value-free manner, in which, for example, health and agriculture programs focus on local institutional strengthening with no concern for human rights or democracy, could risk even more harmful political consequences than no political involvement at all.

THE DANGER OF POLITICAL SUPERFICIALITY

Those pushing for wider application of political methods within development aid also face a core conundrum as the integration agenda advances. Should political methods be simplified to ease their wide application, or is it preferable to insist on a high level of analytic depth even if that means less analysis gets done? Politically smart programming is difficult. It requires nuanced political understanding as well as the ability to navigate politically in often treacherous and ever-changing waters. It is hard to believe that a how-to note or one-day training could equip a practitioner without previous experience in governance or politics to take on such tasks effectively.

Proponents of political methods tend to focus on trying to get what might be called "good enough understanding" to as many projects as possible. They argue that so little political knowledge exists within most programs that even basic political insights can be helpful. A transportation program in Mozambique might touch on a set of contending interests and institutions in the transportation sector of such complexity that fully understanding the political context would require a huge effort, much less figuring out what to do about it. But even gaining just some basic insight into how the main institutions operate would still be helpful. Yet there is disagreement about what "good enough" means. Some governance specialists are happy to encourage more widespread use of fairly basic stakeholder analysis, seeing that as a clearly useful and easy-to-apply tool with appeal for sectors. Others insist that more complete political economy analysis is important if sector programs are to understand how their interventions fit into the broader context and whether they are focusing on the right entry points. Methods advocates complain of the uneven quality of political analyses within their agencies and the misnaming of technocratic institutional analyses as political economy studies.

Some observers take a more critical stance, warning that the techno-cratic impulses of aid are more likely to depoliticize the application of polit-ical methods than political methods are likely to transform the technical nature of aid. They argue that donor political economy analysis is often superficial and that development agencies continue to underrate the need for political expertise. They worry that simplifying political methods and presenting them in economistic language in order to make them broadly appealing to practitioners will leave the impression that extremely complex political issues can be easily analyzed and applied by amateurs. Adrian Leftwich argues, for example, that "the variety of 'tools' that pass for politi-cal economy analysis are a bit like giving you or me instruction in how to do surgery or take out an appendix without our having any understanding of the underlying physiology, anatomy or neurological structure."[21] Sam Hickey similarly critiques donor moves toward using political analysis, arguing that "the analytical approaches that can offer rigorous insights into the complex issue of power and politics tend to be the most difficult to operationalize, while the easiest to operationalize (e.g., political capital) tend to lack intellectual credibility."[22]

David Booth criticizes "the toleration often shown to the dissemina-tion by economists of ideas about governance and social relations which have a 'common sense' basis, and are offered in ignorance of the relevant literature," noting that economists would never tolerate political scientists making similar claims about their discipline.[23] David Hudson and Adrian Leftwich also observe that the persistent preference to think about politics in economic terms undermines the utility of political economy tools, leading to an excessive focus on rational choice incentives at the expense of deeper attention to the role of power, agency, ideas, and contingency—factors that may be more important in explaining how political actors are likely to behave.[24]

The issue of depth also arises as practitioners move from political under-standing to political engagement, particularly in bottom-up governance work. Demand-side methods—which originated from the political idea that citizen pressure is needed to change the behavior of power holders—have in many cases translated into citizen report cards and other standard tools that are applied in a wide range of programs without much regard to the specific context. Booth sharply criticizes the "powerful incentives to simplify and be upbeat" within the development community as leading to "the use of simple, partial-equilibrium propositions (e.g., 'information empowers') when reality has general-equilibrium properties, or where causality is multiple and complex."[25] Concerns also come from advocates of bottom-up approaches, who are torn between wanting to encourage such principles as participation within all programs and worrying that they will be applied superficially. One of the architects of the World Bank's KDP program in Indonesia, for example, warned that "from being an innovative project idea intended to test some hypotheses about social capital in development, KDP is now at risk of being mainstreamed in both Indonesia and the World Bank, with all the rigidities and complacencies that mainstreaming entails."[26] The superficial adoption of political methods without an accompanying awareness of their limits could be dangerous, leading to a proliferation of programs that insert themselves into recipient country politics without a clear idea of what they are doing or what the consequences will be.

Some political economy advocates are trying to refine and deepen the analytic tools available to socioeconomic programs. The focus within some agencies on creating political resource people is supposed to address this shortcoming. But political expertise remains thin and undervalued at major aid agencies. They continue to employ many more technical sector specialists than political scientists or other governance experts.[27] This is in itself not a problem; aid organizations need socioeconomic sector specialists to carry out much of their work. But politics and governance, unlike socioeconomic specialties, are seen as topics that can be adequately taught in a short course and constitute extra rather than core skill sets. The idea that understanding process is as central to success as knowledge of good technical policy solutions—and is thus worthy of similar human resource investments—has not gained wide purchase within development agencies.

RANDOMIZED TRIALS IN DEVELOPMENT: TECHNOCRACY STRIKES BACK?

The push to mainstream and deepen attention to political goals and methods across aid programming is complicated by the fact that the renewed push on politics is by no means the only or the most powerful intellectual trend attempting to reshape development assistance. Advocates of political approaches compete not just with other crosscutting concerns but also with different underlying visions of how to advance aid effectiveness.

The most significant challenge comes from the rising popularity of randomized control trials (RCTs) as a method both for assessing the impact of specific aid programs and for learning about development generally, the result of pathbreaking work by MIT's Abdul Latif Jameel Poverty Action Lab (J-PAL). RCTs seek to control for all factors relating to a development outcome by isolating a particular intervention as the independent variable and comparing results in a control group and a "treatment" group. RCTs represent an important and in many ways productive addition to the study of development, questioning some common assumptions about what types of programs work well and highlighting how certain micro-level policy changes can lead to improved outcomes for poor people. RCTs address somewhat different problems in development aid than do political goals and methods and could in theory complement them. Yet when conceived as a broader reform agenda aimed at transforming how to think about development—which is the larger ambition of its proponents—the randomization approach cuts against the renewed push on politics. It emphasizes the search for generalizable technical solutions over context-specific processes, micro reforms over attention to broader systems, and how to identify good policies rather than how to get policy recommendations approved and implemented. This perspective is powerfully appealing to development practitioners skeptical of the complications inherent in the politics agenda and eager for definite answers.

RCTs as Monitoring and Evaluation Tools

The growth in randomized control trials and their perceived rigor has sparked interest in their use in evaluating the success of specific development projects. This push poses new challenges to political aid and integrated programs already struggling to demonstrate results within current donor evaluation frameworks. RCTs can provide rigorous assessments of the effects of highly specific, bounded aid interventions—such as the health effects of distributing clean cook stoves in certain villages in a particular region. But they require a strict regimen of operational characteristics:

preset objectives, potential for randomization, and clear outcome indicators. These conditions are usually absent in politically oriented programs. RCTs would not be useful, for example, to assess the success of an extended assistance relationship between a Western political foundation and a counterpart party in a new democracy aimed at stimulating gradual changes in internal party structures, mindsets, and behaviors through ongoing, interactive consultations, exchange visits, formal and informal training exercises, and other means. Nor would they be helpful for evaluating a multiyear effort intended to support the policy advocacy of a diverse coalition of actors pushing for reforms in the health sector and adapting their specific objectives to take advantage of changing political opportunities.

Even in cases when political programs are susceptible to randomization requirements, measuring success still presents difficulties. The Committee on Evaluation of USAID Democracy Assistance Programs, for example, looked at existing USAID democracy programs to try to identify promising pilots for impact evaluation. It suggested a decentralization program in Peru would be well adapted to this type of assessment because program planners could randomly assign municipalities to receive or not receive assistance and then compare levels of citizen satisfaction with local government over time in the treated and untreated localities.[28] The problem with such an approach is that while significant differences in citizen satisfaction between localities would provide convincing evidence of the success of the program, a lack of statistically significant differences would not necessarily indicate that the program was useless. It may have helped build the capacity of certain local officials but been too small or short-term to have an impact on aggregate levels of citizen satisfaction. After an expensive and time-consuming evaluation process, the aid planner would thus be uncertain whether the program should be given more funding and more time, or be canceled.

Yet despite recognition in principle of the limited applicability of RCTs and the value and need for mixed evaluation methods, randomized trials are increasingly considered the gold standard within donor agencies. USAID's 2011 evaluation policy, for instance, acknowledges the value of both qualitative and quantitative methods and notes that "no single method will be privileged over others" but then says that "for impact evaluations, experimental methods generate the strongest evidence. Alternative methods should be utilized only when random assignment strategies are infeasible."[29]

Randomized trials are still used only infrequently as aid program evaluations because of their cost and difficulty, but they have become the ideal to which other evaluation techniques are compared. Many political specialists thus worry that they will not be able to provide the same "hard evidence" of impact as their colleagues working on more narrowly defined interventions and that it may become increasingly difficult to justify their own programs and to convince sector specialists to take risks with integrated efforts.

RCTs and Learning About Development

Proponents of greater use of RCTs are interested in doing more than evaluating individual projects—they want to build up evidence to inform development policy and practice more broadly. But this approach to learning is largely technocratic and clashes with more political approaches to aid. J-PAL has carried out assessments of governance-related policies and is attempting to build up knowledge around several key politically oriented issues, including the impact of citizen participation and anticorruption measures on development outcomes. One early randomized study by Raghabendra Chattopadhyay and J-PAL co-founder Esther Duflo, for example, looked at the impact of quotas for the representation of women in India. It found that in villages in West Bengal where quotas mandated that a woman head the local council, female leaders were more likely to invest in priorities of particular interest to women (in this case drinking water, fuel equipment, and roads) over others (education). Village women were also more likely to participate in town meetings in localities with female leaders.[30] Another randomized trial in Brazil found that giving voters information from audits about municipal irregularities reduced votes for incumbents in municipalities where corruption was reported and this effect was particularly strong in places with local radio stations.[31]

While these governance studies have reached a number of interesting findings, they are working at a granular level that is still far from producing insights about broader governance challenges. Crucially, they assume that different contexts are similar enough to allow for conclusions that transcend very particular places. But this is a problematic idea with regard to more political interventions, both with regard to goals and methods. Much of the cutting-edge research on the political economy of development points to the need to focus on highly context-specific features of governance such as informal institutions, as well as the interaction among governance elements that reinforce or undermine each other. The central message of politically smart methods is knowledge of and adaptation to particularly political contexts.

As we have seen in previous chapters, the success of efforts to improve governance through citizen participation—one of J-PAL's priority areas of research—has been highly dependent on the specific political environment and the existence of other opportunities for citizen empowerment and mobilization. Public information tools such as the citizen report cards pioneered in Bangalore have proved useful in a number of places, but they have had limited effect in contexts where public officials have no incentive to respond to public pressure. The results of an ongoing RCT in Sierra Leone looking at whether hosting candidate debates before elections provides voters with useful information on the performance of incumbents and challengers and as a result decreases reliance on ethnic party ties will be informative regarding that particular country at that time.[32] Its application to different countries with different sets of political actors, differently educated citizens, and other contrasting features, however, is unclear.

Context specificity is a major obstacle to learning through micro-level trials even outside the governance arena. As Nancy Cartwright observes, a disconnect exists between the high level of internal rigor of randomized trials and the willingness of some RCT enthusiasts to stretch specific conclusions to apply to places that vary in any number of ways from the experimental group.[33] As she argues, "There is no a priori reason to favour a method that is rigorous part of the way and very iffy thereafter over one that reverses the order or one that is less rigorous but fairly well reasoned throughout."[34] Dani Rodrik makes a similar point with specific reference to development assistance. He cites a study showing that distributing free bed nets to women visiting prenatal clinics in Kenya was more successful than selling bed nets in encouraging bed net usage. Rodrik argues that while the experiment provides suggestive evidence that free distribution is a good idea, it does not mean that a similar intervention would have the same effect with a wider population or in a different context. As a result, "the randomized field evaluation cannot settle the larger policy question which motivated it."[35]

Randomized trials also provide little guidance on the why and how of successful interventions, questions central to more politically informed approaches. As Angus Deaton argues, randomized trials can tell us that certain programs work, but their focus on success rates do not contribute to our understanding of why they work and how their impacts differ on different subgroups.[36] RCTs by definition have to focus on a bounded set of interventions and cannot provide much insight on how programs interact with each other and the broader political system, or how the incentives and circumstances may change as they are scaled up.

Even if such studies are able to come up with some generalizable truths, their focus on evidence and on identifying effective policies leaves out the crucial question of whether host governments will be willing and able to implement these recommendations. As noted in the previous chapter, J-PAL founders Abhijit Banerjee and Esther Duflo argue that it is more productive to focus on micro-level policy changes than systemic political economy issues because policy progress is possible even in otherwise bad political environments.[37] Yet as Daron Acemoglu and James Robinson highlight, "small market failures may be only the tip of the iceberg … The policymakers and bureaucrats who are supposed to act on well-intentioned advice may be as much a part of the problem, and the many attempts to rectify these inefficiencies may backfire precisely because those in charge are not grappling with the institutional causes of the poverty in the first place."[38]

Even the sharpest critics of RCTs concede that they can contribute to an understanding of what works in development in certain ways, and even the strongest proponents do not claim that their findings are universally applicable. RCTs and political approaches can complement each other if they are conceived as partial answers to the broader challenge of improving development effectiveness. For example, political methods can help fill the gap between policy recommendations arising out of RCTs and the need to win political support for implementation. On their end, RCTs can highlight innovative governance interventions worth trying out elsewhere. But randomized trials are often presented not as a partial solution but as a transformative tool. Within a development aid community starved for definite answers and empirical rigor (or at least the appearance of rigor), enthusiasm around RCTs risks feeding into broader technocratic mindsets that development progress is primarily about finding scientifically correct solutions to precisely defined problems and persuading people in developing countries to apply them.

CONCLUSION

Twenty years after major aid providers began embracing political aid programming, many of them are starting to get serious about mainstreaming insights and approaches from their political work into traditional areas of socioeconomic focus. They usually formulate this task as "governance integration" and talk about inserting an understanding of and attention to governance in other sectors. Development agencies have already undertaken a number of steps to encourage integration through analytic tools, staff trainings, joint operational programs, and other efforts.

The integration agenda follows a strong logic—it clearly makes sense to ensure that the political and socioeconomic dimensions of aid programs work together to address complex development challenges. Yet, it nevertheless goes against the organizational grain of many aid providers, where separate silos have long operated on the political and socioeconomic sides, with rival budgets and separate subcultures. The conceptual argument persists over what integration means and what it would require. Integrating a democracy dimension, rather than just a governance dimension, into socioeconomic work remains a bridge too far politically for most aid organizations. At the same time, some specialized democracy aid groups are starting to look for ways to incorporate socioeconomic concerns into their work and build stronger ties to other development efforts.

The temptation of the technical continues to hold strong appeal within development agencies and can easily overwhelm nascent attempts at integrating political methods and goals within socioeconomic sectors, potentially rendering them superficial or even counterproductive. While the rising popularity of randomized trials as a way of testing program impact and learning about what works in development has usefully pushed the aid community forward in some respects, it also reinforces many of its technocratic instincts. Advocates of political approaches must continually make the case within their organizations that serious attention to political economy factors and a willingness to adapt to local circumstances is crucial to the success of all development programs. They simultaneously feel pressure to simplify their insights and tools to make them as widely applicable as possible and to advocate for investments in more rigorous studies. Managing this delicate balance will require committed leadership on the issue from the top and a willingness to tackle structural constraints as well as a sustained effort to change organizational culture.

CONCLUSION

CHAPTER 9

THE LONG ROAD TO POLITICS

INTRODUCTION

The road to politics in development aid—the journey away from early apolitical mindsets and approaches toward the incorporation of political thinking and action into both the goals and methods of assistance—has turned out to be remarkably long. It has stretched on already for at least five decades and an uncertain distance still lies ahead. Important movement has taken place along that road over the last twenty years, movement that may even constitute an unfolding revolution in the development enterprise. After long eschewing a commitment to political goals, the mainstream aid community now widely pursues such objectives alongside its efforts to help reduce poverty and foster socioeconomic development generally. After far too many years of relying on technocratic approaches that failed to either adapt to complex local contexts or to spark and sustain locally rooted processes of change, a growing number of practitioners within major aid organizations are taking seriously the challenge of operationalizing politically smart methods that do both.

Yet substantial as it is, progress along the political road is still only partial and in many ways tentative. Debates and doubts persist within development agencies about the value of political approaches and how far such changes can or should go. Worries among developmentalists about being "too political" remain common. Many people within aid-receiving countries are wary of donors' intentions when they talk about politics or attempt to act politically. Some elements of a multilateral effort to define principles of aid effectiveness may actually clash with politically smarter approaches. Moreover, changes in the overall international political context are undercutting some of the fundamental assumptions about the West's place in the world that helped open the door to politics in development in the first place. Nevertheless, moving further along the political road is both possible and necessary.

PROGRESS OVER THE DECADES

The initial apolitical cast of development aid was strong. As the mainstream aid community began operating in the 1950s and 1960s, it settled quickly on economic goals, above all trying to stimulate economic growth in the countries of what was then known as the Third World. Political purposes were certainly very much present in the rapidly growing new enterprise of foreign aid, led in those years by the United States and its major allies. Worried that Third World poverty might breed Third World communism, Western policymakers hoped that fostering economic development in poor countries would inoculate them from leftist subversion. But they pursued this broader political purpose as an extension of the core economic task of aid.

The swelling pool of economists, agronomists, public health experts, public administration specialists, and others who entered the ranks of newly established development agencies usually preferred to insulate their work from the specific political objectives of donor governments. They saw their true cause not as achieving certain political outcomes but as reducing economic misery in poor countries. They worried that in a Cold War context of acute sensitivities about Western political interventionism, directly associating aid with political goals would undercut its legitimacy and access. Moreover, the rising tide of authoritarianism in the developing world during the 1960s dampened hopes of easy political progress in the Third World and obliged aid providers to work mostly in repressive contexts where open discussion of political issues was forbidden.

The apolitical framework of development goals was matched by a technocratic outlook on methods. Aid providers operated under the assumption that the governments they were assisting—many of which were headed by first-time leaders of recently decolonized states—were committed to their countries' development and just needed more capital and the right technical knowledge to get there. And these were goods that Western aid organizations could provide. Development practitioners operated under a strong temptation to design and carry out their programs as technical endeavors free from political complications, and this apolitical approach quickly established itself as the dominant mode of operating. Aid agencies hired staff and established organizational practices, such as the core project method, based on the idea of aid as a mechanistic process proceeding from technical analysis, design, and planning to rationalistic, orderly implementation.

In the early 1970s rising attention to basic human needs grafted itself onto the 1960s orthodoxy of state-led economic takeoff. That orthodoxy was superseded in the 1980s by the overriding focus on market-centered or neoliberal approaches. But these broad changes in development frameworks did not overturn the underlying apolitical impulse, either with respect to goals or methods. If anything, they reinforced it, albeit in different ways. Some developmentalists tried to present the basic human needs agenda in broad political terms, as a transformative imperative to empower the poor and enable them to claim a greater share of their countries' wealth. But mainstream aid organizations approached this agenda much more technocratically, interpreting it as helping states deliver socioeconomic goods and services more effectively and to more people. The market-based development orthodoxy that took the development world by storm in the 1980s was formally agnostic about politics—it held that the key to development was getting governments, of whatever political stripe, to shrink their states and adopt certain market-friendly economic policies. It encouraged a belief in blueprint technical solutions to economic problems, bolstering the notion that the essence of external assistance is the provision of timely doses of capital and key morsels of policy knowledge.

Some development practitioners and scholars in those early years pushed back against this technocratic consensus. They pointed out that recipient government commitment to development could not be taken for granted, that Western institutional models and recommendations usually failed to take root in developing countries, and that carrying out development projects without even a vague idea of the relevant local political dynamics was an exercise in futility. They also highlighted the harmful effects for developing countries (and for donor legitimacy) of aid programs designed and implemented in ignorance of their political consequences. Yet these remained lonely voices in a development community deeply committed to technocracy.

The door to politics in development aid finally opened in the 1990s. Changed thinking about the application of the market approach in poor countries provided an initial push. Faced with the frequent experience of market policies floundering in developing countries because of weak state capacity to implement reforms, endemic corruption, and inadequate legal protections for market activity, the mainstream aid community embraced the need to strengthen state capacity. It quickly defined this imperative in terms of promoting good governance. Aid providers originally tried to construe strengthening governance as a technical endeavor. But once into the business of trying to change how states operate, they found themselves pulled into more political conceptions of the task.

The startling changes in the international context in those years opened the door to politics more fully. The end of the superpower rivalry, the apparent triumph of the Western economic and political model, and the dramatic spread of democracy in the non-Western world all encouraged Western governments to view political and socioeconomic development as mutually reinforcing processes and to use aid to advance political goals alongside socioeconomic ones. They began applying aid conditionality to further these ends. Mainstream aid organizations also constructed a whole new range of explicitly political aid programs aimed at fostering what they believed to be the constituent elements of democratic governance or democracy itself. They adopted these new goals out of parallel instrumental and intrinsic rationales: the belief that political reforms would contribute to the realization of aid's traditional socioeconomic goals and the conviction that building more transparent, inclusive, and accountable political systems was a worthwhile aid objective in and of itself.

As the goals of aid became more political, the methods gradually followed suit. The initial wave of programs that mainstream aid organizations designed to foster better governance and democratic change often operated from the same penchant for technical solutions as other areas of aid, emphasizing the transmission of technical knowledge and the export of Western institutional blueprints. Many such programs foundered on the complex shoals of developing country contexts where power holders often had little real interest in positive transformation or where Western models were a manifestly poor fit. In response, aid providers began getting politically smarter. They improved their understanding of local political realities, both through informal accumulation and application of political knowledge and more formal political economy analyses. They started trying to use assistance to facilitate processes of change rather than reproduce static institutional models, which led them to greatly expand the range of actors with which they worked. They shifted some aid toward the nongovernmental side in the hope of creating pressure for positive political change and stimulating innovations in governance from the bottom up. They developed more participatory approaches across the aid domain, taking much more seriously the idea of citizens rather than states being the essential locus of developmental change.

In the second half of the last decade, some practitioners and scholars committed to helping the aid community think and work more politically felt that existing efforts in this area were reaching significant limits and began pushing to go further in new ways. They have focused on politically smart assistance methods, trying to refine and widen the use of political analysis and explore more sophisticated ways of supporting processes of change. They are pushing for better integration of political thinking across assistance programming, trying to ensure that not just democracy and governance specialists but also health, education, agriculture, infrastructure, and other socioeconomic development experts implement programs in a politically informed fashion. Advocates of a strong place for political goals also hope to mainstream attention to governance (and often democracy and human rights) throughout development programming. Many have pointed to the Arab Awakening, in particular the fall of governments in Tunisia and Egypt that had been championed by some aid actors as economic reformers, as new proof of the importance of giving equal attention to the political dimensions of development.

In sum, development aid has traveled a considerable distance from its original apolitical framework. The aid world is today suffused with talk about the importance of politics in development, the need to take politics into account, and the value of working politically. And many efforts exist to translate that talk into action. Yet serious questions persist about the strength of this movement toward politics. Proponents of political approaches within aid organizations speak frequently in private about a continued sense of uphill struggle against entrenched mindsets and bureaucratic structures that remain wary of both political goals and methods. How far, in fact, has the aid community moved along the road to politics?

HOW FAR ON GOALS?

Every aid-receiving country now finds itself the recipient or (in the view of some host country governments) the target of at least some externally sponsored aid programs specifically designed to affect its political development.[1] These programs might be intended to improve the efficiency of the civil service, rationalize public financial management, assist the administration of elections, bolster constituency outreach by parliamentarians, strengthen independent television and radio stations, increase political participation by women, foster more interaction between villagers and their local governments, empower public interest advocacy groups, reform civic education, or do any number of other similar things. In quite a few developing countries, it is hard to find any sector relevant to political life where external aid actors are not involved at least to some extent.

Every major aid organization asserts some political goals alongside its socioeconomic ones. Most frame such goals with an emphasis on democratic governance or democracy and human rights. The World Bank, while formally prohibited by its charter from engaging in political work, nevertheless seeks to advance better governance in developing countries and interprets this goal in politically normative ways, stressing values such as accountability, transparency, and participation that conform closely with the democratic governance agenda of other aid providers.

Despite all this activity, political goals remain of secondary importance compared with the socioeconomic goals that have long made up the heart of the development aid endeavor. Totaling in the neighborhood of $10 billion annually, spending on political aid remains a modest share of overall aid flows, between 5 and 15 percent at most major aid organizations. More important, many aid programs that are formally categorized as political aid are in fact technocratic institutional reform efforts with only minimal political character. The general domain of "governance" covers an extremely wide range of issues, and there is a large difference in the degree of political content between a program designed to provide better equipment and training on evidence procedures to police officers and one aimed at mobilizing citizens to assert their rights to demand better services from the government. Additionally, mainstream aid organizations have been slow to integrate political goals into their socioeconomic programs, treating their work on democracy and governance as a distinct sector rather than an integral element of all areas of development. This leaves many large-scale aid activities only lightly touched by political objectives. It also means that aid providers make too little systematic effort to prevent their socioeconomic programs from doing democratic or governance harm—by helping legitimize autocratic regimes, putting excessive and competing demands on weak governments, skewing the accountability of civil society organizations, and much else.

In addition to these general limitations, the provision of political aid varies significantly across developing country contexts. Although at least some political aid programs reach every aid-receiving country, spending on democracy and governance programs is often highly concentrated in a few countries of heightened strategic concern to the major donors, leaving only small amounts of funding for countries whose profiles are not as high. Moreover, mainstream aid organizations are frequently willing to downplay their stated political goals for the sake of supporting socioeconomic progress in countries where politically noxious governments demonstrate some commitment to socioeconomic reforms (or are diplomatically helpful to donor governments). Aid providers' use of aid selectivity as a tool to further political goals is weak, with various other factors quite distant from democracy and governance dominating decisions about aid allocations.

Why does the fusion of political and socioeconomic goals in development aid remain so partial more than twenty years after the initial opening of aid to politics? The spirit of the early 1990s pointed to an urgent, compelling synthesis of economic and political concerns, with policymakers repeatedly declaring with evident conviction that democracy, good governance, and human rights are vital to development and that political and economic development naturally go hand in hand.

The answer has two main parts. First, Western donor governments have a wide range of interests that shape their relations with governments in the developing world, spanning a host of economic, strategic, diplomatic, cultural, and other issues. In many cases these interests point to a perceived need to get along with undemocratic or manifestly badly functioning governments—leading donors to put their stated interest of supporting democratic governance or democracy itself on the back burner. In other words, the imperative to support political goals is often trumped by other interests guiding the foreign policies of the main funders of development aid.

Second, even when countervailing interests are not present and the path is clear for aid providers to focus on political goals, many people within the mainstream aid organizations do not want to pursue such objectives. They are still either unsure about or actively against the view that helping countries improve their political life should be a priority for development aid, no matter what the official policy documents emanating from their organizations say. These skeptical voices are not convinced by the instrumental argument that certain types of political institutions and reforms are necessary for socioeconomic progress. Nor are they swayed by the intrinsic case for political goals.

Although they may agree that democratic governance is a good thing in many ways, they believe development aid should remain primarily focused on its traditional task of reducing poverty. And they do not accept an expanded conception of development that incorporates freedom and other political values as equal elements alongside the core socioeconomic agenda. In short, behind the doors of development agencies that formally support political goals as a way of furthering socioeconomic progress lie widely different beliefs about the wisdom and feasibility of such an approach. The significant and in some places rising distrust within developing countries toward donors pursuing political goals—rooted not just in authoritarian resistance but also a whole series of historical and contemporary experiences with political inconsistency, hypocrisy, and malfeasance on the part of donor governments—only reinforces these doubts among aid providers.

HOW FAR ON METHODS?

Most aid providers, especially in the last ten years, have come to recognize the shortcomings of solely technocratic methods of designing and implementing aid. They are making an effort to explore and adopt politically smarter methods. One manifestation of that change is their increasing use of analytic tools—whether in the form of political economy analyses,

governance assessments, conflict assessments, or stakeholder analyses—
to assess the political complexities of local contexts where they are operating or intend to operate. Another is the widespread shift away from a
default mode of treating developing country governments as near-exclusive
partners toward working extensively with nongovernmental actors in
such countries, not simply as substitute service providers for weak states
but as generators of ideas about and pressure for developmental progress.
An increasing number of aid efforts are specifically designed to take into
account the complex mix of interests and capacities of key local players and
to nurture and facilitate domestic processes of change. After fifty years of
repeatedly hearing the same overarching core "lesson learned"—that aid
should be tailored to the local context—aid providers are in many places
finally attempting to seriously act on it.

The movement toward politically smart methods is rooted in a strong aid
effectiveness rationale. Aid practitioners believe that thinking and working
more politically will help them better achieve their goals and overcome
once and for all the dismaying tendency of aid to perform poorly in the
face of unanticipated adverse political realities. Despite this compelling
logic, however, politically smart methods are still struggling to gain a wide
hold. Many practitioners continue to feel that political methods provide
insights without answers. They complain that political analyses can highlight likely obstacles or help explain why a development program has failed
to meet its goals but rarely illuminate a clear path to positive change. This
is partly a problem that can be solved through better focused analysis, and
donors have found that more specific problem- or sector-focused studies
tend to be more useful in practice than general country-level studies. But
at a deeper level, any political context is going to be complex and difficult
to navigate, and analyses will always be limited in the extent to which
they can provide definite operational answers. The same is true of process-
focused programs attempting to build coalitions of local actors to push for
specific developmental reforms. These efforts may be more likely to succeed
at changing policy than browbeating recipient governments with the same
politically infeasible recommendations for years on end, but they hold no
guarantees of success.

Politically informed methods thus imply a whole set of operational characteristics—such as flexibility, open-endedness, toleration of uncertainty,

labor intensiveness, significant investments in preparatory analysis, and devolution of control—that cut directly against many of the central imperatives and habits of mainstream aid organizations. Although political methods can be adopted incrementally as small-scale changes, taken together they represent a fundamental challenge to long-established ways of operating. Yet like the deep reserves of belief among many practitioners that development aid should focus on socioeconomic rather than political issues, the established edifice of institutional mindsets and mechanisms that control how aid is carried out has considerable staying power. It not only hinders wider adoption of political methods but also tends to dilute what new methods are put in place, leading, for example, to superficial political economy analyses or the reduction of bottom-up assistance into technocratic exercises that avoid core political obstacles.

HOW POLITICALLY ASSERTIVE?

The question of how far aid providers have moved along the road toward politics also raises the issue of donor assertiveness. Some observers express frustration over what they see as excessive caution or timidity on the part of most mainstream aid organizations concerning their political goals and methods. They point to various manifestations of this tendency:

- Most aid operates on the basis of direct, friendly partnerships with host governments in which aid providers refrain from blunt assessments of corruption, overly centralized power structures, and other problems and limit themselves to soft responses. Even though a political focus for aid arose in the 1990s out of the perceived need to overcome reform blockages within governing institutions, much such aid has ended up working politely around the edges of these very obstacles, often partnering with the sources of the problems.

- When aid providers reach out to the nongovernmental sector, they frequently limit themselves to comfortable circles of Western-oriented NGOs that pursue limited agendas for change that match the interests and perspectives of major donors. These groups generally confine themselves to unchallenging methods such as technical advice to government actors or participation in formal consultation processes, while avoiding more assertive strategies like mass mobilization, confrontation, and civil disobedience. Aid programs supporting change coalitions or other experiments with process-oriented mechanisms often emphasize cooperative assemblages of actors that seek only incremental change through legal or regulatory reform.

- Donor governments raise attention to key political issues as the importance of holding credible elections, but then impose no real negative consequences on governments that violate widely accepted international standards.

- Aid organizations pursue different elements of political aid in any one country mostly as sector-specific endeavors, such as media law reform, democratic civic education, or judicial strengthening. They do not design or implement them as elements of a larger strategy of deep-reaching political change, in which the various parts build on each other to exert significant pressure against existing power holders.

- Political aid focuses too much on the forms of political systems and not enough on the underlying power structures. Simply revising political forms without directly addressing the underlying socioeconomic roots of inequality, marginalization, and other fundamental problems will not produce meaningful pro-poor change.

There is considerable truth in these observations. Much of what mainstream aid providers do when they work politically is unassertive in some or all of these ways. Yet the fact that the politics agenda in aid remains relatively unassertive does not mean it is insignificant. Reshaping development aid so that it directly focuses on the reform of political institutions, works directly with civic actors to broaden the base of pressure for reform, operates from a genuine understanding of the local political realities, and focuses on facilitating local drivers of change is a significant advance, even if it remains largely nonconfrontational and often uncertain about how hard to push against obstacles to change.

Some Exceptions From Democracy Aid

There are, of course, exceptions regarding the general pattern of donor unassertiveness. First, in at least some cases, major Western aid organizations do deploy political aid in pointed ways to challenge recipient governments.

This usually occurs when an authoritarian or semiauthoritarian regime that the West has no reason to befriend is clearly driving its country to socio-economic ruin or is defying donor governments diplomatically on disputed political issues. Where such a strongman is facing an election—an election that he hopes will lend him legitimacy but which he clearly intends to manipulate enough to ensure his continuing hold on power—Western aid organizations sometimes pursue a politically tough strategy that challenges the government's effort to control the election. They do so by supporting independent domestic election monitors, opposition political parties, get-out-the-vote campaigns that target opposition strongholds, independent media, and civic activists calling attention to governmental wrongdoing. In some cases, these various parts contribute meaningfully to local move-ments that are exerting serious pressure on the government. Western aid to Serbian actors challenging Slobodan Milosevic in the run-up to the Serbian elections of 2000 represents the archetypical case of this type of aid (which was part of a larger Western diplomatic strategy of challenging Milosevic's rule). Other aid campaigns with at least some of these elements have unfolded in Chile in 1988, Slovakia in 1998, Georgia in 2003, Ukraine in 2004, and Belarus across multiple recent elections.[2]

Second, in various types of political contexts, mainstream donors some-times support enough local NGOs in enough different sectors of a country over a long enough time to help the NGO sector become a genuine coun-terweight to governmental power. This can occur even when the NGO sector is made up mostly of Western-funded groups with constrained agendas and methods. The extensive Western aid for the NGO sector in the Philippines is one such example. This support has continued for more than two decades, helping underwrite what has become in certain ways a politically assertive and capable sector, one that has strongly challenged successive presidents on corruption and other key issues. The extreme sen-sitivity of nondemocratic governments in Ethiopia, Russia, Zimbabwe, and elsewhere to Western funding of NGOs reflects how seriously they take the potential power of civil society.

Third, although most of the main aid agencies and foreign ministries that fund bilateral aid programs and the larger multilateral aid institu-tions are politically cautious, some Western governments fund organiza-tions specialized in political aid that operate at arm's length from these governmental development aid institutions and are able to be more openly political in their assistance. Examples of such organizations include the U.S. National Endowment for Democracy, the German and Swedish political foundations, and various European multiparty institutes devoted to political party support such as the Netherlands Institute for Multiparty Democracy, the Westminster Foundation for Democracy, the Danish Institute for Parties and Democracy, and (possibly) the new European Endowment for Democracy. These groups work directly with both ruling and opposition political parties in developing countries, often through sustained partnerships, and also sometimes with human rights activists and other local actors who are openly critical of their governments.

Explaining Non-Assertiveness

Examples of highly challenging political aid are largely confined to the democracy sphere, however, and usually do not extend to assertive political methods to promote socioeconomic development goals. Some academic critics on the left argue that the unassertiveness of much of the mainstream aid community's efforts reflects problematic Western political realities. Because Western aid providers proceed from an elite-based conception of democracy, they contend, one that often coexists with significant concentrations of socioeconomic power, their political aid inevitably tends to support liberal political and economic systems abroad that tolerate or even foster high levels of inequality, exclusion, and injustice. Political aid providers are thus sometimes willing to be assertive with regard to elections but are not willing to help poor people directly challenge political power structures in pursuit of economic redistribution.[3] In other words, an inclination toward democratic form over substance and unassertiveness vis-à-vis entrenched elites is baked into the assistance pie.

Other critics point to the fact that the aid community as a whole is still primarily rooted in a model of cooperative relations with host governments. While aid actors do reach out to non-state actors, they usually coordinate or clear those efforts with recipient governments. As a result they typically take a cautious line with regard to what sorts of nongovernmental actors they work with. Natural limits on the degree of political assertiveness are thus built into the basic structures of aid relationships.[4]

Both of these explanations have some validity. And there are other factors. The interest that donor governments have in the development of the countries to which they provide aid is simply not strong enough to induce them to engage in the difficult, risky, and unpopular business of directly challenging entrenched ruling elites in aid-receiving countries—even when donors do not have any larger strategic interests that point them toward maintaining good relations with problematic governments. Multilateral organizations such as the World Bank and UNDP are not directly subject to these kinds of bilateral foreign policy considerations but their accountability to a broad range of member states makes them if anything more cautious in dealing with recipient governments. Development aid lives with a punishing gap between the strength of the basic developmental interest that lies behind it and the strength of the forces that block progress toward development in many countries.

Furthermore, aid has sharp limits as a means of challenging entrenched power, above all the fact that it is fairly easily stopped if recipients feel threatened by it. The ongoing backlash against democracy assistance in a number of countries, including Bolivia, Egypt, Ethiopia, Russia, and Uzbekistan, highlights the fact that when host governments start to feel that external aid may actually create serious pressure for change, they will erect barriers to such aid, whether by enacting tight restrictions on aid actors, arresting them, or expelling them.

And finally, while it is certainly true that the existing power structures in many developing countries are an obstacle to economic development, it is far from certain that aid could lead to a significant reordering of such structures. Also unclear is whether the new order emerging from such a fundamental restructuring would in fact be more developmental. In other words, even if aid providers were determined to somehow change the core power structure in a society and get to the roots of its developmental shortcomings, they lack the kind of definite knowledge about how such foundational change might occur. Vague ideas about mass-based popular empowerment or sweeping socioeconomic redistribution are insufficient in this regard. The "good guys/bad guys" mentality that motivated much early thinking around reform champions and demand-side work—the idea that aid providers should support altruistic reform-oriented actors in pressuring entrenched antidevelopmental elites—has proved too simplistic.

Instead, practitioners increasingly recognize that developmental change is a complex process that requires the buy-in of many different actors and can happen in multiple ways. The key question is thus not necessarily how assertive aid actors can be but how serious they are in thinking through possible entry points and acting consistently and in a sustained way to advance developmental political reform.

CLASHING AID EFFECTIVENESS AGENDAS

Greater aid effectiveness is one of the driving motivations behind the movement to make aid more political. Surprisingly and unfortunately, however, some of the major elements of the formal international aid effectiveness agenda (enshrined first in the 2005 Paris Declaration on Aid Effectiveness and then in related follow-up accords at Accra in 2008 and Busan in 2011) and of corresponding reform efforts within development agencies complicate political approaches. These trends—including the emphasis on country ownership, accomplishing more with fewer resources, and demonstrating results—could in theory be entry points for more attention to politics. But in practice they are interpreted in ways which tend to work against the movement to embed political goals and methods into development aid.

Promoting Country Ownership

The principle of country ownership, a mainstay of the Paris process, represents a fraught issue for the politics agenda. On the one hand, recognizing the central role of governments in their countries' development is fundamental to a more political conception of development assistance. The critical insight of the 1990s that aid needs to be locally rooted helped drive the rediscovery of the state as well as more participatory and bottom-up approaches. It reflected the idea that sustainable development progress comes not from the accumulation of isolated independent projects—build a school in one village, set up a health clinic in another, push a specific economic reform— but from building up effective institutions and strengthening local capacity. It also constitutes long overdue recognition that it is domestic actors and not donor governments that should be setting priorities and development plans.

Moreover, if recipient governments are to have more direct control over the aid resources flowing into their countries, it is only natural that donors become increasingly concerned with how they are governed and learn more about how to influence them. These factors point clearly both to greater incorporation of political goals related to governance and an enhanced need for political understanding.

On the other hand, in the multilateral process leading up to the Paris Principles, country ownership came to be conceived as giving recipient governments more control over aid with fewer conditions attached or questions asked. This was a response to the highly problematic and often counterproductive conditionality of the 1980s and 1990s, but it also represented in some ways a swing back to the prevailing aid ethos of the 1960s: assume that governments are well-intentioned and give them the resources and flexibility to use aid to promote the development of their countries. Under this understanding, country ownership can cut against efforts by aid providers to pursue political goals that involve challenges to problematic power holders. It can also hinder attempts at critical political analysis or operational methods that reach beyond the host government to engage with other domestic actors. Where aid-receiving governments oppose democracy or governance programming, it can further impede those objectives.

If country ownership is interpreted differently, as implying society-wide or democratic ownership rather than host government ownership, then the conflict recedes.[5] Yet while the various aid effectiveness declarations coming out of Paris, Accra, and Busan acknowledge the importance of societal forces outside the government, they continue to be widely interpreted as prioritizing host country governments—particularly executive branches—and the use of governmental systems in aid delivery. A number of major aid providers, such as DFID, have backed away at least somewhat from direct budget support after initial enthusiasm at the beginning of the Paris process, but country ownership remains the rhetorical backdrop of most international aid discussions.

Doing More With Less

Also associated with the larger push on aid effectiveness is ever-greater pressure on aid organizations to "do more with less." This usually means reducing administrative management costs while maintaining or even increasing program expenditures. For example, DFID's program budget has increased significantly over the last several years while its operating budget has not moved in parallel fashion. The World Bank has lived for over a decade with a flat administrative budget and considerable internal pressure to do more with less. The shaky public support for development assistance in most donor countries creates a strong imperative to show skeptical publics that aid providers are operating efficiently.

Yet for development agencies, operating in politically smart ways can entail new administrative costs, whether for more analyses, additional staff time to manage augmented relationships with local actors, or new specialists to cover areas of knowledge not well developed within the organizations. Proponents of the politics agenda argue that overall they *can* do more with less, in terms of achieving better development results with fewer total resources. It is cheaper to fight corruption in the justice sector by supporting some capable nongovernmental organizations focused on judicial corruption than to mount a traditional large-scale training program for judges on why corruption is a bad thing, an intervention that is likely to be both expensive and ineffective. Yet this more political approach might entail new administrative costs or a higher ratio of administrative to program costs than a technical assistance program and thus run afoul of the imperative to operate more efficiently. In short, praiseworthy though it sounds in theory, "doing more with less" can end up working against needed innovations within aid agencies to make greater use of politically smarter methods. Over the longer term, it can result in the preservation of old habits that entail doing less with more.

Proving Results

Perhaps the most challenging element of current debates around aid effectiveness for the politics agenda is the sharply heightened imperative to define, monitor, and assess results with a high degree of precision. This movement has seized most mainstream aid organizations as they seek to justify their value to skeptical publics and parliaments, becoming an enormous preoccupation in donor circles that is consuming an ever-increasing amount of time and energy. Theoretically, closer attention to results could encourage the use of more political goals and methods. Given that project success is often hindered by political obstacles, practitioners should have greater incentive to invest in prior political analysis and craft more politically informed interventions if they know they will be held closely accountable for their results. Interpreting the results agenda more broadly than just assessing specific projects to encompass learning about what types of approaches and strategies work well in what contexts could highlight the importance of political methods and build the evidence base on the relationship between political and socioeconomic outcomes.

Yet as the focus on "results management" takes hold in the aid community, it unfortunately usually manifests itself in ways that reduce rather than increase space for the flexibility and innovation in aid programming crucial to incorporating political goals and methods. As discussed in the previous chapter, the growing enthusiasm around randomized control trials as a means for rigorous project assessment poses a number of challenges for political aid programs. But even outside such experimental techniques, project evaluation frequently takes shape as close, sometimes myopic scrutiny of the near-term impact of specific projects, while neglecting the accumulation of broader learning about how aid works and how it can be improved.

Tightly constructed monitoring and evaluation schemes require aid providers to accept only outcomes that can be narrowly defined and quantitatively measured, to impose precise, usually short-term, timetables and to insist on clear, direct lines of expected attribution between aid input and predetermined developmental outcomes. Such schemes may work for some technical interventions. But politically focused, process-oriented programs usually have more open-ended, less easily quantifiable intended outcomes, require greater flexibility and time in implementation to match the serpentine nature of local political reform processes, and involve issues where the causality of intended effect is likely to be blurred by complex clusters of explanatory variables. Moreover, the more deeply aid interventions immerse themselves in locally rooted processes of change, and the wider their reach across diverse local actors, the more difficult and also politically sensitive it becomes to ascribe causal effects and take credit for successes.

Proponents of political approaches contend that they can define goals and assess results with rigor but need more flexibility than is often allowed in the new focus on clear, quantifiable results. In an in-depth study of the challenges of evaluating politically oriented aid programming, Chris Roche and Linda Kelly criticize the one-sided emphasis on quantitative assessments and randomized control trials, arguing instead for utilizing a mix of evaluative methods that better fits the complexities of more politically oriented approaches:

> [E]xperience suggests that performance assessment of programs engaged in working politically, and through networks of development actors, require[s] different sorts of assessments at different points of time, and across various different domains of programs. ... The challenge is to ensure that donors and those they work with, or through, have the range of skills, knowledge and expertise to be able to draw upon an appropriate mix and range of methods that such an approach to assessment requires.[6]

Roche and Kelly set forward and analyze a number of different potential methods, which can be used separately or together, including network mapping, quasi-experimental approaches (attempting to establish a counterfactual without randomization), narrative analysis, participatory evaluations, and action-reflection studies. In *Evaluating Democracy Assistance*, Krishna Kumar further probes the frequent pitfalls of applying to political programs evaluation methods that were designed for technocratic socioeconomic assistance efforts. Kumar also proposes an eclectic approach that fully takes into account the complexities of change processes and the difficulty of causal attribution when aid programs utilize political methods.[7] Yet donors have yet to demonstrate that they are willing to invest in these kinds of sophisticated mixed-method evaluation techniques, especially when results may be longer in coming and more difficult to interpret.

THE SHIFTING INTERNATIONAL GROUND

The opening to politics in development aid gained impetus from the optimistic international political, economic, and strategic landscape that emerged in the early 1990s and seemed to point to an emergent liberal world order. Yet fundamental facilitating elements of that landscape are now in question or already overturned.

To start with, the sense of triumph about the Western political and economic model that so strongly fueled the optimism of the early 1990s is gone. Both the United States and Europe have taken significant hits to their credibility as global models in the past five to ten years. The United States suffered grave damage to its reputation as a country that respects the rule of law and human rights during the last decade as a result of its detention facility at Guantánamo Bay, the scandal relating to the Abu Ghraib prison, drone strikes, and many other elements of U.S. counterterrorism policies. Additionally, blame for triggering the global financial crisis in 2008 and the discouraging picture from recent years of a political system beset by polarization and gridlock have contributed to growing doubts in many quarters about the health of U.S. economic and political governance. The protracted European economic crisis and its attendant sociopolitical woes, as well as the loss of impetus for European unification, mean that Europe is faring no better in the world's eyes.

In addition, alternative forms of governance that depart significantly from Western models are now attracting global attention. Aid-receiving countries are actively engaging with other international actors to learn about and sometimes adopt elements of their governance approaches. China in particular is clearly an appealing model for many leaders who are interested in promoting development (or appearing to promote development) but are skeptical of democratic governance prescriptions. The relative developmental success of some nondemocratic governments in Africa such as Rwanda reinforces this view. In the Arab world, the emergence of Islamist-led governments through elections in Tunisia and Egypt has further weakened earlier assumptions about the triumph of the Western liberal model.

The place of Western aid in the international system is also no longer what it was two decades ago. Development aid from OECD donor governments is still significant, amounting to more than $100 billion per year annually. Yet it constitutes well under one-third of total capital flows to developing countries, significantly outstripped by private capital. The large majority of private investment goes to East and South Asian developing countries, but Africa and Latin America have also seen steep increases in foreign direct investment over the past decade.[8] In addition, remittances to developing countries now exceed $400 billion per year.[9] China has become a major lender and investor in Africa and other parts of the developing world. It is still a relatively small donor in terms of traditional development assistance but its aid budget is increasing and in a few countries rivals or exceeds Western assistance.[10] South-South cooperation more generally, both with regard to aid and to trade and investment, is on the rise.[11] Traditional donors have acknowledged these trends, at least rhetorically, and called for rethinking assistance in a world where development is driven primarily by non-aid factors and where rising global powers will play an increasingly important role.[12]

Additionally, the suddenly greater openness in the 1990s toward external actors working across borders on sensitive political issues—what was framed as part of a broader phenomenon in international relations of a generalized decline of sovereignty—is no more. Concerns about sovereignty and efforts to safeguard it are once again on the rise in today's international environment. Sensitivity, skepticism, and outright hostility toward politically related assistance began spreading in the last decade in what became and continues to be a serious backlash against such assistance. Thus even as proponents of political approaches push mainstream aid agencies to incorporate and pursue political goals more vigorously, those organizations operate in a world where a growing number of recipient governments are less and less receptive to externally generated actions that might be seen as challenges to their rule. Even domestic actors who might once have been receptive to political aid are increasingly skeptical. The mixed record of democracy and governance assistance in producing positive results—particularly with respect to helping shaky democratic systems consolidate their institutions and deliver the goods for their citizens—has diminished enthusiasm in many places about what such programs can contribute. The too often clumsy and uncoordinated implementation of such aid has also hurt its legitimacy.

Of course, not all positive propulsive elements of the international context of the early 1990s have faded. The rise of civil society in most parts of the developing world, which has opened up many new potential partnerships for aid providers and made bottom-up political change a more widespread reality, is still unfolding. The spread of enhanced communications methods resulting from the information technology revolution continues, facilitating the dissemination of political ideas and increased cooperation across borders. The notable expansion of and innovation in work relating to social accountability in the developing world—due in some part to aid programs but more importantly to the efforts of domestic actors—reflects the influence of these two continuing trends. Yet it remains a sobering fact that while aid actors have been slowly working out over the last twenty years how to fully act on the crucial breakthrough regarding political thinking and action in aid, the ground that initially fostered this opening has shifted under their feet, creating yet further obstacles and challenges.

GOING FURTHER

The movement over the last two decades to incorporate political thinking and action into development aid is not a fad. It is not one more item in the seemingly ever-changing series of development fashions that capture the attention of aid providers before quickly fading away. It is, potentially at least, a fundamental advance in the aid community's conception of the substance and process of development itself and how outside actors can play a useful role. But as we have attempted to show in this book, it remains a partially realized revolution, at best. The surge of momentum that surrounded the opening of the door to politics in the 1990s has led to many changes in policy and practice but still falls short of systematic incorporation of political goals or methods into the overall development aid enterprise.

Some practitioners and scholars who believe strongly in the political agenda are deeply uncertain and frustrated about its prospects. They feel the weight of the obstacles blocking the way forward, including the countervailing incentives, habits, and mindsets within development agencies as well as the headwinds arising from adverse developments in the larger international political context. They question whether it is possible for aid providers to fully internalize political thinking within programs or if nascent political efforts will be overwhelmed by technocracy. Some believe that the development enterprise remains the "anti-politics machine" James Ferguson described nearly two decades ago, destined to depoliticize everything it touches and fundamentally incapable of taking politics seriously.[13]

Political advocates further wonder if mainstream aid organizations will ever pursue their stated political goals with anything like the commitment that they show to their socioeconomic goals. They also disagree among themselves about what going further should mean. Proponents of more political methods sometimes feel that being politically smart actually points toward the need to seriously question conventional political goals, such as achieving Western-style governance. Enthusiasts of political goals are divided with regard to the relative priority they attach to democracy, governance, and rights. They further differ on whether they believe that their political goals should be considered part of the definition of development, or as valuable elements separate from a conventional socioeconomic conception of development.

Despite these challenges, we believe that going further on both political goals and methods is both necessary and possible. Aid organizations have many frustratingly persistent limitations as drivers of developmental progress—ranging from instinctively technocratic outlooks and inflexible structures to clumsy implementation and resources inadequate to the magnitude of the challenges they are trying to address. But the recent evolution toward more political goals and methods in development aid has not been trivial. And as long as donors continue to spend tens of billions of dollars a year in assistance, it remains crucial to try to improve aid practice, with all the constraints and frustrations that entails.

A transformative leap toward much greater attention to politics in development aid in the future is highly unlikely. A focus on small, iterative steps connected to a larger framework of ambition is the better approach. Despite the various ways that political goals and methods can be separated, we believe that the record of the past twenty years demonstrates that they ultimately do have deep interconnections and should be pursued as complementary efforts.

On Goals

A more robust approach to the pursuit of political goals will require building greater consensus about what political goals development agencies can and should pursue. This will depend on whether the core rationales for the political side of development aid gain wider acceptance among mainstream aid practitioners and their partners in developing countries. We believe that the intrinsic case for embracing democratic governance or democracy as a development goal is powerful. Political conditions within a country affect human welfare as much as economic conditions do, and Amartya Sen's argument for conceiving of political freedom as part of human development is persuasive. Surveys consistently show that citizens in developing countries value or aspire to freedom, the rule of law, accountability, and other core elements of democratic governance, including democracy itself. They are also generally unhappy with how their political systems currently operate.[14] It is true that political goals put development actors into the role of making normative choices, but so, too, do economic goals. When aid providers make choices about the relative level of emphasis to put on economic growth versus equity, or investments in health versus education, they are swimming in normative waters as deep and murky as those surrounding political goals. Importantly, choosing *not* to pursue or pay attention to political goals is also a normative choice. If development actors continue to fund governments that routinely violate democratic standards, they risk supporting that behavior, no matter what their claims to technocratic neutrality. If donors do not pay attention to the impact of their own programs on human rights or drivers of conflict, they are also making political choices, whether they acknowledge them or not.

With regard to the instrumental case for a politics lens on development, the research picture regarding the impact of democratic governance or democracy on socioeconomic development is, as analyzed in chapter 7, mixed. We believe that it makes sense to view this unclear analytic glass as half full rather than half empty. There is substantial evidence that politics has significant and multiple impacts on socioeconomic outcomes and that capable, accountable, and pro-poor governance is centrally important, even if the amount of very specific knowledge under that general finding is not yet what practitioners need.

Closing the door to the political side due to a lack of clear-cut answers would make little sense, especially since understanding of the social and economic sides of development also continues to evolve. The answers that may emerge over time on the political-economic nexus will likely not point to any simple conclusions wholly supporting or opposing the basic instrumental case for political aid. Instead, researchers working at the cutting edge of the issue converge around the complexity of the relationship and the need for nuanced context-specific answers and approaches. It seems almost certain that a fuller understanding of these issues will only deepen the imperatives for greater attention to politics in the development enterprise and more sophisticated integration of political and socioeconomic perspectives. What is all too clear is that socioeconomic programs ignore governance issues—whether this means absent performance management in hospitals, corruption in food delivery, or poor road maintenance—at their own peril.

In the midst of uncertainty about the overall relationship between governance and development, it makes sense to err on the side of aid programs that expand space for democratic governance and respect for human rights. There is little evidence that democratic governance or democracy is *bad* for socioeconomic progress. To the extent that elections or other elements of democracy are associated with conflict and political fragmentation, it is unclear that there is a viable authoritarian alternative that would work better. This does not mean that the good governance paradigm should be mechanistically applied in every development project. Citizen participation will not automatically solve corruption, inclusive consultation processes can sometimes slow down decisionmaking, and elections by themselves are not sufficient mechanisms of accountability.

But efforts to enhance the transparency and accountability of governments on a systemic level—to create a more inclusive society, to allow a place for substantive citizen participation in decisions that affect their lives, to increase government responsiveness—are all likely to improve development outcomes. Moreover, strengthening legitimate democratic processes remains the only way to escape the enduring quandary of country ownership: aid programs require domestic buy-in to function effectively but donors in autocratic countries lack partners who can speak for society.[15] The various efforts aid providers have made to overcome this dilemma through technocratic measures—such as setting up artificial consultative processes that reach only a narrow band of civil society actors—have failed to provide broad legitimacy or sustainable domestic commitments.

Betting on developmental authoritarians is also a dangerous game. Donors have a long history of embracing governments that appear to be committed to their country's development, only to get burned somewhere down the road. Tunisia and Egypt are the most recent examples of governments that seemed to be making developmental progress without corresponding political progress but then crumbled when accumulated citizen discontent erupted. Others have suffered less dramatic but still highly troubling falls from grace. Uganda, for example, attracted large amounts of aid as a result of its perceived effectiveness in fighting HIV/AIDS, but recent performance declines and corruption scandals have put that record into serious question.[16] Even Rwanda, the paradigmatic case of developmental authoritarianism in Africa, has proved to be a problematic aid partner. While development results continue to be strong, Rwandan support to rebels in the Democratic Republic of Congo as well as persistent human rights violations are putting pressure on donors to rethink their assistance policies.[17]

Going further on political goals is mostly about aid organizations fulfilling commitments they have repeatedly made on paper or in public declarations. This would entail multiple interrelated measures:

- Maintaining spending on the political side of the aid ledger and striving to distribute it more according to political needs and the opportunity for positive impact and less in service of other, divergent interests.

- Strengthening support for the political agenda at the top level of major aid organizations, including greater efforts by senior leaders to communicate to staff that political goals are a substantive and not just rhetorical priority.

- Taking forward the still nascent initiatives at most mainstream aid providers to integrate democracy and governance approaches and perspectives into the full spectrum of programming.

- Investing in the necessary internal organizational resources for staff training in political programming, both to increase specialized knowledge about such assistance and to spread greater understanding of it among all practitioners.

- Ensuring that all aid programs are designed and implemented with full awareness of their potential impact on domestic political systems, especially harm to democracy or human rights.

- Minimizing the trading away of political goals for the sake of near-term socioeconomic objectives in countries with politically problematic leaders that are showing some signs of economic success, including maintaining serious conversations with such governments on political shortcomings even when working with them on other matters.

- Engaging more actively with a wider range of people in aid-receiving countries to develop a greater shared understanding of the proper role and potential value of donor political goals.

On Methods

With respect to the methods of assistance, going further is largely a question of putting into more systematic practice the insights and ideas raised by thoughtful observers for decades about the deep shortcomings of technocratic approaches. It is astonishing, for example, that debates persist within major aid organizations about whether investing the needed resources to gain a strong understanding of the political realities of a particular local or national context before proceeding to invest or implement aid programs there is worthwhile. It is equally remarkable that more than fifty years into the aid endeavor, development practitioners still often rely on the old default method of trying to model institutions in other societies to conform to Western examples.

Going further on political methods will not be achieved through any single advance. It must entail the continued application of insights and innovations on multiple practical fronts. But it must also be underpinned by a coherent vision of what politically smarter methods require rather than the haphazard adoption of certain superficial aspects of the agenda. Making progress involves taking forward the central elements of political methods—improving political understanding, working with a greater diversity of local actors, and using aid to facilitate domestically driven processes—and trying to incorporate them more widely in development programs. But as we have seen, particularly with regard to demand-side methods, some of these elements can be interpreted in rather apolitical ways that take on board a political insight (for example, citizen pressure can lead to better governance) but fail to ground it in a broader understanding of the political context or the realistic prospects for change.

There is no single model for good political methods. Development practitioners should be armed with the best political analysis possible; they must also be aware that no study can tell them exactly how political actors in any particular country will behave and that they will need to adapt to changing circumstances. Aid programs should engage with a greater variety of partners in recipient countries; they must also understand that no particular set of partners can speak for "society" as a whole or is likely to fully share donor priorities. And aid providers should try to insert themselves into and productively influence local processes of change, but with an understanding that this could lead in multiple directions and requires some real willingness to allow local actors to take the lead rather than try to engineer "country-owned" results through artificially constructed processes.

Even within the context of current structural constraints, development actors who want to move forward on political methods can take a number of steps, several of which have already contributed to significant progress within some aid organizations:

- Increasing the use of analytic tools to gain a better understanding of the political dimensions of developing country contexts.

- Making fuller use of sources of political knowledge within recipient countries beyond formal analyses, including the insights of local staff and research institutes.

- Increasing staff training on political tools and fostering more open discussions among staff across sectors about the political challenges they face in their work and experiences gained in the productive use of political methods.

- Hiring or training more staff with the expertise and mandate to support improved political understanding and engagement.

- Incorporating political insights more seriously into strategic planning processes for country programming and combating the tendency to plan interventions without an understanding of the underlying political dynamics of the country in question.

- Moving fully away from treating developing country governments as sole development partners to a broader conception of developing country societies as natural aid partners.

- Rewarding practitioners for taking risks and for trying to engage directly with local processes of political and developmental change, and holding staff accountable for the broader outcomes of their programs, not just narrow outputs.

- Investing in evaluation techniques well suited to illuminate the impact of politically informed interventions on complex development processes.

- Creating institutional space for programming that is genuinely long term, adaptable to changes on the ground, and process-oriented.

Navigating the Headwinds

Those practitioners and scholars trying to take the politics agenda forward have to confront the daunting implications of the current aid context. The shift from the optimistic times of the early 1990s is both striking and sobering. Yet within these challenges may be opportunities to rethink development aid. Rising competition on the international stage regarding political governance models and the presence of more actors exerting political influence across borders could force Western aid providers to up their game politically, both in terms of seriously pursuing their values and genuinely understanding local processes of political change. The declining relative weight of Western aid in the international marketplace of resources could stimulate aid providers to focus more on leveraging the resources they do apply, encouraging politically smart methods instead of old habits rooted in the assumption of a naturally dominant role for Western aid providers. The new tensions and pushback over how much political space is open to aid providers should prompt them to sharpen their responses to resistance and engage aid-receiving countries more thoughtfully in mutual conversations about the means and ends of assistance where space for such discussions exists.

Of course, only so much opportunity exists in adversity. The way forward is certain to be daunting. At the end of the day, development actors need to decide whether they are willing to face this challenge. Political methods and goals do not provide any magic bullets—developmental change is always complex and usually difficult. Although political approaches are not sufficient for sustainable development progress, there is good evidence that taking politics more fully into account is necessary. Proponents of going further who are daunted by the many difficulties and delays on the road to politics can perhaps take some comfort in the fact that rapid revolutions of any type, whether they occur in entire countries or just in individual institutions, often go off track and end up reversed. Slow, sustained pursuit of change, marked by the gradual accumulation of iterative gains and a steady adherence to core principles, is ultimately the more likely way to achieve deep and lasting change, both in development aid and in those countries it seeks to assist.

NOTES

CHAPTER 1

1 Adrian Leftwich, "Bringing Agency Back In: Politics and Human Agency in Building Institutions and States: Synthesis and Overview Report," Research Paper 6 (Developmental Leadership Program, June 2009), 13.

CHAPTER 2

1 Samuel Huntington, *Political Order in Changing Societies* (New Haven, Conn.: Yale University Press, 1968).

2 Harry Truman, "Inaugural Address," Washington, D.C., January 20, 1949.

3 John F. Kennedy, "Special Message to the Congress on Foreign Aid," March 22, 1961, The American Presidency Project, University of California, Santa Barbara, available at www.presidency.ucsb.edu/ws/?pid=8545.

4 Lipset himself warned that the existence of a connection between these factors and democracy did not mean that economic development would necessarily lead to democracy in all cases, but these cautions were not always heeded. See Seymour Martin Lipset, "Some Social Requisites of Democracy: Economic Development and Political Legitimacy," *American Political Science Review*, vol. 53, no. 1 (March 1959): 69–105.

5 Robert Packenham, *Liberal America and the Third World: Political Development Ideas in Foreign Aid and Social Science* (Princeton, N.J.: Princeton University Press, 1973).

6 For further discussion of the Harrod-Domar model and its future implications for development policy, see William Easterly, "The Ghost of Financing Gaps: How the Harrod-Domar Growth Model Still Haunts Development Economics," Working Paper 1870 (Washington, D.C.: World Bank, July 1997). Also see Robert Solow, "Perspectives on Growth Theory," *Journal of Economic Perspectives*, vol. 8, no. 1 (Winter 1994): 45–54.

7 W. W. Rostow, *The Stages of Economic Growth: A Non-Communist Manifesto* (Cambridge: Cambridge University Press, 1990), 7–8.

8   Hollis Chenery and Alan Strout, "Foreign Assistance and Economic Development," *American Economic Review*, vol. 56, no. 4 (September 1966): 679–733.

9   Rostow, *The Stages of Economic Growth.*

10 Chenery and Strout, "Foreign Assistance and Economic Development," 729.

11 Anthony Downs, *An Economic Theory of Democracy* (New York: Harper and Row, 1957), 284.

12 Christopher Adam and Stefan Dercon, "The Political Economy of Development: An Assessment," *Oxford Review of Economic Policy*, vol. 25, no. 2 (2009): 175.

13 David Lindauer and Lant Pritchett, "What's the Big Idea? The Third Generation of Policies for Economic Growth," *Economía*, vol. 3, no. 1 (Fall 2002): 4–5.

14 See Arthur Goldsmith, "Institutions and Planned Socioeconomic Change: Four Approaches," *Public Administration Review*, vol. 52, no. 6 (November-December 1992): 582–87.

15 Committee on Institutional Cooperation, *Building Institutions to Serve Agriculture: A Summary Report of the CIC-AID Rural Development Research Project* (Lafayette, Ind.: Purdue University Press, 1968).

16 James Gardner, *Legal Imperialism: American Lawyers and Foreign Aid in Latin America* (Madison: University of Wisconsin Press, 1980).

17 David Trubek and Marc Galanter, "Scholars in Self-Estrangement: Some Reflections on the Crisis in Law and Development Studies in the United States," *Wisconsin Law Review*, vol. 4, no. 1 (1974): 1062–1102, and Gardner, *Legal Imperialism.*

18 Gardner, *Legal Imperialism.*

19 Trubek and Galanter, "Scholars in Self-Estrangement."

20 Gardner, *Legal Imperialism.*

21 Devesh Kapur, John Lewis, and Richard Webb, *The World Bank: Its First Half Century* (Washington, D.C.: Brookings Institution, 1997), 209–10.

22 Donald Fraser, "New Directions in Foreign Aid," *World Affairs*, vol. 129, no. 4 (January–February–March 1967): 244–45.

23 U.S. Congress, Senate Committee on Foreign Relations and Committee on International Relations, *Legislation on Foreign Relations Through 2002* (Washington, D.C.: U.S. Government Printing Office, 2003), 142.

24 Packenham, *Liberal America and the Third World*, 104.

25 William Gaud, "A.I.D. Progress Toward Title IX Objectives," Statement before the House Foreign Affairs Committee, March 20, 1968, in *Increasing Participation in Development: Primer on Title IX of the United States Foreign Assistance Act* (Washington, D.C.: U.S. Agency for International Development, 1970), 43.

26 USAID, *Increasing Participation in Development.*

27 Packenham, *Liberal America and the Third World.*

28 See USAID, "Report to the Congress on Implementation of Title IX, 1967," in *Increasing Participation in Development*, 45. For a broader critique of the feasibility of democracy promotion, see Packenham, *Liberal America and the Third World*, 190.

29 George Axinn, "The Application of the Institution Building Model: An Overview of IB Programs," paper presented at the Special Session on Institution Building Abroad at the annual meeting of the Rural Sociological Society (Washington, D.C.: 1970).

30 Joel Bernstein, "Institutions and the Political, Social, and Economic Development," in *Institution Building: A Reader*, edited by Amy Mann (Bloomington, Ind.: Program of Advanced Studies in Institution Building and Technical Assistance Methodology, 1975), 5.

31 Committee on Institutional Cooperation, *Building Institutions to Serve Agriculture: A Summary Report of the CIC-AID Rural Development Research Project*, 9–10.

32 C. S. Gulick, "Effectiveness of AID: Evaluation Findings of the World Bank, the Inter-American Bank, U.S. Agency for International Development and the Canadian International Development Agency," draft, August 3, 1984, II–42.

33 Gardner, *Legal Imperialism*.

34 Ibid., 261.

35 Albert Hirschman, *Development Projects Observed* (Washington, D.C.: Brookings Institution, 1967).

36 Ibid., 22.

37 Ian Hamnett, "A Social Scientist Among Technicians," *IDS Bulletin*, vol. 3, no. 1 (October 1970): 24–29.

38 Ibid.

39 Ibid.

40 Hirschman, *Development Projects Observed*, 180.

41 Roger Riddell, *Foreign Aid Reconsidered* (Baltimore: Johns Hopkins University Press, 1987).

42 Kapur et al., *The World Bank: Its First Half Century*.

43 UN General Assembly, *Declaration on the Establishment of a New International Economic Order*, A/RES/S-6/3201, May 1, 1974.

44 Marcos Cueto, "The Origins of Primary Health Care and Selective Primary Health Care," *American Journal of Public Health*, vol. 94, no. 11 (November 2004): 1864–74.

45 *Declaration of Alma-Ata*, International Conference on Primary Health Care, Alma-Ata, USSR, September 6–12, 1978.

46 Overseas Development Institute, "Basic Needs," Briefing Paper no. 5 (London: Overseas Development Institute, December 1978), and Paul Streeten, *First Things First: Meeting Basic Human Needs in Developing Countries* (Washington, D.C.: Oxford University Press and World Bank, 1981).

47 David Morrison, *Aid and Ebb Tide: A History of CIDA and Canadian Development Assistance* (Waterloo, Ontario: Wilfrid Laurier University Press, 1998).

48 Overseas Development Institute, "Basic Needs."

49 Kapur et al., *The World Bank: Its First Half Century*, and Streeten, *First Things First*.

50 Kapur et al., *The World Bank: Its First Half Century*.

51 The Overseas Development Institute explained in 1978 that "in some developing countries, but *in only a few and not those containing many of the world's poor*, aid donors may have sufficient leverage that pressure by them might have a significant effect in altering the recipient government's policy in respect of Basic Needs" (emphasis added). Overseas Development Institute, "Basic Needs," 3–4. For an account of the World Bank's policy advocacy efforts in Brazil, see Kapur et al., *The World Bank: Its First Half Century*.

52 Kapur et al., *The World Bank: Its First Half Century*.

53 Ibid.

54 Streeten, *First Things First*, 58.

55 Overseas Development Institute, "Basic Needs."

56 Ibid.

57 Morrison, *Aid and Ebb Tide*.

58 World Bank, "The World Bank and Institutional Development: Experience and Directions for Future Work," Working Paper 14483 (Washington, D.C.: World Bank, 1980), 4.

59 World Bank, "The World Bank and Institutional Development: Experience and Directions for Future Work," 8.

60 Kapur et al., *The World Bank: Its First Half Century*.

61 See Johnny Morris, "Evsum438: Synthesis of Integrated Rural Development Projects" (London: Department for International Development, 1999); USAID Armenia, "Integrated Rural Development: Lessons Learned" (Washington, D.C.: U.S. Agency for International Development); and Krishna Kumar, "A.I.D.'s Experience With Integrated Rural Development Projects," A.I.D. Program Evaluation Report no. 19 (Washington, D.C.: U.S. Agency for International Development, July 1987).

62 Kumar, "A.I.D.'s Experience."

63 James Ferguson, *The Anti-Politics Machine: Development, Depoliticization, and Bureaucratic Power in Lesotho* (Minneapolis: University of Minnesota Press, 1994).

64 Ibid.

65 Carol Lancaster, "The World Bank in Africa Since 1980: The Politics of Structural Adjustment Lending," in *The World Bank: Its First Half Century (Vol. 2)*, edited by Devesh Kapur, John Lewis, and Richard Webb (Washington, D.C.: Brookings Institution, 1997).

66 Mark McGuire and Vernon Ruttan, "Lost Directions: U.S. Foreign Assistance Policy Since New Directions," Bulletin no. 89–5 (St. Paul: Economic Development Center, University of Minnesota, August 1989).

67 Erik Thorbecke, "The Evolution of the Development Doctrine and the Role of Foreign Aid, 1950–2000," in *Foreign Aid and Development: Lessons Learnt and Directions for the Future*, edited by Finn Tarp (London: Routledge, 2000).

68 Anne Krueger et al., *Aid and Development* (Baltimore and London: Johns Hopkins University Press, 1989).

69 The East Asian cases were later reinterpreted as examples of the potential for strong developmental state intervention in the economy. See Ziya Onis, "The Logic of the Developmental State," *Comparative Politics*, vol. 24, no. 1 (October 1991): 109–26.

70 Tony Killick, *A Reaction Too Far: Economic Theory and the Role of the State in Developing Countries* (London: Overseas Development Institute, 1989), and Riddell, *Foreign Aid Reconsidered*.

71 Lancaster, "The World Bank in Africa Since 1980," 168, and Krueger et al., *Aid and Development*.

72 Jeffrey Hawkins, "Understanding the Failure of IMF Reform: The Zambian Case," *World Development*, vol. 19, no. 7 (1991).

73 Ibid., 847–48.

74 Joan Nelson, "The Political Economy of Stabilization in Small, Low-Income, Trade-Dependent Nations" (Washington, D.C.: Overseas Development Council, March 1984), 2–3.

75 Nelson, "The Political Economy of Stabilization in Small, Low-Income, Trade-Dependent Nations."

76 Philip Ndegwa, "Appendix: A View from Africa, The World Bank in Africa Since 1980: The Politics of Structural Adjustment Lending," in Kapur et al., eds., *The World Bank: Its First Half Century* (vol. 2), 191.

77 Robert Berg, "Foreign Aid in Africa: Here's the Answer—Is It Relevant to the Question?" in *Strategies for African Development: A Study for the Committee on African Development Strategies*, edited by Robert J. Berg and Jennifer Seymour Whitaker (Berkeley and Los Angeles: University of California Press, 1986), 505–43.

78 See Stephan Haggard and Robert Kaufman, "The Politics of Stabilization and Structural Adjustment," in *Developing Country Debt and Economic Performance: The International Financial System*, edited by Jeffrey Sachs (Chicago: University of Chicago Press, 1989); Killick, *A Reaction Too Far*; and Joan Nelson, ed., *Economic Crisis and Policy Choice: The Politics of Adjustment in the Third World* (Princeton, N.J.: Princeton University Press, 1990).

79 Lancaster, "The World Bank in Africa Since 1980," 174–76.

80 Claude Ake, "Rethinking African Democracy," *Journal of Democracy*, vol. 2, no. 1 (Winter 1991): 41–42.

81 Thorbecke, "The Evolution of the Development Doctrine and the Role of Foreign Aid, 1950–2000."

82 See Morrison, *Aid and Ebb Tide*, 189; Berg, "Foreign Aid in Africa," 525; and Kapur et al., *World Bank: Its First Half Century*, 375.

83 Berg, "Foreign Aid in Africa," 525.

84 Goldsmith, "Institutions and Planned Socioeconomic Change."

85 USAID, "Institutional Development," AID Policy Paper (Washington, D.C.: U.S. Agency for International Development, Bureau for Program and Policy Coordination, 1983).

86 Ibid.; Derick Brinkerhoff and Marcus Ingle, "Blueprint and Process: a Structured Flexibility Approach to Development Management," *Public Administration and Development*, vol. 9, no. 5 (November-December 1989): 487–503; and USAID Malawi, "Human Resources and Institutional Development," A.I.D. Evaluation Summary Part I (Washington, D.C.: U.S. Agency for International Development, 1990).

87 Stanley Barnett and Nat Engel, "Effective Institution Building: A Guide for Project Designers and Project Managers Based on Lessons Learned From the AID Portfolio," A.I.D. Program Evaluation, Discussion Paper no. 11 (Washington, D.C.: U.S. Agency for International Development, 1982), and John Tilney and Steven Block, "USAID Efforts to Promote Agricultural Policy Reform and Institutional Development in Developing Countries: Lessons for Design and Implementation," Report no. 317, Agricultural Policy Analysis Project Phase II (Bethesda, Md.: Abt Associates, July 1991).

88 See Barbara Nunberg, "Public Sector Management Issues in Structural Adjustment Lending," World Bank Discussion Paper 99 (Washington, D.C.: World Bank, August 1990); Beatrice Buyck, "The Bank's Use of Technical Assistance for Institutional Development," Working Paper 578 (Washington, D.C.: World Bank, January 1991); and Elliot Berg, "Aid and Failed Reforms: the Case of Public Sector Management," in *Foreign Aid and Development*.

89 World Bank, "Evaluation Results for 1988: Issues in World Bank Lending Over Two Decades" (Washington, D.C.: World Bank, Operations Evaluation Department, 1990), 49–51.

90 Buyck, "The Bank's Use of Technical Assistance for Institutional Development," 20–25.

91 John Mason, "A.I.D.'s Experience With Democratic Initiatives: A Review of Regional Programs in Legal Institution Building," A.I.D. Program Evaluation Discussion Paper no. 29 (Washington, D.C.: U.S. Agency for International Development, February 1990).

92 Thomas Carothers, *In the Name of Democracy: U.S. Policy Toward Latin America in the Reagan Years* (Berkeley: University of California Press, 1991), 221–22. See also Mason, "A.I.D.'s Experience With Democratic Initiatives."

CHAPTER 3

1 USAID, "Democracy and Governance," USAID Policy (Washington, D.C.: U.S. Agency for International Development, November 1991), 6.

2 CIDA, *Cultural Dimensions of Sustainable Development: CIDA's Orientations and Initiatives* (Gatineau: Canadian International Development Agency, June 1998).

3 SIDA, *Making Government Work: Guidelines and Framework for SIDA Support to the Development of Public Administration* (Stockholm: Swedish International Development Cooperation Agency, 1991).

4 World Bank, *Governance and Development* (Washington, D.C.: World Bank, 1992), 1.

5 Ivar Evensmo, "Norwegian Media Assistance: An Integral Part of Democracy Support," in *The "Fourth Estate" in Democracy Assistance: Practices and Challenges of German and International Media Development Cooperation*, edited by Christoph Dietz, Julia Steffenfauseweh, and Angelika Mendes (Berlin: Konrad-Adenauer-Stiftung, November 2010); and Overseas Development Administration, "Taking Account of Good Government," Technical Note 10 (London: Overseas Development Administration, Government and Institutions Department, October 1993).

6 OECD DAC, "DAC Orientations on Participatory Development and Good Governance," OCDE/GD(93) 191 (Paris: Organisation for Economic Co-operation and Development, 1993), 2.

7 World Bank, "Evaluation Results for 1988: Issues in World Bank Lending Over Two Decades" (Washington, D.C.: World Bank, World Bank Operations Evaluation Department, 1990), 28.

8 Douglass C. North, *Institutions, Institutional Change and Economic Performance* (Cambridge, UK: Cambridge University Press, 1990), and Douglass C. North, "The New Institutional Economics and Third World Development," in *The New Institutional Economics and Third World Development*, edited by John Harriss, Janet Hunter, and Colin M. Lewis (London and New York: Routledge, 1995).

9 Tony Killick, *A Reaction Too Far: Economic Theory and the Role of the State in Developing Countries* (London: Overseas Development Institute, 1989).

10 David Dollar and Lant Pritchett, *Assessing Aid: What Works, What Doesn't, and Why, World Bank Policy Research Report* (New York: Oxford University Press, 1998), 83.

11 World Bank, *Sub-Saharan Africa: From Crisis to Sustainable Growth* (Washington, D.C.: World Bank, November 1989), 60.

12 World Bank, *World Development Report 1991: The Challenge of Development* (New York: Oxford University Press, 1991), 4.

13 World Bank, *World Development Report 1997: The State in a Changing World* (New York: Oxford University Press, June 1997).

14 Heather Marquette, *Corruption, Politics and Development: The Role of the World Bank* (New York: Palgrave Macmillan, 2003).

15 James Wolfensohn, *Voice for the World's Poor: Selected Speeches and Writings of World Bank President James D. Wolfensohn, 1995–2000* (Washington, D.C.: World Bank, 2005).

16 See UNDP, "Corruption and Good Governance," Discussion Paper 3 (New York: United Nations Development Programme, Management Development and Governance Division, July 1997); DFID, *Eliminating World Poverty: A Challenge for the 21st Century*, White Paper

on International Development (London: Department for International Development, November 1997); and Marquette, *Corruption, Politics and Development.*

17 *Vienna Declaration and Programme of Action*, World Conference on Human Rights, Vienna, June 14–25, 1993.

18 Ibid.

19 World Bank, *World Development Report 1991*, 4, 9.

20 French President Francois Mitterrand told a French-African conference in La Baule that France would favor countries making democratic progress in its foreign aid allocations. British Foreign Secretary Douglas Hurd similarly told the Overseas Development Council that British aid would favor countries moving toward pluralism and human rights. U.S. Assistant Secretary of State for African Affairs Herman Cohen also announced in 1990 that democratization would be added to economic policy reform and human rights as conditions for U.S. aid. See Claude Ake, "Rethinking African Democracy," *Journal of Democracy*, vol. 2, no. 1 (Winter 1991): 39.

21 U.S. Office of Management and Budget, "Fiscal Year 2013 Historical Tables: Budget of the U.S. Government," www.budget.gov; David Lowe, "Idea to Reality: NED at 25," National Endowment for Democracy, www.ned.org/about/history#12; and Thomas Carothers, *Aiding Democracy Abroad: The Learning Curve* (Washington, D.C.: Carnegie Endowment for International Peace, 1999).

22 OECD Development Assistance Committee, "DAC Orientations on Participatory Development and Good Governance," 2.

23 USAID, *Strategies for Sustainable Development* (Washington, D.C.: U.S. Agency for International Development, March 1994), 18.

24 CIDA, *Government of Canada Policy for CIDA on Human Rights, Democratization and Good Governance* (Gatineau: Canadian International Development Agency, December 1996), 3.

25 Adam Przeworski and Fernando Limongi, "Political Regimes and Economic Growth," *Journal of Economic Perspectives*, vol. 7, no. 3 (Summer 1993): 51–69; Adrian Leftwich, "Governance, Democracy and Development in the Third World," *Third World Quarterly*, vol. 14, no. 3 (1993): 605–24; and Mick Moore and James Putzel, "Politics and Poverty: A Background Paper for the World Development Report 2000/1" (Brighton: Institute of Development Studies, September 1999).

26 Bardhan, writing in 1993, noted that while India has been more successful at preventing famine, China has a better record of dealing with endemic hunger and malnutrition. See Pranab Bardhan, "Symposium on Democracy and Development," *Journal of Economic Perspectives*, vol. 7, no. 3 (Summer 1993): 45–49. Also see Leftwich, "Governance, Democracy and Development in the Third World," 605–24.

27 USAID, *Strategies for Sustainable Development*, 4–5.

28 CIDA, *Government of Canada Policy for CIDA on Human Rights, Democratization and Good Governance*, and Sida, "SIDA's Programme for Peace, Democracy and Human Rights: Part A" (Stockholm: Swedish International Development Cooperation Agency, 1997).

29 Thomas Carothers, "The Elusive Synthesis," *Journal of Democracy*, vol. 21, no. 4 (October 2010): 12–26.

30 CIDA, *Review of Governance Programming in CIDA: Synthesis Report* (Gatineau: Canadian International Development Agency, Performance and Knowledge Management Branch, April 2008).

31 Michael McFaul and Sarah Mendelson, "Russian Democracy: A U.S. National Security Interest," *Demokratizatsiya*, vol. 8, no. 3 (2000): 330–53.

32 See GAO, "Harvard Institute for International Development's Work in Russia and Ukraine," GAO/NSIAD-97-27 (Washington, D.C.: United States General Accounting Office, November 1996), and Janine Wedel, "U.S. Assistance for Market Reforms: Foreign Aid Failures in Russia and the Former Soviet Bloc," *Independent Review*, vol. 4, no. 3 (Winter 2000): 393–418.

33 World Bank, *Governance and Development*, 1.

34 Overseas Development Administration, "Taking Account of Good Government," para. 2.5.

35 Roberto Dañino, *Legal Opinion on Human Rights and the Work of the World Bank* (Washington, D.C.: World Bank, January 27, 2006). The European and Inter-American development banks do not have the same institutional prohibition regarding politics and adopted some modest democracy-related programs in addition to governance work.

36 World Bank, *Governance and Development*, 5–6.

37 Martin Doornbos, "'Good Governance': The Metamorphosis of a Policy Metaphor," *Journal of International Affairs*, vol. 57, no. 1 (Fall 2003): 3–17, and World Bank, *Governance: The World Bank's Experience* (Washington, D.C.: World Bank, May 1994).

38 Dollar and Pritchett, *Assessing Aid*.

39 Mick Moore, "Declining to Learn From the East? The World Bank on 'Governance and Development,'" *IDS Bulletin*, vol. 24, no. 1 (January 1993): 39–50.

40 Marquette, *Corruption, Politics and Development*, and Ann Hudock, *Laying the Foundation for Sustainable Development: Good Governance and the Poverty Reduction Strategy Paper* (Washington, D.C.: World Learning, August 2002).

41 John Gaventa, "Introduction: Exploring Citizenship, Participation and Accountability," *IDS Bulletin*, vol. 33, no. 2 (2002): 1–14.

42 UNDP, *Human Development Report 1993* (New York and Oxford: Oxford University Press, 1993), 1–2.

43 Jeremy Holland, Mary Ann Brocklesby, and Charles Abugre, "Beyond the Technical Fix? Participation in Donor Approaches to Rights-Based Development," in *Participation: From Tyranny to Transformation? Exploring New Approaches to Participation in Development*, edited by Samuel Hickey and Giles Mohan (London: Zed Books, 2005).

44 Gaventa, "Introduction: Exploring Citizenship."

45 See, for example, Jonathan Isham, Deepa Narayan, and Lant Pritchett, "Does Participation Improve Performance? Establishing Causality With Subjective Data," Policy Research Working Paper 1357 (Washington, D.C.: World Bank, September 1994), and World Bank, *Governance and Development*.

46 Dollar and Pritchett, *Assessing Aid*, 4.

47 Maria Aycrigg, "Participation and the World Bank: Success, Constraints, and Responses," Social Development Paper 29 (Washington, D.C.: World Bank, November 1998).

48 Carothers, *Aiding Democracy Abroad*, 101–102.

49 See Dollar and Pritchett, *Assessing Aid*; Doornbos, "Good Governance," 3–17; and Carlos Santiso, "Governance Conditionality and the Reform of Multilateral Development Finance: The Role of the Group of Eight," *G8 Governance*, no. 7 (March 2002): 2–36.

50 World Bank, *Governance and Development*, 11.

51 World Bank, *Governance and Development*.

52 Catherine Weaver, *Hypocrisy Trap: The World Bank and the Poverty of Reform* (Princeton, N.J.: Princeton University Press, 2008), 114.

53 Weaver, *Hypocrisy Trap*.

54 Derick Brinkerhoff and Benjamin Crosby, *Managing Policy Reform: Concepts and Tools for Decision-Makers in Developing and Transitioning Countries* (Bloomfield, Conn.: Kumarian Press, 2002).

55 Samuel Paul, "Making Voice Work: The Report Card on Bangalore's Public Services" (Washington, D.C.: World Bank, Development Research Group, 1998); World Bank, *Economic Growth in the 1990s: Learning From a Decade of Reform* (Washington, D.C.: World Bank, 2005), and Dollar and Pritchett, *Assessing Aid*.

56 Marquette, *Corruption, Politics and Development*.

57 Cynthia Hewitt de Alcántara, "Uses and Abuses of the Concept of Governance," *International Social Science Journal*, vol. 50, no. 155 (March 1998): 105–13; Weaver, *Hypocrisy Trap*; Rita Abrahamsen, *Disciplining Democracy: Development Discourse and Good Governance in Africa* (London: Zed Books, 2000); and David Craig and Doug Porter, *Development Beyond Neoliberalism? Governance, Poverty Reduction and Political Economy* (New York: Routledge, 2006).

58 Santiso, "Governance Conditionality and the Reform of Multilateral Development Finance," 2–36.

59 World Bank, *Economic Growth in the 1990s*, and Marquette, *Corruption, Politics and Development*.

60 World Bank, *Economic Growth in the 1990s*, and Santiso, "Governance Conditionality and the Reform of Multilateral Development Finance," 2–36.

61 Leftwich, "Governance, Democracy and Development in the Third World," 620.

62 Moore, "Declining to Learn From the East?" 39–50; Adrian Leftwich, *Democracy and Development* (Cambridge, UK: Polity Press, 1996); and Doornbos, "Good Governance," 3–17.

63 Hewitt de Alcántara, "Uses and Abuses of the Concept of Governance," 105–13, and Paul Hoebink, "European Donors and 'Good Governance': Condition or Goal?" *European Journal of Development Research*, vol. 18, no. 1 (March 2006): 131–161.

64 Hickey and Mohan (eds.), *Participation*, and Holland et al., "Beyond the Technical Fix?"

65 Andy Norton et al., "A Rough Guide to PPAs: Participatory Poverty Assessment: An Introduction to Theory and Practice" (London: Overseas Development Institute, 2001).

66 Maria Aycrigg, "Participation and the World Bank: Success, Constraints, and Responses," Social Development Paper 29 (Washington, D.C.: World Bank, November 1998).

67 Aycrigg, "Participation and the World Bank," and Norton et al., "A Rough Guide to PPAs."

68 Aycrigg, "Participation and the World Bank," and James Manor, *The Political Economy of Democratic Decentralization* (Washington, D.C.: World Bank, 1999).

69 See, for example, Paul Francis et al., "State, Community and Local Development in Nigeria," World Bank Technical Paper no. 336, Africa Region Series (Washington, D.C.: World Bank, 1996).

70 Tony Evans, "If Democracy, then Human Rights?" *Third World Quarterly*, vol. 22, no. 4 (August 2001): 623–42.

71 Hickey and Mohan (eds.), *Participation*.

72 Hickey and Mohan (eds.), *Participation*; Ghazala Mansuri and Vijayendra Rao, "Community-Based and -Driven Development: A Critical Review," *World Bank Research Observer*, vol. 19, no. 1 (2004): 1–39; and Manor, *The Political Economy of Democratic Decentralization*, 115.

73 Hickey and Mohan (eds.), *Participation*.

74 Anthony Gaeta and Marina Vasilara, *Development and Human Rights: The Role of the World Bank* (Washington, D.C.: World Bank, September 1998), 27–28.

75 World Bank, *The World Bank Participation Sourcebook*, Environmentally Sustainable Development Publications (Washington, D.C.: World Bank, February 1996), and Francis et al., "State, Community and Local Development in Nigeria."

76 Harry Blair, *Spreading Power to the Periphery: An Assessment of Democratic Local Governance*, Assessment Report no. 21 (Washington, D.C.: USAID Center for Development Information and Evaluation, September 1998), and Carothers, *Aiding Democracy Abroad*.

77 Ghazala Mansuri and Vijayendra Rao, *Localizing Development: Does Participation Work?* World Bank Policy Research Report (Washington, D.C.: World Bank, 2013), 29–30.

78 John Cohen and Stephen Peterson, "Methodological Issues in the Analysis of Decentralization," Discussion Paper no. 555 (Cambridge, Mass.: Harvard Institute of International Development, 1996); Manor, *The Political Economy of Democratic Decentralization*; and Blair, "Spreading Power to the Periphery."

79 Carothers, *Aiding Democracy Abroad*. James Manor stresses that the impetus for decentralization in developing countries came from government officials and was very rarely the result of either donor pressure or grassroots advocacy from citizens. See Manor, *The Political Economy of Democratic Decentralization*, 29–31.

80 Kent Eaton, Kai Kaiser, and Paul Smoke, *The Political Economy of Decentralization Reforms: Implications for Aid Effectiveness* (Washington, D.C.: World Bank, 2010), 3.

81 Blair, "Spreading Power to the Periphery."

82 Independent Evaluation Group, *Decentralization in Client Countries: An Evaluation of World Bank Support 1990–2007* (Washington, D.C.: World Bank, 2008), xv.

83 Ibid., 25.

84 Blair, "Spreading Power to the Periphery."

85 Ibid., vii.

86 Blair, "Spreading Power to the Periphery," and Manor, *The Political Economy of Democratic Decentralization*.

87 Mansuri and Rao, *Localizing Development: Does Participation Work?*

88 Edward Miguel, "Tribe or Nation? Nation Building and Public Goods in Kenya Versus Tanzania," *World Politics*, vol. 56, no. 3 (April 2004): 327–62.

89 Blair, "Spreading Power to the Periphery," and Manor, *The Political Economy of Democratic Decentralization*.

90 World Bank, "Strengthening World Bank Group Engagement on Governance and Anticorruption" (Washington, D.C.: World Bank, March 2007).

91 Blair, "Spreading Power to the Periphery."

92 Mansuri and Rao, *Localizing Development: Does Participation Work?*

CHAPTER 4

1 UNDP, *A Guide to UNDP Democratic Governance Practice* (New York: United Nations Development Programme, 2010).

2 Commission of the European Communities, "Governance in the European Consensus on Development: Towards a Harmonised Approach Within the European Union," Communication from the Commission to the Council, the European Parliament, the European Economic

and Social Committee and the Committee of the Regions (Brussels: European Commission, August 2006).

3   The Australian development agency, AusAID, places its work under the broad category of "effective governance" but refers to democratic governance as a principle of Australian aid. See AusAID, "Effective Governance: Thematic Strategy" (Canberra: Australian Agency for International Development, November 2011), and Ministry of Foreign Affairs of Japan, "Good Governance: Japan's Action," Sectoral Development Policy, last updated November 19, 2007, www.mofa.go.jp/policy/oda/sector/governance/action.html.

4   Séverine Bellina, Hervé Magro, and Violaine De Villemeur (eds.), *Democratic Governance: A New Paradigm for Development?* (London: Hurst and Company and Ministère des Affaires Étrangères, 2009).

5   Commission of the European Communities, "Governance in the European Consensus on Development," 5.

6   Ministère des Affaires Étrangères, "Governance Strategy for French Development Assistance" (Paris: Ministère des Affaires Étrangères, December 2006), 5.

7   Alan Hudson and GOVNET Secretariat, "Background Paper for the Launch of the Work-stream on Aid and Domestic Accountability" (Paris: Organisation for Economic Co-operation and Development, DAC Network on Governance, March 2009).

8   The EBRD and IDB do not have the same institutional prohibition regarding politics and adopted some modest democracy-related programs in addition to governance work.

9   World Bank, "Strengthening World Bank Group Engagement on Governance and Anticorruption" (Washington, D.C.: World Bank, March 2007).

10 In 2006–2007 DFID appeared to make a strong commitment to supporting democracy, but this has only partially translated into assistance programming. See Hilary Benn, "Making Politics Work for the Poor: Democracy and Development," Speech at Demos, Westminster Hall, October 23, 2006, www.demos.co.uk/files/File/HB_speech_-_final.pdf, and DFID, *Governance, Development and Democratic Politics: DFID's Work in Building More Effective States* (London: Department for International Development, 2007).

11 DFID, *Eliminating World Poverty: Making Governance Work for the Poor*, White Paper on International Development (London: Department for International Development, 2006), 22.

12 Thomas Carothers, "A Tale of Two Cultures: Democracy, State, and USAID," *Foreign Service Journal*, vol. 78, no. 2 (February 2001).

13 World Bank, *World Bank Group Work in Low-Income Countries Under Stress: A Task Force Report* (Washington, D.C.: World Bank, September 2002), 1.

14 DFID, *Why We Need to Work More Effectively in Fragile States* (London: Department for International Development, January 2005), 7.

15 USAID, "Fragile States Strategy" (Washington, D.C.: U.S. Agency for International Development, January 2005), 1.

16 OECD DAC, *Supporting Statebuilding in Situations of Fragility and Conflict: Policy Guidance* (Paris: Organisation for Economic Co-operation and Development, Development Assistance Committee, 2011), 11.

17 Nick Chapman and Charlotte Vaillant, "Synthesis of Country Programme Evaluations Conducted in Fragile States," Evaluation Report EV709 (London: Department for International Development, February 2010), 4.

18 Ibid.

19 Claire Vallings and Magüi Moreno-Torres, "Drivers of Fragility: What Makes States Fragile?" PRDE Working Paper no. 7 (London: Department for International Development, April 2005), 2.

20 World Bank, *World Development Report 2011: Conflict, Security, and Development* (Washington, D.C.: World Bank, 2011), 2.

21 OECD DAC, *International Engagement in Fragile States: Can't We Do Better?* (Paris: Organisation for Economic Co-operation and Development, Development Assistance Committee, 2011).

22 DFID, "Building Peaceful States and Societies," DFID Practice Paper (London: Department for International Development, 2010), 22. See also Alan Whaites, "States in Development: Understanding State-Building," DFID Working Paper (London: Department for International Development, 2008).

23 Laure-Hélène Piron, *The Right to Development: A Review of the Current State of the Debate for the Department for International Development* (London: Overseas Development Institute, April 2002).

24 Amartya Sen, *Development as Freedom* (Oxford: Oxford University Press, 1999), 3.

25 OECD DAC, *The DAC Guidelines: Poverty Reduction* (Paris: Organisation for Economic Co-operation and Development, Development Assistance Committee, 2001), 38.

26 Sida, *Perspectives on Poverty* (Stockholm: Swedish International Development Agency, October 2002), 7.

27 Laure-Hélène Piron, *Integrating Human Rights into Development: A Synthesis of Donor Approaches and Experiences* (London: Overseas Development Institute, September 2005), 8–9.

28 DFID, "Realising Human Rights for Poor People: Strategies for Achieving the International Development Targets" (London: Department for International Development, October 2000), 18.

29 UNDP, "Integrating Human Rights With Sustainable Human Development," UNDP Policy Document (New York: United Nations Development Programme, January 1998).

30 DFID, "Realising Human Rights for Poor People," 18.

31 Sara Brun, Karin Dawidson, Karolina Hulterström, and Susanne Mattsson, *Integrating the Rights Perspective in Programming: Lessons Learnt From Swedish-Kenyan Development Cooperation* (Karlstad: Swedish Agency for Development Evaluation, 2008), ii.

32 Author (Carothers) interview with Sida officials in Stockholm, June 2010.

33 UNDP, "Integrating Human Rights With Sustainable Human Development."

34 Commission of the European Communities, "Governance in the European Consensus on Development," 20.

35 The 2000/2001 World Development Report, for example, presented empowerment as one of the three aspects of a poverty reduction strategy, alongside promoting opportunity and enhancing security. See World Bank, *World Development Report 2000/2001: Attacking Poverty: Opportunity, Empowerment, and Security* (Washington, D.C.: World Bank, 2000).

36 See for example, David Dollar and Lant Pritchett, *Assessing Aid: What Works, What Doesn't, and Why*, World Bank Policy Research Report (New York: Oxford University Press, 1998).

37 Gordon Crawford, *Foreign Aid and Political Reform: A Comparative Analysis of Democracy Assistance and Political Conditionality* (New York: Palgrave Macmillan, 2001), 241.

38 William Easterly and Tobias Pfutze, "Where Does the Money Go? Best and Worst Practices in Foreign Aid," Global Economy & Development Working Paper 21 (Washington, D.C.: Brookings Institution, June 2008), 14.

39 Daniel Kaufmann and Veronika Penciakova, "How Selective Is Donor Aid? Governance and Corruption Matter and Donor Agencies Should Take Notice," Brookings Institution, July 17, 2012, www.brookings.edu/research/opinions/2012/07/17-donor-aid-kaufmann.

40 U.S. Department of State, "Congressional Budget Justification Volume 2: Foreign Operations" (Washington, D.C.: U.S. Department of State, February 2012), and www.foreignassistance.gov.

41 Netherlands Ministry of Foreign Affairs, "Letter to the House of Representatives Outlining Development Cooperation Policy" (The Hague: Netherlands Ministry of Foreign Affairs, November 26, 2010).

42 CIDA, "Countries of Focus," Canadian International Development Agency, www.acdi-cida. gc.ca/countriesoffocus.

43 OECD DAC, "Sweden: Development Assistance Committee Peer Review" (Paris: Organisation for Economic Co-operation and Development, 2009), and Swedish Ministry for Foreign Affairs, "Focused Bilateral Development Cooperation" (Stockholm: Swedish Ministry for Foreign Affairs, August 27, 2007).

44 Sida, "Our Work in Vietnam," Swedish Agency for International Development, October 2010, www.sida.se/English/Countries-and-regions/Asia/Vietnam/Our-work-in-Vietnam.

45 "MCC Board of Directors Votes to Reinstate Compact With Malawi," Millennium Challenge Corporation, June 21, 2012, www.mcc.gov/pages/press/release/release-062112-boardmeeting.

46 Sheila Herrling and Steve Radelet, "The Millennium Challenge Account: Making U.S. Foreign Assistance More Effective?" *Development Outreach*, vol. 11, no. 1 (February 2009): 16.

47 Millennium Challenge Corporation, "Congressional Budget Justification 2013" (Washington, D.C.: Millennium Challenge Corporation, 2012), and "U.S. Agency for International Development: Planned Stage," http://foreignassistance.gov/Agency_USAID.aspx?budTab=tab_ Bud_Planned.

48 Curt Tarnoff, "Millennium Challenge Corporation," CRS Report for Congress (Washington, D.C.: Congressional Research Service, April 12, 2012), 7.

49 Margaret Dennis, "A New Approach to Foreign Aid: A Case Study of the Millennium Challenge Account," IILJ Emerging Scholars Paper 12 (New York: Institute for International Law and Justice, New York University School of Law, 2008), 31.

50 Nadia Molenaers and Leen Nijs, "From the Theory of Aid Effectiveness to the Practice: The European Commission's Governance Incentive Tranche," *Development Policy Review*, vol. 27, no. 5 (2009): 561–80.

51 Countries can also get extra 5 percent bonuses for agreeing to supplemental measures like the African Peer Review or to compensate for state fragility. See Ibid.

52 European Commission, "Supporting Democratic Governance Through the Governance Initiative: A Review and the Way Forward," Commission Staff Working Paper (Brussels: European Commission, January 2009), 9.

53 For a detailed discussion of the potential negative effects of budget support on democracy in aid-receiving countries, see Anna Lekvall, *Development First, Democracy Later?* (Stockholm: International Institute for Democracy and Electoral Assistance, forthcoming 2013).

54 Anna Lekvall, *Development First, Democracy Later?*

55 DFID, "Government to Suspend General Budget Support to Malawi," Press Release, Department for International Development, July 14, 2011, www.dfid.gov.uk/news/ press-releases/2011/government-to-suspend-general-budget-support-to-malawi.

56 This category includes aid to public sector administrative and financial management, decentralization, anticorruption, legal and judicial development, democratic participation,

elections, legislatures, media, human rights, and women's equality. It does not include conflict, peace, and security assistance, which the DAC also categorizes under government and civil society aid. It reports higher aid amounts for the United States than U.S. government sources due to differences in categorization. For example, in 2009 the United States budgeted $2.7 billion for democracy, human rights, and governance assistance, while the OECD DAC cites a much higher figure of approximately $4.6 billion, which indicates that the latter uses a broader definition of governance and civil society aid. See OECD DAC, "Creditor Reporting System," OECD.Stat Extracts, and "U.S. Agency for International Development: Fiscal Year 2009 Appropriations," www.foreignassistance.gov.

57 UNDP, "Annual Report 2011/2012: The Sustainable Future We Want" (New York: United Nations Development Programme, Bureau of External Relations and Advocacy, June 2012), 5.

58 The World Bank supports governance through various different funding mechanisms and sectors. In the area of public sector reform, for example, the World Bank between 1990 and 2006 approved 467 lending projects with significant public sector reform components. Total funding for these 467 projects represented approximately $47 billion in commitments, or about 13 percent of the World Bank's total project lending over the same period. The number of public sector reform programs doubled from 19 per year in 1990–1999 to 40 programs per year in 2000–2006. See Independent Evaluation Group, "Public Sector Reform: What Works and Why?" (Washington, D.C.: World Bank, 2008), 21.

59 UNDP, *A Guide to UNDP Democratic Governance Practice*, 9.

60 OECD DAC, "Table 19: Aid by Major Purposes in 2010," Organisation for Economic Cooperation and Development, www.oecd.org/dac/aidstatistics/statisticsonresourceflowstodevelopingcountries.htm, and AusAID, "Governance Annual Thematic Performance Report: 2009–10" (Canberra: Australian Agency for International Development, 2011), 1.

61 Foreignassistance.gov, "Foreign Assistance by Country Office," www.foreignassistance.gov./CountryIntro.aspx.

62 The share of other subsectors of DAC governance and civil society aid in 2009 were as follows: 6 percent to public financial management, 6 percent to decentralization and subnational governments, 1 percent to anticorruption organizations, 5 percent to elections, 7 percent to human rights, and 4 percent to women's organizations. See OECD DAC, "Creditor Reporting System," OECD.Stat Extracts.

63 USAID, *Ethiopia Country Development Cooperation Strategy 2011–2015: Accelerating the Transformation Toward Prosperity* (Washington, D.C.: U.S. Agency for International Development, March 2012), 53.

64 Human Rights Watch, *Development Without Freedom: How Aid Underwrites Repression in Ethiopia* (New York: Human Rights Watch, 2010).

65 European Commission, *Ethiopia Country Strategy Paper and National Indicative Programme for the Period 2008–2013* (Brussels: European Commission), 6.

66 Sida, "Our Work in Ethiopia," Swedish International Development Agency, January 27, 2011, www.sida.se/English/Countries-and-regions/Africa/Ethiopia/Our-work-in-Ethiopia.

67 World Bank, "Net Bilateral Aid Flows From DAC Donors, Total (Current US$)," http://data.worldbank.org/indicator/DC.DAC.TOTL.CD.

68 U.S. Mission to Zimbabwe, "Zimbabwe 2007 Performance Report" (Harare: U.S. Agency for International Development, November, 2007), 2.

69 Marcus Cox and Nigel Thornton, "DFID Engagement in Countries in Fragile Situations: A Portfolio Review," Evaluation Report EV701 (London: Department for International Development, January 2009), 6.

70 See, for example, Rajiv Chandrasekaran, *Little America: The War Within the War for Afghanistan* (New York: Random House, 2012), and Seth G. Jones, *In the Graveyard of Empires: America's War in Afghanistan* (New York: W. W. Norton, 2009).

71 Thomas Carothers, "The Backlash Against Democracy Promotion," *Foreign Affairs* (March/April 2006): 55.

72 OECD DAC, *International Engagement in Fragile States*, 15.

73 International Dialogue on Peacebuilding and Statebuilding, "A New Deal for Engagement in Fragile States" (International Dialogue on Peacebuilding and Statebuilding, December 2011).

CHAPTER 5

1 David Booth, "Missing Links in the Politics of Development: Learning From the PRSP Experiment," Working Paper 256 (London: Overseas Development Institute, Africa Power and Politics Programme, October 2005), and Joel Lazarus, "Participation in Poverty Reduction Strategy Papers: Reviewing the Past, Assessing the Present and Predicting the Future," *Third World Quarterly*, vol. 29, no. 6 (2008): 1205–21.

2 Jeremy Holland, Mary Ann Brocklesby, and Charles Abugre, "Beyond the Technical Fix? Participation in Donor Approaches to Rights-Based Development," in *Participation: From Tyranny to Transformation? Exploring New Approaches to Participation in Development*, edited by Samuel Hickey and Giles Mohan (London: Zed Books, 2005), 256–57, and Andy Norton et al., *A Rough Guide to PPAs: Participatory Poverty Assessment, an Introduction to Theory and Practice* (London: Overseas Development Institute, 2001), 11.

3 World Bank, *World Development Report 2000/2001: Attacking Poverty: Opportunity, Empowerment, and Security* (Washington, D.C.: World Bank, 2000).

4 Ibid.

5 DFID, "Realising Human Rights for Poor People: Strategies for Achieving the International Development Targets" (London: Department for International Development, 2000), 12.

6 Commission of the European Communities, "Participation of Non-State Actors in EC Development Policy," Communication from the Commission to the Council, the European Parliament, and the Economic and Social Committee (Brussels: European Commission, 2002), 1.

7 Lazarus, "Participation in Poverty Reduction Strategy Papers."

8 UNDP, *Evaluation of UNDP's Role in the PRSP Process, Volume I: Main Report* (New York: United Nations Development Programme, 2003), and DFID, "Realising Human Rights for Poor People."

9 Booth, "Missing Links in the Politics of Development," 4.

10 World Bank, "Participation in Poverty Reduction Strategy Papers: A Retrospective Study" (Washington, D.C.: World Bank, Social Development Department, January 2002).

11 Booth, "Missing Links in the Politics of Development," and World Bank, "Participation in Poverty Reduction Strategy Papers."

12 Ann Hudock, "Laying the Foundation for Sustainable Development: Good Governance and the Poverty Reduction Strategy Paper" (Washington, D.C.: World Learning, August 2002); Lazarus, "Participation in Poverty Reduction Strategy Papers"; and Sam Hickey, "The Return of Politics in Development Studies (I): Getting Lost Within the Poverty Agenda?" *Progress in Development Studies*, vol. 8, no. 4 (2008): 355.

13 World Bank, "Participation in Poverty Reduction Strategy Papers," 10.

14 UNDP, *Evaluation of UNDP's Role in the PRSP Process*; World Bank, "Participation in Poverty Reduction Strategy Papers;" Lazarus, "Participation in Poverty Reduction Strategy Papers"; Arjan de Haan and Max Everest-Phillips, "Can New Aid Modalities Handle Politics?" Research Paper no. 2007/63 (Helsinki: UNU World Institute for Development Economics Research, October 2007); and Rasheed Draman, "Legislating Poverty in Africa: What Role Have Parliamentarians Been Playing in PRSP Implementation and Policy?" (Ottawa: Parliamentary Centre, May 2007).

15 World Bank, "Participation in Poverty Reduction Strategy Papers," and Lazarus, "Participation in Poverty Reduction Strategy Papers."

16 See, for example, David Craig and Doug Porter, *Development Beyond Neoliberalism? Governance, Poverty Reduction and Political Economy* (New York: Routledge, 2006), and Jeremy Gould (ed.), *The New Conditionality: The Politics of Poverty Reduction Strategies* (London: Zed Books, 2005).

17 Lazarus, "Participation in Poverty Reduction Strategy Papers"; World Bank, "Participation in Poverty Reduction Strategy Papers"; and Hickey, "The Return of Politics in Development Studies (I)."

18 Booth, "Missing Links in the Politics of Development," 4.

19 Mansuri and Rao estimate that the World Bank, for example, increased lending for these types of programs from $325 million in 1996 to $2 billion in 2003. See Ghazala Mansuri and Vijayendra Rao, "Community-Based and -Driven Development: A Critical Review," *World Bank Research Observer*, vol. 19, no. 1 (2004): 2.

20 See Philip Glaessner et al., "Poverty Alleviation and Social Investment Funds: The Latin American Experience," World Bank Discussion Paper 261 (Washington, D.C.: World Bank, September 1994).

21 Mansuri and Rao, "Community-Based and -Driven Development," 2.

22 Mansuri and Rao note that participatory programs pay insufficient attention to "civil society failure," which they define "as a situation in which groups that live in geographic proximity are unable to act collectively to reach a feasible and preferable outcome." See Ghazala Mansuri and Vijayendra Rao, *Localizing Development: Does Participation Work?* World Bank Policy Research Report (Washington, D.C.: World Bank, 2013), 4.

23 Mansuri and Rao, *Localizing Development: Does Participation Work?* 304.

24 World Bank, "Indonesia Kecamatan Development Program," Social Development in East Asia and Pacific, http://go.worldbank.org/9RCD9UBX40.

25 Scott Guggenheim, "Crises and Contradictions: Understanding the Origins of a Community Development Project in Indonesia," in *The Search for Empowerment: Social Capital as Idea and Practice at the World Bank,* edited by Anthony Bebbington et al. (Bloomfield, Conn.: Kumarian Press, 2006).

26 Tania Murray Li, *The Will to Improve: Governmentality, Development, and the Practice of Politics* (Durham and London: Duke University Press, 2007).

27 Scott Guggenheim et al., "Indonesia's Kecamatan Development Program: A Large-Scale Use of Community Development to Reduce Poverty" (Washington, D.C.: World Bank, 2004), 2, and Li, *The Will to Improve.*

28 Guggenheim, "Crises and Contradictions," and Mansuri and Rao, *Localizing Development: Does Participation Work?* 295.

29 John Gaventa and Gregory Barrett, "So What Difference Does It Make? Mapping the Outcome of Citizen Engagement," IDS Working Paper 347 (Brighton: Institute of Development Studies, October 2010), 16; Guggenheim, "Crises and Contradictions"; and Mansuri and Rao, *Localizing Development: Does Participation Work?*

30 Li, *The Will to Improve*, and Thomas Davis, "The Real World of 'Community Empowerment' in International Development," paper prepared at the Australian Political Science Association Conference (Monash University, Australia, September 23–26, 2007).

31 Bernard Wood et al., *The Evaluation of the Paris Declaration Phase Two: Final Report* (Copenhagen: Danish Institute for International Studies, May 2011), 23. The Paris Declaration on Aid Effectiveness includes partner government commitment to "encourage broad participation of a range of national actors in setting development priorities" (Article 38). This commitment is further elaborated in the 2008 Accra Agenda for Action (see Article 13) and the 2011 Busan Partnership for Effective Development Co-operation (see Articles 21 and 22).

32 Donors also sometimes use "social accountability," "voice and accountability," or similar terms to refer to the same types of programs.

33 Participatory budgeting has been particularly popular among Latin American governments, with fifteen countries in the region and about 2,500 localities establishing some kind of participatory budgeting mechanisms. See Benjamin Goldfrank, "Lessons From Latin America's Experience With Participatory Budgeting," in *Participatory Budgeting*, edited by Anwar Shah (Washington, D.C.: World Bank, 2007), and J. Oropeza, "Participatory Budgeting: Citizen Participation for Better Public Policies," ELLA Policy Brief (Lima, Peru: Practical Action Consulting, November 2011).

34 Thomas Carothers and Marina Ottaway (eds.), *Funding Virtue: Civil Society Aid and Democracy Promotion* (Washington, D.C.: Carnegie Endowment for International Peace, 2000).

35 OECD DAC, "Final Report of the Ad Hoc Group on Participatory Development and Good Government: Part 1" (Paris: Organisation for Economic Co-operation and Development, Development Assistance Committee, 1997), 3.

36 DFID, "Realising Human Rights for Poor People," 17.

37 World Bank, *World Development Report 2004: Making Services Work for Poor People* (Washington, D.C.: World Bank and Oxford University Press, 2004).

38 Anuradha Joshi, "Annex 1: Service Delivery," in Rosemary McGee and John Gaventa, *Review of Impact and Effectiveness of Transparency and Accountability Initiatives* (Brighton: Institute of Development Studies, 2010).

39 See for example, World Bank, *Strengthening World Bank Group Engagement on Governance and Anticorruption* (Washington, D.C.: World Bank, March 2007); AusAID, "Australian Aid Approaches to Building Demand for Better Governance" (Canberra: Australian Agency for International Development, December 2007); Commission of the European Communities, "Governance in the European Consensus on Development: Towards a Harmonised Approach Within the European Union," Communication from the Commission to the Council, the European Parliament, the European Economic and Social Committee and the Committee of the Regions (Brussels: European Commission, August 2006); and Alan Hudson and GOVNET Secretariat, "Background Paper for the Launch of the Work-stream on Aid and Domestic Accountability" (Paris: Organisation for Economic Co-operation Development, DAC Network on Governance, March 2009).

40 Sarah L. Henderson, *Building Democracy in Contemporary Russia: Western Support for Grassroots Organizations* (Ithaca and London: Cornell University Press, 2003); Sarah E. Mendelson and John K. Glenn (eds.), *The Power and Limits of NGOs: A Critical Look at Building Democracy in Eastern Europe and Eurasia* (New York: Columbia University Press, 2002); Carothers and Ottaway (eds.), *Funding Virtue*; Ann C. Hudock, *NGOs and Civil Society: Democracy by Proxy?* (Cambridge: Polity Press, 1999); Kees Bierkart, *The Politics of Civil Society Building: European Private Aid Agencies and Democratic Transitions in Central America* (Utrecht/Amsterdam: International Books/Transnational Institute, 1999); and Michael Edwards and David Hulme (eds.), *Beyond the Magic Bullet: NGO Performance and Accountability in the Post–Cold War World* (Bloomfield, Conn.: Kumarian Press, 1996).

41 Sanjay Agarwal, Rasmus Heltberg, and Myrtle Diachok, "Scaling-Up Social Accountability in World Bank Operations" (Washington, D.C.: World Bank, Social Development Department, May 2009); World Bank, *Strengthening World Bank Group Engagement*; Asli Gurkan, "Demand for Good Governance in the World Bank: Conceptual Evolution, Frameworks and Activities" (Washington, D.C.: World Bank, Social Development Department, August 2010); AusAID, "Australian Aid Approaches to Building Demand"; J. Edgardo Campos and Jose Luis Syquia, "Managing the Politics of Reform: Overhauling the Legal Infrastructure for Public Procurement in the Philippines," Working Paper No. 70 (Washington, D.C.: World Bank, 2006); DFID, "Civil Society and Development" (London: Department for International Development, Civil Society Team, February 2006); and Sida, "Independent Press Institute Fights for Freedom of Expression," Swedish International Development Cooperation Agency, January 13, 2012, www.sida.se/English/Countries-and-regions/Asia/Sri-Lanka/Programmes-and-projects1/Independent-press-institute-fights-for-freedom-of-expression.

42 OECD Development Cooperation Directorate, "Creditor Reporting System," Organisation for Economic Co-operation and Development, http://stats.oecd.org/Index.aspx?datasetcode=CRS1.

43 DFID, "Governance Portfolio Review Summary: Summary Review of DFID's Governance Portfolio 2004–2009" (London: Department for International Development, July 2011), 6.

44 DFID, "Civil Society and Development," 3.

45 Jo Hall and Jude Howell, "Working Paper: Good Practice Donor Engagement With Civil Society" (Canberra: Australian Agency for International Development, June 2010), and Heather Marquette, *Corruption, Politics and Development: The Role of the World Bank* (New York: Palgrave Macmillan, 2004).

46 Gurkan, "Demand for Good Governance in the World Bank," and Agarwal et al., "Scaling-Up Social Accountability in World Bank Operations."

47 Mark Robinson (ed.), *Budgeting for the Poor* (Basingstoke: Palgrave Macmillan, 2008).

48 Ibid.

49 Rosemary McGee and John Gaventa, *Review of Impact and Effectiveness of Transparency and Accountability Initiatives: Synthesis Report* (Brighton: Institute of Development Studies, 2010), 21.

50 Gaventa and Barrett, "So What Difference Does It Make?" 28–31.

51 Alina Rocha Menocal and Bhavna Sharma, "Joint Evaluation of Citizens' Voice and Accountability: Synthesis Report," Evaluation Report EV692 (London: Department for International Development, 2008), and PARTICIP, "Evaluation of EC Aid Delivery through Civil Society Organisations: Final Report, Volume 1," Evaluation for the European Commission (Freiburg: PARTICIP, December 2008).

52 Menocal and Sharma note that "voice is often treated as an unproblematic concept, and something that can be easily exercised by the poor and marginalized, without addressing the fundamental question of 'whose voice' is being heard" and that it is essential "to keep in mind that addressing the demands and needs that stem from the population (including the poor) is not necessarily a consensual and conflict-free process." See Menocal and Sharma, "Joint Evaluation of Citizens' Voice and Accountability," xi–xii.

53 A 2008 Sida evaluation, for instance, found that program reports universally failed to demonstrate conscious selection of civil society partners, with programs instead choosing partners based on coincidence, personal contacts, or a sense that there was no other logical partner. See Tom Dahl-Østergaard, Karin Schulz and Barbro Svedberg, "Experiences and Lessons Learnt From Sida's Work With Human Rights and Democratic Governance," Sida Evaluation 29 (Stockholm: Swedish International Development Cooperation Agency, 2008), 22. Robinson and Friedman note that "donors often lack the understanding of the organizations in their environment which would enable them to identify participatory and potentially effective organizations." Mark Robinson and Steven Friedman, "Civil Society, Democratization, and Foreign Aid: Civic Engagement and Public Policy in South Africa and Uganda," *Democratization*, vol. 14, no. 4 (August 2007): 664. Also see Menocal and Sharma, "Joint Evaluation of Citizens' Voice and Accountability."

54 Alan Hudson and GOVNET Secretariat, "Background Paper for the Launch of the Workstream on Aid and Domestic Accountability"; Sam Hickey, "The Politics of Protecting the Poorest: Moving Beyond the 'Anti-Politics Machine'? *Political Geography*, vol. 28, no. 8 (2009): 473–83; David Booth, "Aid Effectiveness: Bringing Country Ownership (and Politics) Back In," Working Paper 336 (London: Overseas Development Institute, Africa Power and Politics Programme, 2011); Centre for the Future State, *An Upside Down View of Governance* (Brighton: Institute of Development Studies, April 2010); and Gaventa and Barrett, "So What Difference Does It Make?"

55 Robinson and Friedman, "Civil Society, Democratization, and Foreign Aid," 643–68.

56 Nicola Banks and David Hulme, "The Role of NGOs and Civil Society in Poverty Reduction," BWPI Working Paper 171 (Manchester: Brooks World Poverty Institute, June 2012), 13.

57 UNDP, "Voice and Accountability for Human Development: A UNDP Strategy to Strengthen Civil Society and Civic Engagement" (New York: United Nations Development Programme and Oslo Governance Centre, August 2009); Gurkan, "Demand for Good Governance in the World Bank"; PARTICIP, "Evaluation of EC Aid Delivery;" and Mansuri and Rao, *Localizing Development: Does Participation Work?*

58 Rosemary McGee and John Gaventa, "Shifting Power? Assessing the Impact of Transparency and Accountability Initiatives," IDS Working Paper 383 (Brighton: Institute of Development Studies, 2011), 21.

59 Menocal and Sharma, "Joint Evaluation of Citizens' Voice and Accountability," and McGee and Gaventa, "Shifting Power?"

60 Robinson and Friedman, "Civil Society, Democratization, and Foreign Aid," 643–68.

61 Gaventa and Barrett, "So What Difference Does It Make?" and McGee and Gaventa, "Shifting Power?"

62 McGee and Gaventa, "Shifting Power?" 21.

63 Brian Levy and Nick Manning, "Institutional and Governance Reviews: A New Type of Economic and Sector Work," PREMnotes no. 75 (Washington, D.C.: World Bank, November 2002).

64 USAID, "Conducting a DG Assessment: A Framework for Strategy Development" (Washington, D.C.: U.S. Agency for International Development, Center for Democracy and Governance, November 2000).

65 See Jonathan Goodhand et al., "Conducting Conflict Assessments: Guidance Notes" (London: Department for International Development, January 2002); USAID, "Conducting a Conflict Assessment: A Framework for Analysis and Program Development" (Washington, D.C.: U.S. Agency for International Development, Office of Conflict Management and Mitigation, April 2005); Tony Vaux, "Conflict-Related Development Analysis" (New York: United Nations Development Programme, Bureau for Crisis Prevention and Recovery, October 2003); Sida, "Manual for Conflict Analysis," Methods Document (Stockholm: Swedish International Development Cooperation Agency, January 2006); Manuela Leonhardt, "Conflict Analysis for Project Planning and Management" (Eschborn: Deutsche Gesellschaft für Internationale Zusammenarbeit, August 2001); and World Bank, "The Conflict Analysis Framework (CAF): Identifying Conflict-Related Obstacles to Development," Dissemination Notes no. 5 (Washington, D.C.: World Bank, Social Development Department, October 2002).

66 Tom Dahl-Østergaard et al., "Lessons Learned on the Use of Power and Drivers of Change Analyses in Development Co-operation" (Paris: Organisation for Economic Co-operation and Development, DAC Network on Governance, September 2005), 4.

67 Ibid., 4–5.

68 See Sue Unsworth and Conflict Research Unit, *Framework for Strategic Governance and Corruption Analysis: Designing Strategic Responses Towards Good Governance* (The Hague: Netherlands Institute of International Relations, October 2007); Netherlands Ministry of Foreign Affairs, "Political Analyses and Development Cooperation: Draft Synthesis of the Power and Change Analyses 2007–2009" (The Hague: Netherlands Ministry of Foreign Affairs, 2010); and Norad, "Political Economy Analysis With a Legitimacy Twist: What Is It and Why Does It Matter?" (Oslo: Norwegian Agency for Development Cooperation, December 2010).

69 David Hudson and Adrian Leftwich argue that these early studies should not be considered "political economy" analyses because they were more societally and historically focused than grounded in economic theory. But this is nonetheless the term that aid providers tend to use. David Hudson and Adrian Leftwich, "From Political Economy to Political Analysis" (Developmental Leadership Program, forthcoming 2013).

70 Alice Poole, "Political Economy Assessments at Sector and Project Levels: How-To Note" (Washington, D.C.: World Bank, March 2011), 1.

71 Conflict assessments, governance assessments, and political economy analyses can also have different priorities. All may examine the patronage system in a country, for example, but reach very different results. A conflict study could see patronage as one of the means of resolving conflict through resource and power sharing. A governance assessment would likely regard the same system as a major barrier to efficient governance. A political economy analysis may conclude that the patronage system is too durable to change and thus examine ways to work around it to achieve socioeconomic results.

72 Conflict assessments usually examine these same issues, but through a conflict-specific lens.

73 Dahl-Østergaard et al., "Lessons Learned," 13.

74 Netherlands Ministry of Foreign Affairs, "Political Analyses and Development Cooperation," 2, 6.

75 A partial exception to this was the joint governance assessment conducted in Rwanda with both a number of development partners and the government of Rwanda participating. This

process helped identify common priorities among the government and donors but also limited—though did not completely prevent—the ability of analysts to probe politically sensitive issues around informal institutions and power relations. A review of this assessment noted that as a result, "the final report adopts a rather technocratic view of good governance, and focuses its recommendations on reform options for improving formal institutions." See Gareth Williams et al., "Carrying Out a Joint Governance Assessment: Lessons From Rwanda," Policy Practice Brief 5 (Brighton: The Policy Practice, January 2009), 6.

76 Arjan de Haan and Max Everest-Phillips noted in 2007, for example, that "much political analysis explains past history and current trajectories, but provides very little, if any, real guidance as to how to create the social cohesion and common interests between elites and the population" required to replicate successful development experiences in East Asia and elsewhere. See de Haan and Everest-Phillips "Can New Aid Modalities Handle Politics?" 12.

77 Netherlands Ministry of Foreign Affairs, "Political Analyses and Development Cooperation," 1.

78 Independent Evaluation Group, "World Bank Country-Level Engagement on Governance and Anticorruption: An Evaluation of the 2007 Strategy and Implementation Plan" (Washington, D.C.: World Bank, 2011), 66.

79 Dahl-Østergaard et al., "Lessons Learned," 15.

80 Ibid.

81 Chris Heymans and Chris Pycroft, "Drivers of Change in Nigeria: A Preliminary Overview" (London: Department for International Development, 2003).

82 Ibid., and DFID, "Political Economy Analysis: How-To Note," DFID Practice Paper (London: Department for International Development, July 2009).

83 Thomas Carothers, "The End of the Transition Paradigm," *Journal of Democracy*, vol. 13, no. 1 (January 2002): 5–21.

84 Greg Power, "The Politics of Parliamentary Strengthening: Understanding Political Incentives and Institutional Behaviour in Parliamentary Support Strategies" (London: Westminster Foundation for Democracy and Global Partners & Associates, 2011), 7.

85 An exception is Greg Power's guide to political analysis for parliamentary programs. See Ibid.

86 Kenneth Wollack and K. Scott Hubli, "Getting Convergence Right," *Journal of Democracy*, vol. 21, no. 4 (October 2010): 37.

87 NDI, *Constituent Relations: A Guide to Best Practices* (Washington, D.C.: National Democratic Institute for International Affairs, 2008).

88 Stephen Golub, "A House Without a Foundation," in *Promoting the Rule of Law Abroad: In Search of Knowledge*, edited by Thomas Carothers (Washington, D.C.: Carnegie Endowment for International Peace, 2006), and Stephen Golub, "The Legal Empowerment Alternative," in *Promoting the Rule of Law Abroad*.

89 Thomas Carothers, *Confronting the Weakest Link: Aiding Political Parties in New Democracies* (Washington, D.C.: Carnegie Endowment for International Peace, 2006), chapter 8.

90 Joerg Forbrig and Pavol Demeš (eds.), *Reclaiming Democracy: Civil Society and Electoral Change in Central and Eastern Europe* (Washington, D.C.: German Marshall Fund of the United States, 2007).

91 Lincoln A. Mitchell, *The Color Revolutions* (Philadelphia: University of Pennsylvania Press, 2012).

92 Thomas Carothers, "Democracy Assistance: Political vs. Developmental?" *Journal of Democracy*, vol. 20, no. 1 (January 2009): 5–19.

CHAPTER 6

1   See Leni Wild and Marta Foresti, "Politics Into Practice: A Dialogue on Governance Strategies and Action in International Development," Conference Report (London: Overseas Development Institute, May 2011), and Sue Unsworth, "What's Politics Got to Do With It? Why Donors Find It So Hard to Come to Terms With Politics, and Why This Matters," *Journal of International Development*, vol. 21, no. 6 (2009): 883–94.

2   Centre for the Future State, *An Upside Down View of Governance* (Brighton: Institute of Development Studies, April 2010), 6.

3   See, for example, David Booth and Ole Therkildsen, "The Political Economy of Development in Africa: A Joint Statement From Five Research Programmes" (Africa Power and Politics Programme; Developmental Leadership Programme; Elites, Production and Poverty; Political Economy of Agricultural Policy in Africa; and Tracking Development, April 2012).

4   See European Commission, "Political Economy at Work" Seminar (Brussels, January 11–12, 2011); Wild and Foresti, "Politics Into Practice"; Adrian Leftwich and Chris Wheeler, "Politics, Leadership and Coalitions in Development," A Research and Policy Workshop Report (Developmental Leadership Program, June 2011); Carnegie Endowment for International Peace, "Toward Better Strategies and Results: Collaborative Approaches to Strengthening Governance: A USAID, DFID, and World Bank Governance Roundtable," Meeting Summary (Washington, D.C., June 9–10, 2011); Danish Institute for International Studies, "The Political Economy of Development in Africa: Five Major Research Programmes Present Policy Implications of Their Work," Danish Institute for International Studies (Copenhagen, March 30, 2012); and Developmental Leadership Program, "Coalitions in the Politics of Development," Research and Policy Workshop Report (Developmental Leadership Program, April 2012).

5   See DFID, "Building the State and Securing the Peace," Emerging Policy Paper (London: Department for International Development, 2009); Thomas Parks and William Cole, "Political Settlements: Implications for International Development Policy and Practice," Occasional Paper no. 2 (Washington, D.C.: Asia Foundation, 2010); and Edward Laws, "Political Settlements, Elite Pacts, and Governments of National Unity: A Conceptual Study," Background Paper no. 10 (Developmental Leadership Program, August 2012).

6   Hilary Benn, "Political Governance, Corruption and the Role of Aid," Remarks at the Royal African Society (London, February 2, 2006), and DFID, *Eliminating World Poverty: Making Governance Work for the Poor*, White Paper on International Development (London: Department for International Development, 2006).

7   DFID, *Eliminating World Poverty: Building Our Common Future*, White Paper on International Development (London: Department for International Development, 2009), 73.

8   See DFID, "Building Peaceful States and Societies," DFID Practice Paper (London: Department for International Development, 2010); DFID, "Governance Portfolio Review Summary: Summary Review of DFID's Governance Portfolio 2004–2009" (London: Department for International Development, July 2011); DFID, *The Politics of Poverty: Elites, Citizens, and States: Findings From Ten Years of DFID Funded Research on Governance and Fragile States 2001–2010*, Synthesis Paper (London: Department for International Development, 2010).

9   World Bank, "Strengthening Governance, Tackling Corruption: The World Bank Group's Updated Strategy and Implementation Plan" (Washington, D.C.: World Bank, March 2012).

10 AusAID, "Effective Governance: Thematic Strategy" (Canberra: Australian Agency for International Development, November 2011), 6.

11 UNDP, "Institutional and Context Analysis – Guidance Note" (New York: United Nations Development Programme, Bureau for Development Policy, Democratic Governance Group, 2012), 4–5.

12 See EuropeAid, "Analysing and Addressing Governance in Sector Operations," Tools and Methods Reference Document no. 4 (Brussels: European Commission, November 2008), and EuropeAid, "Engaging Non-State Actors in New Aid Modalities: For Better Development Outcomes and Governance," Tools and Methods Reference Document no. 12 (Brussels: European Commission, January 2011).

13 See OECD DAC, "Draft Orientations and Principles on Development Co-operation, Accountability and Democratic Governance," DCD/DAC(2012)28 (Paris: Organisation for Economic Co-operation and Development, Development Assistance Committee, July 2012); Tom Dahl-Østergaard et al., "Lessons Learned on the Use of Power and Drivers of Change Analyses in Development Co-operation" (Paris: Organisation for Economic Co-operation and Development, DAC Network on Governance, September 2005); and OECD DAC, "Survey of Donor Approaches to Governance Assessment" (Paris: Organisation for Economic Co-operation and Development, DAC Network on Governance, February 2008).

14 For a more detailed explanation of the different levels of analysis, see Verena Fritz, Kai Kaiser, and Brian Levy, *Problem-Driven Governance and Political Economy Analysis: Good Practice Framework* (Washington, D.C.: World Bank, September 2009), and DFID, "Political Economy Analysis: How-To Note," DFID Practice Paper (London: Department for International Development, July 2009).

15 Authors' interview with DFID Nigeria staff, August 2012.

16 World Bank, "Strengthening Governance."

17 See Fritz, Kaiser, and Levy, *Problem-Driven Governance and Political Economy Analysis*, and Alice Poole, "Political Economy Assessments at Sector and Project Levels: How-To Note" (Washington, D.C.: World Bank, March 2011).

18 See DFID, "Political Economy Analysis."

19 See EuropeAid, "Analysing and Addressing Governance in Sector Operations."

20 This tool explicitly does not refer to itself as "political economy analysis" because it believes that term is too focused on economic issues and political actors, while it wants to take a broader focus. The methodology, issues, and uses of the analysis, however, are quite similar to what other donors call political economy studies. UNDP, "Institutional and Context Analysis Guidance Note," 4.

21 AusAID, "Effective Governance: Thematic Strategy," 15.

22 DFID, the World Bank, the EC, and UNDP organized a joint workshop, for example, to discuss political economy within sectors. See Marta Foresti and Leni Wild, "Analysing Governance and Political Economy in Sectors – Joint Donor Workshop," Workshop Report (London: Overseas Development Institute, 2009).

23 UNDP, "Supporting Country-Led Democratic Governance Assessments: Practice Note" (New York: United Nations Development Programme, February 2009).

24 Independent Evaluation Group, "World Bank Country-Level Engagement on Governance and Anticorruption: An Evaluation of the 2007 Strategy and Implementation Plan" (Washington, D.C.: World Bank, 2011), 75–76.

25 World Bank, "Strengthening Governance," 18.

26 AusAID, "Governance Annual Thematic Performance Report: 2009–10" (Canberra: Australian Agency for International Development, January 2011), 3.

27 Monica Beuran, Gaël Raballand, and Kapil Kapoor, "Political Economy Studies: Are They Actionable? Some Lessons From Zambia," Policy Research Working Paper 5656 (Washington, D.C.: World Bank, Africa Region, May 2011), 12–13.

28 Stephen Jones, "Policymaking During Political Transition in Nepal," Working Paper 3 (Oxford: Oxford Policy Management, 2010), 10.

29 Jones, "Policymaking During Political Transition in Nepal," 13.

30 For best practices and lessons learned on political economy analysis uptake, see DFID, "How-to Note: Lessons Learned—Planning and Undertaking a Drivers of Change Study," DFID Practice Paper (London: Department for International Development, November 2005); DFID, "Political Economy Analysis"; Wild and Foresti, "Politics Into Practice"; EuropeAid, "Analysing and Addressing Governance in Sector Operations"; and OECD DAC, "Survey of Donor Approaches to Governance Assessment."

31 November 2012 e-mail message from a USAID mission director in an African country to headquarters (mission director name withheld on request).

32 Janice Giffen and Ruth Judge, "Civil Society Policy and Practice in Donor Agencies" (Oxford: International NGO Training and Research Centre, May 2010), 9.

33 UNDP, "Voice and Accountability for Human Development: A UNDP Strategy to Strengthen Civil Society and Civic Engagement" (New York: United Nations Development Programme and Oslo Governance Centre, August 2009), 9.

34 See EuropeAid, "Engaging Non-State Actors in New Aid Modalities"; Norad, "Principles for Norad's Support to Civil Society in the South" (Oslo: Norwegian Agency for Development Cooperation, May 2009); Swedish Ministry for Foreign Affairs, "Pluralism: Policy for Support to Civil Society in Developing Countries With Swedish Development Cooperation" (Stockholm: Ministry for Foreign Affairs Information Service and the Department for Development Policy, 2009); DFID, "Civil Society and Development" (London: Department for International Development, Civil Society Team, February 2006); World Bank, "Guidance Note on Bank Multi-Stakeholder Engagement" (Washington, D.C.: World Bank, June 2009); and Giffen and Judge, "Civil Society Policy and Practice in Donor Agencies."

35 Norad, "Principles for Norad's Support to Civil Society in the South," 11–12.

36 EuropeAid, "Engaging Non-State Actors in New Aid Modalities," 11.

37 World Bank, "Strengthening Governance," 17.

38 UNDP, "Voice and Accountability for Human Development," 8.

39 EuropeAid, "Engaging Non-State Actors in New Aid Modalities," 9.

40 AusAID, "Effective Governance: Thematic Strategy," 16.

41 World Bank, "Strengthening Governance," 31.

42 DFID, "Governance Portfolio Review Summary," 18.

43 Swedish Ministry for Foreign Affairs, "Pluralism," 7.

44 EuropeAid, "Engaging Non-State Actors in New Aid Modalities," 15.

45 The OECD DAC's Network on Governance has taken this up as one of its priorities. See Wilson Prichard, "Citizen-State Relations: Improving Governance Through Tax Reform" (Paris: Organisation for Economic Co-operation and Development, DAC Network on Governance, 2010).

46 European Commission, "Preparing the European Commission Communication on Civil Society Organisations in Development," Consultation Paper (Brussels: European Commission, DG Development and Cooperation, March 2012), 8.

47 World Bank, "Guidance Note on Bank Multi-Stakeholder Engagement," 19.

48 The report attempts to lay out a donor consensus on good practice in this area. Based on four case studies and numerous workshops, it faults donors for too often attempting to impose best-practice models from their own countries, focusing on specific institutions in isolation from larger processes, and not engaging fully with fluid political contexts. The report calls "for a focus on substantive functions, not just the form of domestic accountability" and a "move towards an 'accountability systems' approach ... to move beyond a narrow focus on supply-side versus demand-side accountability support, or a focus only on formal institutions." It also calls for more realistic theories of change and a shift away from assuming civil society organizations will be the main drivers of progress to a consideration of the role of other actors—such as parliaments, political parties, and more loosely organized societal groups—as well as the enabling environment. See OECD DAC, "Draft Orientations and Principles."

49 Ramesh Awasthi, "Samarthan's Campaign to Improve Access to the National Rural Employment Guarantee Scheme in India," Partnership Initiative Case Study Series, Study no. 4 (Washington, D.C.: International Budget Partnership, August 2011). See also John Gaventa and Gregory Barrett, "So What Difference Does It Make? Mapping the Outcome of Citizen Engagement," IDS Working Paper 347 (Brighton: Institute of Development Studies, October 2010); and OECD DAC, "Draft Orientations and Principles," 30–33.

50 OECD DAC, "Draft Orientations and Principles," 15.

51 Leftwich and Wheeler, "Politics, Leadership and Coalitions in Development," Research and Policy Workshop Report (Developmental Leadership Program, June 2011).

52 David Booth, *Development as a Collective Action Problem: Addressing the Real Challenges of African Governance*, Synthesis Report (London: Overseas Development Institute, Africa Politics and Power Programme, 2012), 11, 13.

53 Cecilia Cabañero-Verzosa and Helen R. Garcia, *People, Politics, and Change: Building Communication Capacity for Governance Reform* (Washington, D.C.: World Bank, 2011).

54 The Tony Blair Governance Initiative, "Annual Report and Financial Statements" (London: Africa Governance Initiative, December 2010).

55 Laurel MacLaren, Alam Surya Putra, and Erman Rahman, "How Civil Society Organizations Work Politically to Promote Pro-Poor Policies in Decentralized Indonesian Cities," Occasional Paper 6 (Washington, D.C.: Asia Foundation, June 2011), and Jan Douwe Meindertsma et al., "Evaluation of Citizens' Voice & Accountability: Country Case Study: Indonesia," Evaluation Report (Bonn: Federal Ministry for Economic Cooperation and Development, September 2008).

56 Raul Fabella and Jaime Faustino (eds.), *Built on Dreams, Grounded in Reality: Economic Policy Reform in the Philippines* (Makati City, Philippines: Asia Foundation, 2011).

57 Ibid., and interviews with authors.

58 Developmental Leadership Program, "Coalitions in the Politics of Development: Findings, Insights and Guidance From the DLP Coalitions Workshop, Sydney, 15–16 February 2012," Research and Policy Workshop Report, (Developmental Leadership Program, April 2012). Also, author (Carothers) interview with Pyoe Pin staff members, March 2012.

59 PAPEP, "The PAPEP Experience: Strengthening Political Capacities for Development" (New York: United Nations Development Programme, Regional Bureau for Latin America and the Caribbean, October 2011).

60 Authors' interview with World Bank officials working on the Justice for the Poor Program, June 2012.

61 David Booth and the Africa Politics and Power Program have made the most use of the term "with the grain." See for example, David Booth, "Working With the Grain and Swimming Against the Tide: Barriers to Uptake of Research Findings on Governance and Public Services in Low-Income Africa," Working Paper 18 (London: Overseas Development Institute, Africa Power and Politics Programme, April 2011).

62 A CIDA evaluation, for instance, points to the "'ready,' 'fire,' 'aim,' approach to projects" and the pressure to get money out the door as factors limiting the space for analysis. CIDA, "Review of Governance Programming in CIDA: Synthesis Report" (Gatineau: Canadian International Development Agency, 2008), 25.

63 Derick Brinkerhoff and Marcus Ingle, "Integrating Blueprint and Process: A Structured Flexibility Approach to Development Management," *Public Administration and Development*, vol. 9, no. 5 (1989), 489.

64 Beatrice Buyck, "The Bank's Use of Technical Assistance for Institutional Development," Working Paper 578 (Washington, D.C.: World Bank, January 1991), vi, 25.

65 World Bank, "Strengthening Governance," and World Bank, "Operationalizing the 2011 World Development Report: Conflict, Security, and Development," prepared for the April 16, 2011, meeting of the Development Committee (Washington, D.C.: World Bank, April 2011).

CHAPTER 7

1 The World Bank's 2010 Development Policy Review of Tunisia, for example, notes significant progress by policymakers in opening the economy, maintaining macroeconomic stability, improving the business climate, and diversifying the education system. It highlights the need to address persistently high unemployment but does not mention corruption and refers to governance only sparingly and only with reference to economic governance issues such as reducing controls on business and improving the regulatory environment for investment. The report does have a brief section on public services and notes that the government's "public service improvement program reflects a commendable commitment to greater participation by the public." These commitments are, however, rather limited views of participation relating to the ability of citizens to access information, express their opinions and receive responses. Even this degree of participation is qualified by the Bank report, which notes that *"it is however important to indicate the desirable sequencing, which is essential since it is evident that not all seven priorities can be implemented at the same time."* See World Bank, *Republic of Tunisia Development Policy Review*, Report no. 50847-TN (Washington, D.C.: World Bank, Social and Economic Development Group, January 2010), vi, 46.

2 "The Middle East and North Africa: A New Social Contract for Development," Remarks by Robert Zoellick, Peterson Institute for International Economics (Washington, D.C., April 6, 2011), www.worldbank.org/en/news/2011/04/06/middle-east-north-africa-new-social-contract-development.

3 "An Expansion of Human Welfare," Remarks by Rajiv Shah, Democracy, Rights and Governance Conference 2.0 (Arlington, Va., June 20, 2011), http://transition.usaid.gov/press/speeches/2011/sp110620.html.

4 Commission of the European Communities, "Increasing the Impact of EU Development Policy: An Agenda for Change," Communication from the Commission to the European Parliament, the Council, the Economic and Social Committee and the Committee of the Regions (Brussels: European Commission, October 2011), 3.

5   David Cameron, "Speech at Al Azhar University," Jakarta, Indonesia, April 12, 2012, http://ukinindonesia.fco.gov.uk/en/news/?view=News&id=752063682.

6   Shah, "An Expansion of Human Welfare," and USAID, "ADS Chapter 220: Use of Reliable Partner Country Systems for Direct Management and Implementation of Assistance" (Washington, D.C.: U.S. Agency for International Development, March 2012).

7   USAID, "ADS Chapter 220," 14.

8   European Commission, "The Future Approach to EU Budget Support to Third Countries," Communication from the Commission to the European Parliament, the Council, the European Economic and Social Committee and the Committee of the Regions (Brussels: European Commission, October 2011), 9–10.

9   Millennium Challenge Corporation, "Report on the Criteria and Methodology for Determining the Eligibility of Candidate Countries for Millennium Challenge Account Assistance in Fiscal Year 2012" (Washington, D.C.: Millennium Challenge Corporation, September 2011).

10 Global Commission on Elections, Democracy, and Security, *Deepening Democracy: A Strategy for Improving the Integrity of Elections Worldwide* (Stockholm: Global Commission on Elections, Democracy and Security, September 2012), 57.

11 See, for example, Save the Children, "After the Millennium Development Goals: Setting out the Options and Must Haves for a New Development Framework in 2015" (London: Save the Children, April 2012), and OHCHR, "Towards Freedom From Fear and Want: Human Rights in the Post-2015 Agenda," Report for the UN System Task Team on the Post-2015 UN Development Agenda (Geneva: Office of the High Commissioner for Human Rights, May 2012).

12 UN General Assembly, 66th session, "Accelerating Progress Towards the Millennium Development Goals," Annual Report of the Secretary General (New York: United Nations, July 2011), 19.

13 UN System Task Team on the Post-2015 UN Development Agenda, *Realizing the Future We Want for All*, Report to the Secretary General (New York: United Nations, June 2012), 22.

14 OHCHR, "Towards Freedom From Fear and Want."

15 Beyond 2015, "Essential Must Haves—Substance," http://beyond2015.org/essential-must-haves-substance, and Gerard Vives, "Beyond 2015 & GCAP Comment on Post-2015 High-Level Panel," Beyond 2015, August 9, 2012, http://beyond2015.org/news/beyond-2015-gcap-comment-post-2015-high-level-panel-0.

16 Save the Children, "After the Millennium Development Goals," 8.

17 See UNDP, "Measuring Democracy and Democratic Governance in a Post-2015 Development Framework," UNDP Discussion Paper (New York: United Nations Development Programme, August 2012).

18 Nicole Bates-Eamer et al., *Post-2015 Development Agenda: Goals, Targets and Indicators: Special Report* (Waterloo, Canada/Seoul: Centre for International Governance Innovation/Korea Development Institute, 2012).

19 Global Commission on Elections, Democracy, and Security, *Deepening Democracy*, 64

20 See The World We Want 2015, "Governance," www.worldwewant2015.org/governance.

21 See Chuluunbaatar Gelegpil et al., *Millennium Development Goal-9 Indicators and the State of Democracy in Mongolia* (Ulaanbaatar: Institute of Philosophy, Sociology, and Law of the Mongolian Academy of Sciences and UNDP, 2009), and UNDP, "Measuring Democracy and Democratic Governance."

22 Bates-Eamer et al., *Post-2015 Development Agenda*.

23 Gina Bergh et al., "Building Governance into a Post-2015 Framework: Exploring Transparency and Accountability as an Entry Point" (London: Overseas Development Institute, October 2012); Claire Melamed, "Post-2015: The Road Ahead" (London: Overseas Development Institute, October 2012); and Bates-Eamer et al., *Post-2015 Development Agenda.*

24 Advisory Council on International Affairs, *The Post-2015 Development Agenda: The Millennium Development Goals in Perspective* (The Hague: Advisory Council on International Affairs, 2011), 11.

25 Mark Tran, "Human Rights Could Be Faultline in Post-2015 Development Agenda," *Guardian*, November 21, 2012, www.guardian.co.uk/global-development/2012/nov/21/human-rights-faultline-development-agenda.

26 David Cameron, "Combating Poverty at Its Roots," *Wall Street Journal*, November 1, 2012, http://online.wsj.com/article/SB10001424052970204712904578090571423009066.html.

27 George Soros and Fazle Hasan Abed, "Rule of Law Can Rid the World of Poverty," *Financial Times*, September 26, 2012, www.ft.com/cms/s/0/f78f8e0a-07cc-11e2-8354-00144feabdc0.html.

28 International Dialogue on Peacebuilding and Statebuilding, "A New Deal for Engagement in Fragile States" (International Dialogue on Peacebuilding and Statebuilding, December 2011).

29 Lisa Denney, "Security: The Missing Bottom of the Millennium Development Goals? Prospects for Inclusion in the Post-MDG Development Framework" (London: Overseas Development Institute, August 2012).

30 Bergh et al., "Building Governance into a Post-2015 Framework."

31 Open Government Partnership, www.opengovpartnership.org, and Bergh et al., "Building Governance into a Post-2015 Framework."

32 Melamed, "Post-2015"; Richard Morgan and Shannon O'Shea, "Locally-led Monitoring as an Engine for a More Dynamic and Accountable Post 2015 Development Agenda" (New York: UNICEF, Office of Research); and Bergh et al., "Building Governance into a Post-2015 Framework."

33 Jared Diamond, *Guns, Germs, and Steel: The Fates of Human Societies* (New York: W. W. Norton, 1999).

34 Jeffrey Sachs, *The End of Poverty: Economic Possibilities for Our Time* (London: Penguin Press, 2005), and Jeffrey Sachs et al., "Ending Africa's Poverty Trap," Brookings Papers on Economic Activity 1 (Washington, D.C.: Brookings Institution, 2004), 117–240.

35 Abhijit Banerjee and Esther Duflo, *Poor Economics: A Radical Rethinking of the Way to Fight Global Poverty* (New York: Public Affairs, 2011), and Esther Duflo, "Policies, Politics: Can Evidence Play a Role in the Fight Against Poverty?" The Sixth Annual Richard H. Sabot Lecture, Center for Global Development (Washington, D.C., April 2011).

36 Daron Acemoglu, Simon Johnson, and James Robinson, "The Colonial Origins of Comparative Development: An Empirical Investigation," *American Economic Review*, vol. 91, no. 5 (December 2001): 1369–1401.

37 See, for example, Daron Acemoglu and James Robinson, *Why Nations Fail: The Origins of Power, Prosperity, and Poverty* (New York: Crown Publishing Group, 2012); Acemoglu, Johnson, and Robinson, "The Colonial Origins of Comparative Development"; and Pippa Norris, *Making Democratic Governance Work: How Regimes Shape Prosperity, Welfare, and Peace* (Cambridge: Cambridge University Press, 2012).

38 Francis Fukuyama, *The Origins of Political Order: From Prehuman Times to the French Revolution* (New York: Farrar, Strauss and Giroux, 2011), 14.

39 Daniel Kaufmann and Aart Kraay, "Growth Without Governance," *Economía*, vol. 3, no. 1 (Fall 2002): 169–229; Daniel Kaufman, Aart Kray, and Pablo Zoido-Lobatón, "Governance Matters," Policy Research Working Paper 2196 (Washington, D.C.: World Bank, October 1999); and Daniel Kaufmann, Homi Kharas, and Veronika Penciakova, "Development, Aid, and Governance Indicators (DAGI)," Brookings Institution, July 2012, www.brookings.edu/research/interactives/development-aid-governance-indicators.

40 For example, Kurtz and Schrank (2007) argue that cross-national measures of governance are problematic, as they suffer from perceptual biases, adverse selection in sampling, and conceptual conflation with economic policy choices. Arndt and Oman (2006) further criticize the likelihood of error correlation among the data sources used, the indicators' lack of comparability over time and their insufficient transparency. See Marcus J. Kurtz and Andrew Schrank, "Growth and Governance: Models, Measures, and Mechanisms," *Journal of Politics*, vol. 69, no. 2 (2007): 538–54; and Christiane Arndt and Charles Oman, "Uses and Abuses of Governance Indicators," OECD Development Center Study (Paris: Organisation for Economic Co-operation and Development, 2006).

41 William Easterly and Ross Levine, "Tropics, Germs and Crops: How Endowments Influence Economic Development," Working Paper 9106 (Cambridge, Mass.: National Bureau of Economic Research, August 2002).

42 Dani Rodrik, Arvind Subramanian, and Francesco Trebbi, "Institutions Rule: The Primacy of Institutions Over Geography and Integration in Economic Development," Working Paper 9305 (Cambridge, Mass.: National Bureau of Economic Research, October 2002).

43 Stephen Knack and Philip Keefer, "Institutions and Economic Performance: Cross-Country Tests Using Alternative Institutional Indicators," *Economics & Politics*, vol. 7, no. 3 (1995): 207–27.

44 Robert E. Hall and Charles I. Jones, "Why Do Some Countries Produce So Much More Output per Worker Than Others?" *Quarterly Journal of Economics*, vol. 114, no. 1 (February 1999): 83–116.

45 Douglass C. North, John Wallis, and Barry Weingast, *Violence and Social Orders: A Conceptual Framework for Interpreting Recorded Human History* (Cambridge: Cambridge University Press, 2009).

46 Acemoglu and Robinson, *Why Nations Fail*.

47 Adam Przeworski and Fernando Limongi, "Political Regimes and Economic Growth," *Journal of Economic Perspectives*, vol. 7, no. 3 (Summer 1993): 51–69, and Adam Przeworski et al., *Democracy and Development; Political Institutions and Well-Being in the World, 1950–1990* (New York: Cambridge University Press, 2000), 271.

48 Paul Collier, *Wars, Guns, and Votes: Democracy in Dangerous Places* (New York: HarperCollins, 2009). For an opposing perspective on the same issue, see Arthur Goldsmith, "Ballots, Bullets, and the Bottom Billion," *Journal of Democracy*, vol. 23, no. 2 (April 2012): 119–32.

49 Morton H. Halperin, Joseph T. Siegle, and Michael M. Weinstein, *The Democracy Advantage: How Democracies Promote Prosperity and Peace* (New York: Routledge, 2005).

50 Norris cautions, however, that these welfare measures (based on the Human Development Index and education) are based on fairly clear-cut measures that can be susceptible to downward accountability to citizens. Democratic governance may have a less positive impact on more complex developmental challenges. The effect of democracy varies across different MDG targets. See Norris, *Making Democratic Governance Work*.

51 Acemoglu and Robinson, *Why Nations Fail*, 447.

52 Ibid., 460.

53 North, Wallis, and Weingast, *Violence and Social Orders*, 263.

54 Ibid., 264–65.

55 Dani Rodrik and Arvind Subramanian, "The Primacy of Institutions (and What This Does and Does Not Mean)," *Finance & Development,* vol. 40, no. 2 (June 2003): 33.

56 Ziya Onis, "The Logic of the Developmental State," *Comparative Politics*, vol. 24, no. 1 (October 1991): 109–26.

57 Ibid.

58 See Verena Fritz and Alina Rocha Menocal, "Developmental States in the New Millennium: Concepts and Challenges for a New Aid Agenda," *Development Policy Review*, vol. 25, no. 5 (2007): 531–52, and Mushtaq Khan, "Governance, Economic Growth and Development Since the 1960s: Background Paper for World Economic and Social Survey 2006" (New York: United Nations Department of Economic and Social Affairs, 2006).

59 Khan, "Governance, Economic Growth and Development Since the 1960s."

60 Peter Evans and James Rauch, "Bureaucracy and Growth: A Cross-National Analysis of the Effects of 'Weberian' State Structures on Economic Growth," *American Sociological Review*, vol. 64, no. 5 (1999): 748–65.

61 David Booth, *Development as a Collective Action Problem: Addressing the Real Challenges of African Governance*, Synthesis Report (London: Overseas Development Institute, Africa Politics and Power Programme, October 2012).

62 David Booth, "Toward a Theory of Local Governance and Public Goods' Provision in Sub-Saharan Africa," Working Paper 13 (London: Overseas Development Institute, Africa Power and Politics Programme, August 2010).

63 Atul Kohli, *State-Directed Development: Political Power and Industrialization in the Global Periphery* (New York: Cambridge University Press, 2004), 422.

64 David Booth, "Governance for Development in Africa: Building on What Works," Policy Brief 1 (London: Overseas Development Institute, Africa Power and Politics Programme, April 2011), 3.

65 Acemoglu and Robinson, *Why Nations Fail*.

66 Timothy Besley, "Poor Choices: Poverty From the Ground Level," *Foreign Affairs* (January/February 2012): 166.

67 Onis, "The Logic of the Developmental State," and Kohli, *State-Directed Development*.

68 Booth, *Development as a Collective Action Problem*, 48.

69 James Scott, *Seeing Like a State: How Certain Schemes to Improve the Human Condition Have Failed* (New Haven, Conn.: Yale University Press, 1998).

70 Peter Evans, "The State as Problem and Solution: Predation, Embedded Autonomy, and Structural Change," in *The Politics of Economic Adjustment: International Constraints, Distributive Conflicts, and the State,* edited by Stephan Haggard and Robert Kaufman (Princeton, N.J.: Princeton University Press, 1992).

71 Peter Evans, "Constructing the 21st Century Developmental State: Potentialities and Pitfalls," in *Constructing a Democratic Developmental State in South Africa: Potentials and Challenges*, edited by Omano Edigheji (Pretoria: HSRC Press, 2010).

72 Gordon White, "Constructing a Democratic Developmental State," in *The Democratic Developmental State: Politics and Institutional Design,* edited by Mark Robinson and Gordon White (Oxford: Oxford University Press, 1998).

73 Besley, "Poor Choices," 166.

74 Norris, *Making Democratic Governance Work*.

75 Richard Sandbrook, Marc Edelman, Patrick Heller, and Judith Teichman, *Social Democracy in the Global Periphery* (Cambridge: Cambridge University Press, 2007), 24.

76 Merilee Grindle, "Good Enough Governance: Poverty Reduction and Reform in Developing Countries," *Governance*, vol. 17, no. 4 (2004): 525–48, and Merilee Grindle, "Good Enough Governance Revisited," *Development Policy Review*, vol. 25, no. 5 (2007): 533–74.

77 Dani Rodrik, "Thinking About Governance," in *Governance, Growth and Development Decision-making*, edited by D. North, D. Acemoglu, F. Fukuyama, and D. Rodrik (Washington, D.C.: World Bank, 2008), 17–24.

78 Francis Fukuyama and Brian Levy, "Development Strategies: Integrating Governance and Growth," World Bank Policy Research Working Paper no. 5196 (Washington, D.C.: World Bank, January 2010).

79 Fukuyama, *The Origins of Political Order*, 23.

80 Centre for the Future State, *An Upside Down View of Governance* (Brighton: Institute of Development Studies, 2010).

81 Booth, *Development as a Collective Action Problem.*

CHAPTER 8

1   World Bank, "Strengthening World Bank Group Engagement on Governance and Anticorruption" (Washington, D.C.: World Bank, March 2007), i, vii.

2   World Bank, "Strengthening Governance, Tackling Corruption: The World Bank Group's Updated Strategy and Implementation Plan" (Washington, D.C.: World Bank, March 2012), 20.

3   USAID, "USAID Policy: Democracy and Governance" (Washington, D.C.: U.S. Agency for International Development, November 1991), 12.

4   Remarks by Rajiv Shah, "An Expansion of Human Welfare," Remarks at Democracy, Rights and Governance Conference 2.0, Arlington, Va., June 20, 2011, http://transition.usaid.gov/press/speeches/2011/sp110620.html.

5   In 2011–2012, CIDA spent approximately $154 million on advancing democracy and $24 million on security and stability. This compares with $837 million for food security, $1.1 billion on the future of children and youth, and $1.1 billion on sustainable economic growth (in Canadian dollars). See CIDA, "Report to Parliament on the Government of Canada's Official Development Assistance 2011–2012" (Gatineau: Canadian International Development Agency, 2012), 6.

6   CIDA, "Integration of Crosscutting Themes: Gender, Environment, Governance," Canadian International Development Agency, www.acdi-cida.gc.ca/acdi-cida/ACDI-CIDA.nsf/eng/ANN-616124216-MLH.

7   SDC, *Governance as a Transversal Theme: An Implementation Guide* (Berne: Swiss Agency for Development Cooperation, 2007).

8   EuropeAid, "Analysing and Addressing Governance in Sector Operations," Tools and Methods Reference Document no. 4 (Brussels: European Commission, 2008).

9   Carnegie Endowment for International Peace, "Taking Forward the Integration of Governance Into Development Aid: The Cases of Health and Climate Change," Workshop Report (December 8–9, 2011).

10 SDC, "Mini-Toolkit for Addressing Governance as a Transversal Theme in Projects/Domains of SDC" (Berne: Swiss Agency for Development Cooperation, December 2010).

11 Independent Evaluation Group, "World Bank Country-Level Engagement on Governance and Anticorruption: An Evaluation of the 2007 Strategy and Implementation Plan" (Washington, D.C.: World Bank, 2011), 64–66.

12 World Bank, "Strengthening Governance, Tackling Corruption," 64.

13 See, for example, DFID, "How-To Note: Addressing Corruption in the Health Sector," DFID Practice Paper (London: Department for International Development, November 2010).

14 Robert Charlick et al., "Report of the Faisons Ensemble Evaluation, March 2011" (Washington, D.C.: U.S. Agency for International Development Guinea, May 2011).

15 USAID, "USAID Policy Framework 2011–2015" (Washington, D.C.: U.S. Agency for International Development, 2011).

16 World Bank, "Strengthening Governance, Tackling Corruption," 29.

17 Ibid.

18 Kenneth Wollack and K. Scott Hubli, "Getting Convergence Right," *Journal of Democracy*, vol. 21, no. 4 (October 2010): 40.

19 Author (Carothers) interview with Sida officials, June 2010.

20 Laure-Hélène Piron, "Integrating Human Rights Into Development: A Synthesis of Donor Approaches and Experiences" (London: Overseas Development Institute, September 2005).

21 Personal correspondence.

22 Sam Hickey, "The Return of Politics in Development Studies (II): Capturing the Political?" *Progress in Development Studies*, vol. 9, no. 2 (2009): 149.

23 David Booth, "Working With the Grain and Swimming Against the Tide: Barriers to Uptake of Research Findings on Governance and Public Services in Low-income Africa," Working Paper 18 (London: Overseas Development Institute, Africa Politics and Power Programme, April 2011), 12.

24 See David Hudson and Adrian Leftwich, "From Political Economy to Political Analysis" (Developmental Leadership Program, forthcoming 2013). Arjan de Haan and Max Everest-Phillips make a similar point, noting that "as economists attempt to use their theories to explain politics, social scientists (or 'non-economist social scientists') have largely failed to develop alternative analyses to challenge the dominant economics paradigm in universities and development agencies." See de Haan and Everest-Phillips, "Can New Aid Modalities Handle Politics?" Research Paper no. 2007/63 (Helsinki: UNU World Institute for Development Economics Research, October 2007): 11.

25 Booth, "Working With the Grain and Swimming Against the Tide," 10.

26 Scott Guggenheim, "Crises and Contradictions: Understanding the Origins of a Community Development Project in Indonesia," in *The Search for Empowerment: Social Capital as Idea and Practice at the World Bank,*" edited by Anthony Bebbington et al. (Bloomfield, Conn.: Kumarian Press, 2006), 133.

27 Sue Unsworth makes this point, saying that "political scientists have not traditionally been recruited by development agencies, which have depended heavily on expertise from economists and technical advisers, most of them focused on policies rather than process." Sue Unsworth, "What's Politics Got to Do With It? Why Donors Find It So Hard to Come to Terms With Politics, and Why This Matters," *Journal of International Development*, vol. 21, no. 6 (2009): 889.

28 Committee on Evaluation of USAID Democracy Assistance Programs, *Improving Democracy Assistance: Building Knowledge Through Evaluations and Research* (Washington, D.C.: National Academies Press, 2008), 155–62.

29 USAID, "USAID Evaluation Policy" (Washington, D.C.: U.S. Agency for International Development, January 2011), 9.

30 Raghabendra Chattopadhyay and Esther Duflo, "Women as Policy Makers: Evidence From an India-Wide Randomized Policy Experiment," NBER Working Paper 8615 (Cambridge, Mass.: National Bureau of Economic Research, December 2001). J-PAL researchers also reached similar findings in Rajasthan; see J-PAL, "Ain't No Stopping Us Now: Women as Policy Makers," Policy Briefcase No. 1 (Cambridge, Mass.: Abdul Latif Jameel Poverty Action Lab, January 2006).

31 Claudio Ferraz and Frederico Finan, "Exposing Corrupt Politicians: The Effects of Brazil's Publicly Released Audit on Electoral Outcomes," *Quarterly Journal of Economics,* vol. 123, no. 2 (2008): 703–45.

32 J-PAL, "Evaluations," Abdul Latif Jameel Poverty Action Lab, www.povertyactionlab.org/GI/Evaluations.

33 Nancy Cartwright, "What Are Randomized Controlled Trials Good For?" *Philosophical Studies,* vol. 147, no. 1 (2010): 59–70, and Nancy Cartwright, "Are RCTs the Gold Standard?" *BioSocieties,* vol. 2, no. 1 (2007): 11–20,

34 Cartwright, "Are RCTs the Gold Standard?" 19.

35 Dani Rodrik, "The New Development Economics: We Shall Experiment, but How Shall We Learn?" Working Paper RWP08-055 (Cambridge, Mass.: Harvard Kennedy School, October 2008), 15.

36 See Angus Deaton, "Instruments, Randomization, and Learning About Development," *Journal of Economic Literature,* vol. 48, no. 2 (June 2010): 424–55.

37 Abhijit Banerjee and Esther Duflo, *Poor Economics: A Radical Rethinking of the Way to Fight Global Poverty* (New York: Public Affairs, 2011).

38 Daron Acemoglu and James Robinson, *Why Nations Fail: The Origins of Power, Prosperity, and Poverty* (New York: Crown Publishing Group, 2012), 448–49.

CHAPTER 9

1 OECD statistics indicate that all countries that receive official development assistance have also received some aid categorized as "government and civil society" in recent years. See OECD DAC, "Creditor Reporting System," OECD.StatExtracts.

2 Thomas Carothers, "Ousting Foreign Strongmen: The Case of Serbia," in Thomas Carothers, *Critical Mission: Essays on Democracy Promotion* (Washington, D.C.: Carnegie Endowment for International Peace, 2004), ch. 4.

3 For an exploration of this argument, see Christopher Hobson and Milja Kurki (eds.), *The Conceptual Politics of Democracy Promotion* (New York: Routledge, 2011), and Rita Abrahamsen, *Disciplining Democracy: Development Discourse and Good Governance in Africa* (London: Zed Books, 2000).

4 Tania Murray Li sets out this argument in some detail with regard to donor activities in Indonesia. Referencing James Ferguson's *The Anti-Politics Machine,* she contends that little has changed over the decades and that "development interventions can proceed only on the basis that 'the government' is a neutral vessel dedicated to improvement for 'the people.'" See Tania Murray Li, *The Will to Improve: Governmentality, Development, and the Practice of Politics* (Durham and London: Duke University Press, 2007), 134.

5   For an in-depth discussion of this issue, see Anna Lekvall, *Development First, Democracy Later?* (Stockholm: International Institute for Democracy and Electoral Assistance, forthcoming 2013).

6   Chris Roche and Linda Kelly, "The Evaluation of Politics and the Politics of Evaluation," DLP Background Paper 11 (Developmental Leadership Program, August 2012), 7.

7   Krishna Kumar, *Evaluating Democracy Assistance* (Boulder, Colo.: Lynne Rienner, 2012).

8   UNDESA, "Financial Flows to Developing Countries," in *World Economic Situation and Prospects 2011* (New York: United Nations Department of Economic and Social Affairs, 2011), and UNDP, *Towards Human Resilience: Sustaining MDG Progress in an Age of Economic Uncertainty* (New York: United Nations Development Programme, September 2011).

9   World Bank, "Remittances to Developing Countries Will Surpass $400 Billion in 2012," Migration and Development Brief 19 (Washington, D.C.: World Bank, Migration and Remittances Unit, November 2012).

10 Deborah Brautigam estimates that China provided $1.2 billion in aid to Africa in 2008 and $1.4 billion in 2009, roughly similar to Japan ($1.6 billion) but significantly less than the United States ($7.2 billion) and the World Bank ($4.1 billion). Deborah Brautigam, "Chinese Development Aid in Africa: What, Where, Why, and How Much?" In *Rising China: Global Challenges and Opportunities*, edited by Jane Golley and Ligang Song (Canberra: Australia National University Press, 2011), 211. Also see "Crumbs From the BRICs-Man's Table," *Economist*, March 18, 2010, www.economist.com/node/15731508?story_id=15731508.

11 UNDESA, "Financial Flows to Developing Countries"; UNDP, *Towards Human Resilience*, 147–50; and "Crumbs From the BRICs-Man's Table."

12 See, for example, Remarks by Robert Zoellick, "Beyond Aid," George Washington University (Washington, D.C.: September 14, 2011). http://go.worldbank.org/J0VM93C6Z0, and Andrew Mitchell, "Beyond Aid," Wellcome Trust (London, November 11, 2011), http://webarchive.nationalarchives.gov.uk/+/http://www.dfid.gov.uk/News/Speeches-and-articles/2011/Andrew-Mitchell-Beyond-Aid.

13 Tania Murray Li describes this as the tendency of aid agencies to "render technical" social problems. See James Ferguson, *The Anti-Politics Machine: Development, Depoliticization, and Bureaucratic Power in Lesotho* (Minneapolis: University of Minnesota Press, 1994), and Tania Murray Li, *The Will to Improve*.

14 For survey results on opinions on democracy in Africa and Latin America, see Michael Bratton, "Trends in Popular Attitudes to Multiparty Democracy in Africa, 2000–2012," Afrobarometer Briefing Paper no. 105 (Afrobarometer, October 2012), and Corporación Latinobarómetro, "Informe 2011" (Santiago de Chile: Corporación Latinobarómetro, October 2011).

15 For a similar argument, see Anna Lekvall, *Development First, Democracy Later?*

16 See Josh Kron, "In Uganda, an AIDS Success Story Comes Undone," *New York Times*, August 2, 2012, and Samuel Rubenfield, "Uganda Donors Freeze $300 Million in Aid Over Corruption," *Wall Street Journal*, December 4, 2012.

17 DFID, "Rwanda: UK Freezes Budget Support to Government," UK Department for International Development, November 30, 2012, www.dfid.gov.uk/News/Latest-news/2012/UK-aid-to-Rwanda-and-DRC.

BIBLIOGRAPHY

This bibliography lists selected works on major issues relating to political goals and methods in development assistance. It aims to bring together the resources likely to be most useful to those interested in further reading on the topic. It begins with (A) a general section, followed by specific sections on (B) the use of political analysis, (C) participation and bottom-up governance assistance, (D) the political economy of development, and (E) the history of foreign aid in the 1950s through 1980s.

A. GENERAL

Abrahamsen, Rita. *Disciplining Democracy: Development Discourse and Good Governance in Africa.* London: Zed Books, 2000.

Ahmad, Tariq. "The 'Right' Results: Making Sure the Results Agenda Remains Committed to Poverty Reduction." Oxfam Briefing Paper 155. Oxford: Oxfam International, September 2011.

AusAID. "Effective Governance: Thematic Strategy." Canberra: Australian Agency for International Development, November 2011.

Benn, Hilary. "Political Governance, Corruption and the Role of Aid." Remarks at the Royal African Society, London, February 2, 2006.

Booth, David. "Aid Effectiveness: Bringing Country Ownership (and Politics) Back In." Working Paper 336. London: Overseas Development Institute, Africa Power and Politics Programme, August 2011.

———. "Working With the Grain and Swimming Against the Tide: Barriers to Uptake of Research Findings on Governance and Public Services in Low-Income Africa." Working Paper 18. London: Overseas Development Institute, Africa Power and Politics Programme, April 2011.

Brinkerhoff, Derick, and Benjamin Crosby. *Managing Policy Reform: Concepts and Tools for Decision-Makers in Developing and Transitioning Countries*. Bloomfield, Conn.: Kumarian Press, 2002.

Cabañero-Verzosa, Cecilia, and Helen R. Garcia. *People, Politics, and Change: Building Communication Capacity for Governance Reform*. Washington, D.C.: World Bank, 2011.

Campos, J. Edgardo, and Jose Luis Syquia. "Managing the Politics of Reform: Overhauling the Legal Infrastructure for Public Procurement in the Philippines." World Bank Working Paper no. 70. Washington, D.C.: World Bank, 2006.

Carothers, Thomas. *Aiding Democracy Abroad: The Learning Curve*. Washington, D.C.: Carnegie Endowment for International Peace, 1999.

———. "Democracy Assistance: Political vs. Developmental?" *Journal of Democracy*, vol. 20, no. 1 (January 2009): 5–19.

———. "The Elusive Synthesis." *Journal of Democracy*, vol. 21, no. 4 (October 2010): 12–26.

Charlick, Robert, et al. "Report of the Faisons Ensemble Evaluation, March 2011." Washington, D.C.: U.S. Agency for International Development Guinea, May 2011.

CIDA. "Government of Canada Policy for CIDA on Human Rights, Democratization and Good Governance." Gatineau: Canadian International Development Agency, December 1996.

———. "Review of Governance Programming in CIDA: Synthesis Report." Gatineau: Canadian International Development Agency, 2008.

Cox, Marcus, and Nigel Thornton. "DFID Engagement in Countries in Fragile Situations: A Portfolio Review." Evaluation Report EV701. London: Department for International Development, January 2009.

Craig, David, and Doug Porter. *Development Beyond Neoliberalism? Governance, Poverty Reduction and Political Economy*. New York: Routledge, 2006.

Crawford, Gordon. *Foreign Aid and Political Reform: A Comparative Analysis of Democracy Assistance and Political Conditionality*. New York: Palgrave Macmillan, 2001.

Dahl-Østergaard, Tom, Karin Schulz, and Barbro Svedberg. "Experiences and Lessons Learnt From Sida's Work With Human Rights and Democratic Governance." Stockholm: Swedish International Development Cooperation Agency, 2008.

Dañino, Roberto. "Legal Opinion on Human Rights and the Work of the World Bank." Washington, D.C.: World Bank, 2006.

de Haan, Arjan, and Max Everest-Phillips. "Can New Aid Modalities Handle Politics?" Research Paper no. 2007/63. Helsinki: UNU World Institute for Development Economics Research, October 2007.

Developmental Leadership Program. "Coalitions in the Politics of Development: Findings, Insights and Guidance From the DLP Coalitions Workshop, Sydney, 15–16 February 2012." Research and Policy Workshop Report. Developmental Leadership Program, April 2012.

DFID. "Building the State and Securing the Peace." Emerging Policy Paper. London: Department for International Development, 2009.

———. *Eliminating World Poverty: A Challenge for the 21st Century*. White Paper on International Development. London: Department for International Development, November 1997.

———. *Eliminating World Poverty: Building Our Common Future*. White Paper on International Development. London: Department for International Development, July 2009.

————. *Eliminating World Poverty: Making Governance Work for the Poor.* White Paper on International Development. London: Department for International Development, July 2006.

————. "Governance Portfolio Review Summary: Summary Review of DFID's Governance Portfolio 2004–2009." London: Department for International Development, July 2011.

————. "Realising Human Rights for Poor People: Strategies for Achieving the International Development Targets." London: Department for International Development, October 2000.

————. *Why We Need to Work More Effectively in Fragile States.* London: Department for International Development, January 2005.

————. *The Politics of Poverty: Elites, Citizens, and States: Findings From Ten Years of DFID Funded Research on Governance and Fragile States 2001–2010.* Synthesis Paper. London: Department for International Development, 2010.

Dollar, David, and Lant Pritchett. *Assessing Aid: What Works, What Doesn't, and Why.* World Bank Policy Research Report. New York: Oxford University Press, 1998.

Doornbos, Martin. "'Good Governance': The Metamorphosis of a Policy Metaphor." *Journal of International Affairs*, vol. 57, no. 1 (Fall 2003): 3–17.

Easterly, William, and Tobias Pfutze, "Where Does the Money Go? Best and Worst Practices in Foreign Aid." Global Economy & Development Working Paper no. 21. Washington, D.C.: Brookings Institution, June 2008.

Eaton, Kent, Kai Kaiser, and Paul Smoke. *The Political Economy of Decentralization Reforms: Implications for Aid Effectiveness.* Washington, D.C.: World Bank, 2010.

European Commission. "Governance in the European Consensus on Development: Towards a Harmonised Approach Within the European Union." Communication from the Commission to the Council, the European Parliament, the European Economic and Social Committee and the Committee of the Regions. Brussels: European Commission, August 2006.

————. "Increasing the Impact of EU Development Policy: an Agenda for Change." Communication from the Commission to the Council, the European Parliament, the European Economic and Social Committee and the Committee of the Regions. Brussels: European Commission, October 2011.

————. "The Future Approach to EU Budget Support to Third Countries." Communication from the Commission to the Council, the European Parliament, the European Economic and Social Committee and the Committee of the Regions. Brussels: European Commission, October 2011.

Fabella, Raul, and Jaime Faustino, eds. *Built on Dreams, Grounded in Reality: Economic Policy Reform in the Philippines.* Makati City, Philippines: Asia Foundation, 2011.

French Ministry of Foreign Affairs. "Governance Strategy for French Development Assistance." Paris: French Ministry of Foreign Affairs, December 2006.

Frenken, Sarah, and Ulrich Müller, eds. *Ownership and Political Steering in Developing Countries: Proceedings of International Conferences in London and Berlin.* Eschborn/Baden Baden: Deutsche Gesellschaft für Technische Zusammenarbeit and Nomos Publishers, 2010.

Gaeta, Anthony, and Marina Vasilara. "Development and Human Rights: The Role of the World Bank." Washington, D.C.: World Bank, September 1998.

Hewitt de Alcántara, Cynthia. "Uses and Abuses of the Concept of Governance." Paris: United Nations Educational, Scientific and Cultural Organization, 1998.

Hickey, Sam. "The Politics of Protecting the Poorest: Moving Beyond the 'Anti-Politics Machine'?" *Political Geography*, vol. 28, no. 8 (2009): 473–83.

———. "The Return of Politics in Development Studies (I): Getting Lost Within the Poverty Agenda?" *Progress in Development Studies*, vol. 8, no. 4 (2008): 349–58.

———. "The Return of Politics in Development Studies (II): Capturing the Political?" *Progress in Development Studies*, vol. 9, no. 2 (2009): 141–52.

Hoebink, Paul. "European Donors and 'Good Governance': Condition or Goal?" *European Journal of Development Research*, vol. 18, no. 1 (March 2006): 131–61.

Human Rights Watch. *Development Without Freedom: How Aid Underwrites Repression in Ethiopia*. New York: Human Rights Watch, 2010.

Independent Evaluation Group. "World Bank Country-Level Engagement on Governance and Anticorruption: An Evaluation of the 2007 Strategy and Implementation Plan." Washington, D.C.: World Bank, 2011.

Kaufmann, Daniel, and Veronika Penciakova. "How Selective Is Donor Aid? Governance and Corruption Matter and Donor Agencies Should Take Notice." Brookings Institution, July 17, 2012. www.brookings.edu/research/opinions/2012/07/17-donor-aid-kaufmann.

Laws, Edward. "Political Settlements, Elite Pacts, and Governments of National Unity: A Conceptual Study." Background Paper no. 10. Developmental Leadership Program, August 2012.

Leftwich, Adrian, and Chris Wheeler. "Politics, Leadership and Coalitions in Development: Findings, Insights and Guidance From the DLP's First Research and Policy Workshop. Frankfurt, 10–11 March 2011." Research and Policy Workshop Report. Developmental Leadership Program, June 2011.

Lekvall, Anna. *Development First, Democracy Later?* Stockholm: International Institute for Democracy and Electoral Assistance, forthcoming 2013.

Li, Tania. *The Will to Improve: Governmentality, Development, and the Practice of Politics*. Durham, N.C., and London: Duke University Press, 2007.

Manor, James. *The Political Economy of Democratic Decentralization*. Washington, D.C.: World Bank, 1999.

Marquette, Heather. *Corruption, Politics and Development: The Role of the World Bank*. New York: Palgrave Macmillan, 2004.

Ministry of Foreign Affairs of Japan. "Good Governance: Japan's Action." Sectoral Development Policy, November 2007. www.mofa.go.jp/policy/oda/sector/governance/action.html.

Molenaers, Nadia, and Leen Nijs. "From the Theory of Aid Effectiveness to the Practice: The European Commission's Governance Incentive Tranche." *Development Policy Review*, vol. 27, no. 5 (2009): 561–80.

OECD DAC. "DAC Orientations on Participatory Development and Good Governance." OCDE/GD (93)191. Paris: Organisation for Economic Co-operation and Development, Development Assistance Committee, 1993.

———. "Final Report of the Ad Hoc Group on Participatory Development and Good Government: Part 1." Paris: Organisation for Economic Co-operation and Development, Development Assistance Committee, 1997.

————. "Supporting Statebuilding in Situations of Fragility and Conflict." Paris: Organisation for Economic Co-operation and Development, Development Assistance Committee, 2011.

Overseas Development Administration. "Taking Account of Good Government." Technical Note no. 10. London: Overseas Development Administration, Government and Institutions Department, October 1993.

Parks, Thomas, and William Cole. "Political Settlements: Implications for International Development Policy and Practice." Occasional Paper no. 2. Washington, D.C.: Asia Foundation, 2010.

Piron, Laure-Hélène. *Integrating Human Rights Into Development: A Synthesis of Donor Approaches and Experiences.* London: Overseas Development Institute, September 2005.

————. *The Right to Development: A Review of the Current State of the Debate for the Department for International Development.* London: Overseas Development Institute, April 2002.

Roche, Chris, and Linda Kelly. "The Evaluation of Politics and the Politics of Evaluation." DLP Background Paper 11. Developmental Leadership Program, August 2012.

Santiso, Carlos. "Governance Conditionality and the Reform of Multilateral Development Finance: The Role of the Group of Eight." *G8 Governance*, no. 7 (March 2002).

SDC. *Governance as a Transversal Theme: An Implementation Guide.* Berne: Swiss Agency for Development and Cooperation, 2007.

Shah, Rajiv. "An Expansion of Human Welfare." Remarks at Democracy, Rights and Governance Conference 2.0, Arlington, Va., June 20, 2001. http://transition.usaid.gov/press/speeches/2011/sp110620.html.

Sida. *Making Government Work: Guidelines and Framework for SIDA Support to the Development of Public Administration.* Stockholm: Swedish International Development Cooperation Agency, 1991.

————. *Perspectives on Poverty.* Stockholm: Swedish International Development Cooperation Agency, 2002.

————. "SIDA's Programme for Peace, Democracy and Human Rights. Part A." Stockholm: Swedish International Development Cooperation Agency, 1997.

UNDP. *A Guide to UNDP Democratic Governance Practice.* New York: United Nations Development Programme, 2010.

————. "Integrating Human Rights With Sustainable Human Development." UNDP Policy Document. New York: United Nations Development Programme, January 1998.

Unsworth, Sue. "What's Politics Got to Do With It? Why Donors Find It So Hard to Come to Terms With Politics, and Why This Matters." *Journal of International Development*, vol. 21, no. 6 (2009): 883–94.

USAID. *Strategies for Sustainable Development.* Washington, D.C.: U.S. Agency for International Development, March 1994.

————. "USAID Policy: Democracy and Governance." Washington, D.C.: U.S. Agency for International Development, November 1991.

Weaver, Catherine. *Hypocrisy Trap: The World Bank and the Poverty of Reform.* Princeton, N.J.: Princeton University Press, 2008.

Wild, Leni, and Marta Foresti. "Politics into Practice: A Dialogue on Governance Strategies and Action in International Development." Conference Report. London: Overseas Development Institute, May 2011.

Wollack, Kenneth, and K. Scott Hubli. "Getting Convergence Right." *Journal of Democracy*, vol. 21, no. 4 (October 2010): 35–42.

World Bank. *Economic Growth in the 1990s: Learning From a Decade of Reform*. Washington, D.C.: World Bank, 2005.

———. *Governance and Development*. Washington, D.C.: World Bank, 1992.

———. "Strengthening World Bank Group Engagement on Governance and Anticorruption." Washington, D.C.: World Bank, March 2007.

———. "Strengthening Governance, Tackling Corruption: The World Bank Group's Updated Strategy and Implementation Plan." Washington, D.C.: World Bank, March 2012.

———. *Sub-Saharan Africa: From Crisis to Sustainable Growth*. Washington, D.C.: World Bank, November 1989.

Zoellick, Robert. "The Middle East and North Africa: A New Social Contract for Development." Remarks at the Peterson Institute for International Economics, Washington, D.C., April 6, 2011.

B. USE OF POLITICAL ANALYSIS

Beuran, Monica, Gaël Raballand, and Kapil Kapoor. "Political Economy Studies: Are They Actionable? Some Lessons From Zambia." Policy Research Working Paper 5656. Washington, D.C.: World Bank, Africa Region, May 2011.

Dahl-Østergaard, Tom, Sue Unsworth, Mark Robinson, and Rikke Ingrid Jensen. "Lessons Learned on the Use of Power and Drivers of Change Analyses in Development Co-operation." Paris: Organisation for Economic Co-operation and Development, DAC Network on Governance, September 2005.

Development Alternatives, Inc. "Political Considerations: Political Economy Analysis and the Practice of Development." *Developing Alternatives*, vol. 14, no. 1 (Summer 2011): 1–47.

DFID. "How-To Note: Lessons Learned—Planning and Undertaking a Drivers of Change Study." DFID Practice Paper. London: Department for International Development, November 2005.

———. "Political Economy Analysis How-To Note." DFID Practice Paper. London: Department for International Development, July 2009.

EuropeAid. "Analysing and Addressing Governance in Sector Operations." Tools and Methods Reference Document no. 4. Brussels: European Commission, November 2008.

Foresti, Marta, and Leni Wild. "Analysing Governance and Political Economy in Sectors—Joint Donor Workshop." Workshop Report. London: Overseas Development Institute, 2009.

Fritz, Verena, Kai Kaiser, and Brian Levy. *Problem-Driven Governance and Political Economy Analysis: Good Practice Framework*. Washington, D.C.: World Bank, September 2009.

Goodhand, Jonathan, Tony Vaux, and Robert Walker. "Conducting Conflict Assessments: Guidance Notes." London: Department for International Development, January 2002.

Hudson, David, and Adrian Leftwich. "From Political Economy to Political Analysis." Developmental Leadership Program, forthcoming 2013.

Jones, Stephen. "Policymaking During Political Transition in Nepal." Working Paper 3. Oxford: Oxford Policy Management, 2010.

Levy, Brian, and Nick Manning. "Institutional and Governance Reviews: A New Type of Economic and Sector Work." PREMnotes no. 75. Washington, D.C.: World Bank, November 2002.

Netherlands Ministry of Foreign Affairs. "Political Analyses and Development Cooperation: Draft Synthesis of the Power and Change Analyses 2007–2009." The Hague: Netherlands Ministry of Foreign Affairs, 2010.

Norad. "Political Economy Analysis With a Legitimacy Twist: What Is It and Why Does It Matter?" Oslo: Norwegian Agency for Development Cooperation, December 2010.

OECD DAC. "Survey of Donor Approaches to Governance Assessment." Paris: Organisation for Economic Co-operation and Development, DAC Network on Governance, February 2008.

Poole, Alice. "Political Economy Assessments at Sector and Project Levels: How-To Note." Washington, D.C.: World Bank, March 2011.

Power, Greg. "The Politics of Parliamentary Strengthening: Understanding Political Incentives and Institutional Behaviour in Parliamentary Support Strategies." London: Westminister Foundation for Democracy and Global Partners & Associates, 2011.

SDC. "Mini-Toolkit for Addressing Governance as a Transversal Theme in Projects/Domains of SDC." Berne: Swiss Agency for Development and Cooperation, December 2010.

Sida. "Manual for Conflict Analysis." Methods Document. Stockholm: Swedish International Development Cooperation Agency, January 2006.

Tolentino, V. Bruce J. "From Analysis to Implementation: The Practice of Political Economy Approaches to Economic Reform." Occasional Paper no. 3. Washington, D.C.: Asia Foundation, September 2010.

UNDP. "Institutional and Context Analysis—Guidance Note." New York: United Nations Development Programme, Bureau for Development Policy, Democratic Governance Group, 2012.

———. "Supporting Country-Led Democratic Governance Assessments: Practice Note." New York: United Nations Development Programme, February 2009.

———. "The PAPEP Experience: Strengthening Political Capacities for Development." New York: United Nations Development Programme, Regional Bureau for Latin America and the Caribbean, October 2011.

Unsworth, Sue, and Conflict Research Unit. *Framework for Strategic Governance and Corruption Analysis: Designing Strategic Responses Towards Good Governance.* Netherlands Institute of International Relations, October 2007.

USAID. "Conducting a Conflict Assessment: A Framework for Analysis and Program Development." Washington, D.C.: U.S. Agency for International Development, Office of Conflict Management and Mitigation, April 2005.

———. "Conducting a DG Assessment: A Framework for Strategy Development." Washington, D.C.: U.S. Agency for International Development, Center for Democracy and Governance, November 2000.

Vaux, Tony. "Conflict-Related Development Analysis." New York: United Nations Development Programme, Bureau for Crisis Prevention and Recovery, October 2003.

Williams, Gareth, Alex Duncan, and Pierre Landell-Mills. "Making the New Political Economy Perspective More Operationally Relevant for Development Agencies." Policy Practice Brief 2. Brighton: The Policy Practice, January 2007.

Williams, Gareth, Alex Duncan, Pierre Landell-Mills, Sue Unsworth, and Tim Sheehy. "Carrying Out a Joint Governance Assessment: Lessons From Rwanda." Policy Practice Brief 5. Brighton: The Policy Practice, January 2009.

World Bank. "The Conflict Analysis Framework (CAF): Identifying Conflict-Related Obstacles to Development." Dissemination Notes no. 5. Washington, D.C.: World Bank, Social Development Department, October 2002.

C. PARTICIPATION AND BOTTOM-UP GOVERNANCE

Agarwal, Sanjay, Rasmus Heltberg, and Myrtle Diachok. "Scaling-Up Social Accountability in World Bank Operations." Washington, D.C.: World Bank, Social Development Department, May 2009.

AusAID. "Australian Aid Approaches to Building Demand for Better Governance." Canberra: Australian Agency for International Development, December 2007.

Aycrigg, Maria. "Participation and the World Bank: Success, Constraints, and Responses." Social Development Papers no. 29. Washington, D.C.: World Bank, November 1998.

Banks, Nicola, and David Hulme. "The Role of NGOs and Civil Society in Poverty Reduction." BWPI Working Paper 171. Manchester: Brooks World Poverty Institute, June 2012.

Bergh, Gina, Marta Foresti, Alina Rocha Menocal, and Leni Wild. "Building Governance into a Post-2015 Framework: Exploring Transparency and Accountability as an Entry Point." London: Overseas Development Institute, October 2012.

Booth, David. "Missing Links in the Politics of Development: Learning From the PRSP Experiment." Working Paper 256. London: Overseas Development Institute, October 2005.

DFID. "Civil Society and Development." London: Department for International Development, Civil Society Team, February 2006.

Draman, Rasheed. "Legislating Poverty in Africa: What Role Have Parliamentarians Been Playing in PRSP Implementation and Policy?" Ottawa: Parliamentary Centre, May 2007.

European Commission. "Participation of Non-State Actors in EC Development Policy." Communication from the Commission to the Council, the European Parliament and the Economic and Social Committee. Brussels: European Commission, 2002.

———. "Preparing the European Commission Communication on Civil Society Organisations in Development." Consultation Paper. Brussels: European Commission, March 2012.

EuropeAid. "Engaging Non-State Actors in New Aid Modalities: For Better Development Outcomes and Governance." Tools and Methods Reference Document no. 12. Brussels: European Commission, January 2011.

Gaventa, John. "Introduction: Exploring Citizenship, Participation and Accountability." IDS Bulletin, vol. 33, no. 2 (2002): 1–11.

Gaventa, John, and Gregory Barrett. "So What Difference Does It Make? Mapping the Outcome of Citizen Engagement." IDS Working Paper 347. Brighton: Institute of Development Studies, October 2010.

Giffen, Janice, and Ruth Judge. "Civil Society Policy and Practice in Donor Agencies." Oxford: International NGO Training and Research Centre, May 2010.

Gould, Jeremy, ed. *The New Conditionality: The Politics of Poverty Reduction Strategies*. London: Zed Books, 2005.

Green, Duncan. *From Poverty to Power: How Active Citizens and Effective States Can Change the World*. Oxford: Oxfam International, 2008.

Guggenheim, Scott. "Crises and Contradictions: Understanding the Origins of a Community Development Project in Indonesia." In *The Search for Empowerment: Social Capital as Idea and Practice at the World Bank*, eds. Anthony Bebbington et al. (Bloomfield, Conn.: Kumarian Press, 2006).

Gurkan, Asli. "Demand for Good Governance in the World Bank: Conceptual Evolution, Frameworks and Activities." Washington, D.C.: World Bank, Social Development Department, August 2010.

Hall, Jo, and Jude Howell. "Working Paper: Good Practice Donor Engagement With Civil Society." Canberra: Australian Agency for International Development, June 2010.

Hickey, Samuel, and Giles Mohan. *Participation: From Tyranny to Transformation? Exploring New Approaches to Participation in Development*. London: Zed Books, 2005.

Hudock, Ann. "Laying the Foundation for Sustainable Development: Good Governance and the Poverty Reduction Strategy Paper." Washington, D.C.: World Learning, August 2002.

Hudson, Alan, and GOVNET Secretariat. "Background Paper for the Launch of the Work-Stream on Aid and Domestic Accountability." Paris: Organisation for Economic Co-operation and Development, DAC Network on Governance, March 2009.

Isham, Jonathan, Deepa Narayan, and Lant Pritchett. "Does Participation Improve Performance? Establishing Causality With Subjective Data." Policy Research Working Paper 1357. Washington, D.C.: World Bank, September 1994.

Lazarus, Joel. "Participation in Poverty Reduction Strategy Papers: Reviewing the Past, Assessing the Present and Predicting the Future." *Third World Quarterly*, vol. 29, no. 6 (2008): 1205–21.

MacLaren, Laurel, Alam Surya Putra, and Erman Rahman. "How Civil Society Organizations Work Politically to Promote Pro-Poor Policies in Decentralized Indonesian Cities." Occasional Paper 6. Washington, D.C.: Asia Foundation, June 2011.

Mansuri, Ghazala, and Vijayendra Rao. "Community-Based and -Driven Development: A Critical Review." *World Bank Research Observer*, vol. 19, no. 1 (2004): 1–39.

———. *Localizing Development: Does Participation Work?* World Bank Policy Research Report. Washington, D.C.: World Bank, 2013.

McGee, Rosemary, and John Gaventa. *Review of Impact and Effectiveness of Transparency and Accountability Initiatives: Synthesis Report*. Brighton: Institute of Development Studies, 2010.

———. "Shifting Power? Assessing the Impact of Transparency and Accountability Initiatives." IDS Working Paper no. 383. Brighton: Institute of Development Studies, 2011.

Norad. "Principles for Norad's Support to Civil Society in the South." Oslo: Norwegian Agency for Development Cooperation, May 2009.

Norton, Andy, et al. "A Rough Guide to PPAs: Participatory Poverty Assessment, An Introduction to Theory and Practice." London: Overseas Development Institute, 2001.

OECD DAC. "Draft Orientations and Principles on Development Co-Operation, Accountability and Democratic Governance." DCD/DAC(2012)28. Paris: Organisation for Economic Co-operation and Development, Development Assistance Committee, July 2012.

PARTICIP. "Evaluation of EC Aid Delivery through Civil Society Organisations: Final Report, Volume 1." Evaluation for the European Commission. Freiburg: PARTICIP, December 2008.

Robinson, Mark, ed. *Budgeting for the Poor*. Basingstoke, UK: Palgrave Macmillan, 2008.

Robinson, Mark, and Steven Friedman, "Civil Society, Democratization, and Foreign Aid: Civic Engagement and Public Policy in South Africa and Uganda." *Democratization*, vol. 14, no. 4 (August 2007): 643–68.

Rocha Menocal, Alina, and Bhavna Sharma. "Joint Evaluation of Citizens' Voice and Accountability: Synthesis Report." Evaluation Report EV692. London: Department for International Development, 2008.

Swedish Ministry for Foreign Affairs. "Pluralism: Policy for Support to Civil Society in Developing Countries With Swedish Development Cooperation." Stockholm: Swedish Ministry for Foreign Affairs Information Service and Department for Development Policy, 2009.

UNDP. *Evaluation of UNDP's Role in the PRSP Process, Volume I: Main Report*. New York: United Nations Development Programme, 2003.

———. *Human Development Report 1993*. New York and Oxford: Oxford University Press, 1993.

———. "Voice and Accountability for Human Development: A UNDP Strategy to Strengthen Civil Society and Civic Engagement." New York: United Nations Development Programme and Oslo Governance Centre, August 2009.

World Bank. "Guidance Note on Bank Multi-Stakeholder Engagement." Washington, D.C.: World Bank, June 2009.

———. "Participation in Poverty Reduction Strategy Papers: A Retrospective Study." Washington, D.C.: World Bank, Social Development Department, January 2002.

———. *The World Bank Participation Sourcebook*. Environmentally Sustainable Development Publications. Washington, D.C.: World Bank, February 1996.

D. POLITICAL ECONOMY OF DEVELOPMENT

Acemoglu, Daron, and James Robinson. *Why Nations Fail: The Origins of Power, Prosperity, and Poverty*. New York: Crown Publishers, 2012.

Acemoglu, Daron, Simon Johnson, and James Robinson. "The Colonial Origins of Comparative Development: An Empirical Investigation." *American Economic Review*, vol. 91, no. 5 (December 2001): 1369–1401.

Adam, Christopher, and Stefan Dercon. "The Political Economy of Development: An Assessment." *Oxford Review of Economic Policy*, vol. 25, no. 2 (2009): 173–89.

Arndt, Christiane, and Charles Oman. "Uses and Abuses of Governance Indicators." OECD Development Center Study. Paris: Organisation for Economic Co-operation and Development, 2006.

Banerjee, Abhijit, and Esther Duflo. *Poor Economics: A Radical Rethinking of the Way to Fight Global Poverty*. New York: Public Affairs, 2011.

Bardhan, Pranap. "Symposium on Democracy and Development." *Journal of Economic Perspectives*, vol. 7, no. 3 (Summer 1993): 45–49.

Barro, Robert J. "Determinants of Economic Growth: A Cross-Country Empirical Study." Development Discussion Paper no. 579. Cambridge, Mass.: Harvard Institute for International Development, April 1997.

Besley, Timothy. "Poor Choices: Poverty From the Ground Level." *Foreign Affairs* (January/February 2012).

Booth, David. *Development as a Collective Action Problem: Addressing the Real Challenges of African Governance*. Synthesis Report. London: Overseas Development Institute, Africa Politics and Power Programme, 2012.

———. "Governance for Development in Africa: Building on What Works." Policy Brief 1. London: Overseas Development Institute, Africa Politics and Power Programme, April 2011.

———. "Toward a Theory of Local Governance and Public Goods' Provision in Sub-Saharan Africa." Working Paper 13. London: Overseas Development Institute, Africa Power and Politics Programme, 2010.

Booth, David, and Ole Therkildsen. "The Political Economy of Development in Africa: A Joint Statement From Five Research Programmes." Africa Power and Politics Programme; Developmental Leadership Programme; Elites, Production, and Poverty; Political Economy of Agricultural Policy in Africa; and Tracking Development, April 2012.

Centre for the Future State. *An Upside Down View of Governance*. Brighton: Institute of Development Studies, April 2010.

Collier, Paul. *Wars, Guns, and Votes: Democracy in Dangerous Places*. New York: HarperCollins, 2009.

Diamond, Jared. *Guns, Germs, and Steel: The Fates of Human Societies*. New York: W. W. Norton, 1999.

Duflo, Esther. "Policies, Politics: Can Evidence Play a Role in the Fight Against Poverty?" Richard H. Sabot Lecture at the Center for Global Development, Washington, D.C., April 11, 2011.

Easterly, William. "The Ghost of Financing Gaps: How the Harrod-Domar Growth Model Still Haunts Development Economics." Washington, D.C.: World Bank, July 1997.

Easterly, William, and Ross Levine. "Tropics, Germs and Crops: How Endowments Influence Economic Development." Working Paper 9106. Cambridge, Mass.: National Bureau of Economic Research, August 2002.

Evans, Peter. "Constructing the 21st Century Developmental State: Potentialities and Pitfalls." In *Constructing a Democratic Developmental State in South Africa: Potentials and Challenges*, ed. Omano Edigheji. Pretoria: HSRC Press, 2010.

———. "The State as Problem and Solution: Predation, Embedded Autonomy, and Structural Change." In *The Politics of Economic Adjustment: International Constraints, Distributive Conflicts, and the State*, eds. Stephan Haggard and Robert Kaufman. Princeton, N.J.: Princeton University Press, 1992.

Evans, Peter, and James Rauch. "Bureaucracy and Growth: A Cross-National Analysis of the Effects of 'Weberian' State Structures on Economic Growth." *American Sociological Review*, vol. 64, no. 5 (October 1999): 748–65.

Fritz, Verena, and Alina Rocha Menocal. "Developmental States in the New Millennium: Concepts and Challenges for a New Aid Agenda." *Development Policy Review*, vol. 25, no. 5 (2007): 531–52.

Fukuyama, Francis. *The Origins of Political Order: From Prehuman Times to the French Revolution.* New York: Farrar, Strauss and Giroux, 2011.

Fukuyama, Francis, and Brian Levy. "Development Strategies: Integrating Governance and Growth." Policy Research Working Paper no. 5196. Washington, D.C.: World Bank, January 2010.

Goldsmith, Arthur. "Ballots, Bullets, and the Bottom Billion." *Journal of Democracy*, vol. 23, no. 2 (April 2012): 119–32.

Grindle, Merilee. "Good Enough Governance: Poverty Reduction and Reform in Developing Countries." *Governance*, vol. 17, no. 4 (2004): 525–48.

———. "Good Enough Governance Revisited." *Development Policy Review*, vol. 25, no. 5 (2007): 533–74.

Hall, Robert E., and Charles I. Jones. "Why Do Some Countries Produce So Much More Output per Worker than Others?" *Quarterly Journal of Economics*, vol. 114, no. 1 (February 1999): 83–116.

Halperin, Morton H., Joseph T. Siegle, and Michael M. Weinstein. *The Democracy Advantage: How Democracies Promote Prosperity and Peace.* New York: Routledge, 2005.

Huntington, Samuel. *Political Order in Changing Societies.* New Haven, Conn. and London: Yale University Press, 1958.

Kaufmann, Daniel, and Aart Kraay. "Growth Without Governance." *Economía*, vol. 3, no. 1 (Fall 2002): 169–215.

Kaufmann, Daniel, Aart Kraay, and Pablo Zoido-Lobatón. "Governance Matters." Policy Research Working Paper 2196. Washington, D.C.: World Bank, October 1999.

Khan, Mushtaq. "Governance, Economic Growth and Development Since the 1960s: Background Paper for World Economic and Social Survey 2006." New York: UN Department of Economic and Social Affairs, 2006.

Killick, Tony. *A Reaction Too Far: Economic Theory and the Role of the State in Developing Countries.* London: Overseas Development Institute, 1989.

Knack, Stephen, and Philip Keefer. "Institutions and Economic Performance: Cross-Country Tests Using Alternative Institutional Indicators." *Economics & Politics*, vol. 7, no. 3 (1995): 207–27.

Kohli, Atul. *State-Directed Development: Political Power and Industrialization in the Global Periphery.* New York: Cambridge University Press, 2004.

Kurtz, Marcus J., and Andrew Schrank. "Growth and Governance: Models, Measures, and Mechanisms." *Journal of Politics*, vol. 69, no. 2 (2007): 538–54.

Leftwich, Adrian, ed. *Democracy and Development: Theory and Practice.* Cambridge, UK: Polity Press, 1996.

———. "Governance, Democracy and Development in the Third World." *Third World Quarterly*, vol. 14, no. 3 (1993): 605–24.

Lindauer, David, and Lant Pritchett, "What's the Big Idea? The Third Generation of Policies for Economic Growth." *Economía*, vol. 3, no. 1 (Fall 2002): 1–39.

Lipset, Seymour Martin. "Some Social Requisites of Democracy: Economic Development and Political Legitimacy." *American Political Science Review*, vol. 53, no. 1 (March 1959): 69–105.

Moore, Mick. "Declining to Learn From the East? The World Bank on 'Governance and Development.'" *IDS Bulletin*, vol. 24, no. 1 (1993): 39–50.

Moore, Mick, and James Putzel. "Politics and Poverty: A Background Paper for the World Development Report 2000/1." Brighton: Institute of Development Studies, September 1999.

Norris, Pippa. *Making Democratic Governance Work: How Regimes Shape Prosperity, Welfare, and Peace.* Cambridge, UK: Cambridge University Press, 2012.

North, Douglass C. "The New Institutional Economics and Third World Development." In *The New Institutional Economics and Third World Development*, eds. John Harriss, Janet Hunter, and Colin Lewis. London and New York: Routledge, 1995.

North, Douglass C., John Wallis, and Barry Weingast. *Violence and Social Orders: A Conceptual Framework for Interpreting Recorded Human History.* Cambridge: Cambridge University Press, 2009.

Onis, Ziya. "The Logic of the Developmental State." *Comparative Politics*, vol. 24, no. 1 (October 1991): 109–26.

Przeworski, Adam, and Fernando Limongi. "Political Regimes and Economic Growth." *Journal of Economic Perspectives*, vol. 7, no. 3 (Summer 1993): 51–69.

Przeworski, Adam, Michael E. Alvarez, Jose Antonio Cheibub, and Fernando Limongi. *Democracy and Development: Political Institutions and Well-Being in the World, 1950–1990.* Cambridge and New York: Cambridge University Press, 2000.

Robinson, Mark, and Gordon White, eds. *The Democratic Developmental State: Politics and Institutional Design.* Oxford: Oxford University Press, 1998.

Rodrik, Dani. "Thinking About Governance." In *Governance, Growth and Development Decision-making*, eds. Douglass North, Daron Acemoglu, Francis Fukuyama, and Dani Rodrik. Washington, D.C.: World Bank, 2008.

Rodrik, Dani, and Arvind Subramanian. "The Primacy of Institutions (and What This Does and Does Not Mean)." *Finance & Development*, vol. 40, no. 2 (June 2003): 31–34.

Rodrik, Dani, Arvind Subramanian, and Francesco Trebbi. "Institutions Rule: The Primacy of Institutions Over Geography and Integration in Economic Development." Working Paper 9305. Cambridge, Mass.: National Bureau of Economic Research, October 2002.

Rostow, Walt Whitman. *The Stages of Economic Growth: A Non-Communist Manifesto.* Cambridge: Cambridge University Press, 3rd edition, 1990.

Sachs, Jeffrey. *The End of Poverty: Economic Possibilities for Our Time.* London: Penguin Press, 2005.

Sachs, Jeffrey, et al. "Ending Africa's Poverty Trap." Brookings Papers on Economic Activity 1. Washington, D.C.: Brookings Institution, 2004.

Scott, James. *Seeing Like a State: How Certain Schemes to Improve the Human Condition Have Failed.* New Haven, Conn.: Yale University Press, 1998.

Sen, Amartya. *Development as Freedom.* Oxford: Oxford University Press, 1999.

Solow, Robert. "Perspectives on Growth Theory." *Journal of Economic Perspectives*, vol. 8, no. 1 (Winter 1994): 45–54.

World Bank. *World Development Report 1991: The Challenge of Development.* Oxford: Oxford University Press, 1991.

———. *World Development Report 1997: The State in a Changing World.* New York: Oxford University Press, June 1997.

———. *World Development Report 2000/2001: Attacking Poverty: Opportunity, Empowerment, and Security.* Washington, D.C.: World Bank, 2000.

————. *World Development Report 2004: Making Services Work for Poor People*. Washington, D.C.: World Bank and Oxford University Press, 2004.

E. AID HISTORY: 1950s–1980s

Ake, Claude. "Rethinking African Democracy." *Journal of Democracy*, vol. 2, no. 1 (Winter 1991): 32–44.

Barnett, Stanley, and Nat Engel. "Effective Institution Building: A Guide for Project Designers and Project Managers Based on Lessons Learned From the AID Portfolio." A.I.D. Program Evaluation Discussion Paper no. 11. Washington, D.C.: U.S. Agency for International Development, March 1982.

Berg, Robert, and Jennifer Seymour Whitaker. *Strategies for African Development*. Berkeley and Los Angeles: University of California Press, 1986.

Brinkerhoff, Derick, and Marcus Ingle. "Integrating Blueprint and Process: A Structured Flexibility Approach to Development Management." *Public Administration and Development*, vol. 9, no. 5 (1989): 487–503.

Buyck, Beatrice. "The Bank's Use of Technical Assistance for Institutional Development." Working Paper 578. Washington, D.C.: World Bank, January 1991.

Carothers, Thomas. *In the Name of Democracy: U.S. Policy Toward Latin America in the Reagan Years*. Berkeley and Los Angeles: University of California Press, 1991.

Chenery, Hollis, and Alan Strout. "Foreign Assistance and Economic Development." *American Economic Review*, vol. 56, no. 4 (September 1966): 679–733.

Committee on Institutional Cooperation. *Building Institutions to Serve Agriculture, a Summary Report of the CIC-AID Rural Development Research Project*. Lafayette, Ind.: Purdue University, 1968.

Ferguson, James. *The Anti-Politics Machine: Depoliticization, and Bureaucratic Power in Lesotho*. Minneapolis: University of Minnesota Press, 1994.

Gardner, James. *Legal Imperialism: American Lawyers and Foreign Aid in Latin America*. Madison: University of Wisconsin Press, 1980.

Goldsmith, Arthur. "Institutions and Planned Socioeconomic Change: Four Approaches." *Public Administration Review*, vol. 52, no. 6 (November/December 1992): 582–87.

Gulick, C. S. "Effectiveness of AID: Evaluation Findings of the World Bank, the Inter-American Bank, the Agency for International Development and the Canadian International Development Agency." Draft, August 1984.

Haggard, Stephan, and Robert Kaufman. "The Politics of Stabilization and Structural Adjustment." In *Developing Country Debt and Economic Performance: The International Financial System*, ed. Jeffrey Sachs. Chicago: University of Chicago Press, 1989.

Hamnett, Ian. "A Social Scientist among Technicians." *IDS Bulletin*, vol. 3, no. 1 (1970).

Hirschman, Albert. *Development Projects Observed*. Washington, D.C.: Brookings Institution, 1967.

Kapur, Devesh, John Lewis, and Richard Webb. *The World Bank: Its First Half Century*. Washington, D.C.: Brookings Institution, 1997.

Krueger, Anne, Constantine Michalopoulous, and Vernon Ruttan. *Aid and Development*. Baltimore and London: Johns Hopkins University Press, 1989.

Kumar, Krishna. "A.I.D.'s Experience With Integrated Rural Development Projects." A.I.D. Program Evaluation Report No. 19. Washington, D.C.: U.S. Agency for International Development.

Mason, John. "A.I.D.'s Experience With Democratic Initiatives: A Review of Regional Programs in Legal Institution Building." A.I.D. Program Evaluation Discussion Paper no. 29. Washington, D.C.: U.S. Agency for International Development, February 1990.

Morris, Johnny. "Evsum438: Synthesis of Integrated Rural Development Projects." London: Department for International Development, 1999.

Morrison, David. *Aid and Ebb Tide: A History of CIDA and Canadian Development Assistance.* Waterloo, Ontario: Wilfrid Laurier University Press and North-South Institute, 1998.

Nelson, Joan. "The Political Economy of Stabilization in Small, Low-Income, Trade-Dependent Nations." Washington, D.C.: Overseas Development Council, 1984.

Nelson, Joan, ed. *Economic Crisis and Policy Choice: The Politics of Adjustment in the Third World.* Princeton, N.J.: Princeton University Press, 1990.

Nunberg, Barbara. "Public Sector Management Issues in Structural Adjustment Lending." Discussion Paper 99. Washington, D.C.: World Bank, August 1990.

Overseas Development Institute. "Basic Needs." Briefing Paper no. 5. London: Overseas Development Institute, December 1978.

Packenham, Robert. *Liberal America and the Third World: Political Development Ideas in Foreign Aid and Social Science.* Princeton, N.J.: Princeton University Press, 1973.

Riddell, Roger. *Foreign Aid Reconsidered.* Baltimore: Johns Hopkins University Press, 1987.

Streeten, Paul. *First Things First: Meeting Basic Human Needs in the Developing Countries.* New York: Oxford University Press and World Bank, 1981.

Tarp, Finn, ed. *Foreign Aid and Development: Lessons Learnt and Directions for the Future.* London: Routledge, 2000.

Trubek, David, and Marc Galanter. "Scholars in Self-Estrangement: Some Reflections on the Crisis in Law and Development Studies in the United States." *Wisconsin Law Review*, no. 4 (1974): 1062–1102.

USAID. *Increasing Participation in Development: Primer on Title IX of the United States Foreign Assistance Act.* Washington, D.C.: U.S. Agency for International Development, 1970.

———. "Institutional Development." AID Policy Paper. Washington, D.C.: U.S. Agency for International Development, Bureau for Program and Policy Coordination, 1983

World Bank. "Evaluation Results for 1988: Issues in World Bank Lending Over Two Decades." Washington, D.C.: World Bank Operations Evaluation Department, 1990.

———. "The World Bank and Institutional Development: Experience and Directions for Future Work." Washington, D.C.: World Bank, Projects Advisory Staff, 1980.

INDEX

ABOUT THE AUTHORS

THOMAS CAROTHERS is vice president for studies and also director of the Democracy and Rule of Law Program at the Carnegie Endowment for International Peace. A leading authority on international assistance relating to democracy, governance, the rule of law, and civil society, he is the author of numerous critically acclaimed books and articles on these topics. He has worked on assistance projects and served as a strategic adviser for a wide range of public and private organizations and carried out extensive field research in many countries. He is a regular visiting professor at the Central European University and has been associated with Nuffield College, Oxford University, and the Johns Hopkins School of Advanced International Studies. He previously served as chair of the global advisory board of the Open Society Foundations and is chair of the Open Society Foundations Think Tank Fund. He is a graduate of Harvard Law School, the London School of Economics, and Harvard College.

DIANE DE GRAMONT, a Clarendon Scholar at Oxford University, was previously a researcher in the Democracy and Rule of Law Program at the Carnegie Endowment for International Peace. Her research specialties include international support for democracy and governance, political party development, and comparative democratization. She is a graduate of Harvard College.